JUVENILE JUSTICE IN GLOBAL PERSPECTIVE

Juvenile Justice in Global Perspective

Edited by Franklin E. Zimring, Máximo Langer, and
David S. Tanenhaus

NEW YORK UNIVERSITY PRESS
New York and London

NEW YORK UNIVERSITY PRESS
New York and London
www.nyupress.org

References to Internet websites (URLs) were accurate at the time of writing.
Neither the author nor New York University Press is responsible for URLs
that may have expired or changed since the manuscript was prepared.
Library of Congress Cataloging-in-Publication Data

Juvenile justice in global perspective / edited by Franklin E. Zimring, Máximo Langer, and
David S. Tanenhaus.
pages cm — (Youth, crime, and justice series)
Includes bibliographical references and index.
ISBN 978-1-4798-2653-7 (cl : alk. paper)
ISBN 978-1-4798-4388-6 (pb : alk. paper)
1. Juvenile justice, Administration of. I. Zimring, Franklin E., editor. II. Langer, Máximo,
editor. III. Tanenhaus, David Spinoza, editor. IV. Series: Youth, crime, and justice series.
K5575.J86   2015
364.36—dc23   2015004162

New York University Press books are printed on acid-free paper,
and their binding materials are chosen for strength and durability.
We strive to use environmentally responsible suppliers and materials
to the greatest extent possible in publishing our books.

Manufactured in the United States of America

10 9 8 7 6 5 4 3 2 1

Also available as an ebook

For Toni Mendicino, with our gratitude and admiration

CONTENTS

ACKNOWLEDGMENTS

The central financial and administrative support for this project came from the Criminal Justice Research Program at Berkeley Law with funds from the Berkeley Law School. The planning and scheduling of the volume also had the support of NYU Press.

Our largest personal debts are to the individual scholars who met the novel challenges of contributing chapters to this collection. Many of the profiles in this volume are the first in English for the nations represented, and all of them also involve comparisons between juvenile and criminal justice systems. Most chapters provide empirical data to supplement statutory and doctrinal information, and many of the scholars who prepared these chapters were writing in a second language. The efforts and enthusiasm of our contributors were nothing short of inspirational.

Ricardo Lillo compiled an extensive statistical profile of juvenile and criminal custodial data from several Latin American nations, which enriched the profile of juvenile justice in Latin America.

Toni Mendicino is always an indispensable resource in producing the published work of the Criminal Justice Research Program, but the range of her contributions to this effort was remarkable. She served as administrator, travel planner, content editor, and coordinator and displayed important diplomatic skills at critical junctures.

Introduction

FRANKLIN E. ZIMRING, MÁXIMO LANGER,
AND DAVID S. TANENHAUS

Juvenile courts are both a very recent legal invention and an almost ubiquitous presence in modern nations. The first juvenile court was established by statute in Illinois in 1899 and quickly spread to other American states and to a number of other nations. Both the jurisdictional features and policy ambitions of the Illinois juvenile court were widely emulated in the systems that were established worldwide in the first half of the 20th century. And there is one important feature of every juvenile court's delinquency jurisdiction that complicates the task of creating a comparative law of juvenile courts. When juvenile courts are introduced in a legal system, they remove a segment of young offenders that had been traditionally the responsibility of criminal courts. So every juvenile court becomes part of a dual legal system of responding to criminal offenses—a juvenile court for young offenders and a criminal court for adult offenders. One critical dimension of every nation's juvenile court system is the differences in outcome, process, and philosophy between juvenile and criminal courts. This means that the comparative law of juvenile justice is best regarded as a process of double comparison in which juvenile justice systems are compared both to the juvenile systems of other places and to the criminal courts that they coexist with.

The Usual Suspects

This book has three complementary ambitions. The first goal of the volume is to substantially increase both the number of juvenile justice systems that are profiled in English-language scholarship and the variety of geographical, political, and religious contexts in which juvenile courts have been observed. The modest efforts to date at comparative analysis of juvenile justice have focused on systems found in Western developed nations. There is a substantial literature on a relatively small sample of nations—Canada, England, France, Germany (Tonry and Doob 2004) and (for geographic diversity) eastern Europe (Dünkel and Drenkhahn 2003; Dünkel, Grzywa, Horsfield, and Pruin 2011; Junger-Tas and Decker 2006) and Japan (Muncie and Goldson 2006). But the sample of nations where juvenile justice has been profiled is both small and unrepresentative (Hartjen 2008; Jensen and Jepsen 2006). These are the rich nations, mostly Western and tending toward democracy and political stability.

Our first aim is to create in these pages a much wider world map of juvenile justice systems, one that comes closer to approximating the near universality of juvenile justice in the modern world. We think that profiles of juvenile courts in places such as India, the People's Republic of China, Latin America, and the Middle East can provide readers with a much more representative sample of current systems and a better test of whether the features found in Canada and western Europe are more widely shared and thus qualify as essential characteristics of juvenile justice or are simply a variant found in Western developed democracies. The individual chapters on these understudied systems will be useful in two ways: (1) individually, as an introduction to the specific national systems discussed, and (2) collectively, as a wider sample of the variety of juvenile justice systems now functioning. How many different types of juvenile systems currently exist, and how do they differ? What characteristics other than the common label unify juvenile systems in different regions and in different forms of government?

A second ambition of this study is to seek knowledge of the operations of juvenile justice using the double-comparison perspective that seeks to explore the special features of a nation's juvenile system by comparing it to the operations and ideology of the criminal justice system that it adjoins. So we want to find the special character of a specific juvenile system by comparison with its domestic criminal justice sibling as well as with the juvenile justice systems of other nations. This type of two-dimensional mapping can create a much more complicated location of particular systems but one that provides important clues about why juvenile systems may differ from one another and also why there may be characteristic differences in emphasis and operation among juvenile systems in many different national environments and the criminal systems next door to them. In this context, we have included in our case studies not only politically stable countries but also countries that have undergone major political transitions, to explore whether any relevant differences exist between these two types of political situations. We hope a double-comparison perspective produces important hypotheses in this study even if the data we collect will fall far short of supplying definitive answers.

And there is one central issue we hope a broad survey of varieties of juvenile justice in the modern world can help us consider, and that is whether there is a core contrast between juvenile courts around the world and the criminal justice systems that they adjoin. We know that a dual system of justice is a near universal in modern nations, with almost only the Scandinavian nations operating without distinctive juvenile courts. But why is this? In theory, a single institution could coordinate a variety of different policies for offenders of all ages, but no modern nation has chosen to do this. (The Scandinavians give responsibility for offenders under 15 to social service systems and only process older youth through criminal courts, as discussed in chapter 2.) What are the reasons that have made two separate courts for the same behaviors the nearly universal choice of modern governments?

Fashion or Function?

Not all widely adopted institutional structures have clear functional advantages over alternative arrangements. Sometimes labels and organizations are widely adopted simply because they are in fashion. And the very good press that juvenile courts and the mission of rehabilitation of children received all through the 20th century might have made the label appealing without its carrying any distinctive functional arrangements or ambitions. Under such circumstances, the actual functions of a juvenile court might vary widely from system to system, and the operating priorities of a juvenile system adopted as a fashion statement should closely resemble the priorities found in the same nation's criminal courts.

But if there are instead significant differences between juvenile and criminal court principles and priorities and if the features that distinguish juvenile courts in Argentina and South Korea are similar, then careful study of a wide variety of juvenile systems can help us identify what deep structural priorities and strategies define juvenile courts. In this sense, the attempt to broaden the sample of systems studied in this book and to focus on the distinction between juvenile and criminal courts is a down payment on an ambitious empirical jurisprudence.

A Map of the Book

The studies in this volume are divided into four sections and ten chapters. Part 1 covers the familiar territory of juvenile justice in developed western Europe, but the two chapters in this part cover their topics in unconventional ways. In chapter 1, Frieder Dünkel provides a summary of major features in western European systems with special attention to trends over time. Are there major differences in the operating systems on the continent? Have there been major changes in some or many systems? In chapter 2, Tapio Lappi-Seppälä examines the major features of Scandinavian courts and social agencies that are a special case in modern legal systems. This is juvenile justice without juvenile courts. How does this system differ from the outcomes and criteria in nations with juvenile courts? Could other countries produce outcomes similar to Scandinavia without special courts for young offenders?

Part 2 examines juvenile justice in regions and states where little has been reported in English-language literature. In chapter 3, Weijian Gao narrates the history and current status of juvenile courts in the People's Republic of China. In chapter 4, Ved Kumari provides a portrait of juvenile courts in India. In chapter 5, Mary Beloff and Máximo Langer report on Latin America. In chapter 6, Lena Salaymeh reports on juvenile courts in the Muslim-majority nations of the Middle East and North Africa.

Part 3 concerns three nations where major political changes occurred in the last third of the 20th century. In chapter 7, Barbara Stańdo-Kawecka provides an extensive history of juvenile justice in Poland and traces the apparent impact of the country's transition from socialist satellite that happened in 1989. In chapter 8, Ann Skelton traces the ideological and operational impact of the transition from apartheid to democratic rule in South African juvenile courts. In chapter 9, Jae-Joon

Chung contrasts the impact of legislative change in Japan with the non-legislative shifts that occurred in South Korea after a political transition from long-term governance by right-wing political parties to a decade of left-leaning presidential leadership.

In part 4, a concluding chapter surveys the wide variety of systems and trends that this volume has collected to search for common themes in the global portfolios of juvenile courts and correctional facilities. While there are a large number of variations in juvenile systems, there are important overarching similarities among juvenile courts. The passive virtue at the center of juvenile courts is the effort to minimize the use of secure confinement, rather than to interrupt the process of juveniles' maturation in community settings. This is a strategic adjustment to the demands for penal confinement that goes beyond the boundaries of diminished responsibility and requires a separate institution to protect it.

REFERENCES

Dünkel, Frieder, and Drenkhahn, Kirstin (eds.). 2003. *Youth Violence: New Patterns and Local Responses—Experiences in East and West.* Mönchengladbach, Germany: Forum Verlag Godesberg.

Dünkel, Frieder, Grzywa, Joanna, Horsfield, Philip, and Pruin, Ineke (eds.). 2011. *Juvenile Justice Systems in Europe—Current Situation and Reform Developments.* Vols. 1–4. 2nd ed. Mönchengladbach, Germany: Forum Verlag Godesberg.

Hartjen, Clayton A. 2008. *Youth, Crime, and Justice: A Global Inquiry.* New Brunswick: Rutgers University Press.

Jensen, Eric L., and Jepsen, Jorgen (eds.). 2006. *Juvenile Law Violators, Human Rights and the Development of New Juvenile Justice Systems.* Oxford, UK: Hart.

Junger-Tas, Josine, and Decker, Scott H. (eds.). 2006. *International Handbook of Juvenile Justice.* Dordrecht, Netherlands: Springer.

Muncie, John, and Goldson, Barry (eds.). 2006. *Comparative Youth Justice: Critical Issues.* London: Sage.

Tonry, Michael, and Doob, Anthony (eds.). 2004. *Youth Crime and Youth Justice: Comparative and Cross-National Perspectives.* Vol. 31 of *Crime and Justice: A Review of Research.* Chicago: University of Chicago Press.

PART I

Western Europe

The first two chapters of this volume describe the modern history of legal policy toward young offenders in Europe and Scandinavia. In chapter 1, Frieder Dünkel surveys juvenile justice and youth crime policy throughout Europe. Because western European systems have been the subject of extensive prior study, Dünkel's analysis concentrates on documenting changes in policy over the last generation as well as the developments in nations in central and eastern Europe that experienced political transitions after 1989. What the chapter shows is much more continuity in Europe than change, and Dünkel concludes that "youth justice has successfully resisted a punitive turn."

In chapter 2, Tapio Lappi-Seppälä conducts a detailed analysis of Scandinavian responses to youth crime to investigate the impact of criminal court processing of 15-, 16-, and 17-year-olds in Norway, Finland, Sweden, and Denmark. Why do these traditionally progressive legal systems operate without separate juvenile courts? Do the Scandinavian criminal courts have special policies for these very youngest defendants? Would it be possible to replicate the policies found in Scandinavia in the criminal courts of other nations?

1

Juvenile Justice and Crime Policy in Europe

FRIEDER DÜNKEL

In the past 25 years, youth justice[1] systems in Europe have undergone considerable changes, particularly in the former socialist countries of central and eastern Europe. However, differing and sometimes contradictory youth justice policies have also emerged in western Europe. So-called neoliberal[2] tendencies could be seen particularly in England and Wales and also in France and the Netherlands (Cavadino and Dignan 2006: 215; 2007: 284; Goldson 2002: 392; Tonry 2004; Muncie and Goldson 2006; Bailleau and Cartuyvels 2007; Muncie 2008; Cimamonti, di Marino, and Zappalà 2010). In other countries, such as Germany and Switzerland, a moderate system of minimum intervention with priority given to diversion and of educational measures has been retained (Dünkel, Grzywa, Horsfield, and Pruin 2011; hereafter cited as Dünkel et al. 2011). In many countries, elements of restorative justice have been implemented, such as victim-offender mediation, reparation/restitution orders, and recently different forms of conferencing (Dünkel, Horsfield, and Grzywa 2015).

This chapter[3] evaluates youth justice policies and practice in western Europe from a comparative perspective.[4] The focus is on tendencies in youth justice legislation and on the sentencing practice of prosecutors and judges in youth courts. Attention is also paid to the traditional "welfare" and "justice" models of youth justice and how they have become intertwined in modern European practice. The claim that a "new punitiveness" is the prevailing strategy is questioned, and attention is drawn to the practice of many youth justice systems, which seem to be fairly resistant to neoliberal policies. Sonja Snacken (2012: 247) has recently sought to explain why continental European countries in general have succeeded in resisting "penal populism." In the conclusion, this reasoning is applied to youth justice systems in particular.[5]

Contemporary Trends in Youth Justice Policy

Across Europe, policies based on the notions of the subsidiarity and proportionality of state interventions against juvenile offenders are remaining in force or emerging afresh in most, if not all, countries. Recently, however, in several European countries, we have also witnessed the adoption of a contrary approach. These developments intensify youth justice interventions by raising the maximum sentences for youth detention and by introducing additional forms of secure accommodation. The youth justice reforms in the Netherlands in 1995 and in some respects in France in 1996, 2002, and 2007 should be mentioned in this context, as should the reforms in England and Wales in 1994 and 1998 (Kilchling 2002; Cavadino and Dignan 2007: 284; 2006: 215; Junger-Tas and Decker 2006, 2009; Bailleau and Cartuyvels 2007; Dünkel et al. 2011; for earlier comparative reviews, see Kaiser 1985; Dünkel 1997). The causes of the more repressive or "neoliberal" approach in some countries are manifold. It is likely that the punitive trend in the United States, with its emphasis on retribution and deterrence, has had considerable impact in some European countries, particularly in England and Wales.

These developments at the national level, which is the primary focus of this chapter, have to be understood against the background of international and regional instruments that set standards for juvenile justice. Most important in this regard is the 1989 UN Convention on the Rights of the Child, a binding international treaty that all European states have ratified. It makes clear that the common and principal aim of youth justice should be to act in the "best interests of the child"—with *child* defined for the purpose of this convention as a person under the age of 18 years—and to provide education, support, and integration into society for such children. These ideas are developed further in the 1985 UN Standard Minimum Rules for the Administration of Juvenile Justice and at the European level in the recommendations of the Council of Europe, in particular, the 2003 recommendation regarding new ways of dealing with juvenile offending (Rec. [2003] 20) and the 2008 rules for juvenile offenders subject to sanctions or measures (Rec. [2008] 11; Dünkel 2009; Dünkel, Grzywa, Pruin, and Šelih 2011: 1861).

In the past few years, a remarkable shift toward the educational ideal of juvenile justice can be observed in countries that were claimed to be driven by neoliberal ideas in the 1990s and first decade of the 21st century, such as England and Wales and recently (2014) the Netherlands. From outside Europe, a comparable revival of the traditional youth justice ideas can be observed in the US as well (see Dünkel 2014; Bishop and Feld 2012; for Canada, in spite of a "law-and-order" rhetoric, the judicial practice seems to go in the same direction).

Responsibilization and Neoliberalism

In England and Wales, and to some extent elsewhere, the concept of responsibilization has become a pivotal category of youth justice.[6] Responsibilization is not limited to young offenders, but increasingly parents are held criminally responsible for the conduct of their children.[7] Making parents more responsible may have a positive impact. There is empirical evidence that parental training, combined with child support at an early stage, has positive preventive effects (Lösel et al. 2007). However, it is not necessary to criminalize parents. Ideally, parental training should be offered by welfare agencies (as is the case in Germany and the Scandinavian countries) and not be enforced by penal sanctions (Junger-Tas and Dünkel 2009b: 225).

A positive aspect of making young offenders take responsibility for their actions is that it has contributed to the expansion of victim-offender reconciliation (*Täter-Opfer-Ausgleich*), mediation, and reparation. In the English context, however, it is more problematic as it has been accompanied by the abolition of the presumption that 10- to 14-year-olds may lack criminal capacity. Although in practice the presumption had been relatively easy to rebut, its formal abolition in 1998 was an indication of determination to hold even very young offenders responsible for their actions. The tendencies in English youth justice may be regarded as symptomatic of a neoliberal orientation, which can be characterized by the key terms of responsibility, restitution (reparation), restorative justice, and (occasionally openly publicized) retribution. These "4 Rs" have replaced the "4 Ds" (diversion, decriminalization, deinstitutionalization, and due process) that shaped the debates of the 1960s and 1970s (Dünkel 2008). The retributive character of the new discourse is exemplified by the requirement that community interventions be "tough" and "credible." For example, the "community treatment" of the 1960s was replaced by "community punishment" in the 1980s and 1990s. Cavadino and Dignan attribute these changes to the "neo-correctionalist model" that has come to dominate official English penology (2006: 210; Bailleau and Cartuyvels 2007; Muncie 2008).

There are many reasons for the increase in neoliberal tendencies, as defined by Garland and other authors (2001a, 2001b; Roberts and Hough 2002; Tonry 2004; Pratt et al. 2005; Muncie 2008). Some are to be found in the renewed emphasis on penal philosophies such as retribution and incapacitation and in related sentencing policies that demonize youth violence, often by means of indeterminate sentences. There are also underlying socioeconomic reasons. More repressive policies have gained importance in countries that face particular problems with young migrants or members of ethnic minorities and that have problems integrating young persons into the labor market, particularly where a growing number of them live in segregated and declining city areas. They often have no real possibility of escaping life as members of the "underclass," a phenomenon that undermines "society's stability and social cohesion and create[s] mechanisms of social exclusion" (Junger-Tas 2006: 522, 524). They are at risk of being marginalized and eventually criminalized. In this context, recidivist offending is of major concern. Therefore, many of the more punitive changes to the law were restricted to recidivist offenders in England and Wales, France, and Slovakia, for example.

It should be emphasized, however, that in the case of most continental European countries, there is no evidence of a regression to the classical penal objectives and perceptions of the 18th and 19th centuries. Overall, there is continued adherence to the prior principle of education or special prevention, even though "justice" elements have also been reinforced. The tension between education and punishment remains evident. The reform laws that were adopted in Germany in 1990, in the Netherlands in 1995, in Spain in 2000 and 2006, in Portugal in 2001, in France and Northern Ireland in 2002, in Lithuania in 2001, in the Czech Republic in 2003, and in Serbia in 2006 are examples of this dual approach. The reforms in Northern Ireland and in Belgium in 2007 are of particular interest, as they strengthened restorative elements in youth justice, including so-called family conferencing, and thus arguably contribute to responsibilization in this way without necessarily being "neoliberal" in fundamental orientation (Christiaens, Dumortier, and Nuytiens 2011; O'Mahony and Campbell 2006; O'Mahony and Doak 2009; Doak and O'Mahony 2011).

It must be recognized, however, that even in countries with a moderate and stable youth justice practice, the rhetoric in political debates is sometimes dominated by penal populism with distinctly neoliberal undertones. Nevertheless, this does not necessarily result in a change, as can be demonstrated by a German example. At the end of 2007, several violent crimes in subways (which were filmed by automatic cameras) led to a heated public debate about the necessity to increase the sanctions provided by the Juvenile Justice Act. The leader of the Christian Democratic Party (CDU) of the federal state of Hesse, Roland Koch, made this a core element of his electoral campaign by proposing the use of boot camps and other more severe punishments for juvenile violent offenders. He also used the fact that the offenders had immigrant backgrounds for xenophobic statements. Within a few days, almost 1,000 criminal justice practitioners and academics signed a resolution against such penal populism, and in January 2008, the CDU lost the elections. Since then, penal populism has not been made a major issue in electoral campaigns again. The CDU had gone too far. Muncie (2008: 109) refers to this debate in Germany and interprets it as an indicator for increased punitiveness. Yet youth justice practice in Germany has remained stable, and sentencing levels have remained relatively moderate (Heinz 2009, 2011a, 2011b; Dünkel 2011b).

Diversion, Minimum Intervention, and Community Sanctions

If one regards the developments in the disposals that are applicable to young offenders, there has been a clear expansion of the available means of diversion. However, these are often linked to educational measures or merely function to validate norms by means of a warning (Dünkel, Pruin, and Grzywa 2011). Sometimes, however, the concern for minimum intervention still means that diversion from prosecution leads to no further steps being taken at all.

Everywhere it is proclaimed that deprivation of liberty should be a measure of last resort. In practice, the level of what is meant by "last resort" varies across time and in cross-national comparison. England and Wales, for example, experienced sharp increases of the juvenile prison population in the 1990s until the mid-2000s, but the reduction of immediate custody by 45% from 2007 to 2012 demonstrates a shift in the sentencing policy beyond demographic changes (Horsfield 2015). Spain and a few other countries have also shown increases in the use of youth custody in recent years, but in general, recent developments go in the other direction. This is particularly true for central and eastern European countries. In some of these countries, such as Croatia, the Czech Republic, Hungary, Latvia, Romania, Slovenia, and recently Russia, the high level of diversion and community sanctions and the low level of custodial sanctions characteristic of continental western European and Scandinavian countries have been achieved, whereas others, such as Lithuania and Slovakia, still use deprivation of liberty more often, albeit not as frequently as in Soviet times.

With the exception of some serious offenses, the vast majority of youth offending in Europe is dealt with out of court by means of informal diversionary measures: for example, in Belgium about 80%, in Germany about 70% (Dünkel, Pruin, and Grzywa 2011: 1684). In some countries, such as Croatia, France, the Netherlands, Serbia, and Slovenia, this is a direct consequence of the long-recognized principle of allowing the prosecution and even the police a wide degree of discretion—the so-called expediency principle. Exceptions, where such discretion is not allowed, can be found in some central and eastern European countries, but in these cases, one should note that, for example, property offenses that cause only minor damage are not always treated as statutory criminal offenses. Italy, to take a further example, provides for a judicial pardon that is similar to diversionary exemptions from punishment but is awarded by the youth court judge. So there is a large variety of forms of nonintervention or of imposing only minor (informal or formal) sanctions.

Constructive measures, such as social training courses (Germany) and so-called labor and learning sanctions or projects (The Netherlands), have also been successfully implemented as part of a strategy of diversion. Many countries explicitly follow the ideal of education

(Portugal), while at the same time emphasizing prevention of reoffending, that is, special prevention (as is done by the Council of Europe's 2003 recommendation on new ways of dealing with juvenile delinquency and the role of juvenile justice).

Restorative Justice

One development that appears to be common to central, eastern, and western European countries is the application of elements of restorative justice policies to young offenders (see in summary Dünkel, Horsfield, and Grzywa 2015). Victim-offender reconciliation, mediation, or sanctions that require reparation or apology to the victim have played a particular role in all legislative reforms of the past 15 years. Pilot mediation projects were established in the 1990s in central and eastern European countries such as Slovenia (since 1997) and the Czech Republic. They are predominantly linked to informal disposals (diversion).

In some countries, legislation provides for elements of restorative justice to be used as independent sanctions by youth courts. In England and Wales, for example, this is done by means of reparation or restitution orders, and in Germany by means of so-called *Wiedergutmachungsauflage*, that is, victim-offender reconciliation or restitution as an educational directive (see §§ 10 and 15 of the Juvenile Justice Act). Family group conferences—originally introduced and applied in New Zealand—form part of the law reform of 2007 in Belgium. These conferences are forms of mediation that take into account and seek to activate the social family networks of both the offender and the victim. Even before the Belgian reform project, the youth justice reform in Northern Ireland had introduced youth conferences, which have been running as pilot projects since 2003. In addition, the Northern Irish reform made provision for reparation orders, an idea that had been introduced in England and Wales in 1998 (O'Mahony and Campbell 2006; Doak and O'Mahony 2011).

Whether these restorative elements actually influence sentencing practice or are merely a fig leaf seeking to disguise a more repressive youth justice system can only be determined by taking into account the different backgrounds and traditions in each country. Victim-offender reconciliation has attained great quantitative significance in the sanctioning practices of both the Austrian and the German youth courts and in Finland as well.[8] If one also takes community service into account as a restorative sanction in the broader sense, the proportion of all juvenile and young adult offenders who are dealt with by such—ideally educational—constructive alternatives increases to more than one-third (Heinz 2012).

In Italy, the procedural rules for youth justice introduced in 1988 have led to a move away from a purely rehabilitative and punitive perspective to a new conception of penal procedure. Restorative justice measures have gained much more attention, and victim-offender mediation can be applied at different stages of the procedure: during the preliminary investigations and the preliminary hearing when considering "the extinction of a sentence because of the irrelevance of the offence" or combined with the suspension of the procedure with supervision by the probation service (*Sospensione del processo e messa alla prova*; see Dünkel, Pruin, and Grzywa 2011: 1694).

In general, one can summarize that the idea of restorative justice successfully has been implemented all over Europe but that the numbers remain moderate. Mediation and reparation or restitution orders quantitatively cover only a small part of the juvenile justice system (see Dünkel, Horsfield, and Grzywa 2015).

Youth Justice Models

If one compares youth justice systems from a perspective of classifying them according to typologies, the "classical" orientations of both the justice and the welfare models can still be differentiated (Doob and Tonry 2004: 1; Pruin 2011). However, one rarely, if ever, encounters the ideal types of welfare or justice models in their pure form. Rather, there are several examples of mixed systems, for instance, within German and other continental European youth justice legislation.

There is a clear tendency in youth justice policy in recent decades to strengthen the justice model by establishing or extending procedural safeguards and also by implementing what may be regarded as welfare measures. This tendency includes a stricter emphasis on the principle of proportionality, in the sense of avoiding both sentences and educational measures that are disproportionately harsh.

Emphasizing the justice model also means a clear differentiation of the behavior that is subject to juvenile justice interventions. Most European juvenile justice laws rely on criminal behavior defined by the general criminal law, whereas other forms of problematic behavior that could endanger the juvenile and his or her future development are dealt with by separate welfare or family laws. A unified welfare and justice approach (as in the classic welfare model) in Europe is only to be found in Belgium, Scotland, and Poland.

However, other states have recently passed legislation on certain misbehavior ("antisocial" behavior), which is addressed by civil law (so-called antisocial behavior orders) but with a "hidden" form of criminalization in case of civil law order violations as these violations constitute a criminal offense (Bulgaria, England and Wales, Ireland, Northern Ireland). Status offenses such as truancy or running away from home in the continental European juvenile justice systems are dealt with in separate civil or welfare laws and therefore cannot be "punished" by youth courts (see in summary Pruin 2011: 1553).

Other orientations that are not necessarily based squarely on "justice" or "welfare" are significant too. Restorative justice has already been mentioned. Minimum intervention, too, plays a part, but so also do the "neoliberal" tendencies toward harsher sentences and "getting tough" on youth crime (Albrecht and Kilchling 2002; Tonry and Doob 2004; Jensen and Jepsen 2006; Junger-Tas and Decker 2006; Bailleau and Cartuyvels 2007; Ciappi 2007; Patané 2007; Cimamonti, di Marino, and Zappalà 2010; Pruin 2011). Tendencies toward minimum intervention—that is, the prioritization of informal procedures (diversion), including offender-victim reconciliation and other reparative strategies—can also be viewed as independent models of youth justice: a "minimum intervention model" (Cavadino and Dignan 2006: 199, 205). Cavadino and Dignan (2006: 210) identify not only a "minimum intervention model" (priority of diversion and community sanctions) and a "restorative justice model" (priority of restorative/reparative reactions) but also a "neo-correctionalist model," which, as mentioned previously, is particularly characteristic of contemporary trends and developments in England and Wales.

Here, too, there are no clear boundaries, for the majority of continental European youth justice systems incorporate not only elements of welfare and justice philosophies but also minimum intervention (as is especially the case in Germany; see Dünkel 2006, 2011a), restorative justice, and elements of neo-correctionalism (for example, increased "responsibilization" of the offenders and their parents, tougher penalties for recidivists, and secure accommodation for children). Differences are more evident in the degree of orientation toward restorative or punitive elements. In general, one can conclude that European juvenile justice is moving toward mixed systems that combine welfare and justice elements, which are further shaped by the trends mentioned earlier.

Reform Strategies

Against the preceding background of a range of old and newly prominent ideas combined with somewhat fractured models, one can identify a number of reform strategies. In many western European countries, such strategies seem to have been relatively well planned. In Austria, Germany, and the Netherlands, the community sanctions and restorative justice elements that were introduced by the reforms in 1988, 1990, and 1995, respectively, were systematically and extensively piloted. Nationwide implementation of the reform programs was dependent on prior empirical verification of the projects' practicability and acceptance. The process of testing and generating acceptance—especially among judges and the prosecution service—takes time. Continuous supplementary and further training is required, which is difficult to guarantee in times of social change, as has been the case in central and eastern Europe. Yet reform of youth justice through practice (as developed in Germany in the 1980s) appears preferable to a reform "from above," which often fails to provide the appropriate infrastructure.

As a result of major political changes at the end of the 1980s, more drastic reform was required in the countries of central and eastern Europe. The situation as it existed at the time was not uniform across the region but differed among groups of countries. One group was composed of the Soviet republics, Bulgaria, Romania, and to some degree the German Democratic Republic (East Germany) and Czechoslovakia. These countries had developed a more punitively oriented youth justice policy and practice. On the other hand, there were Hungary, Poland,

and Yugoslavia, which had rather moderate youth justice policies with many educational elements.

Across central and eastern Europe, developments since the early 1990s have been characterized by a clear increase in the levels of officially recorded youth crime. The need for youth justice reform, a widely accepted notion in all of these countries, stemmed from the need to replace old (often Soviet or Soviet-influenced) law with (western) European standards as contained in the principles of the Council of Europe and the United Nations. This process has, however, produced somewhat different trends in criminal policy.

Since the early 1990s, there has been a dynamic reform movement both in law and in practice. It is exemplified not only in numerous projects but also in the appointment of law reform commissions and, in many cases, in the adoption of reform legislation in, for example, Estonia, Lithuania, Serbia, Slovenia, and the Czech Republic.

On the one hand, the development of an independent youth justice system is a prominent feature of these reforms; see, for example, developments in the Baltic states, Croatia, the Czech Republic, Romania, Russia, Serbia, and Slovakia, as well as in Turkey. During the Soviet period, specialized youth courts did not exist. In some countries, so-called youth committees worked on the local level dealing informally with minor juvenile crime (e.g., Bulgaria, Estonia, the former Soviet Union), but they were not courts and not bound by any rule of law. Developing a youth justice system included following the Council of Europe's standards for preserving human rights in the area of juvenile justice. In this connection, the importance of procedural safeguards and entitlements that also take the special educational needs of young offenders into account has been recognized. However, in the Baltic states, there are as yet no independent youth courts. In Russia, the first model youth courts are up and running in Rostow on the Don and in a few other cities (Shchedrin 2011).[9] Such a project has also been established in Romania in Brașov (Păroșanu 2011). However, in general, the required infrastructure for the introduction of modern, social-pedagogical approaches to youth justice and welfare is widely lacking.

In order to deter recidivists and violent young offenders in particular, some of this new legislation not only involves new community sanctions and possibilities of diversion but also retains tough custodial sentences. The absence of appropriate infrastructure and of widespread acceptance of community sanctions still results in frequent prison sentences. However, developments in Russia, for example, show that a return to past sanctioning patterns, in which roughly 50% of all young offenders were sentenced to imprisonment, has not occurred. Instead, forms of probation are now quantitatively more common and are more frequently used than sentences of imprisonment. The numbers of juveniles under 18 in youth prisons recently have been reduced from more than 18,000 in 2001 to roughly 2,300 at the end of 2012 (see Dünkel 2014).What is becoming clear in all central and eastern European countries is that the principle of imprisonment as a last resort (*ultima ratio*) is being taken more seriously and the number of custodial sanctions reduced. However, it has to be noted that youth imprisonment or similar sanctions in the former Yugoslavian republics and to a lesser extent also in Hungary and Poland had already been the exception during the period before the political changes at the beginning of the 1990s.

Regarding community sanctions, the difficulties of establishing the necessary infrastructure are clear. Initially, the greatest problem in this respect was the lack of qualified social workers and teachers. This has remained a problem, as to a great extent the appropriate training courses have not yet been fully introduced and developed (Dünkel, Pruin, and Grzywa 2011). Again, one has to differentiate, as there are exceptions: Poland has a long tradition in social work. Also, in the former Yugoslavia, social workers were trained, following the introduction of "strict supervision" as a special sanction in 1960.

The concept of "conditional" criminal responsibility (related to the ability of discernment)—as long expressed in German and Italian law— has recently been adopted in Estonia (2002), the Czech Republic (2003), and Slovakia (for 14-year-olds; see Pruin 2011: 1566). This is another interesting development, for it reflects a tendency for reforms in the countries of central and eastern Europe to have been influenced by Austrian and German youth justice law as well as by international standards. Despite obvious and undeniable national particularities, there is a recognizable degree of convergence among the systems in western, central, and eastern Europe.

The Scope of Juvenile Justice

Although on the basis of comparative research, one may speak, albeit cautiously, of an emerging European philosophy of juvenile justice, which includes elements of education and rehabilitation (apparent in, for example, the recommendations of the Council of Europe), the consideration of victims through mediation and restoration, and the observance of legal procedural safeguards, there are some issues on which such a development is not as clear. In this regard, we consider the age of criminal responsibility and its corollary, the age at which offenders cease to be regarded as juveniles and are treated as adults. The latter issue also raises the question of whether there should be some mechanism for the converse, namely, allowing juveniles to be tried in adult courts.

Age of Criminal Responsibility

There is no indication of a harmonization of the age of criminal responsibility in Europe. Indeed, the 2008 European rules for juvenile offenders subject to sanctions or measures recommend no particular age, specifying only that some age should be specified by law and that it "shall not be too low" (rule 4).

The minimum age of criminal responsibility in Europe varies between 10 (England and Wales, Northern Ireland, and Switzerland), 12 (Netherlands, Scotland, and Turkey), 13 (France), 14 (Austria, Germany, Italy, Spain, and numerous central and eastern European countries), 15 (Greece and the Scandinavian countries), and even 16 (for specific offenses in Russia and other eastern European countries) or 18 (Belgium). After the recent reforms in central and eastern Europe, the most common age of criminal responsibility is 14 (see table 1.1).

The ages of criminal responsibility have to be defined further: whereas we can talk of a really low age of criminal responsibility, for example, in England and Wales, in many countries only educational sanctions imposed by the family and youth courts are applicable at an earlier age (for example, France and Greece). Also, in Switzerland, the youth court judge can only impose educational measures on 10- to 14-year-olds (who are, however, seen as criminally responsible),

TABLE 1.1. Comparison of the Age of Criminal Responsibility and Age Ranges for Youth Imprisonment

Country	Minimum age for educational measures of the family/youth court (juvenile welfare law)	Age of criminal responsibility (juvenile criminal law)	Full criminal responsibility (adult criminal law can/must be applied; juvenile law or sanctions of the juvenile law can be applied)	Age range for youth imprisonment/ custody or similar forms of deprivation of liberty
Austria		14	18/21	14–27
Belgium		18	16[b]/18	Only welfare institutions
Belarus		14[c]/16	14/16	14–21
Bulgaria		14	18	14–21
Croatia		14/16[a]	18/21	14–21
Cyprus		14	16/18/21	14–21
Czech Republic		15	18/18+ (mitigated sentences)	15–19
Denmark[d]		15	15/18/21	15–23
England/Wales		10/12/15[a]	18	10/15–21
Estonia		14	18	14–21
Finland[d]		15	15/18	15–21
France	10	13	18	13–18 + 6 months/23
Germany		14	18/21	14–24
Greece	8	15	18/21	15–21/25
Hungary		12[c]/14	18	14–24
Ireland		10/12/16[a]	18	10/12/16–18/21
Italy		14	18/21	14–21
Kosovo		14	18/21	16–23
Latvia		14	18	14–21
Lithuania		14[c]/16	18/21	14–21
Macedonia		14[c]/16	14/16	14–21
Moldova		14[c]/16	14/16	14–21
Montenegro		14/16[a]	18/21	16–23
Netherlands		15	16/23	15–24

TABLE 1.1 (*continued*)

Country	Minimum age for educational measures of the family/ youth court (juvenile welfare law)	Age of criminal responsibility (juvenile criminal law)	Full criminal responsibility (adult criminal law can/must be applied; juvenile law or sanctions of the juvenile law can be applied)	Age range for youth imprisonment/ custody or similar forms of deprivation of liberty
Northern Ireland		10	17/18/21	10–16/17–21
Norway[d]		15	18	15–21
Poland	13		15/17/18	13–18/15–21
Portugal	12		16/21	12/16–21
Romania		14/16	18/(20)	14–21
Russia		14[c]/16	18/21	14–21
Scotland	8[e]	12[e]/16	16/21	16–21
Serbia		14/16[a]	18/21	14–23
Slovakia		14/15	18/21	14–18
Slovenia		14/16[a]	18/21	14–23
Spain		14	18	14–21
Sweden[d]		15	15/18/21	15–21[g]
Switzerland		10/15[a]	18[f]	10/15–22
Turkey		12	15/18	12–18/21
Ukraine		14[c]/16	18	14–22

[a] Criminal responsibility resulting in juvenile detention (youth imprisonment or similar custodial sanctions under the regime of the Ministry of Justice).
[b] Only for traffic offenses and exceptionally for very serious offenses.
[c] Only for serious offenses.
[d] Only mitigation of sentencing without separate youth justice legislation.
[e] The age of criminal prosecution is 12, but for children from 8 up to the age of 16, the children's hearings system applies, thus preventing more formal criminal procedures.
[f] Article 61 of the Swiss Criminal Code for adults provides for a special form of detention, a prison sentence for 18- to 25-year-old young adult offenders, who are placed in separate institutions for young adults, where they can stay until they reach the age of 30.
[g] Youth custody. There are also special departments for young offenders in the general prison system (for young adults until about 25 years of age).

whereas juvenile prison sentences are restricted to those aged at least 15. The same is the case in the former Yugoslavian republics of Croatia, Kosovo, Serbia, and Slovenia for 14- and 15-year-old offenders. Further still, some countries, such as Lithuania and Russia, employ a graduated scale of criminal responsibility, according to which only more serious and grave offenses can be prosecuted from the age of 14, while the general minimum age of criminal responsibility lies at 16 (for a summary, see also Pruin 2011). Such a graduation of the age of criminal responsibility must be criticized, as it is contrary to the basic philosophy of juvenile justice that sanctions should refer to the individual development of maturity or other personality concepts rather than to the seriousness of the offense.

Whether these notable differences can in fact be correlated to variations in sentencing is not entirely apparent. For, within a system based solely on education, under certain circumstances the possibility of being accommodated as a last resort in a home or in residential care (particularly in the form of closed or secure centers as in England and Wales and France) can be just as intensive and of an equal or even longer duration than a sentence of juvenile imprisonment. Furthermore, the legal levels of criminal responsibility do not necessarily give any indication of whether a youth justice or welfare approach is more or less punitive in practice. What happens in reality often differs considerably from the language used in the reform debates (Doob and Tonry 2004: 16). Legal changes that formally make the regime more intensive are sometimes the result of changes in practice, and sometimes they contribute to changes in practice. The effect of these changes varies too. Despite the dramatization of events by the mass media that sometimes lead to changes in the law, there is often, in Germany, for instance, a remarkable continuity and a degree of stability in youth justice practice (Dünkel 2006, 2011).

Young Adults

There are also interesting developments in the upper age limits of criminal responsibility (the maximum age at which juvenile criminal law or juvenile sanctions can be applied). The central issue in this regard is the extension of the applicability of juvenile criminal law—or at least of its specifically educational measures—to 18- to 20-year-old young adults, as occurred in Germany as early as in 1953 (see also the recent reforms in Austria, Croatia, Lithuania, and the Netherlands; Pruin 2007; Dünkel and Pruin 2011, 2012; Pruin and Dünkel 2014).

This tendency is rooted in a criminological understanding of the transitional phases of personal and social development from adolescence to adulthood and a recognition that such transitions are taking longer. Over the past 50 years, the phases of education and of integration into working and family life (the establishment of one's "own family") have been prolonged well beyond the age of 20. Many young people experience developmental-psychological crises and difficulties in the transition to adult life, and increasingly such difficulties continue to occur into their mid-20s (Pruin 2007; Dünkel and Pruin 2011, 2012; Pruin and Dünkel 2014). Furthermore, new neuroscientific evidence indicates that maturity and psychosocial abilities are fully developed only in the third decade of life (Weijers and Grisso 2009: 63; Bonnie, Chemers, and Schuck 2012; Loeber et al. 2012: 336), which would justify a juvenile justice system up to the age of 21 or even 24. The Dutch government recently has extended the scope of juvenile justice until the age of 23 (for the respective reform proposals, see Loeber et al. 2012: 368, 394).

An increasing number of states have statutory provisions for imposing educational and other sanctions of the youth justice law on young adults. Historically, however, such laws have not always had the same impact in practice. While in Germany the laws applicable to juveniles are applied in more than 90% of the cases concerning young adults who commit serious crimes (overall average: more than 60%; see Dünkel 2011a: 587), in most other countries this has remained the exception. One reason is that in Germany the jurisdiction of the juvenile court has been extended to young adults, whereas in other countries the criminal court for adults is responsible for this age group but can impose some of the measures otherwise reserved for juveniles (for example, in the former Yugoslavia, which introduced this possibility in 1960; Gensing 2011). The Yugoslavian experience is a good example of how substantive and procedural laws have to be harmonized in order to prevent counterproductive effects of such provisions. There was therefore good reason in 1998 for Croatia, a former Yugoslavian state, to transfer the jurisdiction on young adults to the juvenile courts. Austria took the same step in 2001.

In other instances, keeping young adults fully in the adult framework does not mean that they cannot be treated very much like juveniles in practice. In the Netherlands, for example, the general criminal law provides for a plethora of alternative sanctions, which can be seen as educational or rehabilitative (for example, community service) and which are not provided in German criminal law for adults.

The Council of Europe has taken these new considerations about the prolongation of the transitional phase of young adults into account in its recommendation on "new ways of dealing with juvenile offenders and the role of juvenile justice" of 2003 (Rec. [2003] 20) and in the "European Rules for Juvenile Offenders Subject to Sanctions or Measures" (ERJOSSM) of 2008 (Rec. [2008] 11). Rule 11 of Recommendation (2003) 20 reads as follows: "Reflecting the extended transition to adulthood, it should be possible for young adults under the age of 21 to be treated in a way comparable to juveniles and to be subject to the same interventions, when the judge is of the opinion that they are not as mature and responsible for their actions as full adults."

In September 2004, the International Association of Penal Law (AIDP) held its World Congress in Beijing, China. The final resolution of the Congress emphasizes "that the state of adolescence can be prolonged into young adulthood (25 years) and that, as a consequence, legislation needs to be adapted for young adults in a similar way as it is done for minors." The age of criminal majority should be set at 18 years, the minimum age not lower than 14 years (see no. 2 of the resolution). Under no. 6, the resolution states, "Concerning crimes committed by persons over 18 years of age, the applicability of the special provisions for minors may be extended up to the age of 25."

On 5 November 2008, the Committee of Ministers of the Council of Europe passed the aforementioned Recommendation (2008) 11 on the European Rules for Juvenile Offenders Subject to Sanctions or Measures. As a part of the basic principles, rule 17 states that "young adult offenders may, where appropriate, be regarded as juveniles and dealt with accordingly." The commentary to this rule states that "it is an evidence-based policy to encourage legislators to extend the scope of juvenile justice to the age group of young adults. Processes of education and integration into social life of adults have been prolonged and more appropriate constructive reactions with regard to the particular developmental problems of young adults can often be found in juvenile justice legislation" (Council of Europe 2009: 42).[10]

This widespread European consensus about the role of young adults in juvenile justice legislation is reflected by more and more national legislators (see earlier), in the most far-reaching manner by the Dutch Juvenile Justice reform from 1 April 2014. The United Nations' recommendations until recently did not reflect this issue by just defining the scope of juvenile justice for "children," that is, the age group below 18 years of age (see, e.g., No. 4 of the so-called Beijing-Rules of 1985). However, in a recent proposal for a Model Law on Juvenile Justice of 2013, the authors make an interesting statement: "States should note that a majority of European States have extended the applicability *ratione personae* of their juvenile justice laws to the age of 21 as neuro-scientific evidence and brain development studies have indicated that it is difficult to distinguish between the brain of an older child and that of a young adult." (United Nations Office on Drugs and Crime 2013: 57). The Model Law opens the floor to states that wish to do so to extend the scope also for the age group of young adults. Indeed, there exist a few examples concerning the scope of juvenile justice in non-European countries in that way, as, for example, in Japan, Brazil, and Nicaragua (see Castro Morales 2015).

Transfer to Adult Criminal Courts or Jurisdiction (Waiver Procedures)

While raising the upper limit of the definition of *juvenile* may be seen as a way of imposing more appropriate sentences on immature young adults and extending the scope of youth justice, there is also an opposite trend, most prominent in the United States (Stump 2003; Bishop 2009) but also found in a few European countries (Pruin 2011), of referring children for trial in adult courts. Such referrals have a distinctively punitive purpose.

In some European countries, such as Scotland and Portugal, juvenile offenders from the age of 16 onward can be dealt with in the adult criminal justice system. Beyond that, in other countries, juvenile offenders can be transferred from the youth court to the adult court, where so-called waiver or transfer laws provide for the application of adult criminal law to certain offenses (Stump 2003; Bishop 2009; Weijers, Nuytiens, and Christiaens 2009; Goldson and Muncie 2006: 91; Keiser 2008). This is in fact a qualified limitation of the scope of juvenile justice (Hazel 2008: 35) and a lowering of the minimum age for the full application of adult criminal law.

Some countries provide for the application of adult criminal law for serious offenses, for example, in Belgium for rape, aggravated assault, aggravated sexual assault, aggravated theft, (attempted) murder, and (attempted) homicide by juveniles aged 16 or older. Since the law reform of 2006, before which juveniles had been tried by adult courts, so-called Extended Juvenile Courts now have the competence to conduct such trials.[11] The transfer decision is made by the youth court, which has to give special reasons, as the transfer is to be seen as an exception. A judicial review on this decision is guaranteed. The practice even before the reform of 2006, which further restricted the possibilities of a transfer, was very rare (see later). It has to be emphasized that the transfer of 16- and 17-year-old juveniles in Belgium is not to an adult court (as it had been before 2006) but to an Extended Youth Court, which may apply the general penal law sanctions.

In the Netherlands, the youth court remains competent as well, but the general criminal law can be applied to 16- and 17-year-old juveniles. In 1995, the requirements were relaxed. The seriousness of the criminal offense, the personality of the young offender, or the circumstances under which the offense is committed can lead to the application of adult criminal law. The law provides the judge with a great deal of discretion. In most cases, in practice it is the seriousness of the offense, that leads to the application of adult criminal law.

In England and Wales, juveniles, even at the age of 10, can be transferred to the adult criminal court (Crown Court) if charged with an exceptionally serious offense (including murder and crimes that would in the case of adult offenders carry a maximum term of imprisonment of more than 14 years). The Crown Court has to apply slightly different rules for the protection of juveniles in this case. The number of juvenile offenders who are sent to the Crown Court has fluctuated over the past 25 years, without any indication of a clear-cut trend in either direction.

In Serbia and in Northern Ireland, transfers are limited to juveniles who have been charged with homicide or who are coaccused with adult offenders. In the latter case, there is an interesting alternative as well: the juvenile has to be referred back to the youth court for sentencing following a finding of guilt (O'Mahony 2011). In Ireland, in exceptional cases such as treason or crimes against the peace of nations, but also for murder or manslaughter, juveniles are tried by the Central Criminal Court before a judge and jury.

In France, in contrast, less serious offenses, classed as misdemeanors, are brought before an adult court: since 1945, in cases of misdemeanors (*contraventions des quatre premières classes*), juvenile offenders are judged by the Police Court, which can issue reprimands or fines. Since 2002, the jurisdiction of the Police Court has been conferred on a specific "proximity judge," who is neither a lawyer nor a youth justice specialist but has the competence to "punish" juveniles up to a certain level (Castaignède and Pignoux 2011).

In Scotland, there are no waivers or transfer laws, but the same effect can be achieved in another way. In most severe cases, the juvenile offender will not be transferred to the children's hearings system. Formally, this is not a transfer to the adult criminal court, because the criminal court has original competence to try all cases, even if in practice the vast majority is transferred to the children's hearings system. However, Scotland shares the idea that in very serious cases the offenders should not be dealt with by the juvenile criminal system but in the adult criminal system.

Countries, such as those in Scandinavia, that do not have specialized juvenile jurisdictions thus (naturally) do not have provision for transfers either. It should be emphasized, though, that in general in the Scandinavian countries, the same regulations apply in cases of "aggravated" as well as "normal" offenses.

The application of adult law to juveniles through waivers or transfer laws can be regarded as a systemic weakness in those jurisdictions that allow it (Stump 2003). Whereas normally the application of (juvenile) law depends on the age of the offender, transfer laws or waivers rely on the type or seriousness of the committed offense. The justification for special treatment of juvenile offenders (as an inherent principle of youth justice) is challenged by such provisions (Keiser 2008: 38). The fundamental idea is to react differently to offenses that are committed by offenders up to a certain age, on the basis of their level on maturity or their ability of discernment. Waivers or transfer laws question this idea for serious offenses. On the one hand, the maximum age of criminal responsibility should signify—independently from the type of offense—from which age on a young person is deemed "mature enough" to receive (adult) criminal punishment. On the other hand, however, the introduction of "transfer laws" makes exactly those offenders fully responsible who often lack the (social) maturity to abstain from crime or even fully to differentiate right from wrong. Furthermore, it is hard to imagine that the same juvenile would be regarded as not fully mature when charged with a "normal" offense but fully criminally responsible for a serious offense. As Weijers and Grisso (2009: 67) have put it, "An adolescent has the same degree of capacity to form criminal intent, no matter what crime he commits." A systematic approach would treat all offenses equally.

States with transfer laws or waivers often argue that these laws are justified by the alleged deterrent effect of more severe sanctions on juvenile offenders.[12] Additionally, they claim that waivers are needed as a "safety valve" (Weijers et al. 2009) for the juvenile courts because juvenile law does not provide adequate or suitable options for severe cases.[13] However, so far criminological research has not found evidence for positive effects of transfers or waivers. In fact, research has suggested that transferring juveniles to adult courts has negative effects on preventing offending, including increased recidivism.[14]

The second argument misses the point as well: Does adult criminal law provide adequate or suitable options for reacting to severe criminality? How do we measure effectiveness? If we look at recidivism rates, then long prison sentences—the typical reaction by adult criminal law to serious offending—are relatively ineffective in preventing further crimes (Killias and Villettaz 2007: 213). Research results furthermore show that a lenient, minimum-interventionist juvenile justice system does not produce more juvenile offenders than an active and punitive one does (Smith 2005: 192).

In practice, transfers may be of declining significance in Europe. In the Netherlands, the number of transfers to the adult court has been reduced considerably: whereas in 1995 16% of all cases were dealt with by the adult criminal court, only 1.2% were in 2004 (Weijers et al. 2009: 110).[15] In Belgium, the use of transfers is very limited as well: transfer decisions amount to 3% of all judgments (Weijers et al. 2009: 118, with references to regional differences; Christiaens, Dumortiers, and Nuytiens 2011: 116). In Ireland, adult criminal courts are competent in less than 5% of all cases against juveniles. In Poland, from 1999 to 2004, the number of cases transferred to public prosecutors swung between 242 and 309, which is 0.2%–0.3% of all cases tried by the courts (Stańdo-Kawecka 2011).

It is also important to notice that decisions of a transfer or of applying the general criminal law instead of the juvenile law—at least in the continental European countries mentioned earlier—regularly are based on a (juvenile) court decision, often referring to psychiatric/psychological experts or social inquiry reports, and with the legal prerequisite of a judicial review. Even if waivers and transfer laws are of little significance in practice in most countries, they are nonetheless systemic flaws that ultimately undermine the special regulations for juvenile offenders. Additional safeguards in adult courts are unable to compensate for them (Keiser 2008: 38).[16] Therefore, the UN Committee on the Rights of the Child recommends abolishing all provisions that allow offenders under the age of 18 to be treated as adults, in order to achieve full and nondiscriminatory implementation of the special rules of youth justice to all juveniles under the age of 18 years (Committee on the Rights of the Child 2007: paras. 34, 36, 37, and 38; published also in Belser, Hanson, and Hirt 2009: 185, 194–195; see also Doek 2009: 23).

Reform Trends in Juvenile Justice in Individual Countries

The following survey of national reform trends follows the theoretical distinction between reforms focusing on four major, sometimes contradictory, orientations:

- Procedural reform issues, particularly strengthening legal safeguards, principles of due process and sentencing reforms (e.g., introducing new—not necessarily more intrusive—community sanctions)
- Reforms oriented toward the principle of minimum intervention, particularly expanding diversion strategies

- Reforms oriented toward implementing restorative justice elements such as mediation or family group conferencing
- Reforms oriented toward "neoliberal" strategies of more severe punishment, intensifying social control, also by civil measures (ASBOs, parenting orders, etc.; see Dünkel, Grzywa, Pruin, and Šelih 2011: 1851)

Juvenile law in *Austria* experienced a major reform in 1988 by expanding the possibilities for diversion and restorative justice such as victim-offender mediation and other constructive educational measures. Deprivation of liberty was becoming a measure of last resort. Since 2001, the application of juvenile procedural regulations was extended to young adults. The age of criminal responsibility is 14; juvenile courts are dealing also with cases of young adults at the age of 18 to 20. Diversion and community sanctions by the juvenile court is given strong priority. About 90% of juveniles and 75% of young adults are diverted from the youth court; a small percentage of less than 3% receive a custodial sanction.

Belgium held to its classical welfare approach and expanded the restorative justice approach by mediation and family group conferences in the new Juvenile Code of 2007. The principle of proportionality and procedural safeguards were strengthened and detention in closed welfare institutions further limited. On the other hand, in serious cases, the transfer of 16- and 17-year-olds to adult courts opens the pathway to the general justice system and possibly more repressive sanctions. The track to adult criminal justice is, however, rarely used (see Christiaens, Dumortiers, and Nuytiens 2011).

Bulgaria passed a major law reform in 1996, which on the one hand emphasized due process guarantees and the principle of proportionality concerning placements in correctional institutions and on the other hand incorporated neoliberal tendencies toward crime control by antisocial-behavior orders. A second reform law of 2004 further strengthened procedural safeguards and placed decisions of deprivation of liberty in the hands of judges. New alternative sanctions such as probation were introduced. Prison sentences were mitigated considerably, particularly for juveniles under the age of 16. At the same time, antisocial-behavior orders were extended and parenting orders introduced.

Croatia in 1998 implemented comprehensive juvenile justice legislation emphasizing due process standards on the one hand and diversion and educational measures including mediation on the other. The
reform was influenced by the Austrian and German law reforms. Later
reforms in 2002 and 2006 brought a tougher sentencing approach, but
only for young adults (18 to 20 years of age).

In *Cyprus*, in 1996, the scope of educational sanctions was expanded;
in 2006, the age of criminal responsibility was raised from 10 to 14.

In 2003, comprehensive juvenile justice legislation was passed in the
Czech Republic that enlarged the diversionary reactions and educational
sanctions including mediation. In 2009, the educational approach was
kept, but one more repressive sanction (preventive detention) for very
serious and dangerous offenders was introduced. Against strong political demands, the age of criminal responsibility was not lowered to 14
but kept at 15.

In *Denmark*, no separate juvenile justice system exists, and juveniles
are sentenced by the general courts. Nevertheless, special dispositions
for juveniles exist and have been expanded by the reforms in 1998 and
2001. The so-called youth contract can be characterized as a form of
conditional discharge, which tries to "responsibilize" young offenders.
The so-called youth sanction, with a custodial part and a part served
in the community, could be seen as a strengthening of sentencing as it
might replace former shorter sentences. On the other hand, it can be
seen as a clearer structured and rehabilitation-oriented sanction.

England and Wales are often characterized as the prototype of "neoliberal" reforms, with the introduction of stiffer sanctions and the lowering of the age of criminal responsibility from 14 to 10 by the reform
laws of 1994 and 1998. Closed welfare and justice institutions were
introduced also for 10- to 14-year-olds, antisocial-behavior orders widened the scope of juvenile social control, and the notion of community
sanctions changed toward the "getting tough" approach ("credible" and
tough alternatives). The sentencing practice more than in other countries relied on custodial sanctions. On the other hand, the establishment
of the multiagency approach and the so-called Youth Offending Teams
should not be seen primarily as a "neoliberal" or "repressive" way of
dealing with young offenders. Much of it is in line with the classic idea
of education or, in modern words, "preventing reoffending." Also, the

emphasis given to reparation orders or to mediation may not necessarily be seen as "neoliberal." A recalibration in policy and practice has been in demand in the academic sphere for some time and has recently been highlighted by the 2010 policy paper of the Police Foundation ("Time for a Fresh Start"). The title of the volume edited by David Smith in 2010 (*A New Response to Youth Crime*) also stands for such a rethinking of criminal and penal policy.[17] In spite of the riots in some cities in 2011, the new government did not rely on harsher punishments and the "prison works" philosophy of the 1990s and 2000s and instead developed a new strategy that expanded diversion and restricted custodial sentences. So the "offenders brought to justice" strategy and restrictions on applying diversion ("final warning") were given up by the Legal Aid, Sentencing and Punishment of Offenders Act in 2012.

Estonia in 2001 raised the age of criminal responsibility from 13 to 14. In 2002, major juvenile justice legislation followed, expanding diversion and community sanctions and including restorative justice elements (reparation, mediation). In the same year, an amendment to the Code of Criminal Procedure determined that judges have to decide about the placement of a minor in a "school for students who need special treatment" due to behavioral problems. The juvenile committee has to provide a substantiated application in written form.

Finland—as the other Scandinavian countries—has no separate juvenile court system. Nevertheless, some peculiarities exist in the general framework of the Criminal Code. Already in 1989, the imposition of custodial sentences was further restricted to exceptional cases, and in 1997, special emphasis was given to conditional sentences with supervision (the so-called juvenile punishment order). The general criminal policy in Finland has resulted in one of the lowest prison populations in the world (comparable to the other Scandinavian countries; see Lappi-Seppälä 2007). The general trends in juvenile crime policy are in the same line with the minimum intervention model. A particularity of the Finnish system is that the focus of social control concerning children (ages 10–14) and juveniles (ages 15–17) is on the child welfare system, which also deals with delinquents who in other countries are dealt with by the criminal justice system. Interestingly, the welfare system has experienced similar liberal reforms as the justice system, with a considerable reduction of involuntary placements to closed welfare institutions. The reform of the Child Welfare Act in 2006 strengthened the legal guarantees for those who are taken into public care, particularly in welfare institutions.

Some of the reform movements of the past years in *France* may be characterized by the "getting tough" or "neoliberal" approach. The inability to mitigate sentences for 16- and 17-year-old recidivist offenders or the acceleration of criminal procedures with the declared aim of establishing immediate punishments may be seen in this light. However, the reforms of 2002, 2004, 2007, and 2008 kept the general educational approach of the Ordinance of 1945 and also improved the system of supervision in the community (protection judiciaire). Since 2002, educational (welfare) measures can also be imposed on 10- to 12-year-old offenders. As far as the new closed welfare institutions (since 2002) and the juvenile prisons (since 2007) are concerned, their strong rehabilitative approach has to be recognized. These institutions are of high quality and much better equipped than are most of their counterparts in other countries.

Germany passed a major juvenile law reform in 1990. The possibilities of diversion were expanded, and new "alternatives," which had been developed by the practice in the 1980s, were implemented into the law: mediation, social training courses, community service, and special care and supervision by social workers. Alternatives to pretrial detention were expanded, including legal representation for juveniles detained. A few reforms can be characterized as orientation to more intensive sentencing: in 2006, the possibilities of a joint procedure by the victim was introduced in the Juvenile Justice Act (JJA) but to a lesser extent than in the general criminal procedure against adults. In 2008, preventive detention after an offender has served a juvenile prison sentence of at least seven years was introduced[18]—a mostly symbolic law reform, as probably no cases will arise. In the same year, § 2 of JJA clearly formulated the aim of juvenile justice by strictly prioritizing the prevention of reoffending and the reintegration of juvenile and young adult offenders into society. This is formulated as a basic principle for guiding the sentencing practice as well as the juvenile criminal procedure. In 2013, another symbolic "punitive" reform was passed by introducing the combination of the short-term unconditional detention (up to four weeks) with a conditional youth prison sentence (probation). The conditions for that combination have been formulated very narrowly, so that the application in practice remains rare.

The law reform of 2003 in *Greece* (similar to the German reform of 1990) clearly intended the introduction of diversion, mediation, and other new community sanctions to expand due process rules and to further limit juvenile imprisonment as a measure of last resort. Indeterminate sanctions and measures were abolished. In 2010, the age of criminal responsibility was raised from 13 to 15.

Hungary has special regulations for juveniles in the general Criminal Code. In 1995, a law reform emphasized reintegration into society (special prevention) as the aim of juvenile justice. Procedural safeguards were strengthened and juvenile imprisonment restricted as a measure of last resort. In 2000, the general Mediation Act emphasized restorative justice elements (mediation), which were expanded by the reform of the Criminal Procedure Act in 2007 (extended possibilities of diversion and mediation). In 2011, the scope for the use of mediation and restorative proceedings was again expanded. Since 2009, several reforms in general criminal law intensified the sentencing for adults. However, juveniles and young adults were exempted from these policy changes. On the other hand, according to a law reform of 2010, certain administrative and minor offenses can result in short-term detention of up to 90 days. This also applies to juveniles. The new conservative government is currently discussing a lowering of the age of criminal responsibility, but a decision has not yet been reached.

After almost a hundred years since the introduction of juvenile justice legislation, *Ireland* introduced a major law reform in 2001 giving strong priority to restorative justice (mediation, family group conferences), diversion, and community sanctions. Imprisonment for offenders under 18 years old was abolished. The age of criminal responsibility was raised from seven to 12 but in 2006 lowered again to 10, but only for very serious cases such as murder. Antisocial-behavior orders were also introduced in 2006, but there is also wide discretion for diversion in this area.

The last major reform in *Italy* was the general amendment of the Criminal Procedure Act in 1988 (DPR 488/88), with some specific rules for the juvenile criminal procedure by another legislative decree (of 28 July 1989, no. 272), opening the door for diversion and alternative sanctions including mediation. The new juvenile and adult criminal procedure signified a shift from an inquisitorial to an accusatory model. In 1998, a general reform also affected juvenile offenders: a prognostic assessment in prisons or detention is no longer necessary—that is, prison sentences under three years may be suspended immediately.

Latvia in 1998 passed the Law on the Protection of the Rights of the Child. The orientation on procedural safeguards and the primary aim of reintegration of juvenile offenders are well expressed by the title of the law. In 2002, two further reform laws strengthened the idea of diversion and of expanding the scope of community sanctions such as reparation and community service orders.

In *Lithuania*, the major reform of the Criminal Code in 2003 included the expansion of educational measures and community sanctions for juvenile offenders. Diversion, mediation, and community service became issues of the reform movement, but emphasis was also given to procedural safeguards and to further restrictions on the deprivation of liberty. Another reform law in 2007 emphasized educational measures for and supervision of young offenders.

The reform of 1995 in the *Netherlands* brought a mixture of extended alternative sanctions including diversionary measures on the one hand and a more serious punishment for 16- and 17-year-olds in serious cases on the other, by either being transferred to adult courts or being sentenced for up to two years of juvenile imprisonment (before, the maximum was six months). In 2001, alternatives to pretrial detention were abolished; the 2005 reform, with stricter and tougher application of community sanctions, can be characterized as a "neoliberal" orientation. A totally new direction was followed by the law reform of 1 April 2014: the age of criminal responsibility was raised from 12 to 15, and the scope of juvenile justice was extended to the age of 23. This reform was based primarily on new evidence from neurosciences about brain maturation showing that that the full development of important functions to foresee the consequences of one's behavior and other higher brain functions of the frontal cortex are reached around the age of 25 (see Loeber et al. 2012, with further references). The Netherlands reforms are in line with the recommendations of the Council of Europe to expand juvenile justice to young adults and even to young adults older than 21.

Northern Ireland's Children Order of 1995 brought a separation of welfare and justice procedures and thus an orientation to the justice model by strengthening procedural safeguards and due process regulations for juvenile offenders. At the same time, diversion and the range for community sanctions were expanded. A 1996 reform strengthened the ideas of educational measures for juveniles. In 2001, the statutory basis for youth conferencing (family group conferencing) was created, thus shifting juvenile justice to the restorative justice model, and 17-year-old juveniles were included into the juvenile justice system.

Poland already in 1982 had its major law reform on juvenile justice. The emphasis was on a unique justice and welfare model concerning 13- to 17-year-olds. However, in cases of very serious crimes, juveniles aged 15 and above may be sentenced according to the general criminal law. The juvenile law gives strict priority to educational measures and restricts deprivation of liberty. Due process regulations are of more importance in procedures concerning juvenile offenders (in contrast to juveniles prosecuted for phenomena of "demoralization"), particularly when detention in a correctional institution is to be considered. Mediation and victim-offender reconciliation is emphasized by the Mediation Act of 2000.

In *Portugal*, major juvenile justice law reforms in the year 1999 aimed to extinguish the worst consequences of the pure welfare model that prevailed since 1925, in particular by introducing due process guarantees. Accordingly, since 2001, Portugal follows an educational approach for juvenile offenders between 12 and 15 years of age. The juvenile is deemed responsible for his or her actions but not in a penal way. The court may—after a procedure that follows similar rules as a criminal procedure for adults—apply compulsory educational measures but no criminal sanctions; 16- to 21-year-old offenders are fully criminally responsible, but special mitigating regulations and alternatives have been introduced. In 2007, house arrest (including electronic monitoring) was added as a special alternative for this age group.

In 1992, a reform of the Criminal Code in *Romania* introduced educational measures for juvenile offenders but also provided for harsher punishment. The reform of 1996 was in line with the educational approach through the expansion of community sanctions. The Law on the Protection and the Promotion of the Rights of the Child of 2004 strengthened procedural safeguards and provided a stronger justice orientation, in line with international standards. Mediation became a major issue after the Law on Mediation of 2006 and a further law reform in 2009 (which went into effect in 2011).

The general reform of the Penal Code in *Russia* in 1996 brought special educational measures for juveniles, including diversionary and community-based sanctions (e.g., community service). Procedural safeguards were strengthened by the Basic Principles for Juvenile Offenders passed in 1999, but diversionary measures were also expanded. In 2001, mediation and reparation became a major issue of juvenile law reform.

In 1995 in *Scotland*, statutory regulations of the Children's Hearing System dealing with eight- to 15-year-olds were introduced. The focus is on restorative justice elements including mediation and reparation. In 2004, antisocial-behavior and parenting orders were introduced, but the practice seems to be rarer than in England and Wales. In 2010, the age of criminal prosecution was raised from eight to 12, and the competence of the Children's Hearing System remained unchanged.

Serbia in 2006 established independent and separate juvenile justice legislation. It is strongly oriented toward international standards with regard to the principles of education, minimum intervention, and proportionality. Diversion and restorative justice elements are specially emphasized.

The reform of 2005 in *Slovakia* on the one hand is in line with the European justice and welfare orientation with the expansion of the range of community sanctions, but on the other hand more repressive tendencies clearly can be identified. Sentences for recidivist and violent offenders were increased, and the age of criminal responsibility was lowered from 15 to 14; however, 14-year-olds are only responsible if they display the capacity of discernment concerning the wrongdoing of their behavior.

Slovenia got a major law reform in the context of amendments in the Penal Code in 1995, by which diversion was prioritized and mediation, reparation, and community service were introduced. Also, procedural safeguards have been strengthened. Interestingly, the general law reforms in 1999, 2004, and 2008, which increased the penalties of the general Criminal Code for adults (inter alia, "three-strikes" legislation), left out juveniles.

Spain created a justice-oriented juvenile law for the age group of 12- to 15-year-olds in 1992. In 1995, legislation was amended, and the age group of 14- to 17-year-olds was the subject of Penal Code legislation. The focus was on diversion and restorative justice elements (mediation, reparation). The same orientation to modern juvenile justice principles is to be seen in the separate Juvenile Justice Act of 2000. In 2006, however, some tightening of the law can be identified too. Young adults who according to the draft bill should have been subject to educational measures of the Juvenile Justice Act were excluded again before the specific rule of 2000 came into force. So Spain is one of the few countries that does not provide any special regulations for 18- to 20-year-old offenders (Dünkel and Pruin 2011; Pruin and Dünkel 2014).

Sweden traditionally relies on a welfare orientation by transferring juvenile offenders (aged 15 to 17) regularly to the welfare authorities. Punishments according to the general Criminal Code and particularly imprisonment have become a measure of last resort for 15- to 17-year-old juveniles (see also Dünkel and Stańdo-Kawecka 2011). In 1999, the transfer to social welfare authorities was expanded as a kind of diversion. Closed youth care institutions were established as an alternative to youth imprisonment. In practice, this meant a net widening, as instead of the expected number of around 10 juveniles, more than 100 were found in these institutions. With regard to the principle of proportionality, specific human rights standards (the principle of certainty, that is, determination of the sanction to be expected and of proportionality) have been implemented by extending the court's control over the welfare services in 2007. The reform law of 2007 aimed at reducing fines for young offenders by introducing special juvenile sanctions, the so-called youth service and the youth care. Youth service contains unpaid work (20–150 hours) plus attendance in program work or education. Youth care can mean different forms of treatment organized by the welfare authorities.

The reform in *Switzerland*, with the introduction of a separate Juvenile Justice Act in 2007, is in line with the international standards of emphasizing education, diversion, and a variety of community sanctions including mediation and reparation. Procedural safeguards as well as the principles of minimum intervention and proportionality are emphasized. Youth imprisonment is the measure of last resort; instead, detention in mostly open welfare homes is prioritized. Although the maximum youth prison sentence has been increased to four years (for at least 16-year-olds), the Swiss juvenile justice system can be characterized as a moderate educational and justice approach.

Turkey in 1992 passed a reform of the Criminal Procedure Act strengthening some procedural safeguards for juveniles (e.g., obligatory defense counsels). In 2003, the Children's Courts Act (1979) was amended, expanding the scope of juvenile justice from 12- to 15-year-olds to 12- to 18-year-old juvenile offenders. The Child Protection Law of 2005 expanded diversionary procedures (referrals to the welfare agencies) and the range of community sanctions (e.g., reparation, community service).

In the *Ukraine*, the reform of the general Penal Code in 2001 established special educational sanctions for 14- to 17-year-old juvenile offenders, including diversion, reparation, and community service orders. The reforms in Ukraine—as in the other central and eastern European countries—were inspired by the new membership in the Council of Europe and the ambition to meet the requirements of international juvenile justice standards such as the recommendations of the Council of Europe and the United Nations.

Altogether, the present international comparison shows that in the majority of countries there has in fact not been a reversal from the precept of education and the prevailing aim of preventing reoffending. Also, countries that moved toward the "getting tough" approach have kept their general orientation of dealing with juveniles (and young adults) differently compared to adults. Reforms aimed at more severe sentencing of young offenders regularly are restricted to certain recidivist or violent offenders (e.g., in England and Wales, France, the Netherlands, Romania, and Slovakia).

It also can be deemed as internationally accepted that less intensive interventions, including diversion (if need be in connection with victim-offender reconciliation, reparation, and other socially constructive interventions), better assist the integration of the "normal" juvenile delinquent (characterized by the episodic nature of his or her offending) than intensive (repressive) interventions, especially imprisonment (see Dünkel and Pruin 2009; Dünkel, Pruin, and Grzywa 2011).

On the other hand, the education goal does not allow for long-term indeterminate interventions. Restrictions of educational criminal law through sentencing that is proportional to the offense are necessary, especially concerning custodial sentences. There is no justification to extend custodial sentences because of "educational needs," leading to disproportionate interventions.

Developments of Sentencing Young Offenders

Even if reform developments in juvenile justice legislation do not confirm a "punitive turn," it is possible that sentencing practices in some or many countries follow the "getting tough" approach in order to fulfill public demands for reactions to juvenile delinquency with more severe sanctioning. In order to evaluate this hypothesis, we can observe a general lack of reliable comparative and longitudinal data.[19] In many countries, data on sentencing practices are not complete, comparable, or even accessible, in particular, regarding informal reactions (diversion etc.). If data on diversion are not clear, sentencing statistics of the courts are hardly interpretable. Therefore, we must abstain from a comprehensive cross-national comparison among the 34 countries involved in the study. To evaluate the hypothesis of an increasing "punitiveness," it may be sufficient to evaluate national data in a longitudinal perspective in order to examine the changes in time. Reliable and interpretable data must consider the delinquency structure and qualitative changes in juvenile crime. Often such data were not presented in the national reports in the present study. The decrease of youth imprisonment may be related to diminished youth violence and not necessarily to a milder sentencing practice. The following presentation therefore may only give some indication in favor or disfavor of the hypothesis of a "new punitiveness" (see in more detail Dünkel, Pruin, and Grzywa 2011: 1684).[20]

In *Bulgaria*, since the reform laws of 1996 and 2004, fewer custodial sanctions are imposed, whereas victim-offender agreements increased considerably (more than 40% of all court dispositions). About one-fourth of juvenile delinquents are formally sentenced, almost half of them to deprivation of liberty (before the law reforms, almost 90% of court dispositions were custodial sanctions).

In *Croatia*, in the 1980s, the proportion of juveniles sentenced to imprisonment was about three times higher (16%–22%) than today. As in other countries, deprivation of liberty in a closed setting has therefore become the absolute exception and accounts for only about 2%–3% of all informal and formal sanctions imposed on juveniles.

In *Denmark*, the sentencing practice has not changed significantly after the introduction of the so-called youth sentence in 2002. Still, less than 10 juveniles are in prison departments on a given day.

In the *Czech Republic*, the proportion of custodial sentences decreased from 14% in 1995 to 7% in 2006. The number of youth prisoners correspondingly decreased from 300 to 100 (see Dünkel, Pruin, and Grzywa 2011: 1687).

England and Wales showed a strongly increasing rate of the juvenile prison population during the 1990s until the middle of the first decade of the 21st century. The more punitive sentencing practice included also the imposition of longer sentences and a decline of diversion rates, which was a result of the so-called final warning system introduced in 1998 (excluding diversion for a third-time offense). The prevailing philosophy of "prison works" was translated into the "offenders brought to justice" strategy during the 1990s and early 21st century. This approach has been reversed by abolishing the restrictions of the final warning system and expanding diversion by the Legal Aid, Sentencing and Punishment of Offenders Act in 2012. The practice, however, had already been reversed before the legislative change came into force. The sentencing practice in England and Wales has changed considerably: the number of 10- to 17-year-old offenders sentenced to imprisonment had increased from 4,719 in 1994 to 7,653 in 1999, which means an increase of 62%. Since then, the yearly numbers have been reduced to 4,104 in 2012, a decrease of 46%. This decrease in part is the result of demographic changes, but per 100,000 of the age group, it still represents a 32% decline and is thus very remarkable.[21] It is paradoxically under the new conservative government that a shift from "neoliberal" sentencing has been discussed and that the government definitively has wanted to restrict immediate custody (mainly because of budgetary restrictions).[22] The results are amazing: as mentioned earlier, the numbers of immediate custody (including pretrial detention) have been reduced. Correspondingly, the per diem population in youth custody of 10- to 17-year-old juveniles declined by 43% from 2007 to 2012 for the age group of 15- to 17-year-olds and to only one-third for the age group of 10- to 14-year-olds (see Horsfield 2015). In November 2012, only 1,485 juveniles were deprived of their liberty (a 49% reduction, compared to 2,933 five years before). The reduction was similar for the detention and training order (–45%), for pretrial detention (–40%), and for sentences of at least two years imposed by the Crown Court (–41%, from 533 in custody in 2008 to 313 in 2012; see Horsfield 2015).

In *Estonia*, since the reform of 2002, the proportion of diversionary measures (transfer to so-called youth committees) has tripled and is now more than 80%. Although statistical data are not always clear, the number of custodial sanctions has considerably declined.

In *Finland*, the imposition of prison sentences has declined over the years. While in 1980 3.5% of all cases dealt with by the courts resulted in imprisonment, only 0.8% were in 2006. This implies that Finland is taking the idea of applying imprisonment as a last resort very seriously. As a reason, Lappi-Seppälä sees reforms that he signifies as "humane neo-classicism" (see Lappi-Seppälä 2011). Law reforms in Finland stressed both legal safeguards against coercive care and the goal of less repressive measures in general. In sentencing, the principles of proportionality and predictability have become the central values. The population seems to agree with these objectives and has not voiced any demands for harsher punishments, not even in cases of serious offending. The most frequently used sanction in Finland is the fine, which is quite exceptional compared to the legal situation and practice in other European countries.[23] Fines account for 74% of court sentences issued against 15- to 17-year-old juveniles. The second most relevant sanction in Finland is conditional imprisonment, accounting for over 17% of all interventions in 2005. Overall, one can conclude that Finland follows a strategy of minimum intervention and that there have been no indications that practice has become or is becoming harsher or more severe.

The criminal prosecution system in *France* is traditionally based on the principle of expediency. The prosecutor has the discretion whether or not to prosecute. In 2006, almost 60% of cases were dismissed. The proportion of unconditional prison sentences among all sentences increased from 8% in 1980 to almost 14% in 2003 but subsequently dropped again to 10% in 2006, which is close to the figures of the early 1980s. It has to be considered as well that the social control within the area of community sanctions has been increased by enforced forms of supervision (*protection judiciaire*), which includes electronic monitoring in some cases. However, these changes quantitatively are difficult to measure.

In *Germany*, in the 1980s, a major movement toward diversion and new educational alternative sanctions occurred. Diversion rates increased considerably from slightly more than 40% in the early 1980s to 70% in 2008. Although a considerable number of violent and more serious offenders entered the juvenile justice system in the beginning of the 1990s, an amazing stability of the sanctioning practice remains characteristic. Unconditional juvenile imprisonment accounts for only 2%–3% of all informally (prosecutors and youth courts) or formally (youth courts after a trial) sanctioned juveniles and young adults aged 14–20. However, another 5% of the juveniles and young adults experience the disciplinary measure of short-term detention of up to four weeks (*Jugendarrest*). The sentencing practice in the eastern federal states 20 years after the reunification has adjusted to the "western" style. Altogether, the sentencing practice is oriented to the minimum intervention model (including some restorative elements, mediation, and community service orders).

In some aspects, sentencing practice in *Greece* is different from the countries that have been discussed so far. Informal (diversionary) sanctions such as the absolute discharge, which has only been available since 2003, are only rarely applied. With regard to formal sentencing, educational measures play a pivotal role, with approximately 75% of all cases resulting in the imposition of an educational measure. More specifically, the most common of these measures is the reprimand, accounting for more than 50% of all court dispositions. It is remarkable that imprisonment is the second most commonly ordered sentence in Greece. More than 20% of all dispositions are sentences to imprisonment. Around 70% of prison sentences are less than one month, and 90% are less than six months in duration. This means that short prison sentences are clearly predominant. What is more, they are executed only very rarely because they are often suspended (similar to probation). Fines are almost never issued against juveniles in Greece. The sentencing data make no indication of an intensification or toughening up of Greek practice. Greece, on the other hand, does not seem to follow any strategies of nonintervention. Obviously the Greek system emphasizes warning offenders through formal proceedings and sanctions that are in fact not very invasive on second glance.

Despite poor statistical evidence, it becomes clear that, with the reform of the Children Act of 2001 in *Ireland*, the use of custodial sentences has diminished, and the scope of restorative and other educational measures has been broadened. In conformity with this policy, the numbers of juveniles detained in reformatory and industrial schools on 30 June of each year show an overall downward trend from 159 in 1978 to 41 in 2005.

In *Hungary*, the proportion of diversion in the sense of an unconditional discharge (mostly combined with a reprimand) has increased from 16% in 1980 to 34% in 2007. Other forms of diversion are the postponement of an indictment and the referral to mediation schemes. The result of this orientation to informal reactions is that the proportion of indictments decreased from almost 84% to 58%. The court sentencing practice, too, shows a clear tendency toward less severe punishments. The proportion of (suspended and unconditional) juvenile prison sentences dropped from 34% in 1980 to 27% in 2007. At the same time, the proportion of suspended sentences increased from 47% to 74%. In other words, only 6.3% of all convicted juveniles received an unconditional prison sentence in 2007 (the corresponding figure for 1980 was 18%).[24] Altogether, Hungary has made great progress toward meeting the international standards that emphasize minimum intervention and community sanctions and measures.

Although statistical data are rarely available and not always validated, it seems to be evident that the criminal justice system in *Italy* can still be characterized by its specific leniency and moderate sentencing practice, which results in amazingly low incarceration rates, particularly for juvenile offenders (see in general Nelken 2009, 2010). Populist rhetoric, which from time to time emerges in the political debates in Italy (from Berlusconi and others), does not change this picture. The reform law of 1988 has led to an expansion of judicial diversionary measures (*perdono giudiziare*).

Latvia had a rather stable sentencing practice in the 1990s, but with the introduction of community service in 1999 and further community sanctions such as mediation in 2005, the youth prison population has been reduced from 438 in 2000 to 149 on 1 January 2010 (a reduction of 66%).

In *Lithuania*, the law reform of 2003 has not yet had too much impact. Still, about 30% of sentenced juveniles receive custodial sanctions. However, this proportion is much lower than in Soviet times.

In the *Netherlands*, since the mid-1980s, a "getting tough" approach has emerged insofar as diversion without any intervention has been reduced. The law reform of 1995 introduced longer custodial sanctions (up to one or two years instead of up to six months), which has had some impact on the sentencing practice. The proportion of dismissals or of diversionary transfers to projects is somewhat unclear. Therefore, the relatively large proportion of about 30% custodial sanctions on the court level is difficult to interpret.

In *Northern Ireland*, much emphasis is given to the police diversion schemes that are successful "in managing to keep the number of young people prosecuted through the courts to a minimum" (O'Mahony 2011: 971). The numbers of juveniles sentenced by the courts decreased from 1,254 in 1987 to 722 in 2004, and the proportion of custodial sanctions decreased from 21% to 10% of all court dispositions. The major law reform of 2001 has had further impact on sentencing. Youth conferencing (introduced in 2004) became the major alternative sanction, which further reduced custody.

In *Poland* also, since 1990, the proportion of custodial sanctions has been reduced to a very low level of about 2% of all measures issued by the family court.

In *Romania*, diversion is used extensively. Whereas in 1995 only 28% of the cases involving minors were diverted, the percentage rose to 53% by 1999 and reached 81% in 2007. Concerning the court dispositions, prison sentences are applied relatively often. In 1996, almost half of convicted minors were given prison sentences. In the following years, the number of minors sentenced to prison dropped and accounted for roughly one-quarter of all sentences in 2006. In 2002, a probation service was created, which contributed to an increase of probation sentences.

A trend to use alternative sanctions is visible in *Russia*, too. In Soviet times, 30%–50% of convictions involved custodial sanctions. In 2005, the proportion decreased to "only" 24%, which still reflects a rather severe punishment practice. Diversion until 2005 counted only for 25% of all juvenile criminal cases; that is, the judges relied more on alternative court sanctions than on informal sanctions. Developments in the following years indicate a further dramatic change of the youth justice policy: the number of juveniles in youth prisons declined from 18,677 in 2001 to 2,300 at the end of 2012, a decrease of 88% (see Dünkel 2014).

The developments in *Scotland* can be seen in contrast to England and Wales. Custodial sanctions for 16- to 21-year-old offenders decreased between 1990 and 2006, and the younger age group below 16 also profited from alternative sanctions.

Serbia has extended diversion by the reform of 2005; however, exact statistical data are lacking. Nevertheless, a reduction of custodial sentences was observable already before the law reform.

Interestingly, the sentencing practice in *Slovakia* has not changed very much, although the official crime policy has emphasized more severe punishment of juvenile offenders.

Slovenia belongs in the category of countries with an absolutely moderate sentencing practice. Since 1980, the proportion of custodial sentence has further decreased.

Longitudinal data about *Spain* have not been available. However, there are indicators for a tougher sentencing practice in Catalonia, with an increased proportion of custodial sentences in the 21st century.

In contrast, *Sweden* has kept its policy to avoid imprisonment for 15- to 17-year-old juveniles and 18- to 20-year-old young adults and to use it only as a very last resort. Law reforms led to a less extensive diversion practice. The result is not more severe punishment but an increase of transfers to the Social Welfare Boards (in 2008, two-thirds of all criminal cases).

In *Switzerland*, too, custodial sentences remain the absolute exception. Interestingly, the few youth prison sentences—if ever applied—are very short (almost 80% less than one month). The figures demonstrate that the Swiss sentencing practice is not punitive at all.

Data on the sentencing practice in the *Ukraine* are not easily accessible and are incomplete. An indicator for a change in the sentencing practice of courts may be seen in the reduction of inmates in so-called youth colonies (youth prisons) since 2000. During the 1990s, the number was around 3,300–3,900 per day; in 2007, it declined to about 1,900.

Summary and Conclusion

Juvenile justice systems in Europe have developed in various forms and with different orientations. Looking at sanctions and measures, the general trend reveals the expansion of diversion, combined in some countries with educational or other measures that aim to improve the compliance with the norm violated by the juvenile offender (*Normverdeutlichung*), that is, to prevent reoffending or to strengthen the offender's propensity for a law-abiding life. Mediation, victim-offender reconciliation, and family group conferences are good examples of such diversionary strategies.[25] On the other hand, from an international comparative perspective, systems based solely on child and youth welfare are on the retreat. This is not as evident in Europe, where more or less "pure" welfare-orientated approaches exist only in Belgium and Poland,[26] as in, for instance, Latin American countries, which traditionally have been oriented to the classic welfare approach (Tiffer-Sotomayor 2000; Tiffer-Sotomayor, Llobet Rodríguez, and Dünkel 2012; Gutbrodt 2010).

Across Europe, elements of restorative justice have been implemented, both in countries that to some extent adopt neoliberal or neo-correctional approaches and in those with a relatively strong welfare orientation. In addition, educational and other measures—which try to improve the social competences of young offenders, such as social training courses and cognitive-behavioral training and therapy—have been developed more widely. These developments are in line with international juvenile justice standards. The 2003 recommendation of the Council of Europe on new ways of dealing with juvenile delinquency clearly emphasizes the development of new, more constructive community sanctions also for recidivist and other problematic offender groups. This recommendation maintains the traditional idea of juvenile justice as a special "educational" system of intervention designed to prevent the individual from reoffending.

Although the ideal of using deprivation of liberty only as a measure of last resort for juveniles has been hailed as desirable across Europe, it cannot be denied that in some countries "neoliberal" orientations have influenced juvenile justice policy and, to a varying extent, also practice (see Muncie 2008, with further references). The widening of the scope for youth detention in England and Wales, France, and the Netherlands may be interpreted as a "punitive turn." And indeed the youth prison population in these countries did increase considerably in the 1990s; however, these trends have been reversed in the past few years. Muncie (2008: 110) refers to public debates and statements of academics also in other (including Scandinavian) countries and comes to the conclusion that "such commentaries clearly suggest that not only in the USA and England and Wales but throughout much of Western Europe, punitive values associated with retribution, incapacitation, individual responsibility and offender accountability have achieved a political legitimacy to the detriment of traditional principles of juvenile protection and support."

This conclusion reflects only a facet of the full reality. A different reality emerges, however, when one considers the practice of juvenile prosecutors, courts, social workers, and youth welfare agencies and projects such as mediation schemes. These continue to operate in a reasonably moderate way and thus to resist penal populism. Deprivation of liberty remains the truly last resort in Scandinavia and indeed in most other regions and countries (von Hofer 2004; Storgaard 2004; Haverkamp 2007). This differentiated picture of a "new complexity" (Habermas 1985) is the main message of the research presented by the major comparative study on juvenile justice legislation and sentencing practice in Europe on which this chapter is largely based (see in detail Dünkel, Pruin, and Grzywa 2011; Dünkel, Grzywa, Pruin, and Šelih 2011).

Snacken has sought to explain why many European countries have resisted penal populism and punitiveness (Snacken 2010, 2012; Snacken and Durmontiers 2012). She has emphasized that European states are constitutional democracies strongly oriented toward the welfare state, democracy, and human rights. These fundamental orientations, which can be found most clearly in many continental western European states and particularly in Scandinavian states (Lappi-Seppälä 2007, 2010, and chap. 2 in this volume), serve as "protective factors" against penal populism (see also Pratt 2008a, 2008b).

It is undoubtedly true that penal populism does not halt at the gates of youth justice (Pratt et al. 2005; Ciappi 2007; see also Garland 2001a, 2001b; Roberts and Hough 2002; Tonry 2004; Muncie 2008). Generally speaking, however, the same factors that have allowed such punitiveness to be resisted in many European countries apply even more strongly to youth justice. Moreover, juvenile offending is different from that of adults. Its episodic nature allows for more tolerance and moderate reactions.

The relative invulnerability of youth justice to punitive tendencies is reinforced by the strong framework of international and European human rights standards that apply to it, courtesy of the 1989 UN Convention on the Rights of the Child and the other instruments mentioned earlier. More specifically, these instruments also emphasize the expansion of procedural safeguards, on the one hand, and the limitation or reduction of the intensity of sentencing interventions, on the other hand.

Clearly more needs to be done, and this chapter has highlighted three areas in which policies are still unresolved, at both the international and the European level:

- One step forward would be to raise the age of criminal responsibility to at least the European average of 14 or 15 (see also Hammarberg 2008).
- A second step would be to build on the interesting initiatives to increase the maximum age at which young offenders can be treated as if they were juveniles. This could do much to protect a potentially vulnerable group and to divert them from a career of adult crime. The recent reform of April 2014 in the Netherlands increasing the scope of juvenile justice up to the age of 23 may be seen as the forerunner in juvenile justice reform in this respect.
- Third, the contrary tendency toward trying juveniles as adults should be resisted. It not only is doctrinally dubious, as explained earlier, but holds the risk of increasing the impact of the worst features of the adult criminal justice system on young offenders.

In sum, youth justice policy as reflected in legislation and practice in the majority of European countries has successfully resisted a punitive turn. While there is more work to be done in areas where policy is not yet clear, it is realistic to hope that neoliberal approaches will be moderated. Important signs in this direction can be observed in England and Wales and the Netherlands, where neoliberal policies have rhetorically been prominent in the past decades. A shift to revitalizing the educational aim of juvenile justice and to expand diversion and other alternatives to youth custody can also be recently observed in the United States (see Bishop and Feld 2012: 914; Dünkel 2014) and Canada (see Bala 2015). Therefore, there is some evidence that the ideal of social inclusion and reintegration will be the leitmotiv for juvenile justice reforms of the 21st century in Europe and other continents as well.

NOTES

1. A note on terminology: I use the terms *youth* and *youth justice* as well as *juvenile justice* in this chapter in the same sense. The term *juvenile justice* is in use in a number of international, European, and national instruments, where it usually refers to persons under the age of 18 years. However, the Convention on the Rights of the Child uses the term *child* to refer to anyone under the age of 18 years. I have not followed this usage of *child*, as it is not always appropriate in this context. Finally, I use the term *young adults* to refer to persons between the ages of 18 and 21 who are treated as youths or juveniles as proposed by the European Rules for Juvenile Offenders Subject to Sanctions or Measures (Rec. [2008] 11); see rule 17.

2. The meaning of the term *neoliberal*, which derives from the concept of Garland's "culture of control," contains different concepts and aspects that cannot be simply characterized by more repressive sanctions or sentencing: see Crawford and Lewis 2007: 30. These include the criminalization of antisocial behavior (ASBOs), increased use of youth custody, managerialism, and the reduction of risk by social exclusion rather than by integrating vulnerable offender groups through specific programs.

3. This chapter is an extended and updated version of a chapter in a 2013 edited book on European penology (see Dünkel 2013) and is inspired by the discussion of "new punitiveness" (Pratt et al. 2005) and so-called neoliberal orientations that can be observed in some European and in particular Anglo-Saxon jurisdictions (see among others Tonry 2004), in contrast to Scandinavian countries that are characterized under the label of "penal exceptionalism"; see Pratt 2008a, 2008b; and Lappi-Seppälä, chap. 2 in this volume. This chapter shows that not only Scandinavian countries but a lot of others, and in particular their juvenile justice systems, have succeeded in "resisting punitiveness in Europe" (Snacken and Dumortiers 2012).

4. The comparison is based largely on a survey of 34 countries conducted by the Criminology Department at the University of Greifswald; Dünkel et al. 2011. The project was funded by the European Union (AGIS program) and by the Ministry of Education of the Federal State of Mecklenburg–Western Pomerania in Germany.

5. See also Snacken 2010 and the contributions in Snacken and Dumortiers 2012.

6. See, critically, Crawford and Lewis 2007: 27; and Cavadino and Dignan 2006: 68, with regard to the "managerial" and the "getting tough" approaches.

7. See, for example, the so-called parenting order in England and Wales or similar measures in Belgium, Bulgaria, France, Greece, Ireland, or Scotland; Pruin 2011: 1559.

8. Roughly 8% of all sanctions imposed on juveniles; see Dünkel 2011a: 587; for Austria, see Bruckmüller 2006; for a summary of the development in 36 European countries, see Dünkel, Horsfield, and Grzywa 2015.

9. Recently (2011) the Russian parliament (*Duma*) has rejected a proposal to introduce a separate youth court system on a nationwide base. Opponents including the Russian Orthodox Church had warned of a state instrument of arbitrary prosecution and unwarranted interference in the realm of family. Supporters hoped to see a child-friendly institution that reduces juvenile delinquency and child homelessness and makes parents more responsible for their offspring. Ultimately, the influence of the Orthodox Church was of major importance for denying juvenile justice reforms.

10. In this context, the formal status of international instruments such as the Council of Europe's 2003 recommendation or the ERJOSSM of 2008 should be clarified. Such recommendations, unless they are formally incorporated into national law, are not binding for national legislators; they are sometimes called "soft laws." However, the German Constitutional Court delivered an important decision in May 2006, emphasizing the persuasive force of such recommendations: "It could be an indication that insufficient attention has been paid to the constitutional requirements of taking into account current knowledge and giving appropriate weight to the interests of the inmates if the requirements of international law or of international standards with human rights implications, such as the guidelines or recommendations adopted by the organs of the United Nations or the Council of Europe, are not taken into account or if the legislation falls below these requirements." (Federal Constitutional Court [*Bundesverfassungsgericht*] 2006: 2093, 2097; a similar statement can be found in a decision of the Swiss Federal Constitutional Court in 1992.)

11. See Christiaens, Dumortiers, and Nuyiens 2011, 115; Put and Walgrave 2006. Besides this possibility for waivers, traffic offenses are always judged by (adult) police courts.

12. In Belgium, the possibility of waivers is officially based on the need to compensate for the high age of criminal responsibility, which is set at 18 years (Christiaens, Dumortiers, and Nuyiens 2011: 114). In Germany, the same arguments are used to fight for the application of adult criminal law to young adults, that is, those from 18 to 20 years of age (Dünkel 2011a: 587–593; Dünkel and Pruin 2011, 2012; Pruin and Dünkel 2014).

13. These arguments do ultimately show fear of, and intolerance toward, juveniles' misconduct (Hartjen 2008: 9).

14. Bishop (2009: 97) emphasizes that the negative effects of transfer laws are found among those who receive community sanctions as well.

15. This has to do with the range of youth custody sentences: until 1995, youth courts in the Netherlands had the competence to impose youth prison sentences of up to six months only. The reform law extended it to two years in the case of 16- and 17-year-old juveniles. Therefore, juvenile judges only rarely have to transfer a case in order to arrive at a "proportionate" sentence; Pruin 2011: 1571.

16. The European Court for Human Rights has not found that such trials in adult courts necessarily violate the European Convention of Human Rights, but in *T. and V. v. The United Kingdom* ([2000] 30 E.H.R.R. 121), a case concerning the 10-year-old murderers of James Bulger, a significant minority of the judges took the view that trying such young offenders in an adult court would inevitably violate their rights.

17. See the Report of the Independent Commission on Youth Crime and Antisocial Behaviour of the Police Foundation 2010; Smith 2010. Goldson (2011: 3) has criticized the commission not going far enough, as it—for example—did not question the low age of criminal responsibility and in general the youth justice apparatus and concepts of responsibilization. Furthermore, "the limited coverage of children's human rights within the Commission is noteworthy" (Goldson 2011: 23n8).

18. The German Federal Constitutional Court in its decision of 4 May 2011 (2 BvR 2365/09) judged all forms of indeterminate preventive detention that could be imposed after an offender has served a determinate prison sentence as being a violation of the Constitution; therefore, the legislature had until 1 May 2013 to introduce new regulations for preventive detention that make its application an absolute exception extrema ultima ratio) and that in its execution is clearly distinct from regular prison sentences. Preventive detention must be rehabilitative in its nature (see also § 66c Penal Code of 2012). New legislation has been passed restricting preventive detention for 14- to 18-year-old juveniles to violent or sexual offenders sentenced to at least seven years of imprisonment and to at least five years in the case of young adults (18–21 years of age). It can be imposed only conditionally, and the offender's dangerousness must be judged by a new court hearing at the end of his or her having served the prison sentence. In the whole of Germany, only one young adult offender is in preventive detention (2014).

19. For Germany, see Heinz 2009, 2011b; Dünkel 2011b. For more detail regarding the many methodological problems and the problems of measuring "punitiveness" with regard to sentencing, see Heinz 2011a: 437.

20. There were also some data gaps, as in some countries, longitudinal data were not presented (e.g., for Belgium, Latvia, Portugal, and Turkey). The data on the sentencing practice in various European countries derive from the national reports in the aforementioned research (Dünkel Pruin, and Grzywa 2011).

21. See Ministry of Justice 2013 (own calculations according to Table 2e), and Horsfield 2015.

22. In the academic area, such a shift has been demanded for a long time, but it culminated in the policy paper of the Police Foundation ("Time for a Fresh Start"; see Police Foundation 2010) and the publication edited by David Smith in 2010 (*A New Response to Youth Crime*). Astonishingly, even after the riots in many cities in 2011, the government held this line to emphasize prevention instead of increased punishment and social exclusion.

23. Fines cannot be issued against juveniles in Belgium, Bulgaria, Croatia, Italy, Poland, Scotland, Serbia, and Spain; see Dünkel, Pruin, and Grzywa 2011: 1671, 1681.

24. Author's own calculations from table 3 of the report of Váradi-Csema 2011: 696.

25. However, diversion in the sense of nonintervention has been restricted, particularly for recidivist offenders, in some countries such as England and Wales (with a reverse reform movement since 2012; see Horsfield 2015), France, and the Netherlands. Diversionary restorative justice measures have been expanded in many European countries; for a summary, see Dünkel, Horsfield, and Grzywa 2015.

26. The Scottish practice to send juvenile offenders up to the age of 16 to the children's hearings system could also be characterized as a welfare approach.

REFERENCES

Albrecht, H.-J., and Kilchling, M. (eds.). (2002). *Jugendstrafrecht in Europa*. Freiburg i. Br., Germany: Max-Planck-Institut für ausländisches und internationales Strafrecht.

Bailleau, F., and Cartuyvels, Y. (eds.). (2007). *La justice pénale des mineurs en Europe— Entre modèle welfare et infléxions néo-libérales*. Paris: L'Harmattan.

Bala, N. (2015). Responding to juvenile crime in Canada: Law reform reduces use of courts and custody despite "law-and-order" rhetoric. In: Birckhead, T., and Mouthaan, S. (eds.), *The Future of Juvenile Justice*. New York: NYU Press. 103–124.

Belser, E. M., Hanson, K., Hirt, A. (2009). *Sourcebook on International Children's Rights*. Berne: Stämpfli.

Bishop, D. M. (2009). Juvenile transfer in the United States. In: Junger-Tas, J., and Dünkel, F. (eds.), *Reforming Juvenile Justice*. Dordrecht, Netherlands: Springer. 85–104.

Bishop, D. M., and Feld, B. C. (2012). Trends in juvenile justice policy and practice. In: Feld, B. C., and Bishop, D. M. (eds.), *The Oxford Handbook of Juvenile Crime and Juvenile Justice*. New York: Oxford University Press. 898–926.

Bonnie, R. J., Chemers, B. M., and Schuck, J. (eds.). (2012). *Reforming Juvenile Justice: A Developmental Approach*. Washington, DC: National Research Council of the National Academies.

Bruckmüller, K. (2006). Austria: A protection model. In: Junger-Tas, J., and Decker, S. H. (eds.), *International Handbook of Juvenile Justice*. Dordrecht, Netherlands: Springer. 263–294.

Casteignède, J., and Pignoux, N. (2011). France. In: Dünkel, F., Grzywa, J., Horsfield, P., and Pruin, I. (eds.), *Juvenile Justice Systems in Europe—Current Situation and*

Reform Developments, 2nd ed. Mönchengladbach, Germany: Forum Verlag Godesberg. 483–545.

Castro Morales, A. (2015). *Jugendstrafvollzug und Jugendstrafrecht in Chile, Peru und Bolivien unter besonderer Berücksichtigung von nationalen und internationalen Kontrollmechanismen. Rechtliche Regelungen, Praxis, Reformen und Perspektiven.* Mönchengladbach, Germany: Forum Verlag Godesberg.

Cavadino, M., and Dignan, J. (2006). *Penal Systems. A Comparative Approach.* London: Sage.

Cavadino, M., and Dignan, J. (2007). *The Penal System: An Introduction.* 4th ed. London: Sage.

Christiaens, J., Dumortiers, E., and Nuytiens, A. (2011). Belgium. In: Dünkel, F., Grzywa, J., Horsfield, P., and Pruin, I. (eds.). *Juvenile Justice Systems in Europe— Current Situation and Reform Developments.* 2nd ed. Mönchengladbach, Germany: Forum Verlag Godesberg. 99–129.

Ciappi, S. (2007). *La nuova punitività—Gestione dei conflitti e governo dell'insicurezza.* Soveria Mannelli, Italy: Università Rubbettino.

Cimamonti, S., di Marino, G., and Zappalà, E. (eds.). (2010). *Où va la justice des mineurs? (Allemagne, Espagne, France, Italie, Russie).* Torino, Italy: G. Ciappichelli Editore.

Committee on the Rights of the Child. (2007). *General Comment Nr. 10: Children's Rights in Juvenile Justice.* CRC/CGC/10, 25 April. http://tbinternet.ohchr.org/_layouts/treatybodyexternal/Download.aspx?symbolno=CRC%2fC%2fGC%2f10&Lang=en.

Council of Europe (ed.). (2009). *European Rules for Juvenile Offenders Subject to Sanctions or Measures.* Strasbourg, France: Council of Europe Publishing.

Crawford, A., and Lewis, S. (2007). Évolutions mondiales, orientations nationales et justice locale: les effets du néo-liberalisme sur la justice des mineurs en Angleterre et au Pays de Galles. In: Bailleau, F., and Cartuyvels, Y. (eds.), *La justice pénale des mineurs en Europe—Entre modèle welfare et infléxions néo-libérales.* Paris: L'Harmattan. 23–43.

Doak, J., and O'Mahony, D. (2011). Developing mediation and restorative justice for young offenders across Europe. In: Dünkel, F., Grzywa, J., Horsfield, P., and Pruin, I. (eds.), *Juvenile Justice Systems in Europe—Current Situation and Reform Developments*, 2nd ed. Mönchengladbach, Germany: Forum Verlag Godesberg. 1717–1746.

Doek, J. (2009). The UN Convention of the Rights of the Child. In: Junger-Tas, J., and Dünkel, F. (eds.), *Reforming Juvenile Justice.* Dordrecht, Netherlands: Springer. 19–31.

Doob, A. N., and Tonry, M. (2004). Varieties of youth justice. In: Tonry, M., and Doob, A. N. (eds.), *Youth Crime and Youth Justice: Comparative and Cross-National Perspectives.* Crime and Justice 31. Chicago: University of Chicago Press. 1–20.

Dünkel, F. (1997). Jugendstrafrecht in Europa—Entwicklungstendenzen und Perspektiven. In: Dünkel, F., van Kalmthout, A., and Schüler-Springorum, H. (eds.),

Entwicklungstendenzen und Reformstrategien des Jugendstrafrechts im europäischen Vergleich. Bonn, Germany: Forum Verlag Godesberg. 565–650.

Dünkel, F. (2006). Juvenile justice in Germany—Between welfare and justice. In: Junger-Tas, J., and Decker, S. H. (eds.), *International Handbook of Juvenile Justice.* Dordrecht, Netherlands: Springer. 225–262.

Dünkel, F. (2008). Jugendstrafrecht im europäischen Vergleich im Licht aktueller Empfehlungen des Europarats. *Neue Kriminalpolitik* 20:102–114.

Dünkel, F. (2009). Young people's rights: The role of the Council of Europe. In: Junger-Tas, J., and Dünkel, F. (eds.), *Reforming Juvenile Justice.* Dordrecht, Netherlands: Springer. 33–44.

Dünkel, F. (2011a). Germany. In: Dünkel, F., Grzywa, J., Horsfield, P., and Pruin, I. (eds.). *Juvenile Justice Systems in Europe—Current Situation and Reform Developments.* 2nd ed. Mönchengladbach, Germany: Forum Verlag Godesberg. 547–622.

Dünkel, F. (2011b). Werden Strafen immer härter? Anmerkungen zur strafrechtlichen Sanktionspraxis und zur Punitivität. In: Bannenberg, B., and Jehle, J.-M. (eds.), *Gewaltdelinquenz. Lange Freiheitsentziehung. Delinquenzverläufe.* Mönchengladbach, Germany: Forum Verlag Godesberg. 209–243.

Dünkel, F. (2013). Youth justice policy in Europe—Between minimum intervention, welfare and new punitiveness. In: Daems, T., van Zyl Smit, D., and Snacken, S. (eds.), *European Penology?* Oxford, UK: Hart. 145–170.

Dünkel, F. (2014). Jugendkriminalpolitik in Europa und den USA: Von Erziehung zu Strafe und zurück? In: DVJJ (eds.), *Jugend ohne Rettungsschirm? Dokumentation des 29. Deutschen Jugendgerichtstags.* Mönchengladbach, Germany: Forum Verlag Godesberg.

Dünkel, F., Grzywa, J., Horsfield, P., and Pruin, I. (eds.). (2011). *Juvenile Justice Systems in Europe—Current Situation and Reform Developments.* 2nd ed. Mönchengladbach, Germany: Forum Verlag Godesberg.

Dünkel, F., Grzywa, J., Pruin, I., and Šelih, A. (2011). Juvenile justice in Europe—Legal aspects, policy trends and perspectives in the light of human rights standards. In: Dünkel, F., Grzywa, J., Horsfield, P., and Pruin, I. (eds.), *Juvenile Justice Systems in Europe—Current Situation and Reform developments,* 2nd ed. Mönchengladbach, Germany: Forum Verlag Godesberg. 1839–1898.

Dünkel, F., Horsfield, P., and Grzywa, J. (eds.). (2015). *Restorative Justice and Mediation in Penal Matters in Europe—A Stock-Taking of Legal Issues, Implementation Strategies and Outcomes in 36 European Countries.* Mönchengladbach, Germany: Forum Verlag Godesberg.

Dünkel, F., and Pruin, I. (2009). Community sanctions and the sanctioning practice in juvenile justice systems in Europe. In: Junger-Tas, J., and Dünkel, F. (eds.), *Reforming Juvenile Justice.* Dordrecht, Netherlands: Springer. 183–204.

Dünkel, F., and Pruin, I. (2011). Young adult offenders in the criminal justice systems of European countries. In: Dünkel, F., Grzywa, J., Horsfield, P., and Pruin, I. (eds.), *Juvenile Justice Systems in Europe—Current Situation and Reform Developments,* 2nd ed. Mönchengladbach, Germany: Forum Verlag Godesberg. 1583–1606.

Dünkel, F., and Pruin, I. (2012). Young adult offenders in the criminal justice systems of European countries. In: Lösel, F., Bottoms, A., and Farrington, D. (eds.), *Young adult offenders Lost in Transition?* London: Routledge. 11–38.

Dünkel, F., Pruin, I., and Grzywa, J. (2011). Sanctions systems and trends in the development of sentencing practices. In: Dünkel, F., Grzywa, J., Horsfield, P. and Pruin, I. (eds.), *Juvenile Justice Systems in Europe—Current Situation and Reform Developments*. 2nd ed. Mönchengladbach, Germany: Forum Verlag Godesberg. 1649–1716.

Dünkel, F., and Stańdo-Kawecka, B. (2011). Juvenile imprisonment and placement in institutions for deprivation of liberty—comparative aspects. In: Dünkel, F., Grzywa, J., Horsfield, and P., Pruin, I. (eds.), *Juvenile Justice Systems in Europe—Current Situation and Reform Developments*, 2nd ed. Mönchengladbach, Germany: Forum-Verlag Godesberg. 1789–1838.

Federal Constitutional Court *(Bundesverfassungsgericht)*. (2006). Decision of 31 May, 2 BvR 1673/04; 2 BvR 2402/04. Neue Juristische Wochenschrift: 2093.

Federal Constitutional Court *(Bundesverfassungsgericht)*. (2011). Decision of 4 May, 2 BvR 2365/09. Neue Juristische Wochenschrift: 1931.

Garland, D. (2001a). *The Culture of Control: Crime and Social Order in Contemporary Society*. Chicago: The University of Chicago Press.

Garland, D. (ed.). (2001b). *Mass Imprisonment. Social Causes and Consequences*. London: Sage.

Gensing, A. (2011). Jurisdiction and characteristics of juvenile criminal procedure in Europe. In: Dünkel, F., Grzywa, J., Horsfield, P., and Pruin, I. (eds.), *Juvenile Justice Systems in Europe—Current Situation and Reform Developments*, 2nd ed. Mönchengladbach, Germany: Forum Verlag Godesberg. 1607–1648.

Goldson, B. (2002). New punitiveness. The politics of child incarceration. In: Muncie, J., Hughes, G., and McLaughlin, E. (eds.), *Youth Justice: Critical Readings*. London: Sage. 386–400.

Goldson, B. (2011). "Time for a fresh start," but is this it? A critical assessment of the report of the Independent Commission on Youth Crime and Antisocial Behaviour. *Youth Justice* 11:3–27.

Goldson, B., and Muncie, J. (2006). *Youth, crime and justice*. London: Sage.

Gutbrodt, T. (2010). *Jugendstrafrecht in Kolumbien*. Mönchengladbach, Germany: Forum Verlag Godesberg.

Habermas, J. (1985). *Die neue Unübersichtlichkeit*. Frankfurt/Main, Germany: Suhrkamp.

Hammarberg, T. (2008). *Memorandum Following Visits to the United Kingdom.* 5–8 February and 31 March–2 April 2008. CommDH (2008) 27, Strasbourg, 17 October.

Hartjen, C. A (2008). *Youth, Crime, and Justice: A Global Inquiry.* New Brunswick: Rutgers University Press.

Haverkamp, R. (2007). Neuere Entwicklungen im Jugendstrafrecht in Schweden und Finnland. *Recht der Jugend und des Bildungswesens* 55:167–190.

Hazel, N. (2008). *Cross-National Comparison of Youth Justice*. London: Youth Justice Board. http://www.yjb.gov.uk/publications/Resources/Downloads/Cross_national_final.pdf.

Heinz, W. (2009). Zunehmende Punitivität in der Praxis des Jugendkriminalrechts? Analysen aufgrund von Daten der Strafrechtspflegestatistiken. In: Bundesministerium der Justiz (ed.), *Das Jugendkriminalrecht vor neuen Herausforderungen? Jenaer Symposium*. Mönchengladbach, Germany: Forum Verlag Godesberg. 29–80.

Heinz, W. (2011a). Neue Lust am Strafen. Gibt es eine Trendwende auch in der deutschen Sanktionierungspraxis? In: Kühl, K., and Seher, G. (eds.), *Rom, Recht, Religion. Symposion für Udo Ebert zum 70. Geburtstag*. Stuttgart, Germany: Mohr Siebeck. 435–458.

Heinz, W. (2011b). Neue Straflust der Strafjustiz—Realität oder Mythos? *Neue Kriminalpolitik* 22:14–27.

Heinz, W. (2012). *Das strafrechtliche Sanktionensystem und die Sanktionierungspraxis in Deutschland 1882–2010*. Stand, Germany: Berichtsjahr, 2010. http://www.uni-konstanz.de/rtf/kis/Sanktionierungspraxis-in-Deutschland-Stand-2010.pdf.

Horsfield, P. (2015). *Jugendkriminalpolitik in England und Wales—Entwicklungsgeschichte, aktuelle Rechtslage und jüngste Reformen*. Mönchengladbach, Germany: Forum Verlag Godesberg.

Jensen, E. L., and Jepsen, J. (eds.). (2006). *Juvenile Law Violators, Human Rights, and the Development of New Juvenile Justice Systems*. Oxford, UK: Hart.

Junger-Tas, J. (2006). Trends in international juvenile justice—What conclusions can be drawn? In: Junger-Tas, J., and Decker, S. H. (eds.), *International Handbook of Juvenile Justice*. Dordrecht, Netherlands: Springer. 505–532.

Junger-Tas, J., and Decker, S. H. (eds.). (2006). *International Handbook of Juvenile Justice*. Dordrecht, Netherlands: Springer.

Junger-Tas, J., and Dünkel, F. (eds.). (2009a). *Reforming Juvenile Justice*. Dordrecht, Netherlands: Springer.

Junger-Tas, J., and Dünkel, F. (2009b). Reforming juvenile justice: European perspectives. In: Junger-Tas, J., and Dünkel, F. (eds.), *Reforming Juvenile Justice*. Dordrecht, Netherlands: Springer. 215–233.

Kaiser, G. (1985). International vergleichende Perspektiven zum Jugendstrafrecht. In: Schwind, H.-D., Berz, U., Geilen, G., Herzberg, R. D., and Warda, G. (eds.), *Festschrift für G. Blau*. Berlin: Walter de Gruyter. 441–457.

Keiser, C. (2008). Jugendliche Täter als strafrechtlich Erwachsene? Das Phänomen der "Adulteration" im Lichte internationaler Menschenrechte. *Zeitschrift für die gesamte Strafrechtswissenschaft* 120:25–67.

Kilchling, M. (2002). Vergleichende Perspektiven. In: Albrecht, H.-J., and Kilchling, M. (eds.), *Jugendstrafrecht in Europa*. Freiburg i. Br.: Max-Planck-Institut für ausländisches und internationales Strafrecht. 475–532.

Killias, M., and Villettaz, P. (2007). Rückfall nach Freiheits- und Alternativstrafen: Lehren aus einer systematischen Literaturübersicht. In: Lösel, F., Bender, D., and

Jehle, J. M. (eds.), *Kriminologie und wissensbasierte Kriminalpolitik*. Mönchengladbach, Germany: Forum Verlag Godesberg. 207–225.

Lappi-Seppälä, T. (2007). Penal policy in Scandinavia. In: Tonry, M. (ed.), *Crime, Punishment, and Politics in Comparative Perspective*. Crime and Justice 36. Chicago: University of Chicago Press. 217–295.

Lappi-Seppälä, T. (2010). Vertrauen, Wohlfahrt und politikwissenschaftliche Aspekte—International vergleichende Perspektiven zur Punitivität. In: Dünkel, F., Lappi-Seppälä, T., Morgenstern, C., and van Zyl Smit, D. (eds.), *Kriminalität, Kriminalpolitik, strafrechtliche Sanktionspraxis und Gefangenenraten im europäischen Vergleich*. Mönchengladbach, Germany: Forum Verlag Godesberg. 937–996.

Lappi-Seppälä, T. (2011). Finland. In: Dünkel, F., Grzywa, J., Horsfield, and P., Pruin, I. (eds.), *Juvenile Justice Systems in Europe—Current Situation and Reform Developments*, 2nd ed. Mönchengladbach, Germany: Forum-Verlag Godesberg. 423–482.

Loeber, R., Hoeve, M., Farrington, D. P., Howell, J. C., Slot, W., and van der Laan, P. H. (2012). Overview, conclusions, and policy and research recommendations. In: Loeber, R., Hoeve, M., Slot, W., and van der Laan, P. H. (eds.), *Persisters and Desisters in Crime from Adolescence into Adulthood: Explanation, Prevention and Punishment*. Aldershot, UK: Ashgate. 335–412.

Lösel, F., Stemmler, M., Beelmann, A., and Jaursch, S. (2007). "Universelle Prävention dissozialen Verhaltens im Vorschulalter mit dem Elterntraining von EFFEKT. Eine Wirkungsevaluation." In Lösel, F., Bender. D., and Jehle, J. M. (eds.). *Kriminologie und wissensbasierte Kriminalpolitik. Entwicklungs- und Evaluationsforschung*. Mönchengladbach, Germany: Forum Verlag Godesberg. 357–377.

Ministry of Justice (ed.). (2013). *Sentencing Statistics 2012*. London: Home Office. https://www.gov.uk/government/statistics/sentencing-statistics-annual-ns.

Muncie, J. (2008). The "punitive turn" in juvenile justice: cultures of control and rights compliance in western Europe and in the USA. *Youth Justice* 8:107–121.

Muncie, J., and Goldson, B. (eds.). (2006). *Comparative Youth Justice*. London: Sage.

Nelken, D. (2009). Comparative criminal justice: Beyond ethnocentrism and relativism. *European Journal of Criminology* 6:291–311.

Nelken, D. (2010). *Comparative Criminal Justice—Making Sense of Difference*. Los Angeles: Sage.

O'Mahony, D. (2011). Northern Ireland. In: Dünkel, F., Grzywa, J., Horsfield, P., and Pruin, I. (eds.), *Juvenile Justice Systems in Europe—Current Situation and Reform Developments*, 2nd ed. Mönchengladbach, Germany: Forum Verlag Godesberg. 957–989.

O'Mahony, D., and Campbell, C. (2006). Mainstreaming restorative justice for young offenders through youth conferencing: The experience in Northern Ireland. In: Junger-Tas, J., and Decker, S. H. (eds.), *International Handbook of Juvenile Justice*. Dordrecht, Netherlands: Springer. 93–115.

O'Mahony, D., and Doak, J. (2009). Restorative justice and youth justice: Bringing theory and practice closer together in Europe. In: Junger-Tas, J., and Dünkel, F. (eds.), *Reforming Criminal Justice*. Berlin: Springer. 165–182.

Păroşanu, A. (2011). Romania. In: Dünkel, F., Grzywa, J., Horsfield, P., and Pruin, I. (eds.), *Juvenile Justice Systems in Europe—Current Situation and Reform Developments*, 2nd ed. Mönchengladbach, Germany: Forum Verlag Godesberg. 1077–1114.

Patané, V. (ed.). (2007). *European Juvenile Justice Systems.* Vol. 1. Milan, Italy: Giuffrè Editore.

Police Foundation (ed.). (2010). *Time for a Fresh Start: The Report of the Independent Commission on Youth Crime and Antisocial Behaviour.* http://www.police -foundation.org.uk/uploads/catalogerfiles/independent-commission-on-youth -crime-and-antisocial-behaviour/fresh_start.pdf.

Pratt, J. (2008a). Scandinavian exceptionalism in an era of penal excess, part I: The nature and roots of Scandinavian exceptionalism. *British Journal of Criminology* 48:119–137.

Pratt, J. (2008b). Scandinavian exceptionalism in an era of penal excess, part II: Does Scandinavian exceptionalism have a future? *British Journal of Criminology* 48:275–292.

Pratt, J., Brown, D., Brown, M., Hallsworth, S., and Morrison, W. (eds.). (2005). *The New Punitiveness: Trends, Theories, Perspectives.* Cullompton, UK: Willan.

Pruin, I. (2007). *Die Heranwachsendenregelung im deutschen Jugendstrafrecht. Jugendkriminologische, entwicklungspsychologische, jugendsoziologische und rechtsvergleichende Aspekte.* Mönchengladbach, Germany: Forum Verlag Godesberg.

Pruin, I. (2011). The scope of juvenile justice systems in Europe. In: Dünkel, F., Grzywa, J., Horsfield, P., and Pruin, I. (eds.), *Juvenile Justice Systems in Europe—Current Situation and Reform Developments*, 2nd ed. Mönchengladbach, Germany: Forum Verlag Godesberg. 1539–1582.

Pruin, I., and Dünkel, F. (2014). *Young Adult Offenders in Europe: Interdisciplinary Research Results and Legal Practices.* Department of Criminology, Greifswald, Expertise for the Cadbury Trust.

Put, J., and Walgrave, L. (2006). Belgium: From protection towards accountability? In: Muncie, J., and Goldson, B. (eds.), *Comparative Youth Justice.* London: Sage. 111–126.

Roberts, J., and Hough, M. (eds.). (2002). *Changing Attitudes to Punishment: Public Opinion, Crime and Justice.* Cullompton, UK: Willan.

Shchedrin, N. (2011). Russia. In: Dünkel, F., Grzywa, J., Horsfield, P., and Pruin, I. (eds.), *Juvenile Justice Systems in Europe—Current Situation and Reform Developments*, 2nd ed. Mönchengladbach, Germany: Forum Verlag Godesberg. 1115–1148.

Smith, D. J. (2005). The effectiveness of the juvenile justice system. *Criminal Justice* 5:181–195.

Smith, D. J. (ed.). (2010). *A New Response to Youth Crime.* Cullompton, UK: Willan.

Snacken, S. (2010). Resisting punitiveness in Europe? *Theoretical Criminology* 14:273–292.

Snacken, S. (2012). Conclusion: Why and how to resist punitiveness in Europe? In: Snacken, S., and Dumortiers, E. (eds.), *Resisting Punitiveness in Europe? Welfare, Human Rights and Democracy.* London: Routledge. 247–260.

Snacken, S., and Dumortiers, E. (eds.). (2012). *Resisting Punitiveness in Europe? Welfare, Human Rights and Democracy*. London: Routledge.

Stańdo-Kawecka, B. (2011). Poland. In: Dünkel, F., Grzywa, J., Horsfield, P., and Pruin, I. (eds.), *Juvenile Justice Systems in Europe—Current Situation and Reform Developments*, 2nd ed. Mönchengladbach, Germany: Forum Verlag Godesberg. 991–1026.

Storgaard, A. (2004). Juvenile justice in Scandinavia. *Journal of Scandinavian Studies in Criminology and Crime Prevention* 5:188–204.

Stump, B. (2003). *"Adult Time for Adult Crime"—Jugendliche zwischen Jugend- und Erwachsenenstrafrecht*. Mönchengladbach, Germany: Forum Verlag Godesberg.

Tiffer-Sotomayor, C. (2000). *Jugendstrafrecht in Lateinamerika unter besonderer Berücksichtigung des Jugendstrafrechts in Costa Rica*. Mönchengladbach, Germany: Forum Verlag Godesberg.

Tiffer-Sotomayor, C., Llobet Rodríguez, J., and Dünkel, F. (2012). *Derecho Penal Juvenil*. 2nd ed. San José, Costa Rica: DAAD.

Tonry, M. (2004). *Punishment and Politics*. Cullompton, UK: Willan.

Tonry, M., and Doob, A. N. (eds.). (2004). *Youth Crime and Youth Justice: Comparative and Cross-National Perspectives*. Crime and Justice 31. Chicago: University of Chicago Press.

United Nations Office on Drugs and Crime. (2013). *Justice Matters Involving Children in Conflict with the Law: Model Law on Juvenile Justice and Related Commentary*. New York: United Nations.

Váradi-Csema, E. (2011). Hungary. In: Dünkel, F., Grzywa, J., Horsfield, P., and Pruin, I. (eds.), *Juvenile Justice Systems in Europe—Current Situation and Reform Developments*, 2nd ed. Mönchengladbach, Germany: Forum Verlag Godesberg. 671–720.

von Hofer, H. (2004). Crime and reactions to crime in Scandinavia. *Journal of Scandinavian Studies in Criminology and Crime Prevention* 5:148–166.

Weijers, I., and Grisso, T. (2009). Criminal responsibility of adolescents: Youth as junior citizenship. In: Junger-Tas, J., and Dünkel, F. (eds.), *Reforming Juvenile Justice*. Dordrecht, Netherlands: Springer. 45–67.

Weijers, I., Nuytiens, A., and Christiaens, J. (2009). Transfer of minors to the criminal court in Europe: Belgium and the Netherlands. In: Junger-Tas, J., and Dünkel, F. (eds.), *Reforming Juvenile Justice*. Dordrecht, Netherlands: Springer. 105–124.

2

Juvenile Justice without a Juvenile Court

A Note on Scandinavian Exceptionalism

TAPIO LAPPI-SEPPÄLÄ

Scandinavian (Nordic) countries have a population of around 25 million (9.2 million in Sweden, 5.5 million in Denmark, 5.3 million in Finland, 4.8 million in Norway, and 320,000 in Iceland). The five countries share much common history and many common traits. All have democratic constitutions with governmental power divided among judicial, executive, and legislative branches. All have multiparty political systems in which coalition governments are the norm. Legislative power is vested in national parliaments whose members are elected in multimember districts on the basis of proportional representation. All are what comparative political scientists call consensus as contrasted with conflict political systems.

In the core of the Nordic model of society is the "Nordic welfare state," which is characterized by comprehensive welfare programs and services, investment in human capital, coordinated labor markets, and relatively generous unemployment benefits. Its key features include state responsibility for welfare provision based on principles of universal coverage. Benefits and entitlements are available to every member of the society with no exceptions made on the basis of employment, social status, or family situation (in contrast to most English-speaking countries, where many social programs are means tested and only people below designated income levels are eligible for benefits).

These welfare structures are aimed at ensuring universal provision of basic human needs, stabilizing the economy, maximizing labor force participation, promoting gender equality, maintaining egalitarian and generous benefit levels, redistributing income on a large scale, and using an expansionary fiscal policy liberally. The Nordic countries usually rank high in relation to welfare, the economy, education, competitiveness, social equality, and quality of life. The Nordic welfare state sustains and reflects particular social values and priorities, including high levels of social and institutional trust and high levels of social tolerance.

These features of the welfare state and political system are crucial to understanding Nordic criminal justice system policies and operations, which are characterized by moderate penal policies, low imprisonment rates, low fears, and low public punitivity.[1] The connection between social structure, welfare model, and criminal justice is especially clear in the realm of Nordic youth justice. These countries have developed a system of their own, in which major parts of youth justice lie outside criminal justice. Decisive steps in the evolvement of this model were taken during the shift of the last century. Nordic countries came up with a system of child protection legislation that granted municipal authorities the right to intervene in children's behavior. Children under 14 or 15 were moved from the courts to child welfare boards, whereas children aged 15 to 17 remained under both criminal justice and child welfare.

Today the system stands as it was designed more than a century ago. All offenders under the age of 15 are dealt with only by the child welfare authorities. Young offenders aged 15 to 17 are dealt with by both the child welfare system and the system of criminal justice. Young adults aged 18 to 20 are dealt with by the criminal justice authorities (and to some extent by the child welfare system with provision of aftercare). The Scandinavian youth justice system has one foot in the adult criminal justice system and the other in the child welfare system. Both dimensions need to be taken into account.

The functioning of child welfare and criminal justice is based on fundamentally differing principles. The criterion for all child welfare interventions is the best interest of the child. The system consists of a large variety of open care measures, as well as institutional interventions. All interventions are supportive, and criminal acts have little or no formal role as a criterion or as a cause for these measures. The criminal justice side in the Nordics, on the other hand, makes much less distinction between offenders of different ages. All offenders from the age of 15 are sentenced in accordance with the same Criminal Code. Strictly speaking, there is no separate juvenile criminal system in the sense in which this concept is usually understood in most other legal systems. There are no juvenile courts, and the number of specific penalties only applicable to juveniles has been quite limited, although growing in numbers during the past years. Instead of separate youth courts, in the shift of the last century the Nordic countries adopted a youth justice system, based on municipal child protection boards. This in turn had its foundation in the long-standing tradition of municipal self-governance in the Nordic countries.

Nordic youth justice—as a whole—must be seen in the framework of the Nordic welfare state. It is an integral element of a wider system of universalistic social services that the state provides to all inhabitants. While the child welfare system takes care of functions that belong in many other countries to youth criminal justice, it is important to note that the tasks of the child welfare system go well beyond crime problems. They cover all elements relevant to the well-being and safe development of the child.

This chapter gives an overview of the development and distinct features of Nordic youth justice in Finland, Denmark, Norway, and Sweden.[2] The story starts with a short case study of the birth of the Nordic model at the end of the 19th century. Next follows an overview of major phases in the evolvement of Nordic youth justice from the beginning of the last century until the most recent reform period, around the turn of the millennium. The next two sections give a summary view of the contents of the present criminal sanctions and their implementation practices. Then the role of child welfare interventions is discussed in more detail, using Finland and Sweden as examples. Discussion and conclusions follow in the final section.

The Birth of the Nordic Model

The history of the Nordic model starts in late 19th-century Norway.[3] In 1874, courts were provided with the right to place children under the age of 15 to approved reformatory schools, instead of imprisonment. However, as no such institutions fulfilling the conditions prescribed by the law existed, the practical relevance of this new option remained nonexistent. Shortly, however, the already existing children's homes that had functioned mainly on a charitable and philanthropic basis saw the strategic potential of the new law: adjusting their functions in a manner that fulfilled the prescribed conditions would grant them fiscal support from the state. In a short period of time during the 1880s and early 1890s, new institutions capable of also receiving convicted children were established based on mutual give-and-take agreements between the state and the administration of these institutions (Dahl 1985, 88–89). During the following years, new foundations were established for the cooperation of child protection and criminal law. The birth of this particular model was partly a result of historical coincidences, the personal influence of powerful individuals, social innovations, socioeconomic changes, and professional interests.

The window of opportunity for the establishment of a new model was provided by the ongoing drafting of the new penal code in Norway in the 1880s and 1890s. This reform was combined with two others— the code of criminal proceedings and the child protection act. All reforms were chaired and conducted by the same individual, Bernhard Getz, an active member of the International Association of Criminalists, founded by Franz von Listz. The connection with a highly appreciated and progressive international movement contributed to the aims of restricting the use of imprisonment for juveniles and children. The prison administration had for long, but without success, reported the problems and inhumanities that resulted from placing children with adults in prisons. However, not until the late 19th century had anyone provided a theoretically sound program for rehabilitation. After joining with the rising influential lawyers of the criminalist movement, the prison administration was, for the first time, able to formulate its demands in the form of a coherent program to be presented in highly distinguished platforms.

However, the reforms were not confined to the criminal justice system; there were other interests, demands, and interest groups involved. The reforms were conducted at a time when new ideas regarding dealing with children at risk and social defense (protecting the society from the threat of crime) were crisscrossing in Europe. Social changes and pressures produced by industrialization were pushing general demands for democratization, including of the educational system. In fact, a reform movement that started as a procedural and penal reform was gradually more influenced by issues of how to deal with neglected children. The reform demands included the establishment of a new type of reformatory institution for children in trouble, at the expense of the state. This idea was expressed in full in the proposal for a new child welfare act in 1892. The act was presented to the parliament as an "Appendix to the Criminal Law," signifying the important link between the criminal justice system and child welfare. This proposal included also an important amendment to the previous plans. Whereas in the earlier plans reformatory institutions were intended only for offenders, the 1892 proposal included all children who live in socially and morally risky environments and who "more and more constitute the recruits of the army of criminals" (Dahl 1985, 94). Reformatory institutions became a general device of social defense and child protection, as well.

These costly proposals were accepted without any notable resistance. As pointed out by Tove Stang Dahl (1985), there were strong vested interests of different professions involved. Reformatories came to serve a role in the democratization of the Norwegian school system. By the end of the 19th century, pressures had increased to expand the public school system for all social classes, partly raised by liberals in the name of social equality, partly supported also by the conservatives and the government (in the hope that the raising of the general level of enlightenment would ease the defending of the social order from revolutionary challenges and also work as an instrument against poverty). But to establish a unified school system for pupils from all social classes would demand a segregation of disturbing and "morally susceptible" children from the rest. Reformatories that would include not only criminals but also other "borderline cases" would serve that purpose. The educationalists' interest in a unified public school and the lawyers' interest in social defense met each other in reformatory schools.

As a legislative project, the Norwegian Child Welfare Act became a joint effort for criminologists and educationalists. The proposal was launched as a penal law but was increasingly considered a school law during the debates in the 1890s (Dahl 1985, 130). This shift was also reflected in procedural arrangements. While according to the 1886 proposal the power to order residential placement of children was given to the prosecutor, the final act adopted another view. The specific solution followed the existing tradition of communal self-governance and the system of municipal boards, such as poor relief boards and school boards. The legislators' solution was the establishment a specific child welfare board consisting of municipal authorities, laypeople, and state officials (with a local judge as the chairman).

Since municipal boards as the standard structure of municipal self-government had a long tradition in the Scandinavian countries, the solution was not so radical in the Nordic context (even if rare in international comparison). However, child welfare boards were also granted rights far beyond those of other municipal boards, such as school boards or relief boards. They were also given the right to deprive parents of their parental rights and to place children against their or their parents' will to closed institutions. These are all decisions that come very close to the use of state power, which in other countries had been left in the hands of the courts. However, the ethos of child protection got an upper hand over criminal justice as the reform work progressed. During this process, the terminology in the law was gradually changed from a penal one toward a more open educationalist mode of expressions. It was pointed out, for instance, that child welfare boards were not to be understood as a form of penal courts. Eventually all provisions related to institutional discipline were also removed from the law.

The model of youth justice involving child welfare boards was first formulated in the 1896 child welfare reform (vergårdsloven) in Norway. The reform lifted the minimum age of criminal responsibility from 10 to 14 years (and later to 15 years). Total reform of the criminal code followed in 1902. Sweden, Denmark, and Finland carried out or initiated total reforms of child welfare at the turn of the 20th century according to the principles laid out in the Norwegian reforms. These reforms were carried out in packages, with elements in both child protection legislation and criminal law. Child welfare and criminal law reforms were interlocked, as the exclusion of children from criminal justice could be achieved only by establishing a concomitant child protection system that could take charge of misbehaving and mistreated children.

Major Phases in Nordic Youth Justice

Fixing Age Limits and the Spirit of Penal Rehabilitation

The basic structure of Nordic youth justice were fixed around the turn of the 20th century. Core elements include the establishment of child welfare boards, the fixing of the age of criminal responsibility, and the enactment of specific child protection acts. The age of criminal responsibility was fixed in countries to either 14 or 15.[4] The timing of other reforms varied slightly, depending on political configurations. In Finland, legislative work was stalled first by deteriorating relations with the Russian administration and after that by the civil war in 1918. So while Denmark and Sweden carried out Norwegian-style reforms in child protection in the early 1900s, Finland did not manage to do so until 1936.

Since children were removed from criminal justice to child welfare, there were fewer pressures to develop specific sanctions for the youngest age groups. The starting point was that the same sanction structure was applicable for all offenders under the criminal law. However, due to reasons related to reduced culpability, the 19th-century criminal codes, influenced by the German classical school of criminal law, provided mitigation and reduced penalty scales for younger age groups from the very outset. Early 20th-century youth justice, in turn, came to be inspired by positivist and sociological schools of criminal law from Italy (Enrico Ferri) and Germany (Franz von Liszt), with pressures toward the aims of special prevention and rehabilitation. The Norwegian criminal code in 1902 was the first European code to be based on these principles, with the Danish one to follow in 1930.

Among the innovations inspired by new penological ideologies were the introduction of suspended/conditional sentence (in Norway 1894, Denmark 1904, Sweden 1905, and Finland after the civil war in 1918) and further attempts to divert juveniles aged 15 to 17 from criminal justice to child welfare. These efforts started in Norway and Denmark at the beginning of 1900s, to be developed into a system of nonprosecution and waiver of sanctions in the 1930s and 1940s. Sweden followed this line to the extent that in the 1950s around 70% offenders below the age of 18 were transferred to social welfare. With regard to imprisonment, all Nordic countries established specific juvenile prisons in the 1920s and 1930s, with Denmark being the ideological leader. From the very start, youth prisons included elements of indeterminate sentencing, as the duration of the stay was much dependent on the progress shown in the juveniles' behavior.

The criminal sanction system from 1930s to 1950s was heavily oriented toward special prevention, in terms of both rehabilitation and incapacitation. Youth justice was strongly motivated by the hope of rehabilitating juveniles, either by interventions of "protective education" carried out under the child welfare system or by treatment offered in youth prisons. Sweden, being the most resourceful of the Nordic countries (and not touched by World War II), took this orientation to the limit by passing a proposal of "protection law" in 1956 that would have abolished the concepts of criminal responsibility and criminal punishment for all offender groups and replaced them with interventions constructed purely from the points of view of social protection, education, and rehabilitation. Ultimately, this change never happened, as penal ideologies took another turn during the following decades.

The Turn of the 1960s and the Period of (Humane) Neoclassicism

Doubts about the effectiveness and appropriateness of the extensive use of institutional treatment started to grow in the shift of the 1950s–1960s. During the 1960s, the Nordics experienced heated debate on the results and justifications of involuntary treatment in closed institutions. The first targets of the critics were mental hospitals (Galtung 1959) and the treatment and forced labor of alcoholics (Christie 1960). From there, mistrust on coercive care and institutional treatment expanded to child welfare and the prison system in general (Aubert and Mathiesen 1962; Eriksson 1967).

The results of this movement were manifold. They included an overall decline in the use of imprisonment in Finland, a move that started in the latter half of the 1960s and continued until the early 1990s. The number of juvenile prisoners fell from 350 to around 100 in the age group 18–20 and from 120 to around 10 in the group 15–17 (for details, see Lappi-Seppälä 2001, 2010). Reforms in health care included deinstitutionalization in mental hospitals and abandonment of compulsory care in alcohol treatment in the 1960s and 1970s.

With regard to young offenders, the two most marked changes were the scaling down of closed reformatory schools in child welfare and the abandonment of specific youth prisons. Denmark was the first country to abolish youth prisons in 1973. Norway closed youth prisons in 1974, with reference to arguments related to both ineffectiveness (high reoffending rates) and lack of legal safeguards. Finland abolished the indeterminate element of juvenile prison in 1974 (which had already lost its practical relevance). Sweden conducted the same reform in 1979, with similar motives. It should be noted that the end of youth prison did not indicate any sort of punitive turn. In Denmark, it was pointed out that those who had been sentenced earlier to youth prison should be taken under the child welfare organs in order to avoid the use of (normal) imprisonment as far as possible (Greve 1996, 159). Also, in the other countries, the enforcement of prison sentences for young offenders continued on the same premises as before but without the theoretical possibility of prolonging the sentence.

Eventually these shifts and changes in penal ideologies and penal thinking led to a general reformulation of sanction policies and sentencing principles. The criminal political ideology that followed the period of treatment ideology (labeled in Finland as "humane neoclassicism" in the mid-1970s) stressed both legal safeguards against coercive care and the goal of less repressive measures in general. In sentencing, the principles of proportionality and predictability became the central values. Individualized sentencing and sentencing for general preventive reasons or perceived dangerousness were moved into the background. Since the early 1970s, Nordic sanction systems were reformed from these starting points, however, with differences in degree. In 1973, Denmark abolished all indeterminate sentences as well as treatment orders in special institutions. Finland carried out a sentencing reform in 1976 with clearly formulated neoclassical sentencing principles. Sweden conducted a similar reform in 1988.

Despite individual differences among the countries, main trends were shared. In all countries, youth justice remained more or less a nonissue in the Nordic debate for most of the 1970s and throughout the 1980s. The separation of care and control—as demanded by the neoclassical sanction ideology—had removed rehabilitative interventions to the realm of social work and child protection. The criminal justice system was designed to express society's disapproval in a manner proportional to the seriousness of the offense and the blameworthiness of the offender. However, the Nordic version of "just deserts" rested on different criminal, political, and theoretical foundations, compared to the U.S. counterpart. Criminal sanctions were assumed to serve pragmatic aims, but this effect was deemed to be reached not through fear, deterrence, and sentence severity but through indirect general prevention and the morals-creating and values-shaping effects of criminal sanctions. Emphasis was on norm internalization, perceived fairness, and the legitimacy of the sanction system (in today's terms, on normative compliance). Values related to proportionality and predictability remained central, but these aims could be reached through financial penalties and community sanction and without resort to widespread use of custodial sanctions.

The period of neoclassicism was also a period of penal liberalization, especially in Finland, and mainly for two reasons. First, the Finnish system was in much more need of revision, being still affected by a harsh history and a social and political crisis during the first half of the 20th century. In addition, Finland had much weaker traditions regarding rehabilitative practices (especially compared to Sweden and Denmark). This also may have contributed to the fact that Finland took the neoclassical ideas further than the other Nordic countries did.[5] One may even question whether Sweden, despite the 1988 sentencing reform based on the principle of proportionality, really ever gave up the idea of penal rehabilitation. The sanction system remained more or less the way it was. The abolishment of special institutions in Denmark in 1973 did not end treatment in the Danish criminal justice system, as different types of treatment orders were incorporated back into the traditional sanction system during the 1990s, in the form of treatment programs in custodial settings or as part of conditions in conditional sentencing for specific offender categories (such as drunk drivers, drug offenders, and sex offenders). However, more encompassing modifications in general neoclassical sentencing structures were enacted during the 1990s with the introduction of new community alternatives and the adoption of new penalties targeted especially to juveniles.

Nordic Youth Reforms since the 1990s — Three Stories

The silent years of youth justice ended in the course of the 1990s. All Nordic countries expanded their sanction structures with new community sanctions. Finland, Denmark, and Sweden also introduced new forms of youth sanctions. However, these reforms had different backgrounds and different aims.

Finnish penal reformists had published several proposals for specific juvenile sanctions from the 1960s onward but without success. The proposals were shot down either because of the mixing of care and control (which was not allowed) or because of the inability to offer anything but symbolic denouncement (for which there already were proper measures in the form of fines and conditional sentence). However, in the mid-1990s, this neoclassical deadlock was broken. Impressed by the practical success of community service, legislators wished to expand this model to juveniles, as well. The reform was also pushed by public critics of the existing liberal practice of imposing consecutive sentences of conditional imprisonment for the same juveniles. Legislators assumed that a kind of junior version of community service would offer a constructive positive alternative. It would also have a better public image, compared to simple conditional sentences, which were deemed to lack the required concrete content. However, civil servants and penologists had their doubts about the genuine rehabilitative potential of (any form of) short community sanction. There were also doubts about whether juveniles under the age of 18 with several previous suspended sentences would be motivated to attend the planned programs. Also, the risks of net widening were taken seriously. On the other hand, the new juvenile sanction was considered practical as a means to establish an additional step in the penal "ladders" between conditional imprisonment and custody. In order to avoid net widening and to ensure that the new sanction would really hit the intended target group, its application was restricted in the final draft in 1994 to offenders who already had been sentenced at least once to conditional imprisonment. This would also create an additional "rung" in the system of sanctions that could slow down the movement toward custodial sanctions in case of reoffending. New juvenile punishment was a kind of compromise between neoclassicist and rehabilitative approaches. The sanction had a clear place in the sanction system in terms of severity, but it had also definite social and reintegrative goals. However, the outcome turned out to be a disappointment in numbers. The estimated scope of nationwide application was around 300 cases each year. The first year's caseload was around 100 penalties (in only five district courts), but since then, the numbers fell to around 20 sentences per year. This may partly result from the requirement of issuing this sentence only in high-risk cases. But the main explanation for restrictive application may be found in the role of the child welfare system: juveniles otherwise suitable for juvenile punishment are usually already involved in the child welfare system, perhaps even placed in institutions. In such cases, there is not much that juvenile punishment could add from a rehabilitative point of view.

The second story comes from Denmark. In 2001, a Danish legislator introduced a new half-residential youth sanction for juveniles with a more substantial criminal career. This reform was triggered by a set of serious offenses committed by young offenders (Kyvsgaard 2004, 373; Storgaard 2009, 382). This sanction is imposed by the courts but implemented by the social authorities. It consists of three phases, lasting altogether two years. After a period in secure accommodations, there follows a period in an open residential institution. Both institutional accommodations are managed by the social welfare system. The sanction is aimed to be used instead of a prison sentence for offenders under the age of 18 (at the time of the offense). Even if the sanction is not defined as imprisonment, the restrictions on liberty and the powers of the institution staff are, especially in secure accommodations, very much like those of a prison (for a critical assessment and evaluation, see Storgaard 2009; and Clausen and Kyvsgaard 2009). The annual number of youth for whom this sanction is imposed varied around 100 sentences in the first decade of the 21st century (but since then has slightly declined). This is three times more than the drafters had anticipated (see Vestergaard 2004, 74). Secured confinement lasts usually two months (over 70%), and the placement in open units lasts at least six months.

Compared to other Nordic countries, the Swedish youth justice system had developed more differentiated measures targeted especially for juveniles. Until 2007, the main sanction for juveniles aged 15–17 in Sweden was transfer to the social welfare board. The system had been criticized for its lack of transparency and low predictability. It was also deemed that child welfare was receiving clients who in reality were not in need of the kind of support and treatment that the services could provide. In order to increase transparency and to target the child welfare resources more effectively, the old transfer order was divided in 2007 into two separate sanctions, youth care and youth service. Youth care is a court order for offenders under the age 21 that obligates the social welfare board to take actions that promote the young offenders' future social development and reintegration. Youth service is a junior version of community service. It consists of unpaid work for 20–150 hours plus attendance in program work or education. In Sweden, the 2007 youth reform received a more or less silent reception. Statistical comparisons before and after the reform indicates an increase in the number of youths on whom these new sanctions were imposed in the age group 15–17, from 2,775 (2006) to 4,216 (2008). This increase corresponds to a similar reduction in the number of fines, from 6,350 (2006) to 5,516 (2008). Corresponding figures in 2012 were 3,048 youth sanctions and 3,324 fines (with court fines and prosecutor fines combined). Legislators' third aim—to reduce the use of fines in the youngest age group—seems to have been achieved.

The last example of youth reforms deals with imprisonment. As noted earlier, all Nordic countries had abolished specific youth prisons in the course of the 1970s for reasons related to legal security and the rights of prisoners. However, the UN Convention on the Rights of the Child (ratified in these countries in the 1990s) demanded the separation of juveniles from adult prisoners. Building a separate prison for a small and declining number of young prisoners was not a sensible option (also from the point of view of offering the prisoner the possibility of staying close to his or her family during the enforcement). Denmark solved the problem by enforcing all prison sentences in child welfare institutions or in specific "pensions." The Swedish solution for the same problem was a new sanction called "closed youth care" (adopted in 1999). Closed youth care is enforced not by the prison administration but by the States Institutional Administration (the organization responsible for the administration of all involuntary treatment in institutional settings). The sanction can be used only in cases where the offender would have been sentenced to prison. Enforcement takes place in juvenile homes designed to provide the involuntary treatment and approved for enforcement of closed youth care (six institutions in which the total capacity is 68 juveniles). Juvenile homes used for this purpose have closed as well as more open units. The enforcement starts in a closed unit. However, in the course of time, the juvenile is moved into a more open environment. Closed youth care has been met with a number of criticisms. The aim of the 1999 reform was neither to increase nor to decrease the use of custodial sentences for young offenders. It was assumed that there would be need for around 10 places. However, in a short time, the annual number of sentences reached over 100, a clear sign of net widening (see Kühlhorn 2002, 56).

While the global trends in youth justice generally point to a more punitive direction (see Cavadino and Dignan 2006; Muncie and Goldson 2006; Dünkel et al. 2010), Nordic youth justice reforms during the past 15–20 years provide a more complex picture. Even if some of the reforms have originated form political needs to enhance the credibility of the existing youth system, the actions taken can hardly be characterized as especially punitive ones. In some instances, the Nordic drafters and policy planners seem to have been caught between a rock and a hard place. While the drafters of the Danish youth sanction were well aware of the uncertainties concerning the rehabilitative results of the proposed "structured sociopedagogic program work," this still was deemed to be a better option than the other probable alternatives. As something had to be done, the drafters tailored a plan that would minimize the damages (Vestergaard 2004, 65). New juvenile punishment in Finland was motivated partly by the need to avoid repeated use of conditional sentences and partly by the desire to offer more functional and effective rehabilitation programs. The drafters were less convinced of the rehabilitative effects. However, something had to be offered, and if it had not been a nonresidential juvenile sanction with a social work dimension, the most probable alternative would have been a short-term arrest (which had been proposed in almost all previous reform plans from the late 1960s onward). By defining strict limits for application of the new sanction, the drafters consciously took the risk that there would be difficulties in finding proper candidates. As it turned out, the caseload has reached barely 10%–20% of the intended level. This is mainly due to the fact that children in this target group are already under the programs of the child welfare services.

Were these reforms successful? Much depends on the chosen perspective. The Finnish reform produced less than the anticipated number of convictions; the Danish and Swedish custodial reforms surpassed the expectations in this respect. In both Denmark and Sweden, the net outcome was increased use of custodial treatment, albeit in an environment that corresponds to closed child welfare institutions, not prisons. Net widening was avoided in Finland. However, the Finnish policy planners need to ask themselves whether the investment in separate noncustodial juvenile sanction still serves its purpose in an environment in which these cases are more willingly dealt with under the child welfare system and not by criminal law.

Youth Sanctions Today

Nordic countries apply basically the same sanction system to adults and juveniles. The system consists of fines, different kinds of community sanctions, and imprisonment. In all countries, young age is grounds for mitigation. Each country has also enacted specific sanctions applicable to juveniles only. Sweden has the most differentiated system of juvenile sanctions, while youth-oriented modifications are much more restrictive in Norway and Finland. This section gives a summary overview of the main alternatives (for details, see Lappi-Seppälä 2011, 236–239).

Nonprosecution and Mediation

Nonprosecution. The first-level sanctions for minor offenses consist of warnings given by the police and decisions of nonprosecution. Nonprosecution, in this context, refers to a decision to drop the charge even if there is a known offender and his or her guilt has been established. In Denmark, the decision of nonprosecution can be attached to certain conditions that must be met, with the threat of the case being taken into court. The most common form, however, is unconditional nonprosecution (in all countries). Under the legality principle (applied in Finland and Sweden but not in Denmark and Norway), prosecution must take place in all cases in which sufficient evidence exists of the suspect's guilt. Nonprosecution is possible only for reasons defined in the law. The main grounds relate to the seriousness (petty nature) of the offense and the young age of the offender (offenders under the age of 18). Non-prosecution can also be based on reasons of equity or criminal policy expediency. In Finland, the court may also waive further sanctions for reasons very much similar to those of nonprosecution.

Mediation. Mediation was introduced in the Nordic countries in the early 1980s. Norway was the first to experiment with mediation in 1981, with Finland to follow in 1983. In both countries, mediation had reached widespread application (referrals counted in thousands) by the 1990s. Norway was also the first country to expand the system nationwide by passing a law on "conflict counsels" in 1991. Others followed in the 21st century (Finland 2006, Sweden 2008, and Denmark 2010). The relations between mediation and criminal justice systems have been organized differently in these countries. Mediation has the most official role in Norway, where successful mediation automatically diverts the case from the criminal justice system. In the other countries, the further processing of the case is left to the discretion of the prosecutor.[6] In Finland and Sweden, an agreement or settlement between the offender and the victim is a possible grounds for nonprosecution or waiving or mitigation of punishment by the court. In Denmark, the role and the practical relevance of mediation has remained more restricted.

Mediation is based on volunteer work in all countries. Also, participation in mediation is always voluntary for all the parties. The municipal social welfare authorities usually assist in coordinating the mediation services, but mediators are not considered public officials. In Finland and Norway, the annual number of offenders in mediation comes close to 10,000. The number of juveniles aged 15–17 in mediation is around 2,000–3,000. In Finland, the number of juveniles aged 15–17 in mediation is around 60% of all criminal justice dispositions in courts; in Norway, conflict counsels handle over 3,000 mediation cases with offenders aged 15–17 and less than 800 cases in the courts. The clear majority of mediation cases involve either minor property offenses or minor forms of assault and battery.

Fines

Fines are the most used penalty in all Nordic countries. Denmark, Finland, and Sweden impose fines as day fines (a system adopted in the

1920s and 1930s). The day-fine system aims to ensure equal severity of the fine for offenders of different income and wealth. The number of day fines is determined on the basis of the seriousness of the offense, while the amount of a day fine depends on the financial situation of the offender. Thus, similar offenses committed by offenders of different income will result in (roughly) similar overall severity of the sanction.

A fine may be imposed either in an ordinary trial or, for petty offenses, through simplified summary penal proceedings, by the prosecutor or the police. Some summary fines are imposed both as day fines and as fixed fines. The powers of the police to impose fines are usually restricted to traffic offenses. The majority of prosecutor's fines are also imposed for traffic offenses. However, a substantial number of minor offenses under the general criminal code are also sanctioned by prosecutorial fines. All in all, the vast majority of fines are ordered in a summary process.

Community Sanctions Applicable for All Age Groups

The two main community alternatives, conditional sentence and community service, apply both for adults and for juveniles. Some countries have separate probation and treatment orders (also combined with conditional sentences). Community sanctions restricted only for juveniles form the third main group (see the following section).

Conditional and Suspended Sentences. The lower end of the community punishments consists of suspended sentences or conditional imprisonment, with or without stipulated time. In Finland and Norway, the court imposes the sentence but postpones the enforcement. In Sweden, the court postpones the pronouncement of the sentence for a probation period. In Denmark, both options are in use. In Finland, sentences of imprisonment of at most two years may be imposed conditionally. Norway and Denmark have no formal limits, but conditional sentences lasting more than two years are quite rare.

Conditional imprisonment can be combined with supervision, fines, community service, or—as in Denmark and Norway—prison. Conditional imprisonment may vary also in terms of the conditions involved. In Denmark and Norway, the sentence may be combined with different sort of conditions, such as obligating the offender to participate in rehabilitative programs or mediation, to pay compensation to the victim, or to report regularly to the police. The Swedish suspended sentence can be combined with fines or with community service.

A person who has been sentenced to conditional imprisonment can be ordered to serve his or her sentence in prison if he or she commits a new offense during the probation period (usually one to two years). The thresholds for the revocation of a conditional imprisonment vary. For example, in Finland, revocation is possible only if the court imposes a sentence of imprisonment for the new offense. Thus, a behavioral infraction alone is not enough for the enforcement of a conditional prison sentence.

Community Service. Community service appears in different forms. Finland and Norway treat community service as an independent sanction (although Norway renamed community service in 2001 to "community punishment"). In Denmark and Sweden, community service is attached either to conditional imprisonment or a probation order. In Finland, conditional prison sentences of more than one year may be combined with a short (20–60 hours) community service order. In Denmark, community service can be combined also with fines and unconditional imprisonment. In addition, community service may be combined with separate conditions concerning residence, school attendance, or work. Also, Norway allows specific conditions regarding the offender's dwelling, work, and treatment. The maximum number of community service hours varies from 200 (Finland) to 420 (Norway).

Countries differ also in how strictly community service has been defined as an alternative to imprisonment. Finland has followed the strictest policy in this respect, by adopting a specific two-step procedure. First, the court is supposed to make its sentencing decision by applying the normal principles and criteria of sentencing without considering the possibility of community service. Second, if the result of this deliberation is unconditional imprisonment (and certain requirements are fulfilled), the court may transform the sentence into community service. In principle, community service may therefore be used only in cases in which the accused would otherwise have received a sentence of unconditional imprisonment. Other countries are less strict on this point. In connection with the 2001 reform in Norway, the scope of community punishment was extended to be used not only instead of imprisonment but as a replacement penalty for juvenile offenders who had previously been sentenced to supervised conditional imprisonment.

Probation and Treatment Orders. Sweden is the only Scandinavian country with a separate probation type of sanction. Probation ("protective supervision") means a period of three years, in which the sentenced person is supervised during the first year. Probation may be used alone or combined with other penalties. The Swedish probation is a kind of "frame" penalty. It can be ordered together with fines or with a short prison sentence (14 days to three months). It may also be combined with a treatment order (see the following paragraph) and with community service. Swedish contract treatment (*kontraktsvård*) is targeted primarily to long-term substance abusers when there is a link between the abuse and crime. A contract is made between the court and the client on institutional care, in a home or an open clinic. If the person misbehaves, the sentence can be transformed to a prison sentence. The treatment lasts between six months and two years. Part of the treatment takes place in an institution. In contract treatment, treatment is always voluntary (but the choices are limited: either to go to prison or not).

Denmark is the other Nordic country combining treatment with criminal justice interventions. In Denmark, treatment orders appear together both with conditional imprisonment and as a form of prison enforcement. Conditionally sentenced offenders suffering from substance abuse (an alcoholic or a drug addict) or mental disturbance may be faced with a requirement of treatment for alcohol or drug abuse or a condition of outpatient psychiatric treatment. For those already sentenced to prison, there remains an option to suspend the sentence by undergoing a treatment for substance abuse. Persons who are sentenced to prison for 60 days or less can apply for suspension of the serving of the sentence, if they are in obvious need of treatment for their abuse of alcohol.

Specific Community Alternatives to Juveniles

Specific community alternatives for juveniles include the juvenile punishment in Finland, youth sanction in Denmark, and youth care and youth service in Sweden. The Norwegian community punishment contains elements of many of these. However, it is not designed as a specific penalty applicable only for juveniles.

The Finnish juvenile punishment order is a four- to 12-month-long community sanction comparable in severity to conditional imprisonment. The duration is determined by the court, whereas the detailed content of the sanction is set by the Probation Service. Youth care in Sweden is a court order applied for offenders under the age of 21. It obligates the social welfare board to take actions that promote the young offender's future social development and reintegration. It may include both voluntary and involuntary institutional treatment. Youth care may consist only of supporting and counseling activities, but it may also include placement in a secured child welfare institution. Youth service is targeted mainly to offenders between the ages of 15 and 17. It consists of unpaid work for 20–150 hours plus attendance in program work or education. The choice between these two options is made on the basis of the need for treatment. Youth care is reserved for offenders who are in need of treatment and program work (for more detail, see Borgeke 2008, 405–409). The Danish youth sanction can be defined as a partially custodial sanction (see the following section), as it involves a period of around two months in a similar type of secure child welfare institution, run by the social welfare authorities.

Custodial Sanctions

All countries apply several techniques in order to avoid and to minimize the use of imprisonment in young age groups. Sentencing provisions oblige the courts to impose unconditional prison sentences for offenders under age 18 only for "special" or "extraordinary" reasons. When prison sentences are used, there is a reduction in the length of the prison term compared to adult offenders. In addition, sentences that are formally classified as prison sentences may be enforced outside prison in Denmark. All prison sentences imposed for offenders under age 18 are enforced either in secure child welfare institutions or in specific "pensions" (boarding houses). The latter are small units administered by the Department of Corrections. Sweden has replaced most prison sentences for offenders under 18 with closed youth care, a court-ordered custodial sanction from 14 days to four years.

When sentenced to ordinary prison, juveniles receive mitigations for the length of the prison terms. For adults, Denmark, Finland, and Sweden have a life sentence (which means in practice a prison term of around 15 years). Norway has abolished the life sentence and replaced it with a 21-year maximum term. For offenders under age 18, life sentences are replaced with a determinate prison sentence varying between 10 (Sweden) and 16 (Denmark) years. Otherwise, the maximum penalty for offenders under 18 is reduced usually by one-fourth. If sentences are to be enforced in normal prisons, juveniles are kept separately and, as a rule, placed in open institutions. For each offender, a sentence plan is drafted that is tailored according to the prisoner's needs. Even if youth prison has been abolished as a specific institution, juveniles serve their sentences in units specialized according to their needs.

Youth Process

Juvenile criminal procedure is based on cooperation between the police, prosecutor, mediation services, probation service, social service and child welfare, and the courts. The relationships between different actors are arranged differently in each Nordic country. The following serves as an example from Finland (for details, see Marttunen 2008).

A child under the age of 15 cannot in any case be arrested or remanded in custody. However, he or she can be questioned, and the act can be investigated. Arrest and remand in custody are possible if the juvenile is suspected of a crime of a rather serious nature and it is necessary to prevent the continuation of criminality, the escape of the juvenile, or the destruction of evidence. In practice, arrest is seldom used as a coercive measure against a juvenile. When the person to be questioned is under the age of 18, the custodial parent and child welfare officials must be given the opportunity to be present during the questioning. Police work in close cooperation with child welfare. It is the duty of the police to inform child welfare authorities whenever a person under the age of 18 has been suspected of an offense. The police may also play an active part in sending referrals to mediation.

The handling of juvenile cases places several special duties on the public prosecutor. Extra attention must be paid to the speedy handling of the case. Before proceeding with the case, the prosecutor must consider diversionary options, nonprosecution, and mediation. A decision of nonprosecution may be accompanied by an oral caution, which is communicated to the young offender in the form of a hearing in the prosecutor's office.

For each young offender under the age of 21 charged with an offense that is deemed to lead to a sentence more severe than a fine, a personal investigation report must be prepared. The report is made by either social welfare officials or the Probation Association, but the prosecutor must make the request for such a report. The probation service collects all the relevant information by contacting, for example, the social services, the offender, and usually also the offender's legal guardians before deciding whether to recommend community service or juvenile punishment in that particular case.

There are no juvenile courts in the Finnish system. Juvenile cases are dealt with in ordinary courts. The normal composition of the local court in the juvenile cases is one legally trained judge and three lay judges. Simple criminal cases may also be dealt with in the local court by one legally trained judge sitting alone if the maximum punishment for the offense in question is a fine or imprisonment for 18 months or less. Specific rules apply to handling of the cases involving young offenders. In the court proceedings, cases involving juvenile crimes must be taken to the main court hearing within two weeks of the summons. If the case is tried in a court, a minor has a right to free legal counsel, unless it is obviously unnecessary. This right has to be taken into account ex officio also in cases in which the juvenile him- or herself does not request to have a lawyer. In addition, if the person to be prosecuted is under the age of 18, the custodial parent and child welfare officials must be given the opportunity to be present during the trial.

Sentencing Practice

The following compares the use of different sentencing alternatives and the length of prison sentences, both overall and for specific offenses.

Overview of the Use of Sentencing Alternatives

The number of sentencing alternatives and their combinations range from 7–8 in Norway to well over 20 in Denmark and Sweden. For the sake of simplicity, court-ordered sentencing alternatives are grouped into three categories:

1. Prison. This includes immediate custodial sanctions as well as all combinations with prison and community sentences, youth sanction in Denmark and closed youth care in Sweden.
2. Community sanctions. This group covers conditional and suspended sentences, probation in Sweden, community service, specific juvenile punishment (in Sweden, youth service and youth care and, in Finland, juvenile punishment), as well as all combination of community sanctions and/or fines.
3. Fines. This group covers only fines imposed by courts. Thus, summary fines, imposed as a rule for minor traffic offenses, have been excluded from this overview.

Results are presented both as percentages (penalty shares) and per 100,000 population in the age group (penalty rates), as both indicators need to be used simultaneously.

In the 15–17 age group, the share of fines ranges from 80% in Finland to about 5% in Norway. The share of prison varies from 1% (in Finland) to over 10% (in Denmark and Norway). In the 18–20 age group, fines are still the most common penalty in both Finland and Denmark (around 70%). The share of prison remains marginal in all countries, with the exception of Norway in the 18–20 group (45%). In Finland and Sweden, prison sentences are close to nonexistent in the 15–17 group and represent a very small share also in the 18–20 group.

Some of these differences are explained when sanctions are counted relative to population. Finland imposes the largest number of penalties in the 15–17 age group and Denmark in the 18–20 group. Finland also imposes the largest share of fines in the 15–17 group and Denmark in the 18–20 group. One may assume that the large share of fines in both cases is partly explainable by the fact that countries with fewer

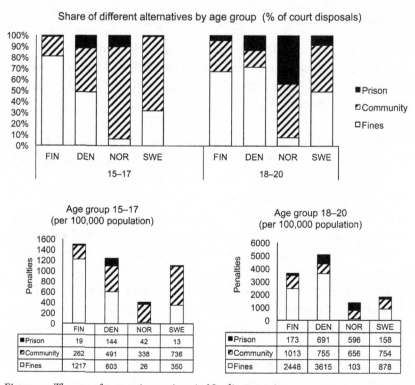

Figure 2.1. The use of sentencing options in Nordic countries, 2011–2012

convictions relative to population have dealt with larger shares of minor offenses outside the court process. This is especially evident in Norway, with around 400 convictions per 100,000 population in the age group, while the number in Finland exceeds 1,500.

When sentences are counted relative to population, the use of imprisonment also looks different. While the share of prison sentences in Denmark and Norway was on the same level in the 15–17 group, Denmark imposes three to four times more prison sentences relative to the size of that age group.

The number of community sanctions is about on the same level in Finland and Norway and clearly highest in Sweden in the 15–17 group. In the 18–20 group, community sanctions have been used in a similar scale in all countries (relative to population).

These comparisons exclude different forms of diversion, which may form an important element in youth justice. Nonprosecution is most widely used in Sweden (around 1,000 per 100,000 population in the 15–17 group and over 500 in the 18–20 group), with Finland being next (with the corresponding figures 500 and 300). However, the statistics from Norway report only conditional nonprosecution (omitting unconditional diversion cases from its statistics).

In addition, one should acknowledge the role of mediation. This applies especially to Norway but also to Finland. In fact, mediation is used most widely in Finland, but it has a stronger role among youth justice alternatives in Norway. In Finland, there are around 1,000 mediation cases per 100,000 population in the 15–17 group (almost as many as fines) and 800 cases in the 18–20 group. Corresponding figures for Norway in the 15–17 age group are even higher. In 2008, there were 3,329 cases mediated (1,800 per 100,000 population), more than fourfold the overall number of court disposals (777, or 406 per 100,000 population in 2011). Since mediation in Norway also replaces other criminal justice interventions, it is clear that especially in the 15–17 age group, the low number of court disposals is explainable by diversion to mediation.

The Overall Use of Imprisonment

The Share of Prison Sentences. Figure 2.2 gives a more detailed picture of the overall use of imprisonment separately for juveniles (15–17), young adults (18–20), and adults (21 and over). The figures confirm the fact

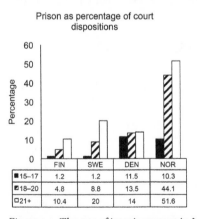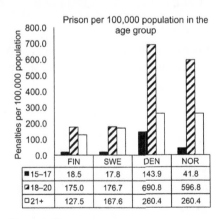

Figure 2.2. The use of imprisonment in Nordic countries, 2011–2012

that Finland and Sweden use imprisonment less often in the 15–17 age group according to both indicators.

In all countries, the share of imprisonment increases together with the age of the offender (left section). This is a logical consequence of a sentencing policy that aims to avoid the use of custodial sanctions in younger age groups. However, the profile of Denmark differs from this pattern, as the share of prison sentences is on the same level in all age groups (around 12%–14%). Denmark does not seem to "spare" juveniles from custodial measures to the same extent that other Nordic countries do. This, however, may well be related to the fact that prison sentences for juveniles in Denmark are enforced in secure child welfare institutions or under other specific arrangements (which may lower the threshold of the use of custody).

Counted relative to age group, both Denmark and Norway impose many more prison sentences for young adults (600–700 per 100,000 population compared to below 200 in Finland and Sweden). Similar, albeit smaller, differences apply also for adults (260 compared to 130–170 per 100,000 population). Denmark and Norway also in general impose more prison sentences, compared to Finland and Sweden.

The Length of Imprisonment. Nordic prison sentences are generally short; in Norway and Denmark, they are exceptionally short. Table 2.1 displays the share of short prison sentences (below six months) as shares and per 100,000 population.

In the 15–17 group, the share of short sentences ranges from 35% in Finland to 59% in Denmark and 69% in Norway (but note that the

TABLE 2.1. Short Prison Sentences (at Most Six Months) by Age Groups (as Percentage and per 100,000 Population)

	Sentences at most six months (% of all prison sentences)			Sentences at most six months (per 100,000 pop. in the age group)		
	15–17	18–20	21+	15–17	18–20	21+
Finland	35.1	50.4	56.4	6.5	88.2	71.9
Sweden	52.9	53.2	65.3	9.4	94.0	109.5
Denmark*	59.1	76.0	80.5	85.1	524.7	209.6
Norway	68.8	81.4	75.1	28.8	485.5	195.6

* Less than six months

TABLE 2.2. Long Prison Sentences (One Year or More) by Age Groups (as Percentage and per 100,000 Population)

	Sentences over one year (% of all prison sentences)			Sentences over one year (per 100,000 pop. in the age group)		
	15–17	18–20	21+	15–17	18–20	21+
Finland	40.5	32.0	26.5	7.5	56.0	33.7
Sweden	20.0	24.3	16.4	0.5	42.9	27.5
Denmark	7.3	10.7	10.6	10.5	74.0	27.5
Norway*	10.0	7.8	12.9	4.2	46.4	33.7

* One year or more

TABLE 2.3. Very Long Prison Sentences (Over Four or Five Years) by Age Groups (as Percentage and per 100,000 Population)

	Sentences over four or five years (% of all prison sentences)			Sentences over four or five years (per 100,000 pop. in the age group)		
	15–17	18–20	21+	15–17	18–20	21+
Finland (five years or more)	2.7	3.2	2.9	0.5	5.5	3.9
Sweden (over four years)	1.5	2.0	2.5	0.3	3.7	4.2
Denmark (over five years)	0.9	0.5	1.3	1.0	3.5	3.3
Norway (five years or more)	2.6	0.7	1.4	1.0	3.7	4.9

Danish figures include only sentences below six months). These patterns repeat in the other age groups. The share of short prison sentences is smallest in Finland, followed by Sweden, and is highest in Norway and Denmark. Figures relative to population (right section) highlight the other differences among the countries. Denmark imposes ten times the number of short prison sentences in the 15–17 group (even if the Danish figures include only sentences less than six months). Tables 2.2 and 2.3 show similar data for long prison sentences (at least one year) and very long sentences (four to five years or more). Figure 2.3 illustrates these differences in more detail (per 100,000 population).

The share of long prison sentences is largest in Finland in all age groups. However, these differences are much smaller when sentences

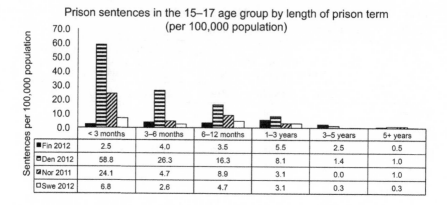

Prison sentences in the 15–17 age group by length of prison term (per 100,000 population)					
	< 3 months	3–6 months	6–12 months	1–3 years	3–5 years	5+ years
■Fin 2012	2.5	4.0	3.5	5.5	2.5	0.5
▣Den 2012	58.8	26.3	16.3	8.1	1.4	1.0
▨Nor 2011	24.1	4.7	8.9	3.1	0.0	1.0
▢Swe 2012	6.8	2.6	4.7	3.1	0.3	0.3

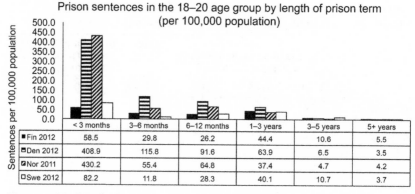

Prison sentences in the 18–20 age group by length of prison term (per 100,000 population)					
	< 3 months	3–6 months	6–12 months	1–3 years	3–5 years	5+ years
■Fin 2012	58.5	29.8	26.2	44.4	10.6	5.5
▣Den 2012	408.9	115.8	91.6	63.9	6.5	3.5
▨Nor 2011	430.2	55.4	64.8	37.4	4.7	4.2
▢Swe 2012	82.2	11.8	28.3	40.1	10.7	3.7

Figure 2.3. The length of prison term for age groups 15–17 and 18–20, 2011–2012

are counted relative to populations. All differences get smaller when the length of prison sentences increases. The share of long-term sentences (over four or five years) varies between 1% and 3% in all age groups in all countries. Neither are there major differences between the countries in the frequency of these sentences per 100,000 population. Figure 2.3 illustrates these patterns. The special position of Denmark (and Norway to a certain extent) as a country with a higher number of prison sentences gets weaker as the length of prison terms increases.

Penalties for Specific Offenses

The following compares sentencing outcomes in three Nordic countries in five major offense categories: assault, theft, robbery, drunk driving, and drugs. Separate results are reported also for aggravated assault and aggravated theft/burglary. Due to data availability, comparisons are restricted to Finland, Sweden, and Denmark. Also, the age categories have been joined into one group of ages 15–20. Table 2.4 displays data for the use of imprisonment.

The share of imprisonment in assault varies from 3% (Finland) to 38% (Denmark) and in robbery from 18% (Finland) to 82% (Denmark). Differences in other offense categories are smaller, but the trend is the same: Danish courts much more frequently use prison sentences compared to Finnish courts. Sweden often finds its place between these two countries. Drunk driving and drug offenses form a partial exception.

Some of these differences disappear when prison sentences are counted relative to population. Now Finnish and Swedish sentencing practices converge in assault and theft but deviate in drunk driving (many more prison sentences in Finland) and drug offenses (more prison sentences in Sweden). However, Denmark retains its position as the leading country in the use of imprisonment. The Danish courts impose ten times the number of prison sentences for robbery compared to Finland, eight times the number for assault compared to Finland and Sweden, and four times the number for theft.

As noted earlier, diversion may play a substantial role in Nordic youth justice, even if statistical data are hard to obtain. The following

TABLE 2.4. The Use of Imprisonment in Three Nordic Countries in Seven Offenses (15–20 Years)

	Share of prison sentences (% of court dispositions)			Number of prison sentences (per 100,000 pop. in the age group)		
	FIN	SWE	DEN	FIN	SWE	DEN
Assault	3.4	7.8	38.0	17.3	15.3	116.5
aggravated assault	20.8	40.2	71.7	6.3	8.9	43.4
Theft	4.3	8.0	7.9	16.1	16.6	82.4
aggravated assault	13.6	27.8	27.6	3.5	8.2	48.8
Robbery	17.9	42.2	81.9	7.5	23.2	75.3
DWI	2.1	5.9	1.2	12.0	2.6	2.5
Drugs	2.2	3.5	3.1	3.8	9.5	25.3

The use of sentencing alternatives (percentage)
Assault, theft, and robbery (ages 15–20)

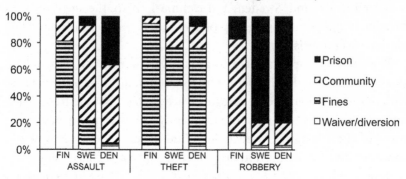

The use of sentencing alternatives (per 100,000 population)
Assault, theft, and robbery (ages 15–20)

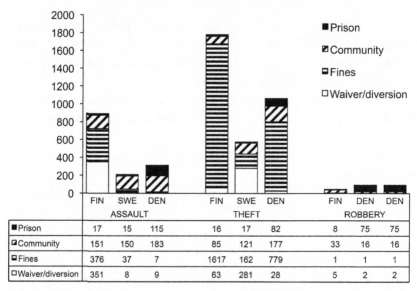

	ASSAULT			THEFT			ROBBERY		
	FIN	SWE	DEN	FIN	SWE	DEN	FIN	DEN	DEN
■Prison	17	15	115	16	17	82	8	75	75
▨Community	151	150	183	85	121	177	33	16	16
▤Fines	376	37	7	1617	162	779	1	1	1
☐Waiver/diversion	351	8	9	63	281	28	5	2	2

Figure 2.4. The use of sentencing alternatives by offense, 2011–2012

comparison includes also existing data on waiver of sanctions and nonprosecution (however, no offense-specific data for mediation are available).

Finland deals with a much larger share of assaults through either nonprosecution or fines, while the share of prison sentences is clearly the lowest. The most telling data can be read from the penalty rates. Finland and Sweden impose an equal number of prison and community sanctions for assault. Denmark imposes the same number of community sanctions but eight times the number of prison sentences. Neither Denmark nor Sweden use fines or nonprosecution for this offense, while these are the standard options in Finland. But at least in comparison to Sweden, one can hardly conclude that the Finnish practice is more lenient, since the number of offenders receiving either a prison sentence or a community sanction is the same. In order to make judgments about the relative severity of sanction practices, we need full-scale information of the levels of recorded crime and the attrition processes (see later).

Theft follows largely similar patterns. Again Finland uses more fines than other countries and imposes more penalties compared to others (with Denmark following fairly close). In this case, Sweden records a high share and number of nonprosecution. The use of prison is, again, on the same level in Finland and Sweden but is clearly higher in Denmark.

Penalties for robbery also differ. These crimes are punished mainly by prison in Denmark and Sweden (80%) and mainly by community sanctions (around 60%) in Finland. These differences remain also when sentences are counted relative to population. Unlike in the former offense categories, the number of tried cases is smallest in Finland. The number of prison sentences is around 15% of that in Denmark and Sweden, but the number of community sanctions is about double that in these countries.

Sentences Relative to Crime: Comparing Finland and Sweden

If we compare the number of sanctions relative to population imposed for juveniles in Finland and Sweden, it appears that Finnish juvenile delinquents outnumber the Swedish ones by three to one in both assault and theft. Associated with the fact that Finland imposes fines much

TABLE 2.5. Processing the Cases in Finland and Sweden by
Offense and by Age Group

	1. Reported		2. Cleared		3. Suspects		4. All dispositions		5. Courts	
	Fin.	Swe.	Fin.	Swe.	Fin.	Swe.	Fin.	Swe.	Fin.	Swe.
I. Ages 15–20 (*per 100,000 pop.*)										
Assault					1,477	721	694	210	501	205
Theft					2,809	1,320	1,473	581	408	489
Robbery		Data n/a			110	168	47	55	47	55
Drugs					938	2,271	533	858	188	521
DWI					571	236	496	91	496	45
II. All age groups (*per 100,000 pop.*)										
Assault	713	955	552	438	601	237	267	90	191	86
Theft	2,587	4,326	931	778	1,121	534	576	256	126	128
Robbery	30	98	16	33	27	24	10	10	10	10
Drugs	375	1,053	337	805	356	704	152	258	74	111
DWI	357	290	355	261	355	229	301	123	300	66

more often, one is tempted to conclude that juvenile crime in Finland
is more frequent and that this has something to do with Finland's more
lenient sentencing practice. This, however, may not be true. Higher conviction rates in Finland may just be a result of the fact that the Finnish
criminal justice system processes a much larger share of cases through
the whole system. This dynamic can be traced by comparing the rates
of recorded crime, cleared offenses, detected suspects, and all disposals
by criminal justice officials. The following brief comparison between
Sweden and Finland summarizes these differences.

Comparisons between reported crime (1) and offenses sentenced in
courts (5) reveal the main differences. Sweden reports more assault than
Finland (Sweden 955, Finland 713), but Finland imposes more sanctions
(all disposals: Finland 267, Sweden 90; and court-ordered sentences:
Finland 191, Sweden 86). The same pattern applies to theft. A major part
of these differences results from differences in the clearing rates. Either

the Finnish police clear up crime more effectively, or bookkeeping rules on what counts as a "cleared case" are different. Whatever the explanation is, the initial level of recorded crime is not higher in Finland compared to Sweden, even if the number of imposed sanctions is. In fact, crime rates are higher in Sweden, but penalty rates are lower.

These observations concern all age groups, not specifically juveniles (for obvious reasons, there are no age-specific data for total recorded crime; age-specific data starts only from cases with detected suspects). However, comparing the data for steps 3–5 in the 15–20 age group with the total population gives reasons to assume that the same filtering processes that work among the total population apply also to juvenile crime.

Survey results confirm these conclusions. Overall, International Crime Victimization surveys find very small differences among the Nordic countries; violent crime and robbery occur at the same level in Finland and Sweden, while all property-offense indicators show higher rates in Sweden (see Lappi-Seppälä and Tonry 2011, 159). This is confirmed also by data from Nordic youth surveys (see table 2.6). Self-reported crime in the 13–16 age group is largely on the same level in all Nordic capitals, with the exception of Copenhagen, which has both higher theft and violent rates. Helsinki rates lowest, along with Oslo. More extensive use of nominal sanctions in Finland is not a result of higher crime rates; rather, it relates to the country's more legalistic culture with less "unofficial diversion."

TABLE 2.6. Last-Year Prevalence of Delinquent Behavior in Nordic Countries (Percentage of 13- to 16-Year-Olds)

	Helsinki %	Stockholm %	Copenhagen %	Oslo %
Theft (all except shoplifting)	3	4	10	3
Shoplifting	8	9	9	7
Assault	1	2	2	1
Robbery	1	1	2	2
Violent combined	12	12	18	10
Drug selling	1	1	2	1

Source: Compiled from Kivivuori and Bernburg 2012

Conclusions

While overall trends in the Nordic countries are largely similar, there are differences in details. Denmark imposes many more prison sentences compared to other countries. This applies both to juveniles ages 15–17 and young adults ages 18–20. Also, Norway imposes a high number of prison sentences in the 18–20 age group. Finland and Sweden use imprisonment most sparingly in both age groups.

One specific feature in Finland is the high number of fines imposed there, especially in the 15–17 group. This seems to be in connection with the high number of cases taken through the criminal justice process (less diversion). The Norwegian system differs from others by a high number of cases diverted to mediation in the 15–17 group (and possibly also in the 18–20 group, but no data are available). Mediation is a standard option for juveniles (and for minor offenses more generally) also in Finland, but it has not been able to reduce the use of fines in a similar manner as in Norway. Along with fines, community sanctions form the other standard option for juveniles and young adults in all countries. In the 15–17 group, community sanctions relative to population are most prevalent in Sweden and Denmark.

Prison sentences are generally short in all Nordic countries. In all but Finland, over half of the sentences in both age groups remain under six months. Only 10%–30% of prison sentences exceed one year, and 1%–5% exceed four to five years. This distribution is largely similar in all Nordic countries, with the exception of Denmark imposing more and shorter sentences for younger age groups.

Offense-specific comparisons confirm the general patterns. Finland imposes more fines for all offenses studied, fewer prison sentences (together with Sweden), and slightly fewer community sanctions. Diversion is common in minor assaults in Finland and in minor theft offenses in Sweden. For robbery, Finland uses more community sanctions and less imprisonment.

In offense-specific comparisons, Denmark has a high number of prison sentences. However, even if Denmark frequently imposes prison sentences, the sentences are short (40% being three months or less in the 15–17 group and 60% in the 18–20 group). And with to regard juveniles, none of the prison sentences are enforced in actual prison but in secure children's homes. Thus, a full-scale comparison should, in the end, also take into account differences in institutional enforcement practices. The exceptionally low number of court dispositions in Norway and high number of fines in Finland are explained when the analysis is extended beyond court data. In Norway, cases are diverted from courts by extensive use of mediation. The higher number of cases tried in Finland—when compared to Sweden—is not a result of higher levels of crime but of more effective and legalistic processing of cases: a much larger share of reported and solved crime will eventually lead to a criminal sanction in Finland. Finland has traditionally strongly followed legalistic traditions. Also, discretion given to the prosecutors and the police in nonreporting was widened in Finland later than in the neighboring countries. This, together with the fact that clear-up rates of offenses are much higher in Finland, explains both the large number of fines and the higher share of offenses leading to conviction in Finland.

* * *

How do these patterns relate to models of youth justice in different countries? The following presents only a tentative comparison in the use of imprisonment in four offense categories in England and Wales and the three Nordic countries added together.

The share of prison sentences is systematically higher in England and Wales, as compared to joint figures from Finland, Sweden, and Denmark. The differences become even more evident when sentences are

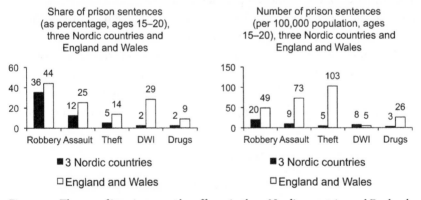

Figure 2.5. The use of imprisonment by offense in three Nordic countries and England and Wales, 2011–2012 (court statistics)

counted relative to population. On the other hand, corresponding rates for Denmark come fairly close to those of England and Wales (in some cases even surpass them). However, differences in the length of prison sentences again widen the differences between the Nordic and English sentencing practices. The average length of all prison sentences in Denmark is 6.3 months, for normal assault 3.0, for aggravated assault 6.6, for burglary 5.6, for robbery 16.5, and for rape 23.5 months (Kriminalitet 2012, table 318). Corresponding figures for England and Wales are 13.7 months for all offenses, for wounding 11.2 months, for burglary 18.4 months, for robbery 33.6 months, and for rape 96.4 months. Prison sentences are two to four times longer in England and Wales.[7] These differences are, of course, reflected also in the number of prisoners. The average absolute number of prisoners under the age of 18 in 2006–2010 was 8.8 in Denmark, 3.2 in Finland, 2.8 in Norway, and 0.4 in Sweden.[8]

Child Welfare Interventions

A balanced overview of Nordic youth justice is possible only by incorporating the functions and interventions of child welfare in the analyses. Child welfare is fundamentally integrated into a massive legislation-based system of welfare benefits and services. This policy covers social security, social services, health, education and training, housing, employment, and so on, with the purpose of ensuring the most basic needs for all. Viewing child welfare from the specific point of view of youth justice opens a narrow perspective on the functions of that system. But it is essential in order to grasp the full picture of the social and rehabilitative work conducted among juveniles (and their families). While the child welfare authorities usually act irrespective of any impulses coming from the criminal justice agencies, these authorities are involved whenever a child is suspected of criminal offenses. Their cooperation is also needed in dealing with the case in the criminal process.

Open Care Measures and Transfer of Guardianship

The first step in child welfare consists of different open care measures, such as support interventions in community care. The authorities are obliged to undertake community-based supportive measures without delay if the health or development of children or young people is endangered or not safeguarded by their environment, or if they are likely to endanger their own health or development. In less problematic cases, these measures are usually limited to one discussion or a series of discussions with the young offender and his or her parents. If it becomes apparent through these discussions that there are serious problems in the home (economic problems, internal conflicts, etc.), an attempt is made to resolve these problems. The list of open care measures is extensive. In addition to economic and social support for the parents, they may include also psychological support and psychiatric services, substance abuse programs, school-related work, structured open care programs for the children (for example multisystemic therapy), appointment of contact persons (mentors), and so on.

The most intrusive child welfare measures are transfer of guardianship and placement in a foster home or in residential care. Foster care orders can be imposed on both a voluntary and an involuntary basis. In a clear majority of cases, all parties (the child and the parents) agree on the matter. The conditions for an involuntary care order and institutional placement are roughly similar in all Nordic countries, while the types and names of institutions vary (see Bengtsson and Jakobsen 2009). Thus, in Finland, an involuntary care order can be issued if the following three conditions are met: (1) the child's health or development is risked either by (a) environmental reasons (often the parents' own behavior and substance abuse problems) or (b) the child's own behavior, (2) open care measures are deemed to be insufficient, and (3) the care order is in the best interest of the child. The Swedish law separates two forms of involuntary care orders. Orders based on environmental grounds can be issued, if "due to physical or mental abuse, exploitation, neglect or some other circumstance in the home, there is a palpable risk of detriment to the young person's health or development" (Care of Young Persons Act § 2). The order can be issued also for behavioral reasons, when the "young person exposes his health or development to a palpable risk of injury through the abuse of addictive substances, criminal activity or some other socially degrading behavior" (Care of Young Persons Act § 3). Both grounds apply to children under 18 without restrictions. In both Finland and Sweden, involuntary orders are decided by the administrative court by the application of the social welfare authorities. The court decides on the care order, but the treatment and placement are decided by the child welfare board.

The duration of the care order depends on the child's conditions, as well as on the conditions in his or her home environment. In Finland, foster care orders are in force until they are terminated by the decision of the leading social worker. The grounds for the care orders must be reexamined at least once a year in connection with the redrafting of the individual care plan. In addition, the parents and the child (over 12 years) always have the right to contest the care order and demand its termination from the leading social worker. For this request, a reasoned decision must be given with a right to appeal to administrative court.

Care orders are terminated when the child reaches the age of 18. Even after that, the local welfare board is obliged to provide necessary aftercare services (including on the request of the child). This obligation terminates once the person reaches the age of 21.

Child Welfare Institutions

To be taken into foster care means that the child is placed outside his or her home. This may mean many things. The system is fairly complex and consists of several different types of arrangements and institutions. Thus, in Finland, the child may be placed in the custody of the his or her relatives, in another family, in professional (private) family homes, in children's homes, in special children's homes, in juvenile homes, or in reformatory schools. A clear majority of the children are placed in families and private family homes. However, for children in need of more intensive care and supervision, there are also special children's homes and juvenile homes. Also, the structure of this "heavy end" of the child welfare system varies in different Nordic countries.

In Finland, the most secured institutions, designed for older children and teenagers, are the state reformatory schools. State reformatory schools have traditionally served the function of the "last institution" in the chain of different child protection measures. Unlike in the past, punitive motives have no role in deciding the placements. Neither are the reformatory schools closed institutions, in the sense that the term is understood in most jurisdictions. However, there are restrictions for movement in various degrees (such as going to town). The daily teaching program is also quite fixed. The law lists all possible restrictions and the preconditions for their application in detail. None of these restrictions are allowed to be used as punishments. As a rule, written decision is required with reasons provided for the use of any of these measures. The decision must be attached with instructions for appeal.

In Finland, there are six state reformatory schools with around 300 children altogether. The average size of one school is 50 beds. However, the law prohibits having more than 25 beds in one building complex and more than seven beds in one unit. All children must have a room of their own. The majority of children in the state reformatories are also there on a voluntary basis. Reformatory schools are first and foremost schools. The basic aim is to ensure the child's completion of the curriculum of the ground school and ability to pursue studies also after that.

For children with the highest risk of endangering themselves or others, there are provisions of intensive specific care (ISC). ISC provides the most intensive form of control under the Child Welfare Act. The overall number of beds with the required facilities for intensive care under the Child Protection Law runs at the moment in between 20 and 30. In practice, the placement in ISC may take place in cases when the child is constantly absconding from his or her regular placement unit and thereby seriously endangers his or her own health or development. The aim of intensive care is to interrupt a cycle of self-destructive behavior and to improve the child's own ability to take responsibility for his or her own life. ISC is not to be used for punitive purposes. However, the child's freedom of movement and contacts with the outside world may be subjected to restrictions, which the child may, undoubtedly, feel as punitive or repressive. For this reason, the preconditions and process for ISC is defined in detail in the law. The placement decision is taken by the leading social worker for voluntary placements and by the administrative court for involuntary orders. All placements are based on a multiprofessional assessment made by experts in education, social work, psychology, and medicine. The decision may be reviewed by the appeals court. Constant bookkeeping is required for actions and interventions as well as an assessment of their effects and impact on the child. The maximum duration for ISC is 30 days. This can be extended by 60 days by a new decision for exceptional reasons. In the ISC units, there is significantly more staff than in other student units. The average number of staff in three- to four-bed units is 12–14. The staff includes educators with various education backgrounds.

In Sweden, there are 33 secured children's homes (special approved homes) with a little over 600 places to take care of those involuntary placements for which a more secured environment is needed. These homes are run by a specific organization—the Swedish National Board of Institutional Care. These 33 homes are not alike. The common feature is that all inmates have serious psychosocial problems, often with elements of criminal behavior and substance abuse. Some institutions are specialized, concentrating, for example, on young persons with immigrant backgrounds, boys with aggression problems, or adopted children. Some approved homes admit girls only, others boys only. Methods of treatment vary from one approved home to another, according to the clientele. Methods include environmental therapy, functional family therapy, cognitive behavioral therapy, and programs for substance abuse. Some approved homes have emergency and examination departments where activities are concentrated on immediately suspending a destructive pattern of living. All institutions have access to a psychologist, psychiatrist, doctor, and nurse. The approved homes also give youngsters the opportunity to supplement inadequate schooling by studying at compulsory school level. These activities are supervised by the National Agency for Education. Lengths of stay in these residential treatment centers vary from a few weeks to two years, and care orders have to be reviewed every six months. About half the admissions are concluded within two months (see the SIA website: http://www.stat-inst.se/om-webbplatsen/other-languages/the-swedish-national-board-of-institutional-care/).

There are also status differences between special approved homes. Some of these (six in all) are also authorized to receive juveniles sentenced to closed youth care. In addition, some of these homes have specific secure reception units and secure treatment units for juveniles with more serious problems. Also, those young offenders who have been given long sentences, who are in need of special treatment, or who are deemed to be dangerous are placed in a secure treatment unit. These arrangements also blur the distinction between criminal justice and child welfare in the Swedish system in a manner that cannot be detected in Finland or Norway but can be seen to some extent in Denmark, too.

Children in Secured Child Welfare Institutions

Counting juveniles in foster care and in residential care in the Nordic countries does not count juveniles in youth prisons elsewhere. The institutions, their conditions, and their aims differ fundamentally, from voluntary family placements due to family reasons to placements in intensive specific care or secure units in secure children's homes due to a child's offending behavior. However, at some points of the scale, secure detention centers elsewhere and Nordic child welfare institutions may overlap; where exactly and how much is hard to define. Therefore, it is difficult to give a definite answer to the question of how many children in the Nordic countries are confined in closed institutions due to their offending behavior and under conditions that equal "youth prisons" elsewhere.

The first problem deals with differences between the institutions. There is a large number of institutions in each Nordic country with different labels. Finding something that would correspond with the commonsense assumption of a "closed institution" is difficult, as some countries do not have that concept at all (e.g., Finland). Both Sweden and Denmark have specifically classified secured institutions with an officially established number of beds. However, these institutions are also occupied by children for reasons other than crime. In addition, children are placed in other institutions as well for committing criminal offenses (for example, as a part of youth care in Sweden). The next problem concerns the reason for placement. Court-ordered placements (in Sweden and Denmark) are easy to classify, but placements by social welfare authorities are not. Some Nordic statistics have information about care orders based on behavior (in contrast to those based on environment); others do not. In addition, behavior covers not only criminal offending but also other behavioral problems (truancy, prostitution, substance abuse, severe anorexia, etc.).

Thus, in reading the child welfare statistics, one needs to remember that (1) only part of the public care orders are involuntary, (2) only part of the involuntary treatment orders are based on behavior, (3) only part of the involuntary orders based on behavior are based on criminal offending, and (4) only part of these placements are conducted in "closed" institutions (if such institutions exist in the first place). With

TABLE 2.7. Children Aged 15-17 Placed in Child Welfare Institutions in Finland and Sweden (per 100,000 Population in the Age Group, Situation at the End of the Year)

Sweden 2008 (absolute)	15-17 (per 100,000 pop.)	Finland 2006 (absolute)	15-17 (per 100,000 pop.)
All placements 5,517	1,437	All placements 3,313	1,650
Voluntary (SoL) 3,879	1,010	Voluntary 2,916	
Involuntary (LVU) 1,701	443	Involuntary 397	
Of all involuntary placements	(443)	Of all placements (% involuntary)	(1,650)
Family home (invol.) 830	216	Private family homes 1,023 (15%)	519
Private (HVB, invol.) 413	108	Children's homes 918 (9%)	466
Special approved homes (HVB) 314	82	Juvenile homes 640 (12%)	325
Of these: closed youth care 68	18	Reformatory schools 199 (13%)	101
		Offense-based involuntary 150 (100%)	76
		Intensive specific care 25 (30%)	13

Source: Lappi-Seppälä 2011, 251

these reservations, the following aims to compare Finnish and Swedish child welfare institutions.

From the viewpoint of the security dimension (but not work orientation), the Swedish special approved homes may come fairly close to the Finnish reformatory schools. Also, the conditions in closed youth care may partly be comparable with the restrictions placed on inmates in intensive specific care, although the purposes of these two type of interventions are quite different (in more detail, see Bengtsson et al. 2009).

In Sweden, around 1,400 children in the 15–17 age group (all figures are relative to 100,000 population in the age group) were placed in child welfare institutions. Out of these 1,400, around 450 were placed involuntarily. Out of all involuntary placements, 82 were placed in special approved homes. These placements typically include children with behavioral problems (offending behavior as the primary cause of care order). Out of these 82, around 18 were serving a punishment in the form of closed youth care.

The Finnish figures start roughly from the same level, with 1,650 juveniles placed in institutions. However, the share of involuntary placements is much smaller (12%, compared to 31% in Sweden). This may well reflect more differences in system structures than true differences in the distribution between voluntary and involuntary placements. One may also question the degree of voluntariness in some cases, as the children may not resist the placement because they feel that their views are not heard in any case. For that reason, comparisons with the Swedish figures are based on all placements and not only on those classified as voluntary. In addition, the share (%) of involuntary placements in each type of institution is placed in parentheses. All in all, Finland at the end of the year 2006 had around 800 children in the age group in children's homes and juvenile homes and 100 in reformatory schools. Out of these 900 children, 75–80 are placed in institutions involuntarily and partly due to offense-based reasons. In addition, some 10–15 are placed in intensive specific care (many of them included already in the previous figure). To this, we might also need to add children placed in mental health institutions. Again the distinction between voluntary and involuntary placements becomes unclear, as does the way the number of patients is counted. In 2007, the Finnish psychiatric hospitals had a patient flow (treatment periods) of 2,275 children aged 13–17. The average duration of treatment was around 40 days. This gives a daily population of around 250 patients of the 13–17 age group. Since 20%–22% of these placements are involuntary, we end up at around 60 involuntary patients in the 13–17 age group on any given day.[9]

All in all, there are around 80 juveniles either in special approved homes in Sweden or placed involuntarily in child welfare institutions partly due their own behavior in Finland. Out of these children, about 10–20 juveniles are either in closed youth care (Sweden) or intensive specific care (Finland). This is the most "closed" and restricted form of institutional treatment to be found in these countries. From the point of view of behavioral and physical restrictions and surveillance, these groups may be compared to "juvenile prisoners" in many other countries. But the comparability is much worse once the aim and purpose of confinement (and the conditions within the institutions) is taken into consideration. This difference also applies partly to Finland and Sweden. Children in Finnish secured institutions are not serving a punishment, while those in the Swedish ones are.

Conclusion and Discussion

With regard to international obligations to restrict the use imprisonment for juveniles, Nordic countries have a clean record. This achievement cannot be nullified with reference to the relatively high number of institutional placements in child welfare institutions. Children's homes are not juvenile prisons, and these institutions do not enforce punishments. Having said this, one needs to acknowledge the risk of the expansion of "benevolent institutional care." The other case of concern relates to poor transparency of child welfare, as compared to criminal justice. The welfare framework may also lead to less vigilance in controlling and monitoring the implementation of closed accommodation.

While the basic model is the same in all Nordic countries, a closer look reveals differences. Finland and to a certain extent Norway have remained more consistent in their efforts to separate punishment and treatment. Child welfare institutions have no role in the execution of criminal punishments. The Swedish and Danish systems mix child welfare and the criminal justice functions more freely. Criminal sanctions are enforced in both countries in child welfare institutions. A large number of juveniles under age 18 are sentenced each year in Sweden's youth care, consisting of interventions that are standard options for child welfare authorities in other Nordic countries (including placement in child welfare institution). Swedish and Finnish systems form a clear contradiction when it comes to the use of fines for offenders under age 18. For the Finns, a fine of 30–80 euros seems to be a standard option, while the Swedish system either diverts these cases from the criminal justice system or replace fines with child welfare interventions.

The Danish and Norwegian courts impose substantially more prison sentences for juveniles compared to the Finnish and Swedish courts. In Norway, this difference applies only to young adults, but in Denmark, it covers both age groups. The number of prison sentences for offenders under age 18 in Denmark and Norway is eight to ten times more than that in Finland and Sweden. This deviation from the common Nordic line may become even more apparent in the future, as Norway has taken actions to reduce the use of prison sentences in the 15–18 age group. Since 2014, young offenders who previously received prison sentences may be sentenced to a new type of nonresidential juvenile punishment, which will include both mediation meetings and a plan for activities for a period between six and 24 months. Thus, the custody threshold is lower in Denmark especially for younger age groups. This may partially be explainable also by the fact that prison sentences for offenders under age 18 are enforced in "sociopedagogic institutions," instead of prisons.

The development of Nordic youth justice is dependent of both general child welfare and criminal justice practices. Changes in these two fundaments will also change youth justice. The risk of a "punitive turn" is clearly smallest within the child welfare system. This system is also less visible and less vulnerable to populist political maneuvers. "Talking tough" in an environment devoted to the best interest of the child would not go far. It is harder to hide the iron fist in a velvet glove in today's child welfare system—even if things may have been quite different in the past. Proposals with manifestly punitive aims are absent in the current Nordic youth justice debate. The recent proposal in Sweden to treat young adults (aged 18–20) according to the same standard as adults is a clear exception from this trend. Another exception was offered by the Danish legislature in 2010, when the age of criminal responsibility was lowered from the common Nordic line of 15 to 14. The reform was done in order to satisfy the radical right-wing party, whose support was needed in order to reach a budgetary agreement. Two years later, a new government lifted the age limit back to 15 (stating that the reform was ill founded). This is a curious episode of political horse trading but also a sign of hope, indicating that the popularity of criminal punishment in solving children's problems still remains low in the Nordics.

TABLE 2.8. The Application of Different Sentencing Alternatives by Age Group, All Offenses, 2011–2012

	Absolute figures			Per 100,000 pop. in the age group			Percentages (court dispositions)		
	15–17	18–20	21+	15–17	18–20	21+	15–17	18–20	21+
Finland 2012 (offense age)									
All	21,278	45,207	456,528	10,617.9	22,795.2	11,310.2			
Courts	3,129	7,266	49,406	1,561.4	3,663.8	1,224.0	100.0	100.0	100.0
Court-ordered sanctions									
Imprisonment	37	347	5,148	18.5	175.0	127.6	1.2	4.8	10.4
Supervision order	0	9	157				0.0	0.1	0.3
Community service	7	151	2,229	3.5	76.1	55.2	0.2	2.1	4.5
Conditional imprisonment	510	1,859	12,213	254.5	937.4	302.6	16.3	25.6	24.7
Of which . . .									
Without fines	*429*	*1,095*	*5,811*	*214.1*	*552.1*	*144.0*	*13.7*	*15.1*	*11.8*
With fines	*77*	*739*	*6,253*	*38.4*	*372.6*	*154.9*	*2.5*	*10.2*	*12.7*
With community service	*4*	*25*	*149*	*2.0*	*12.6*	*3.7*	*0.1*	*0.3*	*0.3*
Juvenile punishment	9	1	0	4.5	0.5	0.0	0.3	0.0	0.0
Court fines	2,439	4,854	29,170	1,217.1	2,447.6	722.7	77.9	66.8	59.0
Waiver of sanctions	127	45	489	63.4	22.7	12.1	4.1	0.6	1.0
Summary sanctions									
Prosecutors fines	10,495	19,769	161,219	5,237.1	9,968.3	3,994.1			
Police fines	7,316	12,929	249,416	3,650.7	6,519.3	6,179.1			
Nonprosecution	1,025	655	4,521	512.5	330.8	112.0			
Included in previous sentence	8	26	266	4.0	13.1	6.6			
Mediation (2012)	2,053	1,536	8,716						
Population 2009	200,398	198,318	4,036,436						

Norway 2011 (offense age)

All	5,109	19,592	292,200	2,671.2	10,328.4	8,334.1			
Courts	777	2,572	17,678	406.2	1,355.9	504.2	100.0	100.0	100.0
Court-ordered sanctions									
Prison	43	881	7,337	22.5	464.4	209.3	5.5	34.3	41.5
Prison and conditional	37	251	1,792	19.3	132.3	51.1	4.8	9.8	10.1
Community punishment	308	429	1,784	161.0	226.2	50.9	39.6	16.7	10.1
Conditional imprisonment	339	816	5,025	177.2	430.2	143.3	43.6	31.7	28.4
Of which . . .									
Conditional with fines	*163*	*594*	*3,606*	*85.2*	*313.1*	*102.8*	*21.0*	*23.1*	*20.4*
Conditional without fines	*176*	*222*	*1,419*	*92.0*	*117.0*	*40.5*	*22.7*	*8.6*	*8.0*
Court fines	50	195	1,740	26.1	102.8	49.6	6.4	7.6	9.8
Summary sanctions (prosecutor)									
Summary fine	2,301	7,695	45,529	1,203.0	4,056.6	1,298.6			
Simplified summary fine	821	9,033	227,732	429.2	4,762.0	6,495.3			
Conditional nonprosecution	1,209	286	1,221	632.1	150.8	34.8			
Unconditional nonprosecution	—	—	—						
Mediation (2009)	3,329	—	—						
Population 2009	191,265	189,690	3,506,081						

Denmark 2012 (conviction age)

All	10,272	24,184	191,864	4,912.0	12,177.1	4,684.6	100.0	100.0	100.0
Courts	2,618	10,141	76,247	1,251.9	5,106.2	1,861.7	100.0	100.0	100.0

(continued)

TABLE 2.8 (*continued*)

	Absolute figures			Per 100,000 pop. in the age group			Percentages (court dispositions)		
	15–17	18–20	21+	15–17	18–20	21+	15–17	18–20	21+
Court-ordered sanctions									
Unconditional prison sentence	301	1,372	10,665	143.9	690.8	260.4	11.5	13.5	14.0
Of which . . .									
Imprisonment alone	103	913	8,157	49.3	459.7	199.2	3.9	9.0	10.7
Partly suspended sentence	107	234	614	51.2	117.8	15.0	4.1	2.3	0.8
Partly suspended with community service	3	55	145	1.4	27.7	3.5	0.1	0.5	0.2
Prison and fines	12	130	1,553	5.7	65.5	37.9	0.5	1.3	2.0
Sentence served on remand	9	40	191	4.3	20.1	4.7	0.3	0.4	0.3
Preventive detention	0	0	5	0.0	0.0	0.1	0.0	0.0	0.0
Juvenile punishment	67	0	0	32.0	0.0	0.0	2.6	0.0	0.0
Institutional treatment	28	93	763	13.4	46.8	18.6	1.1	0.9	1.0
Conditional imprisonment	1,027	1,499	8,055	491.1	754.8	196.7	39.2	14.8	10.6
Of which . . .									
Suspended sentence alone	883	871	3,733	422.2	438.6	91.1	33.7	8.6	4.9
With community service	35	342	1,246	16.7	172.2	30.4	1.3	3.4	1.6
With fines	91	184	1,374	43.5	92.6	33.5	3.5	1.8	1.8
With fines and community service	18	102	1,702	8.6	51.4	41.6	0.7	1.0	2.2
Fine	1,237	6,523	42,730	591.5	3,284.5	1,043.3	47.2	64.3	56.0
Fine and disqualification	25	654	14,034	12.0	329.3	342.7	1.0	6.4	18.4
Summary sanctions									
Agreement of summary fine	65	124	978	31.1	62.4	23.9			
Ticket fines	5,862	11,068	98,455	2,803.2	5,573.0	2,403.9			
Nonprosecution	262	330	2,177	125.3	166.2	53.2			
Transfer to social service	33	10	0	15.8	5.0	0.0			
Other	172	318	2,177	82.2	160.1	53.2			

Nonprosecution/youth contract	57	2	0	27.3	1.0	0.0			
Population 2009	209,119	198,602	4,095,644						
Sweden 2012 (conviction age)									
All	10,283	14,024	105,827	2,688.8	3,671.1	1,522.8			
Courts	4,490	6,848	57,688	1,174.0	1,792.6	830.1	100.0	100.0	100.0
Court ordered sanctions									
Prison	7	589	11,540	1.8	154.2	166.1	0.2	8.6	20.0
Closed youth care	43	15	0	11.2	3.9	0.0	1.0	0.2	0.0
Mental care	0	9	210	0.0	2.4	3.0	0.0	0.1	0.4
Probation	31	1,124	5,683	8.1	294.2	81.8	0.7	16.4	9.9
Of which . . .									
With prison	3	86	94	0.8	22.5	1.4	0.1	1.3	0.2
With contract care	0	49	804	0.0	12.8	11.6	0.0	0.7	1.4
With community service	3	274	1,169	0.8	71.7	16.8	0.1	4.0	2.0
Conditional sentence	21	1,394	9,746	5.5	364.9	140.2	0.5	20.4	16.9
With community service	0	565	3,976	0.0	147.9	57.2	0.0	8.3	6.9
Youth care	1,447	143	0	378.4	37.4	0.0	32.2	2.1	0.0
Youth service	1,601	220	0	418.6	57.6	0.0	35.7	3.2	0.0
Court fines	1,340	3,354	30,509	350.4	878.0	439.0	29.8	49.0	52.9
Included in previous sentence	9	323	1,712	2.4	84.6	24.6			
Summary sanctions									
Prosecutors fines	1,984	4,722	30,566	518.8	1,236.1	439.8			
Nonprosecution	3,796	2,126	15,830	992.6	556.5	227.8			
Ticket fine (police)									
Population 2009	382,437	382,007	6,949,501						

TABLE 2.9. The Length of Prison Sentences by Age Group

Finland 2012

Prison terms		15–17 N = 37	18–20 N = 347	21+ N = 5,148	All N = 5,532
Months	< 1	1	21	242	264
	1–2	3	63	811	877
	2–3	1	32	634	667
	3–4	6	29	561	596
	4–5	2	17	393	412
	5–6	0	13	262	275
	6–7	2	19	227	248
	7–8	1	12	263	276
	8–9	0	3	15	18
	9–10	1	4	93	98
	10–11	3	8	131	142
	11–12	0	6	47	53
	12	2	9	107	118
	12–18	0	27	256	283
	18–24	2	27	277	306
	24	2	4	75	81
Years	> 2	5	21	352	378
	≥ 3	5	13	170	188
	≥ 4	0	8	85	93
	≥ 5	0	3	43	46
	≥ 6	1	0	21	22
	≥ 7	0	3	7	10
	≥ 8	0	0	20	20
	≥ 9	0	0	13	13
	≥ 10	0	1	11	12
	11–12	0	0	10	10
	12+	0	0	7	7
	Life	0	4	15	19
Mean months		16.3	11.8		11.6

TABLE 2.9 (*continued*)

Norway 2011

Prison terms		15–17 N = 80	18–20 N = 1,132	21+ N = 9,129	All N = 10,341
Months	1–3	46	816	5,964	6,826
	3–6	9	105	893	1,007
	6–12	17	123	1,092	1,232
Years	1–3	6	71	867	944
	3–5	0	9	176	185
	5–7	1	5	59	65
	7–9	1	1	28	30
	9–11	0	0	22	22
	11+	0	2	28	30

Denmark 2012

Prison terms		15–17 N = 301	18–20 N = 1,372	21+ N = 10,665	All N = 12,338
Days	< 14	9	89	1,034	1,132
	15–21	9	68	843	920
	22–30	34	178	1,224	1,436
	31–60	35	309	2,684	3,028
Months	2–3	36	168	1,282	1,486
	3–4	24	92	669	785
	4–6	31	138	847	1,016
	6–9	19	106	493	618
	9–12	15	76	453	544
	12–15	2	35	208	245
	15–18	6	33	197	236
	18–24	5	32	241	278
Years	2–3	4	27	202	233
	3–4	3	10	96	109
	4–5	0	3	46	49
	5–6	2	2	26	30
	6–8	0	1	41	42
	8–12	0	4	50	54
	12+	0	0	18	18
	Life	0	0	3	3
Juvenile sanction		67	1		68

(*continued*)

TABLE 2.9 (continued)

Sweden 2012

Prison terms		Conviction age				Closed youth care
		15–17 N = 10	18–20 N = 675	21+ N = 11,646	All N = 12,331	N = 58
Months	< 1	0	27	322	349	
	1	4	113	3,378	3,495	6
	1–2	1	89	1,894	1,984	3
	2–3	2	85	1,033	1,120	10
	3–4	0	32	744	776	7
	4–6	0	13	236	249	3
	6	0	32	734	766	5
	6–12	1	76	924	1,001	12
Years	1	0	44	469	513	4
	1–2	0	109	1,021	1,130	8
	2–4	1	41	598	640	
	4–10	1	13	238	252	
	10+	0	1	49	50	
	Life	0	0	6	6	
Mean months		12.0	10.0		8.5	7

NOTES

1. See in more detail Lappi-Seppälä 2007; Lappi-Seppälä and Tonry 2011; and Pratt and Ericksson 2013.

2. Iceland had to be excluded from the analyses for linguistic reasons and due to the availability of data.

3. The full story is told in Dahl 1985; for an abridged version, see Lappi-Seppälä 2011.

4. The minimum age was fixed at 15 in Sweden in 1864 and in Finland in 1889 (however, in Finland, children between 7 and 15 could be subject to disciplinary measures and protective education by the social welfare authorities). In Norway, the age limit was initially 10 in 1842 and was lifted to 14 in 1902 and then to 15 in 1987. In Denmark, the minimum age in the 1866 code was 10, lifted to 14 in 1905 and to 15 in 1930. In 2011, the age was reduced—as part of a political bargaining process—to 14 but was lifted again back to 15 in 2013. An overview of the development of youth justice is

given in Lappi-Seppälä 2011; especially for Sweden, see Janson 2004 and, for Denmark, Kyvsgaard 2004.

5. Nordic sentencing theory and sanction practices are discussed in detail in Lappi-Seppälä 2001; and Hinkkanen and Lappi-Seppälä 2011, with references.

6. In complainant offenses (offenses that cannot be prosecuted without the request of the victim), a successful mediation automatically means that the prosecutor drops the case.

7. See UK Ministry of Justice, *Criminal Statistics Annual Report*, 4 May 2012, https://www.gov.uk/government/publications/criminal-statistics-annual-report-ns. These differences are, of course, finally reflected also in the number of prisoners. For details, see Lappi-Seppälä 2011, 242.

8. But on top of these figures, one needs to add placements in secure child welfare institutions. For details, see Lappi-Seppälä 2011, 242, and the following text.

9. The figures given by Pitts and Kuula (2005) deviate substantially from these calculations. This, however, is based on the mixing of treatment periods with daily patient populations (see Lappi-Seppälä 2011). Regarding the most intensive form of treatment in the Finnish child welfare system, see Pösö, Kitinoja, and Kekoni 2010.

REFERENCES

Aubert, Vilhelm, and Thomas Mathiesen. 1962. "Forbrytelse og sykdom." *Tidsskrift for Samfunnsforskning* 3:169–192.

Bengtsson, Tea, and Turf Jakobsen. 2009. *Institutionsanbringelse af unge I Norden. Det Nationale Forskningscenter for Velfaerd.* Copenhagen: SFI.

Borgeke, Martin. 2008. *Att besfämma pdföljd för brott.* Norstedts Juridik.

Brå. 2008. *Medling vid brott: En sammanfattning av Brå:s femåriga regeringsuppdrag.* Stockholm: Brå.

Cavadino, Michael, and James Dignan. 2006. *Penal Systems: A Comparative Approach.* London: Sage.

Christie, Nils. 1960. *Tvangsarbeid og alkoholbruk.* Oslo: Universitetsforlaget.

Clausen, Susanne, and Britta Kyvsgaard. 2009. *Ungdomssanktionen: En Effektevaluering.* Justitsministeriets Forskningskontor February 2009.

Dahl, Tove Stang. 1985. *Child Welfare and Social Defense.* Oslo: Norwegian University Press.

Dünkel, Frieder, Joanna Grzywa, Philip Horsfield, and Ineke Pruin, eds. 2010. *Juvenile Justice Systems in Europe: Current Situation and Reform Developments.* In collaboration with Andrea Gensing, Michele Burman, and David O'Mahony. Schriften zum Strafvollzug, Jugendstrafrecht und zur Kriminologia 36. Godesberg, Germany: Forum.

Eriksson, Lars D., ed. 1967. *Pakkoauttajat.* Helsinki: Kustannusosakeyhtiö Tammi.

Galtung, Johan. 1959. *Fengelssamfunnet.* Oslo: Universitetsforlaget.

Greve, Vagn. 1996. *Straffene.* Denmark: Jurist- og Økonomforbundets Forlag.

Hinkkanen, Ville, and Tapio Lappi-Seppälä. 2011. "Sentencing Theory and Sentencing Research in the Nordic Countries." In *Crime and Justice: A Review of Research*, vol. 40, edited by Michael Tonry and Tapio Lappi-Seppälä. Chicago: University of Chicago Press.

Janson, Carl-Gunnar. 2004. "Youth Justice in Sweden." In *Youth Crime and Youth Justice: Comparative and Cross-National Perspectives*, Crime and Justice 31, edited by Michael Tonry and Anthony N. Doob, 391–441. Chicago: University of Chicago Press.

Kivivuori, Janne, and Jon Gunnar Bernburg. 2011. "Delinquency Research in the Nordic Countries." In *Crime and Justice: A Review of Research*, vol. 40, edited by Michael Tonry and Tapio Lappi-Seppälä, 405–477. Chicago: University of Chicago Press.

Kriminalitet. 2012. *Danmarks Statistik.* Copenhagen, 2013.

Kühlhorn, Eckart. 2002. "Sluten ungdomsvård" (Youth Custody). In *Rättsliga reaktioner på de ungas brott fore och efter införandet 1999.* Report no. 5:1–88. Stockholm: SiS.

Kyvsgaard, Britta. 2004. "Youth Justice in Denmark." In *Youth Crime and Youth Justice: Comparative and Cross-National Perspectives*, Crime and Justice 31, edited by Michael Tonry and Anthony N. Doob, 349–390. Chicago: University of Chicago Press.

Lappi-Seppälä, Tapio. 2001. "Sentencing and Punishment in Finland: The Decline of the Repressive Ideal." In *Punishment and Penal Systems in Western Countries*, edited by Michael Tonry and Richard Frase, 92–150. New York: Oxford University Press.

Lappi-Seppälä, Tapio. 2007. "Penal Policy in Scandinavia." In *Crime and Justice: A Review of Research*, vol. 36, edited by Michael Tonry, 217–295. Chicago: University of Chicago Press.

Lappi-Seppälä, Tapio. 2010. "Finland." In *Juvenile Justice in the European Union Countries*, edited by I. Pruin, J. Grzywa, and F. Dünkel, 422–483. Schriften zum Strafvollzug, Jugendstrafrecht und zur Kriminologie 36. Greifswald, Germany: Greifswald University.

Lappi-Seppälä, Tapio. 2011. "Nordic Youth Justice: Juvenile Sanctions in Four Nordic Countries." In *Crime and Justice: A Review of Research*, vol. 40, edited by Michael Tonry and Tapio Lappi-Seppälä, 199–264. Chicago: University of Chicago Press.

Lappi-Seppälä, Tapio, and Michael Tonry. 2011. "Crime, Criminal Justice, and Criminology in the Nordic Countries." In *Crime and Justice: A Review of Research*, vol. 40, edited by Michael Tonry and Tapio Lappi-Seppälä, 1–32. Chicago: University of Chicago Press.

Marttunen, Matti. 2008. *Nuorisorikosoikeus* (Juvenile Criminal Justice). Research reports 236/2008. National Research Institute of Legal Policy.

Muncie, John, and Barry Goldson. 2006. *Comparative Youth Justice: Critical Issues.* Thousand Oaks, CA: Sage.

Odén, Niklas, Lottie Wahlin, Eleonore Lind, and Eva Carling. 2007. *Medling vid brott: En handbook.* Edited by Lottie Wahlin. Stockholm: Brå.

Pitts, John, and Tarja Kuula. 2005. "Incarcerating Young People: An Anglo-Finnish Comparison." *Youth Justice* 5, no. 3: 147–164.

Pösö, Tarja, Manu Kitinoja, and Taru Kekoni. 2010. "Locking Up for the Best Interest of Child: Some Preliminary Remarks on 'Special Care.'" *Youth Justice* 10, no. 3: 245–257.

Pratt, John, and Anna Eriksson. 2013. *Contrasts in Punishment: An Explanation of Anglophone Excess and Nordic Exceptionalism.* London: Routledge.

Storgaard, Anette. 2009. "The Youth Sanction: A Punishment in Disguise." In *Scandinavian Studies in Law*, vol. 54, edited by Peter Wahlgren, 381–396. Stockholm: Stockholm Institute for Scandinavian Law.

Vestergaard Jørn. 2004. "A Special Youth Sanction." *Journal of Scandinavian Studies in Criminology and Crime Prevention* 5, no. 1: 62–84.

PART II

Major Understudied Systems

The four chapters in this part of the book rather dramatically expand the nations and regions where scholarship is available in English on the institutions and principles of juvenile justice. In chapter 3, Weijian Gao profiles the recent and rapid development of juvenile courts in the People's Republic of China and provides preliminary data on the contrast between sanctions in juvenile and criminal justice. Chapter 4 presents a profile of the principles of youth justice in India, and Ved Kumari investigates the comparative scale of arrest and disposition in juvenile and criminal courts. In chapter 5, Mary Beloff and Máximo Langer introduce readers to the main features of separate juvenile court systems that are found in Latin America, provide data on rates of custody in juvenile and criminal courts, and analyze the effect on confinement levels of the Chilean juvenile justice reform as a case study on the wave of juvenile justice reforms that spread throughout Latin America in the past 25 years. In chapter 6, Lena Salaymeh considers the evolution of juvenile courts in the Middle East and North Africa with special attention to the influence of religion on juvenile justice policy in Muslim-majority nations.

These chapters represent an important first installment on learning about the principles and institutions of juvenile justice in the modern world, but there are major gaps in the available information in a number of these countries that will require substantial further research and analysis. The legal framework for juvenile courts is much easier to explore than are the institutional practices that produce real-world outcomes, especially in countries where governments and the administration of justice do not collect data on a regular, consistent, and systematic basis.

3

The Development and Prospect of Juvenile Justice in the People's Republic of China

WEIJIAN GAO

There are many reasons why the history and current conditions of juvenile justice in the People's Republic of China (PRC) are not well known to the citizens of other nations. Juvenile courts were not a part of the legal order for more than a generation after the creation of the PRC in 1949 and were the product of local initiatives rather than national legislation. The gradual and decentralized process that produced thousands of juvenile courts in the 1980s has not received extensive publicity within the PRC or widespread notice abroad. The national legislation that recognized and encouraged juvenile courts in the 1990s has also not been widely noticed.

There are, however, two reasons why Chinese juvenile justice deserves wider notice. The first reason that Chinese institutions and practices are important is the sheer size of the PRC—whatever the character of juvenile justice in the PRC, it is the world's largest system or set of systems. The second reason the particular history of juvenile justice in the PRC demands attention is the distinctive timing and political context of its development.

The Chinese system came into existence not in the very early 20th century but three generations later. The Chinese juvenile court evolved also in an Eastern socialist state instead of a Western democracy. What differences do these features produce? What similarities in emphasis and output span the vast differences in context that separates Chinese juvenile justice from the systems in Western nations?

This chapter documents the recent history of juvenile justice in the PRC and contrasts the Chinese systems with their Western counterparts.

The Early History of Chinese Juvenile Justice

The People's Republic of China got off to a rather late start by international standards in creating principles and institutions of juvenile justice. There are two reasons that juvenile courts were deferred until the last quarter of the 20th century. The first explanation is demographic—the rural character of China at midcentury. The second factor was drastic political changes at midcentury and during the "Cultural Revolution."

The growth of cities and the anonymous and disorganized nature of big-city life was the spur to juvenile courts at the turn of the 20th century in the West. In the United States, it was no coincidence that the explosive growth of Chicago was the setting for the invention of juvenile justice. China, by contrast, was a rural nation well into the middle of the 20th century. Figure 3.1 tells this story with census data. In 1953, the percentage of Chinese living in urban areas was 13.3%, while Zimring's study reports that about 55% of Americans under 20 lived in urban areas by 1955 (Zimring 1982, 42, fig. 3.1). It was not until 2011 that a majority of Chinese lived in cities.

The second circumstance that delayed the development of juvenile courts was two radical political transitions: the victory of the

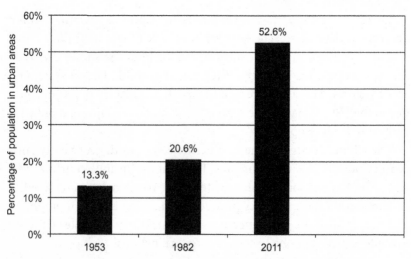

Figure 3.1. Percentage of Chinese living in urban areas, 1953–2011. *Source*: Chinese Census Reports.

Communists in 1948–1949 and the antilegal era of the Cultural Revolution from 1967 to 1977. The Nanking government had already started to explore the creation of juvenile courts in China in the 1930s, but these first steps were erased by the revolution. But there was some interest in juvenile justice in the early years of the Communist government. Appendix A provides my translation in summary of an article published in 1958 reporting legal processes of juvenile justice in Shanghai. This article is the only article about juvenile justice published between 1950 and 1976 that could be found by researchers in the PRC today. But this kind of initiative was undone by the Cultural Revolution, not because that movement was specifically hostile to juvenile courts but because the revolution was hostile to all formal legal institutions.

The demographic, economic, and legal circumstances of the 1980s were the launching pad for the growth of juvenile courts at the initiative of local governments.

1. In the 1980s, rapid urbanization, poverty, unemployment, and lack of education were troubling the nation and led to a lot of social problems, including juvenile delinquency and youth crime.
2. The demographic and political circumstances were ripe for innovation at the local level, particularly in big cities.
3. While revolution and the Cultural Revolution had delayed the creation of juvenile courts in China, the demographic and economic changes after 1980 created a demand for urban juvenile courts, and that development happened rather swiftly.

The First Court

In early 1980s, a prominent Chinese juvenile justice scholar, Xu Jian (徐建) at the East China University of Politics and Law (ECUPL), with its Youth Crime Research Institute, initiated the work to set up the first juvenile court in Mainland China. In October 1984, the Judicial Committee of Changning (长宁) District Court in Shanghai made a decision to set up the Juvenile Offender Collegiate Bench (少年犯合议庭), which has been regarded as the first juvenile court in Mainland China. The Juvenile Offender Collegiate Bench later changed its name to the Juvenile Criminal Cases Collegiate Bench (审理未成年人刑事案件合议庭).

In November 1984, the first juvenile court in Mainland China started to process juvenile criminal cases with some special procedures and treatments for juvenile suspects, defendants or offenders, such as separate control and custody, education procedures, a moderate court atmosphere, and community participation.

One may ask why the first Chinese juvenile court was set up in Changning District, Shanghai, instead of somewhere else. The answer to this question is similar to the answer to the question of why the first juvenile court was set up in Cook County, Chicago, Illinois, in the United States. There were three features that favored Shanghai.

First, Shanghai was a well-industrialized large city. We know that juvenile delinquency is one of the byproducts of industrialization and urbanization, which calls for juvenile protection, education, and justice. No doubt, Shanghai and Chicago were among the cities that needed juvenile courts the most.

Second, there was in Shanghai an urban elite to advocate for creating a juvenile court. In Shanghai, considerable academic research about juvenile delinquency, criminology, and law science had been conducted and favored a new legal initiative. We know that Chicago was famous not only for its industries but also for its universities, for Hull House, and for the Chicago School of Sociology. Shanghai has been the most industrialized and the biggest city in China ever since 1930s. In Shanghai, several very famous universities in China were also located, such as Fudan University, Tongji University, Jiaotong University, East China Normal University, and East China University of Politics and Law. In these universities, there were a number of scholars who specialized in subjects such as criminology, juvenile delinquency, law science, education, and child developmental psychology.

Finally, a city that innovates in juvenile justice should have a spirit that welcomes legal reform. One feature that sets Shanghai apart from other big cities in China is a history of welcoming reform. Chicago was not only a well-industrialized, well-culturalized city but also an important source of Progressive political activity. Shanghai has also been a very special city in China, not only for its industry and population but also for its culture (海派文化), which has been characterized as pragmatic, innovative, and always ready to embrace overseas innovations. Its rich and distinctive history since 1840s, the International Settlements, the Westernization Movement, and so on, made Shanghai the most important center to import Western sciences and philosophies. In the reformative era since late 1970s, overseas juvenile justice theories and juvenile court practices were noticed by observers in Shanghai.

After the establishment of the Changning District juvenile court in 1984, the Public Security Bureau in Changning District in 1986 set up its special juvenile police organization, named the Juvenile Suspects Interrogation Group (少年嫌疑犯预审组), and the Changning District Procuratorate in 1987 set up its special juvenile prosecution organization, named the Juvenile Criminal Cases Prosecution Group (少年刑事案件起诉组). With the negotiation of an agreement about juvenile justice between the Changning Juvenile Court and the Shanghai Juvenile Reformatory, a juvenile justice system composed of a public security bureau (juvenile police), procuratorate (juvenile prosecutors), court (juvenile judges), and justice enforcement department (juvenile correctional officers) was established to staff the new court. In many respects, this was more coordinated than the systems developed since the 1990s elsewhere in the PRC.

The local initiative model became the pattern also for the other courts created in the 1980s. The Changning juvenile justice initiative attracted broad attention from the media, as well as from the top leaders of the nation, whose responses were overwhelmingly positive. In the National Courts Work Conference held in June 1987, the Changning initiative was officially recognized by the national court authority, which proposed that more juvenile courts should be set up in the qualified courts nationally.

The Proliferation of Local Courts

After the National Courts Work Conference was held in 1987, the juvenile courts in Mainland China experienced rapid growth from 1988 to 1995. Figure 3.2 shows the growth in the number of juvenile courts in Mainland PRC from 1984 to 1998. By the time of the National Juvenile Court Conference in Shanghai in May 1988, about 100 juvenile courts had been set up nationwide.

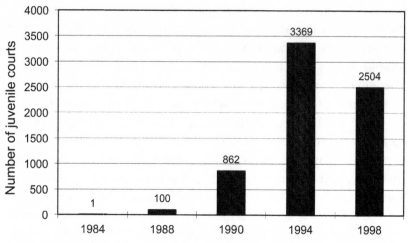

Figure 3.2. Number of juvenile courts in Mainland China, 1984–1998

In July 1988, the Changning District Court upgraded its Juvenile Criminal Cases Collegiate Bench into a bigger and more formal institution, named the Juvenile Criminal Court (少年刑事审判庭), which was administratively equal to the Criminal Court, the Civil Court, the Administrative Court, and so on, in the District Court. This juvenile criminal court was regarded as the symbol of a new era of the juvenile justice system in Mainland China.

By the time of the second National Courts Work Conference in 1990, the number of juvenile courts had reached 862, including six situated in the high courts, 144 in the intermediate courts, and 712 in the district/county courts. Also, 14 high courts created Juvenile Courts Steering Groups (少年法庭工作指导小组).[1] The Nanjing Conference communicated juvenile court work experiences to its audience, probed into related new issues, and discussed the drafts of two normative documents still in preliminary form, the People's Supreme Court's *Regulations on Juvenile Criminal Cases Procedures* (*Trial Implementation*) (关于未成年人刑事案件审判程序的若干规定(试行)) and *Regulations on Forming Juvenile Criminal Case Processing System* (关于办理少年刑事案件建立相互配套工作体系的意见) by the Ministry of Public Security, the People's Supreme Procuratorate, the People's Supreme Court, and the Ministry of Justice of the PRC.

The Nanjing Conference accelerated the creation of juvenile courts. By the end of 1992, the number of juvenile courts had reached more than 2,700. Moreover, according to statistics announced in the third National Courts Work Conference held in May 1995 in Fuzhou, by the end of 1994, the number of juvenile courts had reached 3,369, with more than 10,000 staff, distributed nationwide. Among them, there were more than 2,500 courts of first instance, 540 juvenile criminal courts, and 249 juvenile comprehensive courts, which were dealing with not only juvenile criminal cases but also juvenile civil cases and juvenile administrative cases. With the increasing numbers of juvenile courts and their staff, staffing of juvenile specialists in related institutions (public security bureaus, procuratorates, justice bureaus, and government-related social organizations) also increased correspondingly.

A National Legislative Mandate

The early 1990s also saw the creation of a national mandate for juvenile courts that put the central government on record for standards of juvenile justice.

1. *Regulations on Juvenile Criminal Case Procedures* (*Trial Implementation*) (关于办理少年刑事案件的若干规定(试行)), by the People's Supreme Court, enacted in January 1991.
2. *Joint Regulations on Jurors in Juvenile Criminal Cases* (关于办理少年刑事案件聘请特邀陪审员的联合通知), by the People's Supreme Court's, the Labor Union, the Youth League, and the Women's Federation of the PRC, enacted in April 1991.
3. *Regulations on Forming Juvenile Criminal Case Processing Systems* (关于办理少年刑事案件建立相互配套工作体系的意见), by the Public Security Department, the People's Supreme Procuratorate, the People's Supreme Court, and the Justice Department, enacted in June 1991.
4. *Juvenile Protection Law* (未成年人保护法), by the Seventh Standing Committee of People's Congress in its 21st session, enacted in September 1991. The law explicitly stipulated the principles of juvenile protection, with independent chapters dealing with family

protection, school protection, community protection, and juridical protection. In the chapter on juridical protection, the law explicitly stipulated the principles, the institutions, and some important regulations of the juvenile justice system, which formally created ambitions for the juvenile justice system of Mainland China.

With few exceptions, the national legislation of 1991 sought to encourage the creation and set the tone for juvenile courts rather than to establish systematic performance standards for institutions. Much of the 1991 legislation is an expression of sentiments that should inform decisions rather than rules.

Article 2 provides, in its entirety, "Legal proceedings for juvenile delinquency cases must be based on facts and law, combine punishment and education, follow the guidelines of education, persuasion, and reformation, and adhere to comprehensive measures for social security control." Article 29 admonishes, "No berating, sarcasm, or threat shall be made toward the juvenile defendant during the trial. In the event of such actions, the court shall stop them immediately." Article 34 provides a universal wish of juvenile justice in the form of a command: "In pronouncing a conviction, enlightenment shall be provided to the juvenile defendant so as to ensure him to accept the sentence and reformation and begin to improve himself."

The 1991 legislation also provides a series of procedural standards for juvenile trials, such as mitigation of penalty, a preference of nonconfinement sanctions, no penal liability for defendants under the age of 14, and restricted criminal liability for only the eight most serious crimes for defendants under the age of 16. The system that was favored in the 1991 legislation was based on several design elements.

1. Two coordinated process systems. The Coordinated Juvenile Case Process System involved the police, the procuratorate, the court, and the justice bureau; the Coordinated Juvenile Social Help and Education System involved labor unions, the youth league, the women's federation, schools, and local governmental branches.
2. Diversified juvenile courts. There were different sorts of juvenile courts, not only juvenile collegiate benches but also juvenile

trial courts, not only juvenile criminal courts but also juvenile comprehensive courts.

3. A policy of educate, rehabilitate, and save. The policy emphasized that punishment is just a kind of auxiliary method to treat juvenile delinquents; the predominant idea is to educate, to rehabilitate, to help out, and to preserve the chance for juveniles' future development. The policy was supported by a series of strategies, such as social report, social help and education, court hearing education, the preference of nonpenal sanctions and probation, compulsory liability and punishment mitigation, and so on.

4. A policy of comprehensive treatment. It was stressed that juvenile justice should not stop at case handling but needs to extend its work to finding the causes of juvenile delinquency and related social problems, so as to apply multiple measures to address the problems and to prevent juvenile delinquency.

5. A principle of dual protection. It was stressed that juvenile justice not only should emphasize the protection to juveniles but also should pay attention to the protection of society.

A Broader Base

The transition to national legislative recognition of juvenile courts in 1991 involved not only the Shanghai juvenile justice constituency but also professionals from other cities and criminologists. So it was more than just a process of rounding up the usual suspects.

Table 3.1 shows that the biggest cities in China are all now universally using juvenile courts for young offenders. For each city, the chart shows when a court for juvenile crimes was created, when its jurisdiction was expanded to other juvenile cases so that it became "comprehensive," and whether the court was at the district or intermediate level.

The organizational structure of juvenile courts is not hard to characterize, and the rhetorical emphasis in legislation tries to balance education with the suppression of crime. How this balance is carried out in practice is an important question, but there are not systematic data available to compare outcomes in juvenile courts with outcomes for similar offenses in Chinese criminal courts. So there is little hard data that can test the extent to which the juvenile courts have a special

TABLE 3.1. The Types and Dates of Origin of Juvenile Courts in the Ten Biggest Cities in the PRC

City	Juvenile courts	Types	Creation year	Court created
Shanghai	Yes	Criminal	1984	Changning District (长宁区)
		Comprehensive	2006	Intermediate (第一中级人民法院)
Beijing	Yes	Criminal	1987	Chaoyang District (朝阳区)
		Comprehensive	2006	Intermediate (第二中级人民法院)
Shenzhen	Yes	Criminal	1995	Longgang District (龙岗区)
		Comprehensive	2007	Bao'an District (宝安区)
Guangzhou	Yes	Criminal	1987	Liwan District (荔湾区)
		Comprehensive	2006	Intermediate (中级人民法院)
Suzhou	Yes	Criminal	1988	Pingjiang District (平江区)
		Comprehensive	2006	Intermediate (中级人民法院)
Chongqing	Yes	Criminal	1990	Shapingba District (沙坪坝区)
		Comprehensive	2007	Shapingba District (沙坪坝区)
Tianjin	Yes	Criminal	1991	Hexi District (河西区)
		Comprehensive	2006	Hexi District (河西区)
Wuhan	Yes	Criminal	1991	Hanyang District (汉阳区)
		Comprehensive	2007	Intermediate (中级人民法院)
Chengdu	Yes	Criminal	2004	Wuhou District (武侯区)
		Comprehensive	2008	Wuhou District (武侯区)
Xi'an	Yes	Criminal	1996	Beilin District (碑林区)
		Comprehensive	2008	Weiyang District (未央区)

character in the PRC. This type of data is also very hard to get in many other justice systems, of course, so the lack of comparative data on sanctions is not a peculiarity of the PRC.

A Dual System? Deference to Police Powers in Minor Cases

The basic model of a juvenile court for delinquents that was used in the 1980s was quite similar to the court created in Illinois in 1899, with aspirations of helping juveniles and an emphasis on avoiding the

vocabulary and rhetorical assumptions of criminal courts. But the jurisdiction in Chinese delinquency courts was much narrower than in Illinois for three reasons. Misdemeanors were included in U.S. juvenile
courts as part of the new court's delinquency jurisdiction. In the PRC,
these offenses had been the responsibility of local police and remained
a police matter excluded from court jurisdiction. And what came to
be called "status offenses" in the United States (noncriminal acts and
family conflict) are also a police matter in the PRC, usually defined as
"public security administration law violations." Finally, any acts by persons under 14 are not within the jurisdiction of juvenile courts in the
PRC, but here again this immunity (from punishment) is not complete
because the police can use "shelter and rehabilitation" powers and processes for underage offenders (from the ages of 11 to 16). In practice,
the "shelter and rehabilitation" system is quite similar to the "indoctrination through labor" system (for offenders over the age of 16), with
differences in education emphasis (such as compulsory education) and
the provision of material amenities, although in theory the two systems
should be very different. That is, the one for juvenile offenders should
be based on the ideal of *parens patriae*, while the one for older offenders should be based on the idea of social security measures. With the
enactment of the Decision on Abolishing the Laws about Indoctrination
through Labor, on 28 December 2013, by the 12th Standing Committee
of People's Congress in its sixth session, the system of "indoctrination
through labor" that lasted for more than half a century was ended. With
that decision, the practice of "shelter and rehabilitation" was probably
also undermined. In the view of some observers, the "shelter and rehabilitation" system, based on the ideal of *parens patriae*, should have a
space to survive. But how might this system be justified with juvenile
courts as an alternative?

The authority of local police could be a substantial limit on both the
power and the moral authority of juvenile courts in the PRC. That is, if
many cases of younger offenders and less serious offenses actually get
processed by local police, that could produce millions of police interventions independent of juvenile court standards or review. And the
bite of "shelter and rehabilitation" can be as substantial as a custodial
sentence from a juvenile court. Even if the police are not inclined to be
aggressive in big cities in these less serious cases, the behavior of police

in rural areas and small cities may differ substantially. This could create substantial disparity across different parts of the nation.

And the powers given to police might undermine the moral authority of juvenile courts as the experts on young offenders and their treatment. This is not a small matter for an institution and a mission that has only a short history in Chinese government and society.

While there was a good reason for those who were building juvenile courts to avoid a direct challenge to established police powers, the more established the juvenile criminal court becomes and the more educated and professionalized the juvenile court judges become, the more problematic the continued autonomy of police will appear. What can explain a juvenile court that is "comprehensive" but does not have authority for minor crimes, status offenses, and offenses by the very young? But if the separate authority of local police in such cases is limited, should that reduce government intervention in status and misdemeanor cases, or should these cases expand the jurisdiction of juvenile courts? This is one of the many open questions in 2014 in the evolving system as the government ends education through labor.

Patterns of Criminal Sentencing in Juvenile Court

With the exception of the death penalty (unavailable for persons under 18 at the time of the crime) and the general principle of mitigation for younger offenders, the same national penal legislation governs persons who appear before juvenile and criminal courts. But specific information on the distribution of penal sanctions for juvenile offenders is not well publicized, nor are specific statistics published on patterns of punishment for older offenders convicted in criminal courts. Judges (and prosecutors) have wide discretion to determine outcomes once formal conviction or adjudication occurs. As a tentative step toward obtaining a profile of dispositional patterns in criminal and juvenile courts, I researched reports on the sentences of all juveniles and adults convicted of theft crimes in the five years from 2008 to 2012. Table 3.2 reports the distribution of sentences for the convicted juveniles and adults in Chongqing.

Theft was selected for this sanction comparison because it generates a high volume of cases for both juvenile and adult arrests. Table

TABLE 3.2. Postconviction Sentences for Theft Offenders in
Chongqing, 2008–2012

	Juveniles	Adults
No custody	41.5%	22.7%
Custody 4 years or less	47.6%	67%
Custody 5–9 years	1.7%	5.8%
Custody over 10 years	.5%	4.6%
Total	100%	100%
	(2,287)	(23,130)

Source: Weijian Gao study, 2013.

3.2 shows that the contrast we find in Chongqing between juvenile and adult sentences happens at both ends of the severity extremes. More than 40% of the juveniles receive a noncustodial sentence after a theft conviction, which is almost double the rate for adult theft convictions. The smallest difference between the two groups is for a confinement sentence with a maximum of four years or less: two-thirds of the adults receive this punishment, as compared to just under half of the juveniles. This is the modal outcome for both juveniles and adults.

The largest statistical difference between the two groups is for the most lengthy sentences. More than three times as many adults receive prison terms of five to nine years as do juveniles (5.8% versus 1.7%). For the most severe custody sentences, 10 years or more, the proportion of adults receiving these terms is 4.6%, just over nine times the percentage of these very long terms given to juvenile offenders (0.5%).

The absence of extremely long terms for juveniles reflects a reluctance to totally sacrifice the life chances of persons under 18 in all but exceptional cases. The almost two-to-one ratio of adults versus juveniles receiving noncustodial terms also shows that juvenile courts in Chongqing are more reluctant to incarcerate than are criminal courts. Still, the rate of penal confinement we find in this Chinese juvenile court system is much higher than would be typical of juvenile courts in Europe, the United States, Japan, or the Commonwealth nations, where the majority of theft offenders typically receive noncustodial sentences. In part, this reflects the fact that the mix of cases tried in juvenile courts in the PRC excludes very young defendants and misdemeanor cases.[2] But the extensive use of penal confinement for postadjudication dispositions is probably also an indication of substantive punishment policies in Chinese juvenile courts. To what extent this is a transitional phenomenon that will be reduced as the PRC's juvenile courts mature is an open question.

And of course, it will be necessary to obtain data on many crimes and from many more Chinese courts before any firm conclusions can be made about the sentencing philosophies of juvenile court judges in the PRC.

The Future Course of Juvenile Justice in the PRC

While juvenile courts in most developed nations are entering their second century of history and institutional momentum, the juvenile courts of the PRC are only in their second generation of development. For this reason, there are many more contingencies yet to occur that have already determined the nature and policy of courts elsewhere. This brief concluding section outlines one certainty in the development of juvenile courts in the People's Republic and several important contingencies.

The certainty is that juvenile courts have a future as China develops. The PRC is an urban nation, and juvenile courts are both ubiquitous and necessary in a modern, urban China. There is also now a substantial constituency of judges, professors, and government officials who regard the institution as important and have personal interests in its continuity. So the juvenile court is a permanent part of modern China.

But what kind of juvenile court? There are three important contrasts in future development that have not yet been determined:

1. Local versus national influence
2. Derivative versus autonomous youth crime policy
3. Emphasis on youth welfare or social control

What Level of Government for Reform?

Throughout most of the short history of the juvenile courts in the PRC, the major source of innovation and impetus for reform has been at the local level of government, as opposed to provincial or national institutions. This is a marked contrast to other nations and to the tradition of powerful central governance in many concerns in the PRC. Even the famous Chicago juvenile court, which was inspired at the local level, required enabling legislation from the state government. While many of the rules and institutions that are used in juvenile justice in the PRC, such as the penal codes and institutions of confinement, are the product of national law, the special character of the juvenile courts was created in cities and in the district courts. The 1991 national legislation seemed as much about encouraging the direction of local institutions as about creating any national-level administrative control or financial support.

One important question is whether this tradition of local self-determination will continue or whether the national or provincial governments will try to exert more control over the operations and policies of juvenile courts. The comprehensive juvenile courts pilot reform started in 2006 and directed by the Supreme Court is one indication of a larger role for the national government in further reform. While the local level has done a great deal, changes in the legal structure of juvenile sanctions and in the financial support for programs will require the involvement of the national government. The other significant movement that might suggest a stronger central government role in policy change is the recent announcement by the central government of the abolition of "indoctrination through labor" programs. Because police have retained jurisdiction (and the potential for "shelter and rehabilitation") for younger offenders and less serious youth crime, a national campaign to eliminate this sanction should produce one of three policy outcomes. Either police will be left with the formal jurisdiction but without tools of enforcement, or the central government will formally abolish state intervention for one or more of the three categories of juvenile conduct, or the central government will give jurisdiction over younger or less serious offenses to juvenile courts. If the juvenile courts get expanded jurisdiction, they will also need legal authority to intervene if the behavior is not now prohibited in the penal code. So reforms that have their primary focus outside juvenile justice may necessitate a larger involvement of the central government in juvenile court matters.

Would a larger central government role help or hinder the prospects for desirable reforms? The national legislation of 1991 was a case study of sophisticated local judges and experts using national institutions to foster desirable reforms. And the locally powerful actors who might resent expansion of juvenile courts (such as police) might have less influence if decisions are taken in a central arena.

Derivative versus Autonomous Youth Crime Policy

The people who created juvenile courts in the PRC were concerned with the special status and special needs of young offenders. But the legal framework for the operation of juvenile courts was the nation's penal code for all persons. In this important respect, the legal framework for juvenile courts was derivative, an offshoot of the penal law for all criminals, with the same terms of potential confinement and the same judicial discretions. The sentiments expressed in the 1991 legislation were an attempt to alter this derivative framework but without any explicit change in the types of sanctions or their length. An alternative foundation for sanction policy can be found in those many juvenile court laws that create special categories and terms for juvenile sanctions rather than apply penal code provisions. This model, which I call an "autonomous youth crime policy," cannot be created at local levels of government, which lack the jurisdiction to legislate sanctions, so any transition to autonomous youth sanction policy would have to involve the legislative intervention of the national government.

Further, any sustained attempt to model the evolving systems of juvenile justice in the PRC on the systems in other developed nations would depend on shifting from reliance on the provisions of the general penal code to autonomy in legislative design of special sanctions, terms, and criteria for juvenile offenders.

Youth Welfare versus Social Control

The 1991 national legislation in the PRC endorses the same two objectives that headline every system of juvenile justice in the civilized world—social control of crime and the facilitation of the healthy development and welfare of the young persons before the juvenile court. So there is no novelty and no conflict involved in identifying and endorsing these governmental objectives. The real conflict comes when these two different goals must compete for emphasis in government policies toward young offenders. How much more or less important should youth welfare be than the social defense against crime?

The competition between youth welfare and social defense against crime is present in all juvenile justice systems, and there is substantial variation in relative emphasis between different nations' systems and sometimes in the same nation at different times. Probably the key indicators of the relative emphasis on welfare versus social control is the extent to which secure confinement is used as a standard response to youth crime and the length of custodial terms imposed. Social control puts emphasis on severity of sanctions and on the incapacitation of persons who might otherwise reoffend. But those who emphasize youth development and welfare distrust penal confinement and seek to limit both its use and its duration.

So a shorthand measure of which set of policies are favored in a particular system is how often secure confinements are imposed and for how long. Good data on these questions are not well publicized in the PRC at the present time. The pilot study I did on theft in Chongqing showed a greater reluctance to impose custodial terms on juveniles than on adults and a great reluctance to impose extremely long terms of confinement on juveniles. But the majority of juveniles convicted of theft were sentenced to penal confinement. So there is evidence of some special concern for youth welfare, but the use of penal confinement is an important policy even in juvenile courts.

Appendix A: Summary of 1958 Article on Juvenile Justice in the PRC

Guilong Shen and Hongliang Xiao, *How the Political and Legal Departments in the Yulin District of Shanghai Dealt with Juvenile Crime Problems,* vol. 6 (1958). (沈贵龙、肖洪亮 : "上海市榆林区政法部门是怎样处理青少年犯罪问题的", 载《法学》1958 年第 6 期。).

How to deal with juvenile crimes properly had been a difficult, unsolved problem for a long time. It was always felt that juvenile offenders were too young to be dealt with, but doing nothing was causing the people's dissatisfaction. Since administrative detention could not solve the problem, some practitioners tended to push juvenile offenders out the door, doing nothing, while other practitioners tended to arrest all of the juvenile offenders, feeling the problems were serious. In Shanghai Yulin (榆林) district, during the first two months of 1958, the number of juvenile offenders arrested constituted 53.6% of the total number of arrests, 10.9% more than the last two months of 1957. But the actual problems remained unsolved.

The problem attracted the attention of officers from the public security, the procuratorate, and the court of Yulin district. They recognized that reducing and controlling juvenile crimes was not only an important key issue to lower the criminal case rate but also a serious political task to protect the younger generations from harm. Doing nothing or simply punishing were both wrong and did not match the party's overall policy. So the three institutions held meetings, set up an investigation group, did special research in factories, schools, communities, and public areas, visited teachers and parents, and interrogated suspects; they analyzed the possible causes of juvenile crime and adopted eight effective countermeasures to deal with the problems. From March 27 to April 20, they conducted 41 activities, involving more than 15,500 people, and got some outstanding positive results.

Through investigation and analysis, the researchers identified some possible causes for juvenile crimes:

1. Negative social influences were doing harm to juveniles; some adults were inducing juveniles to commit crimes; moreover, pornographic books and drawings were causing juvenile crimes.
2. Some families were improperly educating their children or were indulging or even inducing crimes.
3. Schools and factories were failing to provide the proper political spirit and education in Communist virtue, which left some young workers and students contaminated by capitalist values, leading to criminal behaviors.
4. Some officers from the legal institutions were dealing with juvenile criminal cases improperly, either doing nothing or simply

punishing, without addressing the real causes of juvenile crimes and doing little about education and rehabilitation.

Eight countermeasures were adopted:

1. Strongly push forward social reform work, eliminating the negative social influences and thwarting the harm and influence of capitalist values; send adults who are bad influences to the countryside to labor under supervision; seriously punish those who were inducing juveniles to commit crimes.
2. Depend on organizations to activate teachers and strengthen their sense of responsibility to educate students.
3. Advance the way of work, collaborate with community organizations, and educate the people about preventing juvenile crimes.
4. Hold meetings with parents or pay families individual visits to address existing problems, to explain the causes, and to activate parents to properly educate their children.
5. Strengthen out-of-school activities, setting up students' study or activity groups and recruiting either teachers or parents to be the tutors.
6. Depend on organizations, such as schools, community organizations, labor unions, and police stations, to activate people, such as neighbors, parents, teachers, and friends, to collaborate on helping out misbehaving juveniles.
7. Depend on the branches of the Communist Party—the administration, the labor union, and the youth league—to address the status and characteristics of young workers by providing labor discipline and education in Communist values.
8. Punish according to the law juvenile offenders who had committed serious and really harmful crimes and who were proved to be incorrigible; expand publicity of these cases in order to educate the people.

The countermeasures proved to be effective. The proportion of juvenile crimes dropped precipitously in Yulin district. The April data showed that the proportion of crimes committed by juveniles had dropped 66.1% from the first three months of the year. Moreover, from the end of April to the middle of May, not a single juvenile criminal case was filed.

Appendix B: Regulations on the Creation of the Juvenile Court System

Public Security Department, the People's Supreme Procuratorate, the People's Supreme Court, and the Justice Department, *Regulations on Forming Juvenile Criminal Case Processing Systems* (关于办理少年刑事案件建立相互配套工作体系的意见), enacted in June 1991; translated by Weijian Gao.

The High People's Courts, the Procuratorates, the Public Security Bureaus, the Justice Bureaus:

In recent years, juvenile crimes have become a more serious problem that is attracting attention from the whole society, as well from the justice institutions. Institutions in some areas have taken active roles in exploring practical measures to address the characteristics of juvenile crimes and have had some good experiences. At present, public security bureaus, procuratorates, courts, and justice administrative institutions in some regions have preliminarily constructed a system to process juvenile criminal cases, as well as to discipline juvenile offenders, which has generated very good social effects and has had positive effects on social security comprehensive treatment, on preventing and reducing crimes, and on social stability.

To further carry out the policy of educating, rehabilitating, and saving juvenile offenders and to improve the juvenile justice system of our country, public security bureaus, procuratorates, courts, and justice administrative institutions should enhance mutual coordination, develop systematic institutions to process juvenile criminal cases, and reinforce the work of juvenile crime prevention and treatment. Therefore, rules are made as follows:

1. The detention house shall strictly follow "Detention House Regulation" and separate juvenile offenders from adult offenders in

detention, and if the detention house does not support such separation, officials also shall do what they can do to avoid imprisoning the juvenile offenders with offenders who are recidivists and difficult to rehabilitate.

For the investigation of juvenile offenders' cases, the public security shall have specialists or officers who focus on dealing with juvenile delinquency cases, or if possible, the public security can establish specialized agencies. The public security shall take different interrogation measures and approaches for juvenile offenders compared to adult offenders. The public security shall do patient and meticulous education and counseling during interrogation. The public security shall learn the criminal motives and causes of juvenile offenders' actions and record them in order to accumulate information, summarize experiences, and advance the work.

2. People's procuratorate shall handle juvenile delinquency cases according to their characteristics and requirements, gradually setting up specialized agencies. Currently, the requirements of setting up specialized agencies are not satisfied; the people's procurate shall appoint specialists to respond to this type of case.

When dealing with juvenile delinquency cases, the procuratorate shall strengthen its connection with the relevant ministry and educate, persuade, and rehabilitate the juvenile defendants patiently and meticulously.

People's procuratorate shall strengthen supervision over the investigation activities, trial activities, and juvenile prisons to ensure that the laws are correctly implemented and that the juvenile defendants' legal rights and benefits are protected.

3. When the people's courts handle juvenile delinquency cases, they shall strictly implement criminal law, criminal procedural law, and certain provisions on the handling of juvenile delinquency cases (trial). The people's courts shall set up juvenile courts or appoint specialized persons to handle juvenile delinquency cases. During the trial, the courts shall take different measures and approaches for juvenile defendants from adult defendants according to the juvenile defendants' physical and psychological characteristics. The court shall emphasize counseling and educate throughout the trial, combine punishment and education, and correctly, legally,

and promptly determine the *corpus delicti*, verify the evidence, and assist juvenile defendants to recognize the causes of their crimes and the harm to society of their criminal conduct. Juvenile courts shall provide legal representatives or other custodians and endeavor to persuade them to coordinate with the education and reformation of the juvenile defendant. For the sentenced juvenile offenders, juvenile courts can take different measures and forms to organize revisiting, inspecting, and admonishing work. After the people's courts conclude juvenile delinquency cases, they shall carefully and exhaustively fill in the closed registration form and send the transcript of the verdict in force together with the enforcement notice to the juvenile reformatory.

4. To educate the juvenile to comply with discipline and the laws and to prevent and reduce juvenile delinquency, the administrative organs of justice shall strengthen the legal propaganda work.

Juvenile delinquency defendants shall have lawyers to attend their defense. If possible, legal firms shall have specialized lawyers to defend juvenile offenders. During the process of defense, the lawyers shall make efforts to educate and reform juvenile defendants.

The juvenile reformatory shall carefully implement the policy of "relying mainly on educating and reforming while imposing light physical labor as subsidiary," insisting on the policy of half-day studying and half-day doing physical labor. The juvenile reformatory shall implement separate management and detention of different types of juvenile delinquency as much as possible. The juvenile reformatory shall designate specialized personnel to teach juvenile offenders culture, laws, and labor skills so that they can find jobs much more easily when they return back to the society. The juvenile reformatory shall strengthen the connection and cooperation with the juvenile courts and provide information to juvenile courts for reforming the juvenile offenders.

5. For juvenile offenders' qualified commutation and parole, the executive organs shall promptly provide written submissions to the people's court to verify and adjudicate. The reforming of juvenile offenders is different from that of adult offenders. The juvenile offenders are easy to rehabilitate and change quickly. Compared

with the commutation and parole of adult offenders, the people's court can moderately relax the standard of the penalty to the extent that the court sees fit.

For the appeal of the detained juvenile offenders and their family members, the people's court or the people's procuratorate shall appoint specialized personnel to promptly handle the appeal. For the appeal of juvenile reformatory transfers, the people's court shall reply to the juvenile reformatory as soon as possible.

6. Handling juvenile delinquency cases requires establishing a work system for mutual support. Public security, procuratorate, court, and the administrative organs of justice shall carefully implement this work and appoint one person to manage it. All departments shall play their own function fully, educate and reform juvenile offenders from various aspects, and use the overall advantages political and law departments to achieve the best results of correcting and reforming juvenile offenders. If necessary, the four political and law organs can establish a joint conference system.

All departments shall create conditions to promptly implement the above requirements. If there are any problems, they shall timely report the situation to superior departments to resolve.

NOTES

1. Jian-long Yao, *Growing to Adults: The Construction of the Juvenile Justice System* (Beijing: Chinese People's Public Security University Press, 2003), P67. (姚建龙 : 《长大成人 : 少年司法制度的建构》 , 中国人民公安大学出版社 2003 年版 , 第 67 页。)

2. According to the Penal Code of the PRC in this period (2008–2012), only persons age 16 and older should have criminal liability in theft crimes, and theft behavior should only be considered as a crime for a single theft behavior with a certain amount (500–2,000 RMB, according to the economic status of the region) or for more than three theft behaviors in a year. Also, the concept of theft crime in the PRC includes burglary, shoplifting, purse cutting, and other kinds of property-stealing behaviors.

REFERENCES

Jian-long Yao. *Growing to Adults: The Construction of the Juvenile Justice System*. Beijing: Chinese People's Public Security University Press, 2003.
(姚建龙 : 《长大成人 : 少年司法制度的建构》 , 中国人民公安大学出版社 2003 年版。)

Xu Jian. *Juvenile Jurisprudence: A New Perspective.* Beijing: Chinese People's Public University Security Press, 2005. （徐建：《青少年法学新视野》，北京：中国人民公安大学出版社 2005 年版。）

Zimring, Franklin E. *The Changing Legal World of Adolescence.* New York: Freedom Press, 1982.

4

Juvenile Justice in India

VED KUMARI

The term "juvenile justice" is used narrowly to refer to the adjudication, reformation, and rehabilitation process after a child has committed an offense. In its wider sense, it includes preventive measure before the advent of delinquency. In India, the Juvenile Justice Act of 2000 covers the wider field of prevention of delinquency by bringing children in need of care and protection within its ambit as well as making provision for dealing with children who are alleged or found to have committed an offense. This chapter, however, examines the theory and practice of the provisions relating to children who have committed offenses and makes only contextual reference to provisions dealing with children in need of care and protection.

Children who commit offenses in India have long been recognized as different from adults who commit offenses, even before the advent of British laws. Separate punishments were prescribed for children under the old Hindu law as well as the Muslim law. The modern history of juvenile justice in India begins from 1850, when the first law was enacted dealing with children under the age of 15 who committed petty offenses or were found vagrant. It began modestly by providing for binding such children over as apprentices to learn some trade but soon expanded by establishing separate residential facilities for reforming children. Children's courts followed not long after the segregation of children from adult offenders during adjudication. These courts came into their own and severed their ties with the criminal justice system with the passing of the first uniform legislation for the whole of India[1] to provide for care, protection, reformation, and rehabilitation of delinquent and neglected children and to prohibit the sending of children to prison or the use of jails and police stations under any circumstances.

The segregation of juvenile justice from criminal justice has been further consolidated by the Juvenile Justice Act (JJA) of 2000, which replaced the Juvenile Justice Act of 1986. It came into force on April 1, 2001, and now governs and regulates all matters concerning juvenile justice in India. It has been amended twice, in 2006 and 2011, to ensure inclusion of all children within its purview.

The JJA 2000 provides that all children under the age of 18 at the time of the offense will be governed by the provisions of the act. Over the years, the Indian legislature and judiciary gradually worked toward including all children below the specified age within the protective umbrella of juvenile justice. However, the inclusive nature of the JJA 2000 came under tremendous challenge when a young girl was brutally gang-raped by five persons. One of the accused was a child aged 17 years and 10 months. While the cases against the adults accused were transferred to fast-track court, the child was sent to the Juvenile Justice Board (JJB) to be dealt with according to the provisions of the JJA 2000. Print and other media were replete with articles for and against children being dealt with under the JJA 2000, and there were reports of heated debates and consultations among children's rights activists, victim support groups, and the Ministry for Women and Child Development. The accused child was demonized by the media as being the most brutal of the perpetrators, even though the same media later on reported that this was not so.[2] The session judge pronounced the death penalty for the adults accused and convicted for the gang rape, while the juvenile offender was sent to a special school by the JJB.

Flavia Agnes, the noted women's rights lawyer, referred to the media coverage as "a never-ending, voyeuristic media spectacle" and bemoaned, "The media laments that there is no closure as the juvenile went 'scot free.' This goading continues though the juvenile was punished as per the provisions of law, as per the norms of a country ruled by law. The sensational reportage makes us believe that we must become a nation ruled by emotions, by public sentiment, and not by the rule of law."[3]

Dispassionate analysis is needed to explore long-term solutions for the challenges facing juvenile justice in India. This chapter contains a historical overview of important developments leading to the enactment of the JJA 2000. It also highlights the salient features of the JJA 2000 and examines critical questions under the act. Various judicial decisions have been analyzed to bring to the fore issues relating to its scope and implementation. Lastly, the chapter explores the way forward.

Historical Overview

While children committing crimes in India were subject to different and favored treatment in the old Hindu law,[4] as well as under the Muslim law,[5] 1850 saw the first modern law dealing with children who committed offenses. The Apprentices Act 1850 provided that vagrant and children below the age of 15 who committed petty offenses could be bound over as apprentices to learn a trade, craft, or employment instead of being sent to prison. In 1860, the Indian Penal Code (IPC) introduced the presumption of *doli incapax* for children below the age of seven years[6] and a rebuttable presumption of *doli capax* for those between the ages of seven and 12 years.[7] This policy continues today.

The Prison Reforms Committee of 1864 recognized the increasing number of children in prison and recommended passing of the Whipping Act to decrease the population in prisons instead of establishing reformatory schools, as there was a fear that unworthy parents would encourage their children to commit offenses to receive government education.[8] Consequently, the Whipping Act of 1864 was enacted, and it provided for whipping in lieu of any other punishment prescribed by the IPC for juvenile offenders for offenses other than those punishable with death.[9] It further provided that "in the case of an adult, the punishment of whipping shall be inflicted with such instrument in such mode and on such part of the person as the local Government shall direct, and in case of a juvenile offender, it shall be inflicted in the way of school discipline with light rattan."[10] Children were segregated within prisons by amending prison codes in Madras, Bombay, the North Western Provinces, and Bengal.[11]

The reformatory schools were established in 1876, following the observation by Sir Richard Temple, then the lieutenant governor of Bengal, in 1874 that imprisoned juvenile offenders were actually growing up in vice and ignorance.[12] The Reformatory Schools Act was amended in

1897 to give wider powers to the local government to ensure reformation. Reformatory schools were established in many states,[13] but they
were not found satisfactory.[14]

Members of the Indian Jails Committee 1919–20 found that special
magistrates were appointed in the United Province to try children's
cases,[15] and a juvenile court was functioning in Calcutta. However,
the committee did not approve of these, as children had to travel long
distances in the United Province, a different magistrate dealt with children's cases on different days, and one magistrate was not responsible
for all those cases in Calcutta. Instead, the committee recommended
appointment of a senior magistrate, who would hold proceedings at a
time and place different from ordinary courts, so as "to produce in the
mind of the magistrate a clear recognition of the fact that he is dealing
with a case of a special character in which he is expected to assume
a different standpoint, a more paternal attitude, to adopt the American idea, from that which he would employ in trying a case against an
adult."[16] Madras took the lead by passing the first Children Act in 1920.
Even though India was a British colony at that time, the juvenile courts
established thereunder followed the paternal model of the US and did
not permit the presence of a lawyer as a matter of right. The Madras
Children Act, as well as all other states[17] that enacted their Children
Acts until 1949, provided for establishment of a children's court to deal
with neglected and delinquent children, their release on probation,
keeping them in remand homes and certified schools instead of prison
unless their offense was so serious and their nature so depraved as to
justify imprisonment, though acts adopted different cut-off ages for
defining a child.

The independence of India in 1947 saw the partition of the country, coupled with a huge amount of migration and many riots, leaving
many children homeless and without family care. Parliament discussed
in great depth the Children Bill 1953, which was to apply to Part C states,
but it was shelved in 1954 with the reorganization of states.[18]

The Parliament of India passed its first central Children Act in 1960,
but it was applicable to union territories only. It was presented as a
model act, and it indeed was followed by all other states that enacted
Children Acts after 1960.[19] The Children Act of 1960 introduced four
unique features for the first time. First, it introduced a sex-based defini-

tion of "child," making the act applicable to girls below the age of 18 and boys below the age of 16. Second, it provided for the constitution of two separate competent authorities, namely, children's courts to deal with delinquent children and the Child Welfare Board for neglected children. Third, it prohibited the imposition of the death penalty or sending children to imprisonment or keeping them in a police station or jail under any circumstances, including for failure to pay a fine or failure to find sureties and even while proceedings were pending. Fourth, three categories of institutions were established under this act for providing residential care to children, namely, Observation Home for keeping all children falling under the purview of the act while their proceedings were pending before the competent authority; Children Home for keeping children found to be neglected; and Special Home for children found to have committed an offense. Subsequent legislation on the subject has retained the prohibition of imposition of any punishment for children for any offense while introducing some changes in the other features and retaining the two adjudicatory bodies and three kinds of residential institutions.

In 1983, Sheela Barse, a journalist, filed a petition of habeas corpus in the public interest in the Supreme Court of India for release of 1,400 children who, as per official records of the government, were in prisons. She claimed that these children were illegally confined as the Children Acts of various states prohibited keeping children in prisons. The Union of India, all the states, and union territories were made party to this petition. Legal aid committees and district judges were given the responsibility of filing reports on the state of affairs in each district. The Supreme Court noted that the differences in the Children Acts of various states, especially the differential in the cut-off age defining "child," was resulting in differential treatment for children in different states. For example, a child of 17 years who committed an offense in Bombay was to be dealt with by the adult criminal court, as the cut-off age defining "child" was 16 under the Bombay Children Act of 1924, but another child of the same age who committed the same offense in West Bengal was to be dealt with by the children's court, which applied to all children until the age of 18. The Supreme Court suggested to the Union of India that it should pass a uniform legislation for children across the territory of India to remove such inequality.[20]

Soon thereafter, Parliament passed the first uniform legislation, namely, the Juvenile Justice Act of 1986. It applied to the whole of India, except the state of Jammu and Kashmir.[21] It retained the basic features of the Children Act of 1960, including the sex-based definition of "child" as well as the complete prohibition of keeping children in prisons, jails, or police stations under any circumstances.

Prior to the enactment of the JJA 1986, questions were raised about the jurisdiction of the children's court to deal with serious offenses in view of section 27 of the Code of Criminal Procedure of 1974, which permitted transfer of children below the age of 16 who committed offenses not punishable with death or life imprisonment to children's court. The Supreme Court had clarified and ruled that children's courts were competent to try all offenses including serious offenses punishable with death or life imprisonment.[22] After the enactment of the JJA 1986, its applicability to children who committed offenses under the special laws was challenged in many cases and was decided differently by different courts.

The special laws contained an overriding effect clause stating that the provisions of that act would override any other contrary law in force. The Gauhati High Court, in *Jagdish Bhuyan v. State*,[23] held that the provisions of the Juvenile Justice Act of 1986 were not applicable to a child who committed an offense under the Terrorist and Disruptive Activities Act (TADA) in view of its overriding effect clause.[24] In *Antaryami Patra*,[25] the High Court of Orissa held that the provision of mandatory bail contained in the Juvenile Justice Act of 1986, enacted after the passing of the Narcotics and Psychotropic Substances Act of 1986, was overridden due to the inclusion of the non obstante clause in the Narcotic Drug and Psychotropic Substances Act in 1989. The Kerala High Court in *re Sessions Judge Kalpetta*,[26] however, applied the Juvenile Justice Act to a child who committed an offense under the Schedule Castes and Schedule Tribes (Prevention of Atrocities) Act of 1989, which contained a similar non obstante clause, with the reasoning that an overriding effect clause comes into operation only if two legislations are dealing with the same subject matter. The court opined that the former legislation dealt with offenders, while the latter dealt with offenses, and hence, there was no occasion for conflict in the provisions of the two acts. The Supreme Court held that the Juvenile Justice Act applied to a child who committed an offense under the NDPS Act in *Raj Singh*[27] and to other children who committed an offense under TADA in *Madan Singh*,[28] but these judgments do not examine the contrary judgments of the High Courts on similar issues and do not contain any analyses of any provisions of these special laws. However, these cases did help in consolidating the inclusiveness of juvenile justice, with the aim of not excluding children from the purview of the act.

India ratified the UN Convention on the Rights of the Child (CRC) in 1992, but in 2000, the UN committee under the CRC observed, "Of particular concern to the Committee is the very low age of criminal responsibility under the Penal Code, which is set at seven years; and the possibility of trying boys between 16 and 18 years as adults."[29] Soon thereafter, the Indian Parliament enacted the Juvenile Justice (Care and Protection of Children) Act of 2000, "bearing in mind the standards prescribed in the Convention on the Rights of the Child, the United Nations Standard Minimum Rules for the Administration of Juvenile Justice, 1985 (the Beijing Rules), the United Nations Rules for the Protection of Juveniles Deprived of their Liberty (1990), and all other relevant international instruments."[30] The age of criminal responsibility continues to be seven years to this day.

Salient Features of the JJA 2000

The JJA 2000 declares that its purpose is "to consolidate and amend the law relating to juveniles in conflict with law and children in need of care and protection, by providing for proper care, protection and treatment by catering to their development needs, and by adopting a child-friendly approach in the adjudication and disposition of matters in the best interest of children and for their ultimate rehabilitation and for matters connected therewith or incidental thereto."[31] However, from a historical perspective, the usage of the word "juvenile" in contradistinction to the usage of "child" connotes a negative attitude. The word "juvenile" has acquired a negative value by being associated with delinquency for a long time. The moment a child is referred to as "juvenile," it is assumed that the child has been involved in the commission of crime. The legislation on the subject from 1920 to 1986 had consistently used the word "child" for all children falling within its ambit. "Juvenile" was substituted for "child" in JJA 1986, perhaps influenced by the use of this word in the Beijing Rules adopted by the UN General Assembly in 1985. Choosing to use both "juvenile" and "child" in the same act in contradistinction with each other does not show friendliness to the former group. There is an additional problem with the wording of the phrase "juvenile in conflict with law" over the earlier phrase "juvenile delinquent." While "juvenile delinquent" under the JJA 1986 referred to a child found to have committed an offense, the phrase "juvenile in conflict with law" has been defined as a child "alleged" to have committed an offense.[32] Devoid of this definition, the simple English meaning of the phrase suggests that these children have already been "found" to have committed an offense and stigmatizes these children even before they are found to have committed an offense.

In order for the JJA 2000 to achieve its objectives, it has made many deviations from the ordinary criminal laws applicable to adults regarding the commission of offenses, namely, the Indian Penal Code of 1860, the Code of Criminal Procedure of 1973, and the Indian Evidence Act of 1912.

The JJA 2000 and the IPC

The IPC contains the general definitions of various offenses and provides for punishment thereof. However, it excludes children below the age of seven from its purview by declaring that nothing done by a child below the age of seven is an offense.[33] It further provides that "nothing is an offence which is done by a child above seven years of age and under twelve, who has not attained sufficient maturity of understanding to judge of the nature and consequences of his conduct on that occasion." [34] This means that children above the age of seven are presumed to have attained sufficient maturity, though their action will not be considered an offense if proved otherwise. The JJA 2000 does not change these presumptions as contained in the IPC and does use the definitions of various offenses under the IPC and other special and local laws. However, all children falling within the purview of the JJA 2000 cannot be subject to any punishment prescribed under the IPC or any other law for the time being in force. If children are found to have committed an offense, the only orders that may be passed in relation to them are the ones specified in section 15, read with section 16, of the JJA 2000.

The JJA 2000 and the Code of Criminal Procedure

In the ordinary criminal justice system in India, offenses under the Code of Criminal Procedure (CrPC) are classified[35] as bailable[36] and nonbailable,[37] and cognizable[38] and noncognizable.[39] The JJA 2000 makes no reference to the cognizable and noncognizable offenses, and children may be arrested as per the differential procedure for cognizable and noncognizable offenses. However, the JJA 2000 makes a big departure in the case of bail. It provides that notwithstanding the classification of an offense as bailable or nonbailable under the CrPC or any other law for the time being in force, all children shall be released on bail. Bail may be refused only in three circumstances:[40]

a. When the release will bring the child in contact with known criminals
b. When the release will expose the child to moral danger
c. When the release will be against the interest of justice

It may be noticed that these exceptions have been created to protect the child and are not related to the seriousness of the offense alleged to have been committed by the child. The phrase "ends of justice" was distinguished from "interest of justice" by the High Court of Delhi, which held that the phrase needs to be interpreted in the light of the child-friendly approach of the act and should be understood to protect the best interest of the child.[41]

The CrPC also divides offenses into two kinds, namely, warrant and summons. All offenses punishable with death, life imprisonment, or imprisonment of more than two years are classified as warrant cases,[42] and the others as summons.[43] Trial in warrant cases involves more detailed proceedings, and the judge is required to record the statements of witnesses word for word. In summons cases, the judge may record a summary of statements in his or her own words. The procedure prescribed under the JJA 2000 to be followed by the JJB (and the Child Welfare Committee in the case of children in need of care and protection) is that prescribed for summons cases, subject to the provisions of the JJA 2000.[44] Model Rules 2007, framed after the 2006 amendments, lay down additional measures to be followed by the JJB to ensure a child-friendly environment and support to the child before it.[45] The Model Rules prescribe that "the inquiry is not to be conducted in the spirit of strict adversarial proceedings and it shall use the powers conferred by section 165 of the Indian Evidence Act, 1872 so as to question the juvenile and proceed with the presumptions that favour the juvenile's right to be restored."[46] They further provide that "the Board shall address the juvenile in a child-friendly manner in order to put the juvenile at ease and to encourage him to state the facts and circumstances without any fear, not only in respect of the offence of which the juvenile is accused, but also in respect of the home and social surroundings and the influence to which the juvenile might have been subjected."[47] Even though the proceedings are to be conducted in a nonadversarial environment, the JJB still has to give "due regard to all the due processes guarantees such as right to counsel and free legal aid."[48] This provision has taken forward what was begun in *Kario @ Mansingh Malu*,[49] in which the High Court of Saurashtra struck down as unconstitutional the provision that prohibited the presence of a lawyer as a matter of right in the children's court. However, my interactions with the magistrates working in the Juvenile Justice Board in Delhi suggest ambiguity on this aspect in actual practice. While one magistrate had stated that she did not look at the social investigation reports until a finding of commission of offense was reached, another magistrate agreed that the board usually asked the child to "tell the truth" without thinking about the constitutional right to remain silent.

Another very important variation made from the procedure prescribed in the CrPC is in relation to registration of the first information report in the case of offenses by children. Rule 11 of the Model Rules 2007 prohibits registration of the first information report in case of offenses punishable with less than seven years of imprisonment. Instead, an entry is to be made in the general daily diary kept in the police station, recording "information regarding the offence alleged to have been committed by the juvenile in the general daily diary followed by a report containing social background of the juvenile and circumstances of apprehension and the alleged offence and forward it to the Board before the first hearing."

Differences between Criminal Courts and the JJB

Schedule 1 of the CrPC also contains a column specifying the court that may try the specific offense. Usually serious offenses are tried by the Court of Sessions, while other offenses are triable by magistrates. The JJA 2000 has done away with this classification, and all offenses by children, irrespective of the nature of the offense, are triable by the Juvenile Justice Board constituted under it.

The JJA 2000, like its predecessors, deals with two categories of children and similarly provides for constitution of two separate adjudicatory bodies, namely, the Juvenile Justice Board and the Child Welfare Committee. The children/juvenile children's court for delinquent children and the child/juvenile welfare board established under the earlier legislation have been renamed as the Juvenile Justice Board to deal with children in conflict with law and the Child Welfare Committee to deal with children in need of care and protection under the JJA 2000.

The Child Welfare Committee is constituted by nonjudicial members having special knowledge of child welfare and child psychology, as was the child/juvenile welfare board under the earlier legislation. However, the constitution of the Juvenile Justice Board differs substantially from its prototype child/juvenile court as well as from ordinary criminal courts. The juvenile court under the JJA 1986 consisted of two judicial magistrates functioning as a bench of magistrates. This bench was to be assisted by two social workers. This system indicated a step toward recognizing that judicial decision making needed to be modulated by inputs from social workers. The JJA 2000 took a big leap forward and created a completely different pattern of decision making vis-à-vis children alleged to have committed an offense. The juvenile court has been renamed the Juvenile Justice Board, and it is constituted by one magistrate and two social workers working together as a bench of magistrates.[50] While the judicial magistrate is designated as the principal magistrate and his signature is mandatory on the final order, the decisions are to be taken by majority. The principal magistrate can cast his or her decisive vote only in case of a tie. This means that if the two social workers agree on a decision, they can override the decision of the principal magistrate. In contrast to the Juvenile Justice Boards, there is no concept of a "bench of magistrates" in the ordinary criminal courts or in the special courts, even when dealing with serious offenses such as murder or terrorism. All cases in these courts are decided by a single judicial officer.

All legislation since the Children Act of 1960 have prescribed that at least one member in each of the two adjudicatory bodies must be a woman, perhaps on the assumption that women will have a different or better understanding of children than men do.

In another departure from the ordinary criminal courts, in which appeals may be filed in the higher court against acquittal or conviction, no appeal is permissible against the finding of the Juvenile Justice Board that the child had not committed the offense or that of the Child Welfare Committee that the child is not in need of care and protection.[51] This prohibition ensures that all children so found may revert to their usual life pattern within a period of four months—the time prescribed for completing an inquiry under the act. On the other hand, children found to have committed an offense or found to be in need of care and protection have a right to appeal to the Court of Session and other higher courts as necessary.

The JJA 2000 and the Indian Evidence Act

The JJA 2000 does not contain any specific provisions regarding the standard of proof and burden of proof, and the principles as contained in the Indian Evidence Act of 1912 are observed by the JJB. The primary concern relating to evidence under the JJA 2000 relates to determination of age. Most of the children arrested for offenses under the JJA 2000 come from the lower economic and educational strata,[52] and most of them do not have a birth certificate and are out of school.[53] Hence, it is no surprise that a large number of cases reaching the Supreme Court under the JJA 2000 and other legislation on the subject in force prior to JJA 2000 are related to age determination. Recognizing this difficulty, the Model Rules lay down detailed procedures and hierarchy of evidence for determining age under the JJA 2000.[54]

Penological Differences between the JJA 2000 and the Criminal Justice System

The orders that may be passed by the JJB also differ substantively from orders that may be passed by the ordinary criminal courts. Ordinary or special courts established under the CrPC or special legislation pass the order of "punishment" as prescribed for the offense. An adult offender dealt with under the ordinary criminal justice system may be subjected to the punishment of death, life imprisonment, rigorous or simple imprisonment for different periods, confiscation of property, or fine.[55] In case the juvenile is found to have committed an offense, the orders listed under section 15 of the JJA 2000 are not paired with specified offenses, and any of the orders may be given for any offense committed by the child. Only the following orders may be passed in relation to a child found to have committed an offense by the JJB or any other court in appeal, revision, or otherwise:

(a) allow the juvenile to go home after advice or admonition following appropriate inquiry against and counselling to the parent or the guardian and the juvenile;

(b) direct the juvenile to participate in group counselling and similar activities;

(c) order the juvenile to perform community service;

(d) order the parent of the juvenile or the juvenile himself to pay a fine, if he is over fourteen years of age and earns money;

(e) direct the juvenile to be released on probation of good conduct and placed under the care of any parent, guardian or other fit person, on such parent, guardian or other fit person executing a bond, with or without surety, as the Board may require, for the good behaviour and well-being of the juvenile for any period not exceeding three years;

(f) direct the juvenile to be released on probation of good conduct and placed under the care of any fit institution for the good behaviour and well-being of the juvenile for any period not exceeding three years;

(g) make an order directing the juvenile to be sent to a special home for a period of three years.

Provided that the Board may, if it is satisfied that having regard to the nature of the offence and the circumstances of the case, it is expedient so to do, for reasons to be recorded, reduce the period of stay to such period as it thinks fit.[56]

There is no hierarchy among these various orders, and any order may be chosen in relation to a child found to have committed an offense with a view to his or her reformation and rehabilitation.

Section 16 specifically bars imposition of punishment of death, life imprisonment, or imprisonment in default of payment of fine or furnishing sureties. However, it further provides that if the child found to have committed an offense is over age 16 and the "offence committed is so serious in nature or that his conduct and behaviour have been such that it would not be in his interest or in the interest of other juvenile in a special home to send him to such special home and that none of the other measures provided under this Act is suitable or sufficient,"[57] the Juvenile Justice Board shall keep in safe custody and refer the juvenile's case to the state government to make appropriate arrangement for his or her safe custody. However, the "period of detention so ordered shall not exceed in any case the maximum period provided under section 15 of this Act."[58]

It may be noted that in the preamble of the JJA 2000, punishment of children who commit offenses is not among the objectives of the law. Even though the punishment of a fine is mentioned in section 15, the penal sting has been taken out of it, as no imprisonment may be ordered for failure to pay the fine.[59] This is a measure to secure community placement, as it may be imposed only if the child is above the age of 14 and earning and is not related to the nature of the offense or the harm caused by the offense.[60]

The purpose of these orders is rehabilitation and reintegration of the child into society. The JJA 2000 also provides for sponsorship, adoption, foster care, and aftercare, among additional measures to achieve these objectives.[61]

Age and Applicability of the JJA 2000

As per the CRC norm, the JJA 2000 adopted the uniform age of 18 for boys and girls for defining "child."[62] However, the JJA 2000 left unanswered many questions that had been raised in many cases in the past relating to the applicability of the JJA to children. For example, what is the relevant date for applying the JJA? Is it the date of commission of the offense or of the arrest or of the beginning of proceedings before the court? Who has the duty to determine the age of the accused? At what stage may the plea of juvenility be raised? Would the JJA apply to a child who commits an offense under a special law?

The relevant date for applicability of the act had been an issue in numerous cases in the past, and different High Courts had decided the issue differently.[63] Finally, in *Umesh Chandra v. State of Rajasthan*,[64] a full bench of the Supreme Court held the date of commission of the offense to be the relevant age for applicability of the (then applicable) Children Act. However, a later two-judge bench decision of the same court in *Arnit Das v. State of Bihar*,[65] without referring to *Umesh Chandra*, held the age on the date of first appearance before the judge as the relevant date to determine applicability of the (then applicable) Juvenile Justice Act of 1986. As the applicable Children Act and the Juvenile Justice Act of 1986 contained similar provisions and had the same definition of "child," *Arnit Das* was critiqued in academic writings.[66] B. B. Pande criticized the judgment for being *per incuriam*, being contrary to the decision of the bigger bench in *Umesh Chandra*.[67] I wrote saying that this ruling was obiter dictum in the case, as the issue had not survived for decision after the division bench had held that the accused before it was above the age of 16 on the date of commission of the offense.[68] Soon a review petition was filed, and the matter was referred to a constitutional bench for decision; but the bench refused to decide the issue for being of academic value only on the facts of the case.[69]

After enforcement of the JJA 2000, the question of the relevant date for its applicability again arose in *Pratap Singh v. State of Jharkhand*.[70] This case raised two important issues:

1. What was the date on which a person should be below the age of 18 to be dealt with under the JJA 2000?
2. Did section 20 of the JJA 2000[71] apply to all the pending cases in which the accused was below the age of 18 on the date of offense, even though the offense was committed prior to the law's coming into force?

On the first question, the constitution bench of the Supreme Court agreed with the decision of *Umesh Chandra* and held that the age on the date of commission of the offense was the relevant age for determining applicability of the JJA 2000.

The second issue had arisen due to section 20 of the JJA 2000, which provided that all pending cases of children before ordinary criminal courts would continue in those courts, but if the court found the child had committed the offense, it should transfer the case to the Juvenile Justice Board for final orders under the JJA 2000. Section 64 of the JJA 2000[72] also directed transfer of children who may be undergoing imprisonment pursuant to the orders of ordinary criminal courts to special homes under the JJA 2000. It may be recalled that boys above the age of 16 were excluded from the purview of the JJA 1986, while they were included within the purview of the JJA 2000. The Supreme Court in *Pratap Singh* held that a boy falling in the aforementioned category would be covered under the provisions of the JJA 2000 only if he was still below the age of 18 on the date on which the JJA 2000 came into force, namely, 1 April 2001, but not otherwise.

Soon after this judgment, the JJA 2000 was amended in crucial respects by the Juvenile Justice (Amendment) Act of 2006. The amended definition of "juvenile in conflict with law"[73] left no doubt that it was age on the date of commission of the offense that determined applicability of the act.

An identical explanation was inserted in sections 20 and 64, which nullified the restriction given by the Supreme Court in *Pratap Singh* and provided that the JJA 2000 was to apply to all pending cases of children who were children on the date of commission of the offense irrespective of their age on the date of enforcement of the act.[74] Even so, many judgments of the Supreme Court given after the amendments continued to apply the limitation contained in *Pratap Singh*.[75] Finally, in *Hari Ram*,[76] the Supreme Court recognized that all those judgments either given without referring to the amendments or given by referring to *Pratap Singh* were incorrect and that the true situation was as follows:

The law as now crystallized on a conjoint reading of Sections 2(k), 2(l), 7A, 20 and 49 read with Rules 12 and 98, places beyond all doubt that all persons who were below the age of 18 years on the date of commission of the offence even prior to 1st April, 2001, would be treated as juveniles, even if the claim of juvenility was raised after they had attained the age of 18 years on or before the date of commencement of the Act and were undergoing sentence upon being convicted.[77]

Section 7A was inserted into the JJA 2000 to make provisions for determination of age in case it was claimed that the accused was a juvenile on the date of commission of the offense. It permitted the plea of juvenility to be raised at any stage—even after the final disposal of the case.[78]

A non obstante clause giving overriding effect to the provisions of the JJA was inserted as subsection 4 to section 1,[79] setting to rest the controversies relating to applicability of the JJA to children who commit offenses under the special laws.

Residential Institutions

The JJA 2000 provides for segregation of children in need of care and protection (CNCP) and others alleged or found to have committed an offense. The CNCP are to be housed in a children's home while proceedings are pending as well as postdecision if no community alternative is found suitable. Children in conflict with law while proceedings are pending against them before the JJB may be kept in observation if not released on bail and placed with a parent or guardian. They may be sent to a special home if they are found to have committed an offense.

This scheme differs from that provided under the JJA 1986, which had provided for the establishment of an observation home for all children while their proceedings were pending before the competent authority. Postdisposition, neglected and delinquent children were to be segregated in children's homes and special homes, respectively. The changed scheme of segregating children in conflict with law from those in need of care and protection while the proceedings are still pending suggests a prima facie presumption of adverse influence by the former on the latter group. It goes against the presumption of innocent until proven guilty.

The JJA 2000 has continued placement of children in fit institutions,[80] as was provided under the JJA 1986. The act does not clarify how the "fit institutions" are different from other homes for keeping children as previously specified. However, the nomenclature of these institutions suggests that these should be institutions that are found fit to suit the special needs of a given child and need not be catering to the needs of children alone.

The JJA 2000 has also included shelter homes for temporary care of children without intervention of the competent authority.[81] These may be used as a drop-in center for children in case of emergency.

Special Juvenile Police Unit

A child covered under the provisions of the JJA 2000 may present him- or herself before the competent authority or be brought before it by a police officer, a public servant, Childline,[82] a social worker, or any public-spirited person.[83] Even so, police continue to be the first point of contact for most children coming within the system. The need for sensitization of police has been felt for a long time, and the JJA 2000 makes provision for identification and training of at least one police officer in each police station as a child/juvenile welfare officer to deal with all children who come within the ambit of this act.[84]

Rehabilitation and Social Reintegration

The ultimate aim of dealing with children under the JJA 2000 is their rehabilitation and reintegration into society. This is to be achieved by making an order for long-term care either by restoring the children to their families, finding an appropriate family for their care, or sending them to an institutional home until suitable arrangements for their reintegration into society are made. Chapter IV of the JJA 2000 focuses on rehabilitation and social reintegration, specifically focusing on adoption, foster care, sponsorship, and aftercare as measures for children's rehabilitation and social reintegration.

The UN Convention on the Rights of the Child prescribes that all children have the right to be taken care of by their parents[85] but also obligates the state parties to ensure alternate care that may include "foster placement, *kafalah* of Islamic law, adoption or if necessary placement in suitable institutions for the care of children."[86]

Prior to the JJA 2000, adoption fell within the purview of personal laws. Only Hindus could adopt, and only Hindu children could be adopted as per the provisions of the Hindu Adoptions and Maintenance Act of 1956. In consonance with the CRC, the JJA 2000 opened adoption of all children falling within its purview irrespective of the religion of the child or the adoptive parents.[87] The provision relating to adoption was the most debated topic during parliamentary debates, and questions were raised due to the differences between adoption norms under Hindu law and those prescribed under the JJA. All the objections were brushed aside by Shrimati Maneka Gandhi, then minister of state in the Ministry of Social Justice and Empowerment, who said that adoption under the JJA 2000 was a secular measure aimed at providing family care. She further said that any problems regarding conflict of laws, when they arise, would be taken care of by the courts.[88]

The definition of "adoption" was inserted in the JJA 2000 by the Amendment Act of 2006: "the process through which the adopted child is permanently separated from his biological parents and becomes the legitimate child of his adoptive parents with all the rights, privileges and responsibilities that are attached to the relationship."[89]

In *Shabnam Hashmi v. Union of India*,[90] the petitioner filed a writ petition in 2005 in the Supreme Court, petitioning that the right to adopt and be adopted be recognized as a fundamental right and requesting the court to frame guidelines enabling adoption of children by persons irrespective of religion, caste, creed, and so on and to direct the government to enact an optional law of adoption focusing on children, "with considerations like religion etc., taking a hind seat."[91] The Muslim Personal Law Board, as intervener, objected to this petition on the grounds that Muslim law does not recognize adoption but only the *"Kafala"* system under which the child is placed under a *"Kafil,"* who provides for the well-being of the child, including financial support, and thus is legally allowed to take care of the child, although the child remains the true descendant of his biological parents and not that of the "adoptive" parents.[92] The petitioner accepted that the JJA 2000 as amended in 2006 enabled and facilitated adoption of children irrespective of religion, caste, creed, and so on. Hence, the Supreme Court resorted to the principle of judicial restraint, stating that the time was not opportune for it to give a constitutional interpretation regarding adoption being a fundamental right. However, it did note that "the legislature which is better equipped to comprehend the mental preparedness of the entire citizenry to think unitedly on the issue has expressed its view, for the present, by the enactment of the JJ Act 2000 and the same must receive due respect."[93]

The JJA also makes provisions for short-term or long-term foster care for children for whom appropriate families for adoption have not been found.[94] In case a child is not placed in a family—natural, adoptive, or foster—and has been placed under the care of a home established under the JJA 2000, the After-care Organisation has been charged with the responsibility of preparing an individualized plan enabling the child to lead an honest, industrious, and useful life after release from the home.[95] The JJA 2000 also provides that children placed in families, children's homes, and special homes may be supported by sponsorship programs to meet their "medical, nutritional, educational and other needs . . . with a view to improving their quality of life."[96]

Challenges in Implementation

Implementation of the JJA 2000 is examined from three perspectives: (1) implementation of basic infrastructure, (2) challenges of the judicial mind-set, and (3) the pattern of disposal of cases of children under the JJA 2000.

Implementation of Basic Infrastructure

The Ministry for Women and Child Development is responsible for coordination of all activities concerning the implementation of the JJA 2000. In its third and fourth periodic reports to the UN committee under the CRC, it has noted that

CWCs, JJBs, SJPUs, Childline, NCPCR [National Commission for Protection of Child Rights], National Crime Records Bureau (NCRB) and the judiciary are some of the monitoring mechanisms in place. As per the provision in Section 62 of the JJ (Amendment) Act, 2006, the process is underway for setting up of Central, State, District and city advisory boards, comprising related Government departments, social work-ers, representatives from voluntary organisations and other child wel-fare professionals, for establishing greater inter-agency coordination in implementation and monitoring of the juvenile justice system. The ICPS [Integrated Child Protection Scheme] provides for a well-defined frame-work for this purpose.[97]

However, different data are available from different sources on the status of implementation of the act. The chart on the website of the Ministry of Women and Child Development showing the status of implementation of the JJA 2000 does not indicate the date of the status. However, a perusal of the information indicates the areas/aspects that the government is pursuing for implementation. Table 4.1 shows that many states have not given full information, and in some cases, there is conflicting information; but clearly the JJA 2000 is still in the process of being implemented in most parts of the country. Table 4.1 shows that there is a lot that has yet to be implemented even at the numerical level. Ensuring quality and functionality of those functionaries is another level of implementation. We have no information about the availabil-ity of basic infrastructure needed for functionality of the bodies and institutions established, but if occasional information coming out in the public domain is any indication, a lot more needs to be achieved.[98]

The government of India has sought to bring all services for care and protection of children under one umbrella structure, called the Inte-grated Child Protection Scheme (ICPS).[99] All services under the JJA 2000 have also been brought under this scheme. However, the judiciary has played a pivotal role in ensuring implementation of the JJA 2000. Two public interest petitions have been filed in the Supreme Court for better implementation of the JJA 2000, and the Supreme Court has been passing various directions for implementation of the JJA and seeking compliance reports from the state governments.

The public interest litigation (PIL) *Sampurna Behrua v. Union of India* was filed by the Human Rights Law Network in 2005 to bring to the fore the nonimplementation of the JJA 2000.[100] It was brought on the basis of a detailed analysis of twelve states[101] of India, which highlighted that the JJA was not being implemented. "Most of these states failed to establish the following mandatory provisions: the establishment of

TABLE 4.1. State of Implementation of the JJA 2000 as per the Ministry of Women and Child Development

State/UT	Rules	OH	SH	CH	SH	AC	Ad	JJB	CWC	AB	SJPU	WF	IC	S	T
Andhra	✓	10	2	5	na	1	na	10	5	✓	u/c	✓	na	na	na
Bihar	✓	na	na	na	na	na	na	u/c	u/c	na	na	na	na	na	na
Chhatisgarh	u/c	na	na	na	na	na	na	9	7	na	na	na	na	na	na
Goa	u/c	2	2	3	na	na	na	1	1	na	✓	na	na	na	na
Gujarat	✓	88	13	63	23 ngo	14	20 ngo	✓	✓	✓	wc	u/c	u/c		2
Haryana	✓	1	1	2	2	1	1	4	19	✓	wc	✓	u/c	na	✓
HP	✓		1	1	4	na	na	2	u/c	u/c	u/c	u/c	1	na	u/c
Karnataka	✓	5	2	45	u/c	na	na	5	27	✓	27	✓	✓	na	na
Kerala	na	13 for all	-	-	nil	na	na	14	14	na	na	na	Na	na	na
MP	✓	18	3	3	u/c	2	✓	u/c	u/c	u/c	✓	✓	na	na	na
Maha-rashtra	✓	56		148	na	na	na	30	37	✓	na	na	na	na	na
Manipur	✓	1	1	1	na	na	3	1	1	na	na	na	na	✓	1
Mizoram	✓	2	2	na	na	na	na	1	1	✓	na	na	2	na	na
Meghalaya	✓	3	u/c	3	u/c	u/c	na	7	7	na	na	na	na	na	na
Pondi-cherry	✓	1	1	1	u/c	1	na	✓	✓	na	na	na	na	na	na
Punjab	u/c	2	2	10	na	na	na	u/c	5	u/c	na	✓	u/c		u/c
Rajasthan	✓	2	1	5	u/c	na	na	9✓	9✓	✓	✓	u/c	u/c	na	na
Sikkim	✓	1	na	nil	na	na	na	1	1	na	na	na	1	na	na
Tamil Nadu	✓	8	2	32	na	3	na	8	18	u/c	✓	✓	✓	na	✓
Tripura	✓	1	na	na	na	na	na	✓	u/c	u/c	na	nil	1	na	nil

	1	2	3	4	5	6	7	8	9	10	11	12	13	14
UP*	✓	22	2	19	u/c	4	u/c	25	12	✓	u/c	u/c	u/c	✓
West Bengal	✓	5	5	5	22	8	na	2✓	5✓	na	in some	✓	u/c	na	na
A&N Islands	✓	1	1	†	u/c	na	na	1	1	✓	u/c	✓	u/c	na	na
Chandigarh	✓	✓	✓	†	u/c	1 ngo	na	✓	✓	not needed	u/c wc	nil	✓	na	na
Daman and Diu	✓	na	na	na	na	na	na	u/c	u/c	na	na	na	na	na	na
Delhi	✓	3	✓	11	4	na	u/c	2	5	✓	na	u/c	10	na	✓
Lakshadweep	There is no problem relating to juveniles in the territory. However, they have earmarked a room in Working Women's Hostel at Kavaratti to accommodate such cases, if required.													
D&NH	✓	not required; delinquent, if any, sent to Gujarat		na	na	na	na	1	not needed	na	nil	na	na	nil as no JD	na
Orissa	✓	15	3	12	na	na	na	28	na	na	u/c	na	na	na	na
Jharkhand	Constitution of Juvenile Justice Boards and Child Welfare Committees in seven districts (notification to be issued).													

Source: http://wcd.nic.in/childprot/jjimp.htm (accessed 15 March 2014).

* At another place in the same column, UP mentions. "There are 58 Observation Homes, 23 children homes, 4 Special Homes and 7 After Care organizations in the State."

† Old People Home and Narniketan declared as CH for boys and girls, respectively.

Key: OH = observation homes; SH = special homes; CH = children's homes; SH = shelter homes; AC = aftercare organizations; Ad = adoption; JJB = Juvenile Justice Boards; CWC = Child Welfare Committees; AB = Advisory Board; SJPU = Special Juvenile Police Unit; WF = Welfare Fund; IC = Inspection Committee; S = sponsorship; T = training; wc = women's cells in police station working as SJPU; na = not available; ngo = nongovernmental organizations; u/c = under consideration

TABLE 4.2. Number of CWCs and JJBs in States and Union Territories

State/UT	Number of districts	CWC	JJB
Andaman and Nicobar	3	1	1
Arunachal Pradesh	17	16	16
Bihar	38	32	38
Chhattisgarh	27	26	17
Delhi	9	7	2
Jharkhand	24	24	21
Puducherry	4	3	4
Tripura	8	4	4
Uttar Pradesh	75	72	72

Juvenile Justice Boards (JJB), Child Welfare Committees (CWC) and special Juvenile Police Units."[102] Over the years, the Supreme Court has passed many directives to the states for creation of the basic infrastructure required under the JJA 2000 and sought compliance.[103] So far, the Supreme Court has passed 32 orders in the case.[104] In its order dated 10 September 2013, the Supreme Court listed nine states and union territories that had not established a JJB and CWC in each district, as required by the JJA (see table 4.2).[105]

A second PIL, *Bachpan Bachao Andolan v. Union of India*,[106] was filed for protection of children subjected to physical, emotional, and sexual violence and abuse in circuses, without access to their families. The solicitor general of India on behalf of the government expanded the scope of this PIL to trafficking of children also. The Supreme Court in its order of 18 April 2011 outlined in detail the wide scale of non-implementation of the JJA 2000, the nonestablishment of basic functionaries under the act, insufficient infrastructure, inadequate funds, and so on,[107] and the reasons given by the state for this PIL also have focused on implementation of the JJA 2000 to ensure the promised care to children in need of care and protection.[108]

In addition, the Chief Justices Conference in 2006 and 2009 directed all High Courts to form committees for strengthening the implementation of juvenile justice. The Committee of the High Court of Delhi has been very active and has been constantly monitoring the functioning of various institutions under the JJA 2000. This committee consists of various stakeholders from the government, the correctional administration, the legal services authority, NGOs, and academicians and meets regularly to apprise itself of the progress made and to take necessary steps to remove obstacles. The High Court of Delhi has also taken the lead to ensure implementation of the JJA 2000 in its true letter and spirit and has taken *suo motu* cognizance of many matters and passed orders in the best interests of children.[109] Pursuant to the order of the High Court of Delhi, a committee has been constituted with National Commission for Protection of Child Rights as its head to monitor the functioning of the government-run children's homes for girls in Delhi.[110]

The High Court of Delhi has also involved senior police officers in its Monitoring Committee, leading to major steps being taken to ensure a child-friendly approach by police in Delhi. The Special Juvenile Police Units have been established in all of the 11 police districts in Delhi as well as in Crime and Railways and Indira Gandhi Airport Units, "with a purpose to co-ordinate and upgrade police treatment of the juvenile and the children. Every Police Station has designated two or three police officers with necessary aptitude, appropriate training and orientation as Juvenile or Child Welfare Officer, who handle or deal with the juvenile or child in conflict with law as well as the children in need of care and protection."[111]

The Delhi Police officially launched a website about juvenile justice (www.dpjju.com) on 6 March 2010, which provides important information regarding functions of the police vis-à-vis children, the functioning of Special Juvenile Police Units, the procedure to be followed in handling children, and so on. It has also developed the *Manual for Trainers: Training on Juvenile Justice System for Police Officials*.[112] A detailed "Standing Order" has been issued instructing all police personnel to follow the directions contained therein on important matters such as nonregistration of the first information report in the case of children for offenses punishable with less than seven years of imprisonment; determination of age; steps to be taken on taking charge of the child; appearance before competent authority.[113]

The Delhi government also has been maintaining a record of progress as well as problems faced in implementation of the JJA 2000 and the ICPS through its central-level Monitoring Committee reports.[114]

Challenges of the Judicial Mind-Set

There is no denying the fact that juvenile justice has branched off from the criminal justice system. The criminal justice system started with an "eye for an eye" mind-set with retribution as its primary aim, added deterrence of offenders and potential offenders as its purpose, and later incorporated reformation of the offender as an achievable goal during imprisonment as well as by community-based measures. Juvenile justice in India took a big step in embracing an approach of reformation instead of punishment when it enacted the Children Act of 1960. The same approach has been strengthened by all subsequent legislation, and the juvenile justice system has completely severed all ties with the penal response of the criminal justice system. However, punishment of the offender continues to be the mind-set of many judges and the general public, especially when a child has committed a serious offense.

There is resistance to applying juvenile justice when the offense committed by the child is serious, and this is further reinforced by a range of misconceptions about the nature and scheme of orders under the JJA 2000. The legislation itself creates no hierarchy among the list of orders, and the appropriateness of an order is to be guided by the Social Investigation Report, looking forward to the possibility of reform, rehabilitation, and reintegration of the child into society rather than looking backward at the severity of the offense committed and the harm caused to the victim by the offense. However, judges have yet to embrace and accept this concept and approach. They continue to conceive of institutionalization as equivalent to imprisonment and tend to send a child to a special home when he or she is found to have committed a serious offense. During training programs for judicial officers that I conducted in Delhi, the judges were given identical facts about a child and the evidence available against him except for the offense committed. Exercise 1, given to half the group, stated that the child had committed a petty offense of theft of scrap iron in order to get money to see a popular movie. Exercise 2, given to the other half of the group, stated that the child had murdered four members of the family in which he was a domestic servant.[115] A majority of the judicial officers who participated in the exercise opted for the child's release after due admonition for the child who had committed the petty offense and for sending the child to a special home for the child who was found to have committed a serious offense.[116] As per the scheme of the act, the choice of the order should be guided by the Social Information Report regarding the child and not by the nature of offense, but it was only exceptionally that the judges asked for additional information to make a decision.

Many judicial decisions reflect acceptance of reformation as the appropriate way to deal with children and have promoted an inclusive approach to the law in which interpretations of the law are favorable to the child.[117] However, those who are unable to accept the reformative approach find ways to exclude children from juvenile justice through other means. *Ram Deo Chauhan* is a case in point, as it adopted the route of age determination to exclude a child who had committed a serious offense from the purview of juvenile justice.[118] Ram Deo Chauhan was found to have killed four members of the family for which he was working as a domestic servant in 1993. During trial before the Sessions Court, he claimed to be a child on the date of the offense and, hence, required to be dealt with by the juvenile court under the provisions of the Juvenile Justice Act of 1986. The Sessions Court, by curious reasoning, determined that he was not a child on the date of the offense, even though his school register matched with the medical report given by Medical Board appointed by the court, and sentenced him to death. His death penalty was confirmed by the High Court and unanimously by a division bench of the Supreme Court, without a reexamination of the determination of his age, which was crucial to the trial by the sessions judge.[119] A review petition was filed with the assistance of the author, as the question of age determination was not raised in the appeal before the High Court and the Supreme Court. Ram Deo Chauhan's death penalty was reconfirmed by the majority opinion of two judges against one.[120] The anger of one of the judges is palpable in the judgment, in which he called the offender a beast and said that he was trying to murder the judicial system by taking recourse to review despite knowing that the review was motivated by my intervention. Ram Deo Chauhan moved for an application of mercy, and the governor of Assam commuted his death penalty to life imprisonment. When the victim's family learned about the commutation, they filed a writ petition against it, and Ram Deo Chauhan was sent back to death row by another judge of the Supreme Court, who set aside the order of clemency by the governor.[121]

Another review petition against this judgment opened a window for Ram Deo Chauhan to approach the appropriate authority for age determination once again.[122] A year and a half later, and after knocking at the doors of the Assam JJB and the High Court of Assam, Ramdeo Chauhan was found to be a child on the date of the offense and was released in 2011,[123] after spending more than 18 years in prison, even though, as per the law, he should not have been kept in jail or even in a police station at all at any stage of the proceedings.

Justice P. Sathasivam, writing the judgment for Justice B. S. Chauan in the "Bombay Blast" case,[124] chose another route to exclude application of the JJA 2000 to the child convicted in the case. While the Bollywood actor Sanjay Dutt, who was sent to jail for five years for possessing an illegal weapon in a notified area, against the provisions of the Terrorist and Disruptive Activities Act, hogged the limelight in print and other media, another 12 convicts who were sent to the gallows and one child offender who was sent to life imprisonment on many counts under TADA remained unnoticed. Mohd. Moin Faridulla Qureshi claimed to be 17 years and three months old on the date of the offense, and he claimed that his case should be disposed of in terms of the JJA 2000.[125] The court devoted considerable space in the judgment to highlighting the beneficial and protective nature of the JJA 2000 but refused to apply the law to Qureshi, who was a child on the date of the offense. It sentenced him to life imprisonment under TADA on the reasoning that because TADA had already been repealed, the non obstante clause contained in section 1(4) of the JJA could not have overridden TADA, as it was no longer a "law for the time being in force." This is very strange reasoning. If the court deemed that TADA was in force for convicting and punishing Qureshi under its provisions, how could it declare it not to be in force for the purposes of applying the JJA? On the date of judgment in Mohd. Moin Faridulla Qureshi's case, both TADA and the JJA 2000 as amended in 2006 were in force. In view of section 1(4),[126] read with section 20[127] and the Supreme Court decision in *Hari Ram*, it was clear that the JJA applied to his case as he was below the age of 18 on the date of the offense. In view of section 1(4), the Supreme Court was duty bound to send the child for appropriate orders under the provisions of the JJA 2000. Instead, he was sentenced to "rigorous imprisonment for life long" on four counts, along with periods of imprisonment ranging from two to 14 years. He had already spent 13.5 years in imprisonment. But ironically, the extreme punishment of death was not imposed on him due to his young age. Referring to article 139-A(2) and article 142 of the Constitution, the Supreme Court claimed to be doing complete justice, as despite the defendant's heinous offenses, the court gave him only life imprisonment for full life, while other offenders were given the death penalty for the same offenses. However, the Supreme Court seemed to believe that children committing offenses also needed to be children in need of care and protection to qualify for the protection of the JJA. It said, "the appellant from his conduct referred to above cannot by any stretch of imagination qualify as a child in need of care and protection as the acts committed by him are so grave and heinous warranting the maximum penalty."[128] This reasoning again reflects the penal mind-set of the judges regarding serious offenses and the continuous tension between the criminal justice perception of justice of punishing the offender and the demand of juvenile justice of achieving justice through reformation of the child.

Ajahar Ali v. State of West Bengal[129] presents another area of conflict, namely, the demand of women's rights activists for stricter punishment for offenses against women and for the approach of juvenile justice of reforming children instead of punishing them for the commission of any offense. In this case, the appellant was convicted of forcibly kissing a 16-year-old girl in 1995, and the Supreme Court confirmed the sentence of six months of imprisonment imposed on him by the lower courts. It refused to release him on probation or to apply the JJA 2000, even though he was also 16 years old on the date of the offense. Ajahar Ali pleaded that 18 years had elapsed since the commission of offense; that both the complainant and the convict were well settled in their lives after marriage and had children, and their lives should not be disturbed; that the appellant would lose his job if sent to prison; and that the JJA 2000 applied to him. The Supreme Court reasoned, "the appellant has committed a heinous crime and with the social condition prevailing in the society, the modesty of a woman has to be strongly guarded and as the appellant behaved like a road side Romeo, we do not think it is a fit case where the benefit of the Act 1958[130] should be given to the appellant."[131] It further reasoned that six months' imprisonment was not prejudicial to him, as "the maximum sentence that can be awarded in such a case is of 3 years"[132] under the JJA 2000, and no purpose would be served by applying the JJA at this belated stage.[133] There is no doubt that offenses against women need to be dealt with strictly, but this order, 18 years after the incident, is too late to improve the protection of women in general or to provide any relief to the actual victim in the case. It also reflects the misconceptions of the court, which equates three years in a special home with imprisonment and assumes that this was the order that the JJB should or would have passed if it had considered the matter.

Disposal of Cases

As mentioned earlier, section 15 of the JJA 2000 contains a large set of orders that may be passed in relation to children. The choice of order in a given case is not to be determined with reference to the offense committed but with reference to what is best for the child's rehabilitation. As per the CRC and the Beijing Rules, orders ensuring placement of a child in the community are to be preferred over those sending a child to an institution, and "placement of a juvenile in an institution shall always be a disposition of last resort and for the minimum necessary period."[134] However, as table 4.3 shows, out of the total number of cases disposed of in all of India in 2012, children in more than 40% cases were sent to special homes,[135] which does not seem to be in sync with the direction of the Beijing Rules for use of institutions as a measure of last resort.

TABLE 4.3. Disposal of Cases in 2012

	Number of cases
Total	39,822
Sent to home after advice or admonition	5,927
Released on probation and placed under care of . . .	
Parents/guardians	7,290
Fit institution	2,183
Sent to special homes	9,677
Fined	1,452
Acquitted or otherwise disposed of	2,572
Pending disposal	10,721

The detailed data regarding states show that among the states with more than 1,000 cases of juveniles pending before the JJB in 2012, Rajasthan, Bihar, and Tamil Nadu topped the list by sending more children to special homes—1,257 out of 2,551, 1,177 out of 3,262, and 1,139 out of 3,542, respectively. Maharashtra had a total of 6,639 children before the JJBs, and it restored 1,907 to parents or guardians—the largest number of children among all states and union territories. The number of children sent to special schools in Maharashtra was comparatively less, at 1,790. Andhra Pradesh shows the least use of special homes, with only 269 children sent to special homes, 557 sent home after due admonition, 599 released under the care of parents/guardian, and 61 released under the care of fit institutions, out of the total of 2,372 children before the JJBs.

Among the union territories, Delhi tops the list, with 443 children sent to special schools, but it also released 500 children after due admonition and released 138 children under the care of parent/guardian and 54 under the care of fit institutions, with a total of 1,572 cases still pending before the JJB in 2012. The large number of cases that remained to be disposed of remains a cause of worry, as the JJA 2000 puts a time limit of four months for disposal of cases.

However, there is a dire need to verify the authenticity of these data. According to *Crime in India 2012* statistics, Delhi sent 443 children to special schools, but this figure is substantively at variance from the figure on the ground. As on 31 March 2013, there were eight boys and five girls in the special homes and eight boys in the "place of safety."[136] These figures are similar to what I had found during my first research on homes in Delhi under the Children Act in 1980. At that time, the number of children in the special homes in Delhi was minuscule—fewer than 20 children in the past four years, and it was exceptional that any girls were found in the special homes. For this reason, all the special homes functioned and continue to function to this day from within the premises of the observation homes.

The Way Forward

The adequacy of the orders listed in section 15, specially subsection g, has been the subject of intense media focus and heated debates since the brutal gang rape in Delhi on 12 December 2012 of a 23-year-old girl, who died from her injuries two weeks later. One of the persons accused of this offense was six months short of age 18. Sending the juvenile for three years of "imprisonment" in a special school was considered to be inadequate given the severity of the offense. There were demands for "adult punishment for adult crime."

A number of cases were filed in different courts challenging application of the JJA 2000 to the child accused of gang rape in this case. The constitutionality of the JJA 2000 was challenged before the Supreme Court by many people in *Salil Bali v. Union of India*[137] and again in *Subramanian Swami v. Raju through Member Juvenile Justice Board*.[138] Fortunately, both of these challenges have been dismissed by the Supreme Court. Rejecting the plea in *Salil Bali*, the Supreme Court reasserted,

> The essence of the Juvenile Justice (Care and Protection of Children) Act, 2000, and the Rules framed thereunder in 2007, is restorative and not retributive, providing for rehabilitation and re-integration of children in conflict with law into mainstream society. The age of eighteen has been fixed on account of the understanding of experts in child psychology and behavioural patterns that till such an age the children in conflict with law could still be redeemed and restored to mainstream society, instead of becoming hardened criminals in future.
>
> There are, of course, exceptions where a child in the age group of sixteen to eighteen may have developed criminal propensities, which would make it virtually impossible for him/her to be reintegrated into mainstream society, but such examples are not of such proportions as to warrant any change in thinking, since it is probably better to try and re-integrate children with criminal propensities into mainstream society, rather than to allow them to develop into hardened criminals, which does not augur well for the future.[139]

Another challenge was started by Subramanian Swami, a former Union cabinet minister of commerce, minister of law and justice, and president of the Janata Party, who filed an application in the JJB for being impleaded in the proceedings in the JJB relating to the juvenile accused in the December rape case. He petitioned for transfer of the child accused to an ordinary criminal court for trial so that he could be given more severe punishment as prescribed by the Indian Penal Code, which secures the rights of the victim. He also claimed the blanket inclusion of all offenses within the purview of the JJA to be "completely arbitrary, unreasonable and . . . violative of the fundamental rights guaranteed under Articles 14 and 21 of the Constitution of India."[140] The JJB dismissed the application, stating that it was not within its powers to grant the relief asked. Swami then filed an appeal before the High Court of Delhi. The appeal was dismissed by the High Court, but the special leave petition against this decision was admitted by the Supreme Court to give an authoritative pronouncement on the possibility of excluding children who commit serious offenses from the purview of the JJA 2000, to be tried in regular courts, as per the IPC and CrPC.[141] However, after considering the arguments on both sides in detail, the Supreme Court again dismissed the petition:

> If the legislature has adopted the age of 18 as the dividing line between juveniles and adults and such a decision is constitutionally permissible the enquiry by the Courts must come to an end. Even otherwise there is a considerable body of world opinion that all under 18 persons ought to be treated as juveniles and separate treatment ought to be meted out to them so far as offences committed by such persons are concerned. . . . If the Act has treated all under 18 as a separate category for the purposes of differential treatment so far as the commission of offences are concerned, we do not see how the contentions advanced by the petitioners to the contrary on the strength of the thinking and practices in other jurisdictions can have any relevance.[142]

The JJA 2000 has survived the constitutionality challenge in the recent past both in *Salil Bali* and the Subraminian Swami cases, but the media continues to highlight prominently the involvement of children in serious cases. The situation is not helped with frequent news of rioting, arson, and escapes from observation homes in Delhi.[143] It is expected that there will be continuous pressure on the legislature and the courts to change the all-inclusive and protective nature of the JJA 2000 and similar legislation in different countries. There is a war of terror in the name of the war on terror, and it is no longer limited to the offenses of terrorism but has seeped into other areas of offending also. The Criminal Law Amendment Act of 2013 has introduced harsher punishments for rape in the IPC,[144] namely, the death penalty[145] and life imprisonment for the duration of the natural life of the convict.[146]

However, I believe that an all-inclusive protective and rehabilitative approach is the best way to deal with children, including and especially adolescents who commit serious offenses. I have three reasons for believing so. First, the number of children involved in offending in India is minuscule, and India has sufficient human and other resources to create individualized care plans for each child and to ensure his or her reintegration into society. Second, numerous criminological and penological researchers have found that subjecting children to harsher punishments under ordinary criminal justice does not lead to significant gains in terms of better protection for society. Third, there is now scientific evidence that shows that the adolescent brain functions differently and that children in the age group 14–18 are particularly vulnerable to violent actions, are different from adults, and need to be treated differently.

The Nature and Extent of Juvenile Crime in India

In 2012, approximately 434 million children were below the age of 18 in India.[147] While no clear figures are available for children in need of care and protection, a report submitted to the Supreme Court in the case of *Bachpan Bachao Andolan* by the Ministry of Women and Child Development declared that 40% of India's children were vulnerable or experiencing difficult circumstances.[148] With such a large number of children in need of care and protection, one would expect large numbers of them to get involved in criminal activities. However, the number of children even alleged to have committed an offense is minuscule. A total of 39,822 children were arrested for commission of 31,973 incidents of crime in 2012.[149] Among these children, 35,346 were first-time offenders, while 4,476 were repeat offenders.[150] Out of the total incidents of crime, 27,936 were under the Indian Penal Code (IPC), and 4,037 were under the Special and Local Laws (SLL). Children committed only 1.2% of the total of 2,387,188 crimes in India in that year. Out of 100,000 children, only 2.3 children were arrested for commission of any offense. In the past ten years, juvenile crime has shown only a marginal increase, from its being 1.0% of total crime and the rate of juvenile delinquency being 1.8 in 2000.[151] These figures are remarkably low compared to the United Kingdom and the United States.

In 2011–2012, out of a total of 1,235,028 arrests for notifiable offenses in England and Wales, children between the ages of 10 and 17 accounted for 167,995 arrests, or 13.6%, and these arrested children accounted for 10.8% of all children in England and Wales in this age group.[152] In 2012–2013, 98,837 children were found to have committed an offense, a 28% decrease from the previous year and a 63% decrease since 2002–2003.[153]

In the United States, 1,020,334 children under the age of 18 were arrested in 2011,[154] and they constituted 10.8% of total arrests.[155] The rate of juvenile delinquency is at 4,367 out of 100,000 children in the age group 10–17; the rate was at its peak at 8,476.1 in 1996.[156] Table 4.4 shows the consistently high rate of violent crime by children between the ages of 10 and 18 in the United States over a period of time.

Table 4.4 shows that the rate of violent juvenile crime is very high in the United States. In contrast, the number of *total children arrested* for commission of *all offenses* in India (under both the Indian Penal Code and Special and Local Laws) shows that in some cases the total number of children arrested in a given age bracket in India is similar to the rate of violent juvenile crime in the United States. Table 4.5 shows that this low number in India has been consistently so over the years and that the increase over the years is marginal. It further shows that the number of girls involved in juvenile delinquency is even smaller.

TABLE 4.4. Violent Crime Index Arrests per 100,000 Children in the Age Group 10–18 in the United States in 1980, 1994, and 2011

Age	Number of arrests per 100,000 children		
	1980	1994	2011
10–12	40.8	86.8	34.4
13–14	228.9	464.6	168.5
15	442.8	803.7	309.5
16	563.9	994.4	395.4
17	661.6	1,064.3	458.3
18	676.3	1,100.0	526.2

Source: US Department of Justice, Office of Juvenile Justice and Delinquency Prevention, "Juvenile Arrest Rate Trends," http://www.ojjdp.gov/ojstatbb/crime/JAR_Display.asp?ID=qa05201.

TABLE 4.5. Total Number of Children Arrested for IPC and SLL Crime
(by Age)

Age	1994* Boys + girls	2001 Boys + girls	2012 Boys + girls
7–12 years	3,426 + 268	3,591 + 105	1,153 + 133
12–16 years	10,426 + 627	12,131 + 598	11,474 + 589
16–18 years	2,456 (only girls)	15,573 + 1,630	25,137 + 1,336
Total	13,852 + 3,351	31,295 + 2,333	37,764 + 2,058
Grand total	17,203	33,628	39,822

* The figures for the age group 16–18 are not comparable between years, as the definition of juvenility included boys in the age group 16–18 only since 2001.
Source: Crime in India 1994, table 49, , available at http://ncrb.nic.in/ciiprevious/Data/CII1994/cii-1994/TABLE-49.pdf; Crime in India 2001, table 54, and Crime in India 2012, table 10.8, available at http://ncrb.nic.in/.

TABLE 4.6. Comparative Table of Violent Crime by Age and Sex

Offense	1994* Children under 18	2001 Children under 18	2012 Children under 18	Children ages 16–18, total	Girls ages 16–18	Total violent crime
Murder	288	531	1,281	831	14	68,676
Attempt to murder	166	449	1,132	821	32	82,669
Culpable homicide not amounting to murder	19	34	52	31	2	7,148
Rape	176	399	1,305	887	6	31,117
Kidnapping and abduction	95	122	913	704	35	62,020
Dacoity	32	59	260	207	10	18,422
Preparation and assembly for dacoity	23	51	132	106	0	13,089
Robbery	49	164	977	730	1	38,450
Riots	637	1,228	2,558	2,002	106	348,232
Arson	!	48	96	64	7	12,572
Dowry death	!	50	73	56	23	24,418
Grand total	1,215	3,254	8,779	3,869	236	275,165

* The figures for 1994 are incomparable, as they do not include boys between the ages of 16 and 18, who were not included within the definition of juvenility in that year.
! = Data not collected
Source: Crime in India 2012, table 10.8, read with table 12.1, available http://ncrb.nic.in/; Crime in India 2004, table 10.2, available at http://ncrb.nic.in/ciiprevious/data/cd-CII2004/cii-2004/Table%2010.2.pdf; and Crime in India 1995, table 43, available at http://ncrb.nic.in/ciiprevious/Data/CII1995/cii-1995/Table-43.pdf.

The number of children involved in violent crime in India is in stark contrast to the very high rate of violent crime for children in the United States, as shown in table 4.4. It is also minuscule in comparison to violent crime committed by adults in India in the year 2012, as shown in table 4.6.

After the December rape case, there were demands to exclude from juvenile justice children between the ages of 16 and 18 who commit serious offenses, such as murder and rape by boys. In real terms, we are looking at the figure of 1,698 boys or 1,718 children in the 16–18 age group for transfer to ordinary criminal courts, or a total of 3,869 children in total for all the violent offenses listed in table 4.6. And this number is only of those who were arrested for the offense mentioned. All of them have not been found to have committed the offense.

A look at the disposal of cases shows that the number of children who may need institutional care is even smaller than this.[157] Out of a total 39,822 children arrested in India in 2012, 2,572 were acquitted or otherwise disposed of, and only 18,529 children were found to have committed any offense. The cases of 10,721 children were pending disposal; 9,677 children were sent to special homes. While this means that almost 50% of the children found to have committed the offense were sent to special homes, which is not as per the mandate of the Beijing Rules, it is still a minuscule number compared to 61,423 children in the US placed in residential facilities in 2009–2010.[158] Surely, India with its population of more than 1.2 billion and rising economy can find the required human and other resources to provide for these children's individualized care and rehabilitation.

There is no scientific evidence available to show that these children do not have the potential of reformation or that all these children are beyond redemption. On the contrary, as pointed out by Jonathan Lippman, the chief judge of the state of New York with more than 40 years of experience in the justice system, who submitted a bill to the New York State legislature to raise the age of criminal responsibility in nonviolent crimes to 18 years,

Adolescents, even older adolescents, are different from adults. In particular, their brains are not fully matured. This limits their ability to make reasoned judgments and engage in the kind of thinking that weighs risks and consequences. Teenagers have difficulty with impulse control and with resisting outside influences and peer pressure. They lack the capacity to fully appreciate the future consequences of their actions. At the same time, the systems in the brain that control emotions are highly activated, leading some to describe the teenage brain as "all drive and no brakes." In addition to being more immature, the teenage brain is also more "plastic," meaning that it is more malleable and capable of change.[159]

Transfer to Ordinary Criminal Justice

The critiques of the JJA 2000 demanded transfer of the child offender in the December rape case so that he could be given the adult punishment for the adult crime. Some demanded the death penalty; others demanded imprisonment for him without parole. In the current scenario, a person convicted of rape is liable to be sent to prison for a mandatory minimum sentence of seven years,[160] 10 years,[161] or 20 years,[162] and these sentences are extendable to life imprisonment, life imprisonment without parole, and even death.

These demands are completely against the international development and directions of the UN Committee on the Rights of the Child. From 2005 to 2008, the death penalty was given to children only in Iran, Saudi Arabia, Sudan, Pakistan, and Yemen.[163] The United States, which was among those countries, abolished the death penalty for children in 2005.[164] The death penalty and life imprisonment without parole are categorically prohibited by the CRC for children who commit an offense.[165] As it is, India falls short of the direction of the CRC Committee, which has recommended 12 years as the minimum age of criminal responsibility and nontransfer of children to adult proceedings until the age of 18.[166] India will come under a lot of criticism for introducing such a barbaric and cruel punishment for children.

Long-term imprisonment has long been recognized to result in institutionalized personality traits.[167] It is ironic that we seek to prepare persons for freedom by taking it away, to make them responsible citizens by not giving them any responsibility, to make them independent thinkers by denying them any opportunity for decision making for a long time. Sending a child of around 17 years to prison for seven or 10 or

20 years may provide some short-term satisfaction to the victims and satisfy their demand for "justice," but it has more adverse effects on the protection of individual victims as well as for society at large. The child of 17 years will be released at the age of 24 or 27 or 37 years for rape, depending on the category of rape. At that age, with this history of being in prison, there is little likelihood of the child getting a job; he is more likely to have lost ties and bonding with his family; he will find it difficult to find a suitable marriage partner; he is more likely to have links and relationships with other criminals; and he is likely to be suffering from institutionalized personality traits. Such a person is more likely to be a threat to society than a robust citizen.

The *New York Times* has reported that "teenagers prosecuted in adult courts or who do time in adult jails fare worse in life and can go on to commit more violent crimes than those who are handled by the juvenile justice system. . . . These facts argue for steering adolescents into the juvenile justice system, where they can receive rehabilitative services and be spared adult criminal convictions that banish them to society's margins and make it virtually impossible for them to find jobs."[168]

Transfer of children from juvenile justice is a serious business with serious repercussions for children and society and must not be done without scientific reasons for doing so. Janet C. Hoeffel considers the transfer of a child from juvenile justice as severe as the imposition of the death penalty in the adult criminal justice system and believes it needs to be guided as strictly as the imposition of the death penalty:

> The parallels between the death penalty and juvenile transfer are striking. Both involve a decision to expose a person to the most severe set of penalties available to the relevant justice system: a death sentence for adults in adult court; a transfer to adult court for youth in juvenile court. The decision to send an adult to his death is a decision to end his life; the decision to send a juvenile to adult court is a decision to end his childhood. Both decisions signify a life not worth saving.[169]

Once transfer is permitted, it may lead to transfer of children as young as 10 years old, even though the "breadth of eligibility for children as young as ten defies scientific research as to the competency, culpability, and capabilities of adolescents."[170]

Adolescent Brain

The United States was the pioneer in introducing the concept of juvenile courts with the *parens patriae* doctrine in late 19th century and later reversed its policies, permitting severe punishments for children with the sharp increase in juvenile delinquency in the 20th century.[171] However, the US is now witnessing a reversal, with abolition of the death penalty for juvenile crime in 2005, followed by the abolition of life imprisonment without parole for juveniles. The US Supreme Court in *Roper v. Simmons* while abolishing the death penalty for offenses committed by children below the age of 18, gave three reasons for treating children differently from adults:

1. "A lack of maturity and an underdeveloped sense of responsibility are found in youth more often than in adults and are more understandable among the young."
2. "Juveniles are more vulnerable or susceptible to negative influences and outside pressures, including peer pressure."
3. "The character of a juvenile is not as well formed as that of an adult. The personality traits of juveniles are more transitory, less fixed."[172]

Following *Roper*, the US Supreme Court in *Graham v. Florida* held that the sentence of life in prison without parole for nonhomicidal offenses was cruel and unusual punishment barred by the Eighth Amendment. It observed, "A life without parole sentence improperly denies the juvenile offender a chance to demonstrate growth and maturity."[173] It further extended the prohibition of life without parole for all juvenile crime in *Miller v. Alabama*.[174] "Groups as diverse as the American Psychological Association, the American Academy of Child and Adolescent Psychiatry, the American Psychiatric Association, the Council of Juvenile Correctional Administrators, the American Bar Association, mental health professionals, former juvenile court judges, criminologists, victims, and national advocacy organizations filed amicus briefs in the cases to urge the Court to give children an opportunity to have their sentences reviewed later in life."[175]

Laurence Steinberg was the lead scientist involved in preparation of the amicus brief submitted by the American Psychological Association to the US Supreme Court, which resulted in the historic judgments in *Roper v. Simmons, Graham v. Florida, and Miller v. Alabama*.[176] He presented incontrovertible evidence to show that adolescence is a period of significant changes in brain structure and function. He points out four structural differences between the adult and adolescent brain:

> First, there is a decrease in gray matter in prefrontal regions of the brain, reflective of synaptic pruning, the process through which unused connections between neurons are eliminated. . . . Second, important changes in activity involving the neurotransmitter dopamine occur during early adolescence, especially around puberty. . . . Third, there is an increase in white matter in the prefrontal cortex during adolescence. . . . Fourth, there is an increase in the strength of connections between the prefrontal cortex and the limbic system.[177]

Steinberg further points out that due to these structural differences, the adolescent brain functions differently than the adult brain in the following three ways. First, adolescents are not able to use the wider network of brain regions used by adults while doing tasks requiring self-control. Second, the adolescent brain responds to rewards more actively than occurs in adults or children. This hypersensitivity is more pronounced in the company of friends. Third, very strong feelings are less likely to be modulated by the brain regions that control impulses, planning ahead, and doing cost-benefit analyses for alternative courses of action.

It is opportune that science has now confirmed what was known to all for centuries. For long and for various purposes, law has distinguished children below the age of 18, and 18 years continue to be the age of majority, of marriage for girls, for entering into a contract, and for obtaining a driver's license, to name a few. Now scientific tests have conclusively proved that adolescents do not have the same capacity to control their impulses, especially risk-taking impulses. The case for continuing the all-inclusive and protective approach of juvenile justice in India is not based on juveniles' ability to distinguish right from wrong but on their inability to control their impulses. Their brains are not wired fully in all aspects of their lives, and they may be mature or impulsive in different spheres of their lives at the same time. Their potential for reform is much greater due to their growing capacities, and juvenile justice must secure the space for them to achieve that.

In conclusion, it cannot be overemphasized that what is needed in India is *implementation* and not reform of the law. The Supreme Court has played a key role in the enactment and implementation of the first uniform law governing juvenile justice, namely, the Juvenile Justice Act of 1986. It has been again issuing various directions for implementation of the JJA 2000 in the two public interest litigations before it, namely, *Sampurna Behrua* and *Bachpan Bachao Andolan*, but a lot remains to be accomplished both quantitatively and qualitatively to achieve the laudable objectives of reformation, reintegration, and rehabilitation of children who are dealt with under the JJA 2000. One hopes that while the Supreme Court continues to play its role, the executive branch will also give its prime attention to implementation of the act. What must be recognized is that juvenile justice in India has not achieved what it set out to achieve, due to lack of implementation and not due to faults in the provisions of the JJA 2000 or other legislation preceding it.

Another aspect that requires urgent attention is data relating to all aspects of juvenile justice—from the number of children in each category falling within the purview of the legislation to arrests, time taken for disposing of their cases, duration of their stay in various institutions, recidivism, and rehabilitation and aftercare. The National Crime Records Bureau has been publishing annually its *Crime in India*, but many of the aspects just mentioned are not available in this publication. Important information regarding the religious and community background of children involved in commission of offenses, which had been given up to 1987, has gone missing since 1988, ostensibly because no connection was found between delinquency and the religious and community background of the children arrested.[178] The accuracy of other data is also not beyond suspicion. Accurate and substantive data is a precondition for adequate and effective implementation of the law as well as for future policy and planning.

NOTES

1. The act did not extend to the state of Jammu and Kashmir, which enjoys a special status under article 370 of the Indian Constitution.

2. Smriti Singh and Manoj Mitta, "Nirbhaya Case Juvenile Wasn't 'Most Brutal'?," *Times of India*, 3 October 2013, http://timesofindia.indiatimes.com/city/delhi/Nirbhaya -case-juvenile-wasnt-most-brutal/articleshow/23426346.cms.

3. Flavia Agnes, "The Rule of Sentiments," *Asian Age*, 18 September 2013, http:// www.asianage.com/columnists/rule-sentiment-358.

4. For example, a child throwing filth on a public road was not liable for punishment but only an admonition and made to clean it, while an adult in similar circumstances was required to pay a fine and made to clean the filth, under the Hindu law as contained in Pandit Tulsiram Swamina, ed., *Manusmriti Bharatdesh Bhashanuvad Sanhita*, p. 390 *Shloka* 283 (1982 Vikrami Samvat) (Sanskrit-Hindi translation of Manusmriti).

5. For example, as per C. Hamilton, trans., *The Hedaya or Guide: A Commentary on the Mussulman Law*, 2nd ed. (1870), 187, a young boy committing whoredom with a consenting adult woman under the Muslim law was not subject to punishment.

6. Indian Penal Code § 82.

7. Indian Penal Code § 83.

8. *Indian Jail Committee Report 1864*, 20 (1864).

9. *A Collection of the Acts Passed by the Governor General of India in Council in the Year 1864* (Calcutta: T. Cutter, Military Orphan Press, 1865), Act VI, available at http:// lawmin.nic.in/legislative/textofcentralacts/1864.pdf.

10. Ibid., § X.

11. *Report of the Indian Jail Committee 1889*, April 1889, 20.

12. Legislative Department, proceeding, March 1876, nos. 23–24, National Archives of India.

13. E.g., Madras, Burma, Bihar and Orissa, the Central Provinces, Bombay, and Delhi.

14. *Report of the Indian Jails Committee, 1919–20* (London: H.M. Stationery Office, 1921), 202, available at https://ia700508.us.archive.org/16/items/eastindiajailsco01indi/ eastindiajailsco01indi.pdf.

15. Resolution of the Government of the United Provinces, No. 2985, 2 August 1913, mentioned in ibid., 201.

16. Ibid.

17. Bengal (1922), Bombay (1924), Andhra (adopted the Madras Children Act 1920), Delhi (1941), Mysore (1943), Travancore (1945), Cochin (1946), and Punjab (1949).

18. Prior to this amendment, states were classified as A, B, and C. Later, they were divided into states and union territories.

19. By 1986, when the first uniform legislation for delinquent children was passed in India, all states except Bihar had their own Children Act. Bihar was governed by the Children Ordinance of 1980.

20. *Sheela Barse v. Union of India*, AIR 1986 SC 1773.

21. The state of Jammu and Kashmir has special status under article 370 of the Constitution of India, because of which laws passed by Parliament need to be adopted by the state assembly for application in that state.

22. *Rohtas v. State of Haryana*, AIR 1979 SC 1839; *Raghbir v. State of Haryana*, 1981 Cri LJ 1497.

23. 1992 Cri LJ 3194 (Gau).

24. Section 25 of the TADA provided, "Overriding Effect—The provisions of this Act or any rule made thereunder or any order made under such rule shall have effect notwithstanding anything inconsistent therewith contained in any enactment other than this Act or in any instrument having effect by virtue of any enactment other than this Act."

25. 1993 Cri LJ 1908 (Ori).

26. 1995 Cri LJ 330 (Ker).

27. (2000) 6 SCC 759.

28. AIR 2004 SC 3317.

29. UN Committee on the Rights of the Child, *Concluding Observations of the Committee on the Rights of the Child in India in Its 23rd Sessions* (2000), http://tbinternet.ohchr.org/_layouts/treatybodyexternal/Download.aspx?symbolno=CRC%2fC%2f15%2fAdd.115&Lang=en.

30. JJA 2000, opening statement.

31. Ibid., preamble.

32. Ibid., § 2(l).

33. IPC, § 82.

34. Ibid., § 83.

35. There is no specified criterion for this classification, and one needs to consult schedule 1 of the Code of Criminal Procedure of 1973 to find out the classification, though the general understanding is that serious offenses are nonbailable and cognizable. See CrPC, § 2(a) and (c).

36. Ibid., § 436. The accused is entitled to be released on bail as a matter of right in these cases.

37. Ibid., § 437. The judge has the discretion to grant bail and may grant bail on being satisfied that the accused is not likely to interfere in the investigation and will cooperate in the trial.

38. Ibid., § 2(c). The police may arrest the accused without warrant in this category of offenses.

39. Ibid., § 2(l). An order of magistrate is required for arrest in these cases.

40. JJA 2000, § 12.

41. *Master Abhishek (Minor) v. State*, 2005 VI AD Delhi 18. See also, Dev Vrat (Minor) v. Govt. of NCT of Delhi; Crl. Rev. P. 588/2006 decided on 10.09.2006; Manoj @ Kali v. State of NCT of Delhi, MANU/DE/8755/2006.

42. CrPc, § 2(x).

43. Ibid., § 2(v).

44. JJA 2000, § 54.

45. Model Rules 2007, Rule 13.

46. Ibid., Rule 13(3).

47. Ibid., Rule 13(4).

48. Ibid., Rule 14.

49. 1969 Guj. L.R. 66.

50. JJA 2000, § 4.

51. Ibid., § 52(2).

52. See the annual official publication of the National Crime Records Bureau, Government of India, *Crime in India 2012*, table 10.14, available at www.ncrb.nic.in.

53. As reported in the *Times of India* (New Delhi), 5 November 2007, 17, the National Family Health Survey III, conducted in 29 states, showed that nationally only 41% of children under the age of five had their birth registered with civil authorities. In the households in the lowest wealth strata, the registration of births was 25%, and "only one in ten had a birth certificate."

54. See Model Rules 2007, Rule 12.

55. IPC, § 53.

56. JJA 2000, § 15.

57. Ibid., proviso to § 16(1).

58. Ibid., proviso to § 16(2).

59. Ibid., § 16(1).

60. Ibid., § 15(1)(d).

61. See ibid., chap. IV.

62. Ibid., § 2(k). This clause uses two terms, "child" and "juvenile," to refer to a person who is under the age of 18 and uses "juvenile" in connection with persons under age 18 who are alleged or found to have committed an offense. I have preferred to use the term *child* for all persons under age 18, because of its nonstigmatizing nature.

63. *V. Lakshminarayana v. State*, 1992 Cri LJ 334 (AP); *Sheo Mangal Singh v. State*, 1990 Cri LJ 1698 (Luck Bench); *Umesh Chandra v. State of Rajasthan*, 1982 Cri LJ 994; *Dilip Saha v. State of West Bengal*, 1979 Cri LJ 88 (FB); *Gobinda Chandra v. State of West Bengal*, 1977 Cri LJ 1501 (Cal) (DB).

64. 1982 Cri LJ 994.

65. AIR 2000 SC 2264.

66. Ved Kumari, "In Defence of *Arnit Das v. State of Bihar*: A Rejoinder," (2002) 2 SCC (Jour) 15; Ved Kumari, "Relevant Date for Applying the Juvenile Justice Act," (2000) 6 SCC (Jour) 9; B. B. Pande, "Rethinking Juvenile Justice: Arnit Das Style," (2000) 6 SCC (Jour) 1. *Contra*, R. D. Jain, "In Defence of *Arnit Das v. State of Bihar*: A Critique," (2001) 2 SCC (Jour) 10.

67. Pande, "Rethinking Juvenile Justice."

68. Kumari, "In Defense of *Arnit Das v. State of Bihar*"; Kumari, "Relevant Date for Applying the Juvenile Justice Act."

69. *Arnit Das v. State of Bihar*, 2001 (6) Supreme 461.

70. (2005) 3 SCC 551 (2 February 2005).

71. Section 20 read, "Notwithstanding anything contained in this Act, all proceedings in respect of a juvenile pending in any court in any area on the date on which this Act comes into force in that area, shall be continued in that court as if this Act had not been passed and if the court finds that the juvenile has committed an offence, it shall record such finding and instead of passing any sentence in respect of the juvenile, forward the juvenile to the Board which shall pass orders in respect of that juvenile in accordance with the provisions of this Act as if it had been satisfied on inquiry under this Act that a juvenile has committed the offence."

72. Section 64 read, "Juvenile in conflict with law undergoing sentence at commencement of this Act.—In any area in which this Act is brought into force, the State Government or the local authority may direct that a juvenile in conflict with law who is undergoing any sentence of imprisonment at the commencement of this Act, shall, in lieu of undergoing such sentence, be sent to a special home or be kept in fit institution in such manner as the State Government or the local authority thinks fit for the remainder of the period of the sentence; and the provisions of this Act shall apply to the juvenile as if he had been ordered by the Board to be sent to such special home or institution or, as the case may be, ordered to be kept under protective care under subsection (2) of section 16 of this Act."

73. Section 2(l) as amended reads, "'juvenile in conflict with law' means a juvenile who is alleged to have committed an offence and has not completed eighteenth year of age as on the date of commission of such offence."

74. The explanation inserted in sections 20 and 64 reads, "Explanation—In all pending cases including trial, revision, appeal or any other criminal proceedings in respect of a juvenile in conflict with law, in any court, the determination of juvenility of such a juvenile shall be in terms of clause (l) of section 2, even if the juvenile ceases to be so on or before the date of commencement of this Act and the provisions of this Act shall apply as if the said provisions had been in force, for all purposes and at all material times when the alleged offence was committed."

75. *Jameel v. State of Maharashtra*, AIR 2007 SC 971; *Jyoti Prakash Rai @ Jyoti Prakash*, AIR 2008 SC 1696; *Balu @ Bakthvatchalu*, AIR 2008 SC 1434; *Vimal Chadha*, (2008) 8 SCALE 608; *Babloo Pasi*, (2008) 13 SCALE 137; *Ranjit*, (2008) 9 SCC 453.

76. 2009 (6) SCALE 695.

77. Ibid., para. 37.

78. Proviso to section 7A reads, "A claim of juvenility may be raised before any court and it shall be recognised at any stage, even after final disposal of the case, and such claim shall be determined in terms of the provisions contained in this Act and the rules made thereunder, even if the juvenile has ceased to be so on or before the date of commencement of this Act."

79. Section 1(4) reads, "Notwithstanding anything contained in any other law for the time being in force, the provisions of this Act shall apply to all cases involving detention, prosecution, penalty or sentence of imprisonment of juveniles in conflict with law under such other law."

80. JJA 2000, § 2(h).

81. Ibid., § 37.

82. A toll-free number is manned around the clock by an authorized nongovernmental organization and may be reached by the child or anybody else to inform about a child in need of assistance.

83. JJA 2000, §§ 10, 32.

84. Ibid., § 63.

85. CRC, art. 7.

86. Ibid., art. 20.

87. JJA 2000, § 41.

88. Rajya Sabha Debates, 20 December 2000, 332.

89. JJA 2000, § 2 (aa).

90. Writ Petition (Civil) No. 470 OF 2005, decided 19 February 2014, available at http://supremecourtofindia.nic.in/outtoday/wp4702005.pdf.

91. Ibid.

92. Ibid.

93. Ibid.

94. JJA 2000, § 42.

95. Ibid., § 44(b).

96. Ibid., § 43.

97. Ministry of Women and Child Development, Government of India, *India: Third and Fourth Combined Periodic Report on the Convention on the Rights of the Child* (New Delhi: Government of India, 2011), available at http://wcd.nic.in/crc3n4/crc3n4_1r.pdf.

98. For example, see Justice Amar Saran, Chairman, Committee Dealing with Juvenile Homes, "Report on Homes under the JJA in UP" (12 July 2011). In the recent past, escapes and rioting in the observation and special homes in Delhi have shined a light on the bad conditions in these homes. See Maria Akram, "Juveniles Set Home on Fire, Vandalize Building," *Times of India*, 18 December 2013, http://timesofindia.indiatimes .com/city/delhi/Juveniles-set-home-on-fire-vandalize-building/articleshow/27550159 .cms; Express News Service, "NHRC Calls for Security Review of Juvenile Homes in Delhi," *Indian Express*, 15 March 2014, http://indianexpress.com/article/cities/delhi/ nhrc-calls-for-security-review-of-juvenile-homes-in-delhi/.

99. For details, see the Ministry of Women and Child Development's ICPS website: http://wcd.nic.in/icpsmon/home1.aspx.

100. Human Rights Law Network, "Sampurna Behrua vs. Union of India & Others," last modified 1 July 2008, http://hrln.org/hrln/child-rights/pils-a-cases/4-sampurna -behrua-vs-union-of-india-a-others.html.

101. Punjab, Bihar, Orissa, Madhya Pradesh, Uttar Pradesh, Rajasthan, West Bengal, Maharashtra, Manipur, Gujarat, Karnataka, and Uttaranchal.

102. Human Rights Law Network, "Sampurna Behrua vs. Union of India & Others."

103. For example, see the order of 12 October 2011, focusing on establishment of special juvenile police units, available at http://indiankanoon.org/doc/150571/; and the order dated 19 August 2011, directing free legal aid to children, available at http://judis .nic.in/temp/473200531982011p.txt;

104. These orders are available at http://courtnic.nic.in/supremecourt/caseno_listed_1.asp?cno=473%20&ctype=3&cyear=2005&frmname=causedisp&petname=SAMPURNA%20BEHRUA%20%20%20%20%20%20%20%20%20%20%20%20%20%20%20%20%20%20%20%20%20%20%20%20&resname=UNION%20OF%20INDIA%20&%20ORS.

105. The order is available at http://judis.nic.in/temp/473200531092013p.txt.

106. Writ Petition (C) No. 51 of 2006, order dated 18 April 2011, available at http://indiankanoon.org/doc/1849142/.

107. Ibid.

108. The series of orders passed in this case by the Supreme Court are available at http://courtnic.nic.in/supremecourt/causedisp.asp.

109. For example, *Court on Its Own Motion v. Govt. of NCT of Delhi*, WP (C) 1801/2008, decided 3 March 2009.

110. *Harsh Virmani vs. Government of National Capital Territory Delhi*, WPC No. 6988/2007, decided on 2nd February 2009.

111. Special Police Unit for Women and Children, "Delhi Police and Juvenile Justice," http://dpjju.com/index.php?option=com_content&view=article&id=48:delhi-police-and-juvenile-justice&catid=34:general&Itemid=59.

112. Department of Women and Child Development, *Manual for Trainers: Training on Juvenile Justice System for Police Officials* (October 2009), available at http://dpjju.com/images/stories/pdf1/Manual_for_Trainers.pdf.

113. Delhi Police, Standing Order No. 68/2012, available at http://dpjju.com/images/stories/circularsNso/SO68.pdf.

114. Central Level Monitoring Reports: Quarter II (2012–13), available at http://wcddel.in/pdf/IInd_Format_Central_Monitoring2012_13.xlsx; Quarter I (2012–13), available at http://wcddel.in/pdf/Ist_Quarter_Format2012_13.xlsx; Quarter IV (2011–12), available at http://wcddel.in/pdf/IVth%20QUARTER%2011-12.pdf; Quarter III (2011–12), available at http://wcddel.in/pdf/IIIrd%20QUARTER%2011-12.pdf; Quarter II (2011–12), available at http://wcddel.in/pdf/IInd_QUARTER%2011-12.pdf; Quarter I (2011–12), available at http://wcddel.in/pdf/Ist%20QUARTER%2011-12.pdf.

115. This exercise was motivated by my experience with the case of *Ram Deo Chauhan*. See the text later in the chapter.

116. For more details, see, Ved Kumari, "Construction of Criminality and Children," in *Essex Human Rights Review—UKIERI Special Issue: Realising Children's Rights: Multidisciplinary, Comparative and Practical Perspectives*, December 2010, available at http://projects.essex.ac.uk/ehrr/V7N1/Kumari.pdf.

117. For example, *Umesh Chandra*, AIR 1982 SC 1057; *Rajinder Chandra*, (2002) 2 SCC 287; *Hari Ram*, 2009 (6) SCALE 695; *Salil Bali*, Writ Petition (c) No. 10 of 2013 (judgment date 17 July 2013).

118. For more details, see, Ved Kumari, "Juvenile Justice in Focus," in *Criminal Justice: A Human Rights Perspective of the Criminal Justice Process in India*, 2nd ed., ed. K. I. Vibhute (Oxford: Oxford University Press, forthcoming).

119. *Ram Deo Chauhan @ Rajnath Chauhan v. State of Assam*, (2000) 7 SCC 455.

120. *Ram Deo Chauhan @ Rajnath Chauhan v. State of Assam*, (2001) 5 SCC 714.

121. *Bani Kant Das and Another v. State of Assam and Others*, Civil Original Jurisdiction Writ Petition (Civil) No. 457 of 2005 (date of judgment 8 May 2009).

122. *Ram Deo Chauhan v. Bani Kant Das*, Review Petition (C) No. 1378 of 2009 in Writ Petition (C) No. 457 of 2005 (date of judgment 19 November 2010).

123. Assam High Court, PIL No. 39/2011 (disposed of on 9 August 2011).

124. *Essa @ Anjum Abdul Razak Memon v. State of Maharashtra Tr.Stf, CBI*, decided on 21 March 2013, available at http://indiankanoon.org/doc/145541813/.

125. Criminal Appeal Nos. 653 and 656 of 2008, as part of the judgment given in *Essa @ Anjum Abdul Razak Memon v. State of Maharashtra Tr.Stf, CBI*.

126. Section 1(4) of the JJA 2000 reads, "Notwithstanding anything contained in any other law for the time being in force, the provisions of this Act shall apply to all cases involving detention, prosecution, penalty or sentence of imprisonment of juveniles in conflict with law under such other law."

127. Section 20 of the JJA 2000 reads,

> Special provision in respect of pending cases.—Notwithstanding anything contained in this Act, all proceedings in respect of a juvenile pending in any court in any area on the date on which this Act comes into force in that area, shall be continued in that court as if this Act had not been passed and if the court finds that the juvenile has committed an offence, it shall record such finding and instead of passing any sentence in respect of the juvenile, forward the juvenile to the Board which shall pass orders in respect of that juvenile in accordance with the provisions of this Act as if it had been satisfied on inquiry under this Act that a juvenile has committed the offence. Provided that the Board may, for any adequate and special reason to be mentioned in the order, review the case and pass appropriate order in the interest of such juvenile.
>
> Explanation.—In all pending cases including trial, revision, appeal or any other criminal proceedings in respect of a juvenile in conflict with law, in any court, the determination of juvenility of such a juvenile shall be in terms of clause (l) of section 2, even if the juvenile ceases to be so on or before the date of commencement of this Act and the provisions of this Act shall apply as if the said provisions had been in force, for all purposes and at all material times when the alleged offence was committed.

128. *Essa @ Anjum Abdul Razak Memon vs. State of Maharashtra Tr.Stf, CBI*, para. 383.

129. Criminal Appeal No. 1623 of 2013, available at http://judis.nic.in/supremecourt/imgs1.aspx?filename=40857.

130. That is, the Probation of Offenders Act of 1958, which directs compulsory release of offenders below the age of 21 on probation.

131. Criminal Appeal No. 1623 of 2013 (Arising Out of SLP (Crl.) No. 2817 of 2013), decided on 13 October 2013, para. 12, available at http://judis.nic.in/supremecourt/imgs1.aspx?filename=40857.

132. Ibid., para. 13.

133. Ibid., para. 21.

134. Rule 19, UN Standard Minimum Rules for the Administration of Juvenile Justice 1985.

135. From *Crime in India 2012*, table 10.13, available at http://ncrb.nic.in/.

136. Under section 16(2) proviso of the JJA, a place of protective custody for holding children above the age of 16 who commit serious offenses is referred to as "place of safety" by personnel, though "place of safety" has been defined by section 2(q) differently.

137. Decided on 17 July 2013, available at http://judis.nic.in/supremecourt/imgs1 .aspx?filename=40577.

138. Criminal Appeal No. 695 of 2014, available at http://judis.nic.in/supremecourt/ imgs1.aspx?filename=41356.

139. W.P.(C) Nos. 14, 42, 85, 90, and 182 of 2013 with W.P.(CRL) No. 6 of 2013 and T.C.(C) No. 82 of 2013, decided on 17 July 2013, available at http://judis.nic.in/supreme court/imgs1.aspx?filename=40577.

140. Para. 27 of the application under § 302 of the Code of Criminal Procedure.

141. *Dr. Subramanian Swamy and Ors. v. Raju through Member Juvenile Justice Board*, Criminal Appeal No. 695 of 2014, admitted on 22 August 2013, available at http://indiankanoon.org/doc/170216295/.

142. Quoted with emphasis and approval in the judgment given on 18 February 2014 in *Dr. Subramanian Swamy*, Criminal Appeal No. 695 of 2014, available at http:// judis.nic.in/supremecourt/imgs1.aspx?filename=41356.

143. See Abhinav Garg, "22 Boys Escape after Rioting, Arson at Delhi Juvenile Home," *Times of India*, 7 October 2013, http://timesofindia.indiatimes.com/city/delhi/ 22-boys-escape-after-rioting-arson-at-Delhi-juvenile-home/articleshow/23615860.cms.

144. On 3 April 2014, a sessions judge in Mumbai imposed the death penalty on adult offenders for repeated rape in the Shakti Mills rape case, which has been prominently covered in the national newspapers. See Rebecca Samervel, "Mumbai Shakti Mills Rape Cases: Death Penalty for 3 Repeat Offenders," *Times of India*, 4 April 2014, http://timesofindia.indiatimes.com/city/mumbai/Mumbai-Shakti-Mills-rape-cases -Death-penalty-for-3-repeat-offenders/articleshow/33238680.cms; Puja Changolwala, "Shakti Mills Gang-Rape: 3 Get Death, Another Gets Life," *Hindustan Times*, 4 April 2014, http://www.hindustantimes.com/india-news/mumbai-shakti-mills-gang-rape -case-3-repeat-offenders-get-death-life-term-for-1/article1-1204174.aspx; Sukanya Shantha, "Mumbai Shakti Mills Gangrape: All Three Convicts Sentenced to Death for Repeat Offence," *Indian Express*, 5 April 2014, http://indianexpress.com/article/ india/india-others/mumbai-shakti-mills-gangrape-all-three-convicts-sentenced -to-death-for-repeat-offence/; Rashmi Rajput, "Three Repeat Offenders Get Death Penalty in Shakti Mills Rape Case," *Hindu*, 5 April 2014, http://www.thehindu.com/ news/national/three-repeat-offenders-get-death-penalty-in-shakti-mills-rape-case/ article5871677.ece?textsize=large&test=1. This judgment was issued despite the written opposition by Majlis, the women's rights NGO that supported the victim throughout

the proceedings in court. See Flavia Agnes, "Not in Our Name," *Asian Age*, 28 March 2014, http://archive.asianage.com/columnists/not-our-name-600; and Flavia Agnes, "Opinion: Why I Oppose Death for Rapists," *Mumbai Mirror*, 5 April 2014, http://www.mumbaimirror.com/mumbai/cover-story/Opinion-Why-I-oppose-death-for-rapists/articleshow/33250078.cms.

145. IPC, § 376E. The death penalty is imposed in the case of repeat offenders of rape, even when it has not resulted in the death of the woman.

146. Ibid., §§ 376D, 376E.

147. UNICEF, *State of World's Children 2014*, http://www.unicef.org/sowc2014/numbers/.

148. Para. 49 of Writ Petition (C) No. 51 of 2006, order dated 18 April 2011, available at http://indiankanoon.org/doc/1849142/.

149. *Crime in India 2012*, chap. 10, p. 131, available at http://ncrb.nic.in/CD-CII2012/cii-2012/Chapter%2010.pdf.

150. Ibid., table 10.14.

151. Ibid., table 10.1.

152. Youth Justice Board / Ministry of Justice, "Executive Summary," in *Youth Justice Statistics 2012/13: England and Wales*, 30 January 2014, available at https://www.gov.uk/government/uploads/system/uploads/attachment_data/file/276098/youth-justice-stats-exec_summary.pdf.

153. Ibid.

154. US Department of Justice, Federal Bureau of Investigation, "Arrests by Age," table 38 in *Crime in the United States 2012*, available at http://www.fbi.gov/about-us/cjis/ucr/crime-in-the-u.s/2012/crime-in-the-u.s.-2012/tables/38tabledatadecoverview pdf.

155. US Department of Justice, Federal Bureau of Investigation, "Arrests: Persons under 15, 18, 21, and 25 Years of Age, 2012," table 41 in *Crime in the United States 2012*, available at http://www.fbi.gov/about-us/cjis/ucr/crime-in-the-u.s/2012/crime-in-the-u.s.-2012/tables/41tabledatadecoverviewpdf.

156. US Department of Justice, Office of Juvenile Justice and Delinquency Prevention, "Juvenile Arrest Rates by Offense, Sex, and Race (1980–2011)," available at http://www.ojjdp.gov/ojstatbb/crime/data.html.

157. *Crime in India 2012*, table 10.13.

158. Children's Defense Fund, *The State of America's Children 2014*, 2014, available at http://www.childrensdefense.org/child-research-data-publications/data/2014-soac.pdf?utm_source=2014-SOAC-PDF&utm_medium=link&utm_campaign=2014-SOAC.

159. Jonathan Lippman, "In Search of Meaningful Systemic Justice for Adolescents in New York," *Cardozo Law Review* 35 (2014): 1021, available at http://www.cardozolaw review.com/content/35-3/LIPPMAN.35.3.pdf.

160. IPC, § 375(1) for the offense of rape.

161. Ibid., § 375(2) for custodial rape.

162. Ibid., §§ 376A for causing death or persistent vegetative state of victim; 376D for gang rape.

163. See Human Rights Watch, "Iran, Saudi Arabia, Sudan: End Juvenile Death Penalty," 9 October 2010, http://www.hrw.org/news/2010/10/09/iran-saudi-arabia -sudan-end-juvenile-death-penalty.

164. *Roper v. Simmons*, 543 U.S. 551 (2005), available at http://www.csustan.edu/cj/ jjustice/CaseFiles/ROPER-v-Simmons.pdf.

165. CRC, art. 37(a).

166. UN Committee on the Rights of the Child, "Children's Rights in Juvenile Justice," General Comment No. 10 (2007), 44th session, Geneva, 15 January–2 February 2007, available at http://www2.ohchr.org/english/bodies/crc/docs/CRC.C.GC.10.pdf.

167. "Institutionalized Personality Traits are caused by living in oppressive environment that demands: passive compliance to the demands of authority figures, passive acceptance of severely restricted acts of daily living, the repression of personal lifestyle preferences, the elimination of critical thinking and individual decision making, and internalized acceptance of severe restriction on the honest self-expression thoughts and feelings." Terence T. Gorski, "Post Incarceration Syndrome and Relapse," The Addiction Web Site of Terence T. Gorski, http://www.tgorski.com/criminal_justice/ cjs_pics_&_relapse.htm (accessed 9 April 2014).

168. Editorial Board, "A Court Just for Juveniles in N.Y.," *New York Times*, 16 September 2013, http://www.nytimes.com/2013/09/17/opinion/a-court-just-for-juveniles -in-ny.html?_r=0.

169. Janet C. Hoeffel, "The Jurisprudence of Death and Youth: Now the Twain Should Meet," *Texas Tech Law Review* 46 (2013): 30, available at http://ssrn.com/ abstract=2354353.

170. Ibid., 32.

171. The juvenile arrest rate in the US continues to be very high, at 4,857 in 2010, though it has come down from 8,157 in 1994. The violent crime rate has fallen by 47%, to 224 in 2010 from 497 in 1994. Juvenile offenders were known to be involved in 8% of all homicides in 2010 in the US. National Institute of Justice, "Juveniles," http://www .crimesolutions.gov/TopicDetails.aspx?ID=5 (accessed 24 March 2014).

172. *Roper v. Simmons*, 543 U.S. 551 (2005), available at http://www.csustan.edu/cj/ jjustice/CaseFiles/ROPER-v-Simmons.pdf.

173. *Graham v. Florida*, 560 U.S. ____ (2010), available at http://njdc.info/wp -content/uploads/2013/11/Graham-Slip-Opinion.pdf.

174. *Miller v. Alabama*, No. 10-9646 (2012), with No. 10-9647, *Jackson v. Hobbs, Director, Arkansas Department of Correction*, on certiorari to the Supreme Court of Arkansas, decided on 25 June 2012, available at http://www.supremecourt.gov/ opinions/11pdf/10-9646g2i8.pdf.

175. Equal Justice Initiative, "Miller v. Alabama," http://www.eji.org/childrenprison/ deathinprison/miller (accessed 7 January 2014)..

176. Steinberg is a distinguished professor of psychology at Temple University and has written extensively about adolescents, including brain development, risk taking and decision making, parent-adolescent relationships, school-year employment, high

school reform, and juvenile justice. See his university webpage: https://www.cla.temple
.edu/psychology/faculty/laurence-steinberg/.

177. Laurence Steinberg, "Should the Science of Adolescent Brain Development
Inform Public Policy?," *Issues in Science and Technology*, Spring 2012, http://www
.issues.org/28.3/steinberg.html.

178. Data relating to the religious and community background of children, contained in *Crime in India* for the years 1980 to 1987, consistently reported that percentages of arrested children belonging to Hindu, Muslim, Christian, Sikh, and other
religions and those belonging to schedule castes and schedule tribes were proportionate to their percentage of the total population, and no significant connection was
found between their religion or community and apprehension. For example, see http://
ncrb.nic.in/ciiprevious/Data/CII1980/cii-1980/CHAPTER-5.pdf; http://ncrb.nic.in/
ciiprevious/Data/CII1985/cii-1985/TABLE-45.pdf; http://ncrb.nic.in/ciiprevious/Data/
CII1986/cii-1986/CHAPTER-5.pdf.

5

Myths and Realities of Juvenile Justice in Latin America

MARY BELOFF AND MÁXIMO LANGER

Latin America has been an almost forgotten region in the academic English-speaking literature on comparative juvenile justice systems.[1] A first goal of this chapter is to provide an overview of the history of Latin American juvenile justice systems until today. The evolution of Latin American juvenile justice presents two crucial moments: (1) its creation at the beginning of the twentieth century with the importation of the American model of juvenile courts and (2) its transformation in the past twenty-five years with the incorporation of international human rights law into domestic law. While in the first period Latin American laws conceived children and adolescents as subjects to be saved and treated, in the second period the laws have considered children and adolescents as rights bearers who have the same due process rights as adults and can be held criminally responsible, though subject to special regulations. Despite these differences, the two periods have actually been in agreement on their stated goals of removing children and adolescents from criminal law and responding to their deviant behavior with rehabilitative measures.

The second goal of this chapter is to assess whether the goal of juvenile justice of removing children and adolescents from criminal law has actually been put into action. This type of empirical assessment of Latin American juvenile justice systems is missing even in the Portuguese- and Spanish-speaking literatures. This chapter shows that throughout Latin America children and adolescents in conflict with the law are confined at substantially lower rates than are adults. On the basis of these findings, without denying other problems these systems present, we argue that Latin American juvenile justice systems have advanced their stated goal of removing children and adolescents from criminal law.

The third goal of this chapter is to start to assess the recent wave of juvenile justice reforms in Latin America by taking the Chilean reform as a case study. In the past twenty-five years, Latin American juvenile justice laws have undergone their deepest transformation since the creation of juvenile justice systems in the first half of the twentieth century. These reforms promised to bring more due process protections for juveniles and to use confinement only exceptionally and as a last resort. However, there have been almost no empirical assessments of the outcomes of these reforms, even in the Portuguese- and Spanish-speaking literatures. Even if Latin American juvenile justice systems remove a substantial number of children and adolescents from criminal law, as we show in this chapter, have these reforms made juvenile justice systems remove more or fewer children and adolescents from criminal law? By taking the Chilean law as a case study, this chapter shows that while the Chilean reform has brought more due process protections for deviant youth by reducing the percentage of juveniles in pretrial detention, it has likely substantially increased the absolute and relative levels of juvenile confinement.

Background and Early Regulations (until 1919)

Until the second decade of the twentieth century, Latin American countries did not have a comprehensive and specific mechanism like the juvenile court to deal with youth deviant behavior.[2] During the colonial era, the wars of independence in the early nineteenth century, and the process of constitutionalization in the second half of the nineteenth century, Latin America used medieval Spanish norms to deal with youth deviant conduct. The basic laws were the *Siete Partidas*, compiled in Castilla between 1256 and 1265, and other regulations such as the *Fuero Juzgo*, the *Leyes de Toro*, the *Nueva*, and the *Novísima Recopilación*.[3]

These Spanish regulations presented the following features: (1) they excluded from criminal responsibility and punishment children below the age of ten and a half; (2) they reduced the levels and kinds of punishment applicable to an intermediate category of children who were between ten and a half years and fourteen years, by considering factors such as the type of offense committed and whether the offender was male or female; and (3) they contemplated a few mitigating sentencing factors for young offenders under the age of sixteen by type of offense.

The lack of a substantial concern for juvenile crime as well as the long and complex process of state formation in Latin America help explain why these Spanish rules (in particular, the *Partidas*) regulated the handling of juvenile cases well into the nineteenth century. The passing of the first criminal codes by Latin American independent nations formally replaced the Spanish regulations but were still heavily influenced by them. For instance, in Argentina, such a code was adopted in 1886. In keeping with the *Partidas*, this code established that exempted from punishment were children under ten years of age (article 81(2)) as well as those between ten and fifteen years, "unless they acted with discernment" (article 81(3)).

The Creation and Spread of the Juvenile Court in Latin America (1919–1990)

The U.S. model of juvenile courts was introduced in Latin America in 1919. The adoption of this system (known in Latin America as the "tutelary system") was the most important change in Latin American policies toward youth in conflict with the law until this day. Under this model, youth crime had to be approached differently than adult crime, and the goal of the interventions on youth was supposed to be rehabilitation, not punishment.

Latin American discourse on youth delinquents echoed U.S. ones. For instance, echoing Enoch Wines, it was stated in the parliamentary debate on the Argentine Protection of Minors Bill in 1918, "The extremely high number of children that roam our streets and live like birds on the wastelands, in the public plazas, on the land regained from the river, in the gaps of the doorways and the filthiest slums . . . will become, as a result of the natural evolution of their irregular lifestyle, the largest contingent of the prisons of our Nation."[4]

Under the humanist slogan of "taking the minor away from criminal law" (criminal law understood fundamentally in a retributive sense), the tutelary system was supposed to adopt protective and educational measures for the benefit of the youth that aimed at their rehabilitation.

These criminological trends were supported by the older and well-established idea in civil and common law countries that the state should act in loco parentis—that is, subrogating the parental functions—in cases in which the minor did not have parents or the parents were considered incapable of carrying out their parental duties. For this reason, from the beginning, the juvenile court, as the specialized legal institution that dealt with children and adolescents who committed crimes, was associated with regulations and institutions on the protection of the child, such as the family court.

Between 1919 and the 1940s, almost all Latin American countries passed laws establishing juvenile courts or similar institutions. Inspired by the U.S. juvenile court, Argentina was the first country with the enactment of Law 10.903 (Law for the Welfare of Minors).[5] This law authorized the handing over to federal or provincial authorities of minors younger than eighteen years who had been abandoned, were placed in a situation of "moral or material danger" by their parents or caretakers, or were crime victims or offenders. This protection by the state (called *Patronato* in Argentina) had to be exercised to pursue the "health, security, moral and intellectual education of the minor" whose parents or caretakers did not provide adequate care (art. 4).

Similar mechanisms for the protection of children and adolescents were created in every Latin American country. For example, Brazil passed its first Code for Minors in 1927 and Uruguay in 1934. Chile passed its Law for the Protection of Minors in 1928, Costa Rica passed its Code for Infancy in 1932, Bolivia passed its National Welfare of Minors Agency in 1937, and Venezuela passed its Statute for Minors in 1949. Most of these institutions were placed within the judicial branch, though some countries such as the Andean countries and Mexico implemented their tutelary system as an administrative agency instead.

The criminal regulations on minors went on a somewhat different track. As already mentioned, influenced by the Spanish *Partidas*, the first Argentine Criminal Code of 1886 established ten years as the minimum age of criminal responsibility. It also established that the rule of discernment had to be used to determine whether individuals between ten and fifteen years were criminally responsible. Being less than eighteen years was considered a mitigating circumstance for sentencing purposes. In 1921, a new Criminal Code established fourteen years as the minimum age of criminal responsibility (art. 36). In the mid-1950s, the minimum age of criminal responsibility was raised to sixteen years.[6]

The criminal codes of all Latin American countries adopted similar regulations. A first group had a low minimum age of criminal responsibility (MACR) for the lowest age range, combined with the rule of discernment for the intermediate age range.[7] A second group had a higher MACR, and the tutelary regime for minors dealt with all cases that involved people under that age.[8]

Like juvenile courts in the United States, Latin American juvenile courts (or the administrative agencies that performed the same function) had broad and discretionary jurisdiction that ranged from taking care of abandoned or abused children (exercising the governmental intervention in loco parentis mentioned earlier) to the adjudication of cases of administrative violations and criminal offenses committed by juveniles. Thus, regardless of the minimum age of criminal responsibility, the stated central criterion for judges and administrative authorities to manage and decide on these cases was whether the child or adolescent was abandoned or at risk. If the minor was in one of these situations, he or she could be subjected to a protective measure, even if he or she was under the minimum age of criminal responsibility. Such measures included the institutionalization until the age of majority (twenty-one years old in the case of Argentina) of minors who did not have a family or whose family was incapable of taking care of them.

From the very beginning, one characteristic that distinguished the Latin American model of juvenile courts (either judicial or administrative) from the U.S. one was that Latin American juvenile courts used inquisitorial criminal proceedings to deal with their cases, as did almost all Latin American criminal courts for adults at the time. In the United States, the proceedings of the juvenile court disregarded due process not because adult criminal proceedings were inquisitorial but under a paternalistic rationale.[9] In this sense, the inquisitorial character of juvenile courts in the United States was always considered exceptional and otherwise alien to the U.S. justice system, even before *Kent* and *In Re Gault*. In contrast, in Latin America, both criminal and juvenile courts operated within inquisitorial frameworks until well into the 1990s.[10]

This broader inquisitorial framework may partially explain why the Latin American legal community and case law did not consider problematic the due process limitations of Latin American juvenile courts until the 1990s.[11]

The Recent Wave of Reforms on Juvenile Justice in Latin America (1990-Present)

Background of the Reforms

In the past twenty-five years, almost all Latin American Portuguese- and Spanish-speaking countries have introduced new laws on the rights of the child and on juvenile justice that replaced the laws of the classical tutelary system. The UN Convention on the Rights of the Child and other human rights instruments and transitions to democracy and concerns for juvenile crime in the region opened windows of opportunity for reforms in this area. Domestic, regional, and international reformers characterized the tutelary system as arbitrary and inefficient and, with the support of international donors, proposed reforms to Latin American juvenile justice as part of a broader package of criminal justice reforms.[12]

This process of reforms started with the Brazilian transition to democracy and the passing of the new Brazilian Constitution of 1988 that included two provisions on the rights of the child. Article 227 summarizes the provisions of the Declaration of the Rights of the Child[13] and establishes, among other regulations, that it is the "duty of the family, the society and the State to ensure children and adolescents the right to life, health, nourishment, education, leisure, professional training, culture, dignity, respect, freedom and family and community life, as well as to guard them from all forms of negligence, discrimination, exploitation, violence, cruelty and oppression." Article 228 of the Constitution says, "Minors under eighteen years of age may not be held criminally liable and shall be subject to the rules of the special legislation."[14]

This process of reforms has been influenced by the Convention on the Rights of the Child (CRC, or the Convention) that all Latin American countries ratified within a very short period of time between 1990 and 1991, as shown in table 5.1.

TABLE 5.1. Dates of Signature, Ratification, and Entry into Force of the CRC by Country (Latin America)

Country	Signature	Ratification	Entry into force
Argentina	June 29, 1990	December 4, 1990	January 3, 1991
Bolivia	March 8, 1990	June 26, 1990	September 2, 1990
Brazil	January 26, 1990	September 24, 1990	October 24, 1990
Chile	January 26, 1990	August 13, 1990	September 12, 1990
Colombia	January 26, 1990	January 28, 1991	February 27, 1991
Costa Rica	January 26, 1990	August 21, 1990	September 20, 1990
Cuba	January 26, 1990	August 21, 1991	September 20, 1991
Ecuador	January 26, 1990	March 23, 1990	September 2, 1990
El Salvador	January 26, 1990	July 10, 1990	September 2, 1990
Guatemala	January 26, 1990	June 6, 1990	September 2, 1990
Haiti	January 20, 1990	June 8, 1995	July 8, 1995
Honduras	May 31, 1990	August 10, 1990	September 9, 1990
Mexico	January 26, 1990	September 21, 1990	October 21, 1990
Nicaragua	February 6, 1990	October 5, 1990	November 4, 1990
Panama	January 26, 1990	December 12, 1990	January 11, 1991
Paraguay	April 4, 1990	September 25, 1990	October 25, 1990
Peru	January 26, 1990	September 4, 1990	October 4, 1990
Dominican Republic	August 8, 1990	June 11, 1991	July 11, 1991
Uruguay	January 26, 1990	November 20, 1990	December 20, 1990
Venezuela	January 26, 1990	September 13, 1990	October 13, 1990

Note: Does not include English-speaking countries from Latin America and the Caribbean, whose analysis of juvenile justice is beyond the scope of this chapter.

These data on the ratification process suggest that the Convention was popular across the wide political spectrum of Latin America, where eighteen of the twenty nations ratified the Convention within one year and every country except Haiti within two years. Reformers argued that the ratification of the CRC required the passing of new domestic laws on children's rights in general and on juvenile justice in particular to comply with the Convention's rules and standards. To advocate and argue for reforms, reformers and their allies also relied on the American Convention on Human Rights and on advisory opinions and decisions by the Inter-American Court of Human Rights on the rights of children and adolescents.[15] Reformers and their allies also argued that the tutelary system was undergoing a profound theoretical crisis because academic studies had put into question the etiological theories on criminal deviance and rehabilitation as a goal of juvenile confinement on which the tutelary system was based.[16]

As in the case of the parallel criminal procedure reforms that also spread through Latin America in the same period, broader phenomena also enabled the passing of the new juvenile justice and children's rights laws.[17] Transitions to democracy in the region as well as an increasing awareness about the phenomenon of the "street child" opened windows of opportunity to this reform program that presented the reforms as a way to improve due process and human rights standards for children and adolescents. Reformers maintained that the secrecy and the paternalistic rationales of the tutelary system deprived children and adolescents of their rights and gave room to unchecked discretion and abuses by tutelary system officials. Concerns about juvenile crime also enabled reformers to propose changes to juvenile systems that were perceived as inefficient.[18] Reformers argued that the written and secret proceedings that the classical tutelary system used were too protracted, formalistic, and unaccountable.

The Reforms to Juvenile Justice

Table 5.2 describes the reforms that Latin American countries introduced on juvenile justice in chronological order and including whether the juvenile justice reform was introduced as part of a more comprehensive regulation on the rights of children or in a statute focused specifically on juvenile justice.[19] For countries that have approved two or more laws in the period of study (since the ratification of the Convention until the present day), only the most recent regulation is mentioned.[20]

As can be noticed from this table, the wave of reforms has included not only changes to the juvenile justice system, which deals with children in conflict with the law, but also regulations on the protection of the rights of children through positive endowments by the state. As already mentioned, the arguments for the introduction of new legislation on crime committed by youth included that the classical tutelary system was arbitrary and inefficient and that it did not meet the international human rights standards set by the CRC and other international

TABLE 5.2. Recent Legislation on Juvenile Justice and Rights of the Child in Latin American Countries (1990–2014)

Country	Statute	Date	Type of legislation
Brazil	Statute on the Child and the Adolescent [Estatuto da Criança e do Adolescente], Act 8069, which was later complemented by National System of Socio-educational Services [Sistema Nacional de Atendimento Socio-educativo (Sinase)], Act 12594, which was passed on January 18, 2012	Approved on June 13, 1990	General legislation concerning children's rights
El Salvador	Youth Offender Act [Ley del Menor Infractor], Act 863	Approved on April 27, 1994; amended by Decree 395 of June 28, 2004, regarding its name and some specific articles	Special legislation on juvenile justice
Costa Rica	Juvenile Criminal Justice Act [Ley de Justicia Penal Juvenil], Act 7576	Approved on February 6, 1996; enacted on March 8, 1996; published and entered into force on April 30, 1996	Special legislation on juvenile justice
Honduras	Childhood and Adolescence Code [Código de la Niñez y de la Adolescencia], Act 73-96	Published on September 5, 1996	General legislation concerning children's rights
Nicaragua	The Childhood and Adolescence Code of Nicaragua [El Código de la Niñez y la Adolescencia de Nicaragua], Act 287	Approved on March 24, 1998; published on May 27, 1998	General legislation concerning children's rights
Panama	Special Regime of Criminal Responsibility for Adolescents [Régimen Especial de Responsabilidad Penal para la Adolescencia] (Law no. 40).	Approved on August 26, 1999; amended by Law 46, approved on June 6, 2003	General legislation concerning children's rights
Bolivia	Code of the Children and Adolescent [Código del Niño, Niña y Adolescente], Act 2026	Approved on October 27, 1999	General legislation concerning children's rights
Peru	New Code of the Children and Adolescents [Nuevo Código de los Niños y Adolescentes], Act 27337	Approved on July 21, 2000; enacted on August 2, 2000; published on August 7, 2000	General legislation concerning children's rights

TABLE 5.2. (*continued*)

Country	Statute	Date	Type of legislation
Paraguay	Childhood and Adolescence Code [Código de la Niñez y la Adolescencia], Act 1680/01	Approved on May 8, 2001	General legislation concerning children's rights
Ecuador	Childhood and Adolescence Code [Código de la Niñez y Adolescencia], Act 2002-100	Approved on December 23, 2002; published on January 3, 2003	General legislation concerning children's rights
Guatemala	Comprehensive Protection of the Childhood and Adolescence Act [Ley de Protección Integral de la Niñez y Adolescencia], Act 27-03	Approved on June 4, 2003; enacted on July 15, 2003; published on July 18, 2003	General legislation concerning children's rights
Dominican Republic	Code for the Protection System and the Fundamental Rights of Children and Adolescents [Código para el Sistema de Protección y los Derechos Fundamentales de Niños, Niñas y Adolescentes], Act 136-03	Approved on July 22, 2003; enacted on August 7, 2003	General legislation concerning children's rights
Uruguay	Childhood and Adolescence Code [Código de la Niñez y la Adolescencia], Act 17823	Enacted on September 7, 2004; published on September 14, 2004	General legislation concerning children's rights
Costa Rica	Enforcement of Juvenile Criminal Sentences Act [Ejecución de Sanciones Penales Juveniles], Act 8460	Passed on October 20, 2005; entered into force on November 28, 2005	Special legislation on juvenile justice
Colombia	Childhood and Infancy Code [Código de Niñez e Infancia], Act 1098	Passed and published on August 11, 2006	General legislation concerning children's rights
Mexico (Oaxaca)	Act of Justice for Adolescents of the State of Oaxaca [Ley de Justicia para Adolescentes del Estado de Oaxaca], Decree 306	Published on September 9, 2006.	Special legislation on juvenile justice
Mexico (Nuevo Leon)	Act of the Special Justice System for Adolescents of the State of Nuevo Leon [Ley del Sistema de Justicia Especial para Adolescentes del Estado de Nuevo Leon], Decree 415	Published on September 10, 2006	Special legislation on juvenile justice

(continued)

TABLE 5.2. (*continued*)

Country	Statute	Date	Type of legislation
Mexico (Chihuaha)	Act of Special Justice for Adolescent Offenders of the State of Chihuahua [Ley de Justicia Especial para Adolescentes Infractores del Estado de Chihuahua], Decree 618/06	Published on September 16, 2006	Special legislation on juvenile justice
Mexico (Zacatecas)	Act of Justice for Adolescents of the State of Zacatecas [Ley de Justicia para Adolescentes en el Estado de Zacatecas), Decree 311	Published on September 30, 2006	Special legislation on juvenile justice
Chile	Juvenile Criminal Responsibility Act [Ley de Sistema de Responsabilidad Penal de los Adolescentes], Act 20.084	Enacted on November 2005; published on December 7, 2005; entered into force on June 8, 2007	Special legislation on juvenile justice
Mexico (D.F.)	Law of Justice for Adolescents for the Federal District [Ley de Justicia Para Adolescentes para el distrito Federal]	Published on November 14, 2007; entered into force on October 6, 2008	Special legislation on juvenile justice
Venezuela	Organic Act for the Protection of Children and Adolescents [Ley Orgánica para la Protección de Niñas, Niños y Adolescentes]	Enacted on August 14, 2007; published on December 10, 2007	General legislation concerning children's rights
Mexico	Federal Act of Justice for Adolescents [Ley Federal de Justicia Para Adolescentes]	Published on December 27, 2012; entered into force on December 27, 2014	Special legislation on juvenile justice

documents.[21] The stated goals of the new legislation have included treating juveniles as rights bearers who have to be protected in their development and social integration, while preventing crime.[22]

Even if the new Latin American juvenile laws adopted the principles of the CRC and of other international instruments, these laws did not follow one single coherent theory or model. Leaving aside the Costa Rican legislation, which was heavily influenced by German law, Latin American countries generally drafted their laws using their own legislative models, which evolved based on the experience of other countries of the region that had already made changes to their legislation in this area. In the drafting of the new laws, there were also tensions and compromises between the principles of the classical tutelary system and the principles of the Convention and of the juvenile justice reformers, especially in the early laws. In addition, in the early years, there was no expertise in the region for the drafting of the new laws, given that the older juvenile justice experts had been raised in the classical tutelary system and that criminal law scholars had not been interested in this area.[23]

These factors help to explain why the laws passed at the beginning of the 1990s reveal serious legislative drafting problems and evident theoretical inconsistencies. This is especially evident in the passing of comprehensive codes on the rights of the child.[24] This trend started to change when laws specifically focused on juvenile justice were passed, such as those of El Salvador and Costa Rica,[25] and as a group of experts participated in the drafting of the new laws in more than one country and learned from previous experience.

Despite the fact that some countries such as Brazil have set the age of legal responsibility at eighteen years, this regulation did not eliminate the category of "young offenders." All countries in the region established a minimum criminal age and created a juvenile criminal law system separate from the adult criminal justice system. The formal law of this juvenile system includes diversionary mechanisms, due process protections, and special posttrial measures for juveniles—generally known as "measures" or "socioeducational measures" in the early laws and as "juvenile sentences" in more recent ones. The legislations establish that the term "juvenile offender" can only be used for those who have been declared criminally responsible. Generally, juvenile offenders may not be subjected to measures or sentences of confinement unless no other alternative measures are available.

Regardless of whether the juvenile justice reforms were introduced as part of a more comprehensive regulation of the rights of children or in a statute focused specifically on juvenile justice, both types of legislation broadly follow the same framework originally adopted by the Brazilian statute. Table 5.3 summarizes the main features of this framework, which are further developed in the subsections that follow.

TABLE 5.3. Main Reforms on Juvenile Justice in Latin America
(1990–Present)

Reform	Description
Principle of legality	A child or adolescent may be subjected to the juvenile justice regime only when he or she is accused of having committed a criminal offense.
Restorative and alternative mechanisms	There are measures for dealing with children and adolescents in conflict with the law without resorting to judicial proceedings and punishment.
Minimum age of criminal responsibility (MACR)	Almost all the countries in the region set the MACR at twelve, thirteen, or fourteen years.
Intermediate group	Children and adolescents above the MACR but under eighteen years are criminally liable, but they are presumed to have diminished responsibility due to their age.
Due process	The new laws have extended the due process protections of adults to youth in conflict with the law and have established specific due process protections for youth.
Legal consequences for youth declared criminally responsible	They are supposed to be different from those applied to adults and range from warnings and reprimands to confinement in a specialized institution. Their goals include social reintegration and rehabilitation.
Confinement as a last-resort measure	Pretrial and posttrial confinement should be used only exceptionally and for the shortest possible time.

1. THE COMMISSION OF A CRIMINAL OFFENSE AS A REQUIREMENT TO BE SUBJECTED TO THE JUVENILE JUSTICE SYSTEM (PRINCIPLE OF LEGALITY)

Article 40.2(a) of the CRC says, "No child shall be alleged as, be accused of, or recognized as having infringed the penal law by reason of acts or omissions that were not prohibited by national or international law at the time they were committed." A number of Latin American constitutions establish a similar requirement that has also been included by all the Latin American juvenile justice statutes.[26]

Latin American juvenile justice laws have interpreted that this requirement implies that a child or adolescent may be subjected to the juvenile justice regime only when he or she is accused of having committed a criminal offense. This requirement has been considered a radical change because under the classical tutelary system, authorities could subject minors to sanctions on the basis of broad and vague legal criteria such as "social risk."[27] This requirement also distinguishes Latin American from Anglo-American and continental European juvenile justice systems that deal with not only juvenile offender cases but also children and adolescents who engage in "any specific behavior that would not be punishable if committed by an adult" or are in danger or in need of protection.[28]

Despite this requirement, the new juvenile justice statutes have not specifically addressed the commission of petty offenses and of administrative violations by juveniles that in most Latin American countries are within the jurisdiction of the police and other administrative agencies. As a consequence, it is possible that children and adolescents accused of committing petty offenses and administrative violations are subjected to a harsher regime than the one established by the juvenile justice statute.

2. RESTORATIVE JUSTICE AND ALTERNATIVE PROCEEDINGS

Article 40.3(b) of the CRC establishes, "States Parties shall seek to promote the establishment of laws, procedures, authorities and institutions specifically applicable to children alleged as, accused of, or recognized as having infringed the penal law, and, in particular: . . . (b) Whenever appropriate and desirable, measures for dealing with such children without resorting to judicial proceedings, providing that human rights and legal safeguards are fully respected." The United Nations Guidelines for the Prevention of Juvenile Delinquency (known as the Riyadh Guidelines) recommend the adoption by states of the same principles.[29]

The new Latin American statutes include such a principle by establishing restorative justice measures as an alternative to juvenile criminal law.[30] Latin American legislation aims at implementing this principle of restorative justice through the application of four mechanisms: (a) conciliation and mediation, (b) the opportunity principle, which allows prosecutors to dismiss cases that could be prosecuted, (c) diversion mechanisms, and (d) the institution of remission, established in article 11 of the Beijing Rules, which is just an alternative label for the application of the opportunity principle or diversion mechanisms.[31] While the new juvenile justice legislation of certain countries such as Chile and Costa Rica refers to the criminal procedure code regulations on adults to apply these mechanisms in the juvenile justice context, other Latin American countries such as Honduras and El Salvador regulate these mechanisms directly in the juvenile justice legislation.[32]

These measures are ways to avoid the application of criminal law to juveniles, under the social integration idea that the fewer children and adolescents who are subjected to criminal law, the better, because criminal law is likely to interfere with, rather than to promote, the social reintegration of the juvenile.

Given that rehabilitation has been articulated as one of the goals of the juvenile justice reforms, these mechanisms could also be interpreted as a way to implement rehabilitation ideals in the context of juvenile justice.[33] The main problem with this interpretation of these mechanisms is the absence in most countries of the region of rehabilitation programs or even monitoring programs that check how these mechanisms are applied.[34] The absence of these rehabilitation or monitoring programs has actually led to law-and-order criticisms of these mechanisms under the argument that they are ways to be soft on crime.

3. MINIMUM AGE OF CRIMINAL RESPONSIBILITY (MACR)

Article 40.3.a of the CRC establishes that "States Parties shall seek to promote the establishment of . . . a minimum age below which children shall be presumed not to have the capacity to infringe the penal law." The Committee on the Rights of the Child has understood this provision as an obligation for state parties to set a minimum age of criminal responsibility below which children cannot be held responsible in a penal law procedure.[35] Almost all the countries in the region set the MACR at twelve, thirteen, or fourteen years. The only country that has kept it at sixteen years is Argentina.

These children are immune from prosecution due to their lack of responsibility and are supposed to be referred to children protection systems. When children under the MACR are accused of committing a criminal offense, their cases are automatically diverted to the administrative system of child protection. A number of the new Latin American juvenile justice regulations have established that children may not be put in confinement when they are under the MACR.[36]

4. DIMINISHED CRIMINAL RESPONSIBILITY FOR THE GROUP BETWEEN THE MACR AND EIGHTEEN YEARS

The new Latin American juvenile justice legislations establish that children and adolescents above the MACR but under eighteen years are criminally liable, but they are presumed to have diminished responsibility due to their age.[37] In other words, the children and adolescents who are between the minimum criminal age and eighteen years old are criminally responsible, though subject to a special regime.

Table 5.4 summarizes the minimum age of criminal responsibility as well as the maximum confinement applicable to children above the MACR and below eighteen years in eighteen Latin American countries on the basis of the statutes described in table 5.2.

TABLE 5.4. Minimum Age of Criminal Responsibility and Maximum Confinement for Those above the Minimum Age and below Eighteen Years in Latin America

Country	Minimum age of criminal responsibility	Maximum confinement for intermediate group(s)
Argentina	16	Punishment may be imposed only on those who have turned 18 years and who have been subjected to a minimum of one year of protective treatment.
Bolivia	12	Maximum confinement of three years for 12- and 13-year-old and of five years for 14- and 15-year-olds
Brazil	12	Maximum confinement period of three years. After turning 21 years, he or she must be released.
Chile	14	Maximum confinement of five years for 14- and 15-year-olds and of ten years for 16- and 17-year-olds
Colombia	12	Rehabilitation measures include confinement and may not be longer than three years.
Costa Rica	12	Maximum confinement of ten years for 12- to 15-year-olds and fifteen years for 15- to 18-year-olds
Dominican Republic	12	Maximum confinement of three years for 13- to 15-year-olds and of five years for 16- to 18-year-olds
Ecuador	12	Maximum of four years of confinement
El Salvador	12	Maximum confinement of five years for 12- to 15-year-olds and of seven years for 16 and older
Guatemala	12	Maximum confinement of two years for 13- to 15-year-olds and of six years for 15- to 18-year-olds

(*continued*)

TABLE 5.4. (*continued*)

Country	Minimum age of criminal responsibility	Maximum confinement for intermediate group(s)
Honduras	12	Maximum of eight years of confinement
Mexico (Chihuahua)	12	Maximum confinement of ten years for 14- to 16-year-olds and of fifteen years for 16- to 18-year-olds
Mexico (D.F.)	12	Maximum confinement of five years for 14- to 18-year-olds
Mexico (Federal Act)	12	Maximum confinement of five years for 14- to 16-year-olds and of seven for 16- to 18-year-olds
Mexico (Nuevo Leon)	12	Maximum confinement of six years for 14- to 16-year-olds and of eight for 16- to 18-year-olds
Mexico (Oaxaca)	12	Maximum of nine years of confinement, twelve years on confinement in cases of homicide, rape, kidnapping, and parricide
Mexico (Zacatecas)	12	Maximum confinement of months for 14- to 16-year-olds and of five years for 16- to 18-year-olds
Nicaragua	12	Maximum of six years of confinement
Panama	14	Maximum of five years of confinement
Paraguay	14	Maximum of eight years of confinement
Peru	12	Maximum of six years of confinement
Uruguay	12	Maximum of five years of confinement
Venezuela	12	Maximum of two years for 12- and 13-year-olds and of four years for 14-year-olds or older

Sources: Statutes described in table 5.2.

5. GENERAL AND SPECIFIC PROCEDURAL AND SUBSTANTIVE CRIMINAL RIGHTS

Article 40 of the CRC and other international instruments establish due process protections for youth accused of the commission of a criminal offense.[38] The new Latin American juvenile justice statutes also explicitly establish such due process protections and special child rights, which include, among others, the presumption of innocence; the right to be informed promptly and directly of the charges against him or her and, if appropriate, through his or parents or legal guardians and to have legal or other appropriate assistance in the preparation and presentation of his or her defense; the right to have the matter determined by a competent, independent, and impartial authority or judicial body, in a fair hearing; the right against compulsory self-incrimination, to examine adverse witnesses, and to compulsory process; and the right to privacy.[39]

Not only international instruments but also the criminal procedure reforms that Latin America has undergone in the past twenty-five years have influenced the due process regulations of the new Latin American juvenile justice systems. Under the slogan of replacing inquisitorial by adversarial systems of criminal justice, these criminal procedure reforms have included, among other measures, the introduction of oral and public trials, the elimination of pretrial investigating judges and a transfer of pretrial investigation to prosecutors, a clear distinction between the roles of prosecuting and adjudicating cases, the introduction of prosecutorial discretion and plea-bargaining-like mechanisms, and broader participation rights for the victim in the criminal process.[40] Given that the new juvenile justice legislations establish that regular criminal procedure regulations apply to children and adolescents in conflict with the law, the reforms to Latin American criminal proceedings have also changed the way these children and adolescents are prosecuted and tried.

6. POSTCONVICTION MEASURES FOR THOSE WHO ARE DECLARED CRIMINALLY RESPONSIBLE

The new Latin American legislations establish the possible legal consequences for a child or adolescent who is declared criminally responsible for the commission of an offense. These legal consequences are supposed to be different from those applied to adults and range from warnings and reprimands to confinement in a specialized institution. Rule 18 of the Beijing Rules says that nonconfinement measures should be used to avoid institutionalization to the maximum extent possible, and article 37(b) of the CRC says that the imprisonment of a child should be used only as a measure of last resort and for the shortest appropriate time. The new Latin American juvenile justice legislations reflect these principles by including no confinement measures, ranging from caution to probation, to deal with children and adolescents who are found criminally responsible.[41]

The international legal instruments generally refer to this type of legal consequences as "measures."[42] Depending on each country's legislation, in Latin America they are known as "measures," "socio-educational measures," "punishments," or "juvenile sentences." The laws that were passed at the beginning of the 1990s, which followed the Brazilian model, generally refer to "protection measures" rather than "sentences" in order to distinguish the postconviction consequences for juveniles from those for adults.[43] Some of the later legislations instead use the term "juvenile sanctions."[44]

The new Latin American laws adjust the maximum time for sentences by age groups (e.g., twelve to fourteen and fifteen to seventeen years), under the rationale that time has different implications for the younger and for the older children and adolescents.[45] The most recent laws also establish specific sentencing rules that refer to the sentencing scale of the crimes, not to the maximum of the sentencing scale or to an abstract reference to the "seriousness" of crimes as a ground for the measure or sanction of confinement.[46]

Two of the stated goals of juvenile criminal sentences in the new Latin American laws are the social reintegration of juveniles and their rehabilitation.[47] In practice, one of the problems for the goal of rehabilitation in most countries is the absence of programs and the lack of an adequate institutional infrastructure for allowing these nonimprisonment sentences or measures to try to advance this goal.[48]

7. CONFINEMENT AS A PRETRIAL MEASURE AND AS AN ALTERNATIVE, EXCEPTIONAL, TEMPORARILY LIMITED, AND BRIEF POSTCONVICTION MEASURE

According to international child rights law, the imprisonment of a criminally responsible child or adolescent is an exceptional, alternative measure that must be applied only in the case of very serious crimes and must be of limited duration.[49] Pretrial and postconviction imprisonment must also be as short as possible.[50] The new Latin American laws have also adopted these principles.[51]

Latin American laws establish that children and adolescents may be subjected to (a) weekend imprisonment, (b) house arrest, and (c) imprisonment in a specialized institution. In practice, the only one that is actually applied in most countries is confinement in specialized institutions, as was already the case in the classical tutelary system, since, once again, no well-functioning programs that are sustainable over the long term have been created to ensure that measures (a) and (b) are truly available in most of the region. The new laws also establish that children and adolescents may be deprived of their liberty only in specialized centers, not regular prisons.[52]

From Theory to Practice: Comparing Use of Confinement and Sanctioning Policies in Criminal and Juvenile Courts

The theoretical statements analyzed in the previous sections about the goals of juvenile justice represent only the rhetoric and aspirations of legal policy rather than hard evidence that juveniles who commit offenses face different treatment and punishment outcomes than older offenders do. Most of the discussion of juvenile justice in Latin America has concerned only these rhetorical and aspirational dimensions of policy. But is there evidence from practice that juvenile offenders are deprived of their liberty differently than are defendants in the criminal courts in Latin America countries? Do juvenile offenders face different sanction policies than adults do? Data sources are quite uneven on crime and justice in the region, and no systematic studies have been undertaken. In addition, since the available data are collected and reported by countries with different standards of care, systematization, and consistency, it is important to be cautious while making cross-country comparisons. But an analysis of statistics on confinement and arrest and formal contact with the police suggests that juvenile courts in Latin America rely less on incarceration than criminal courts for adults do.

Table 5.5 begins the survey by showing the population in confinement of persons under eighteen, persons between eighteen and twenty-four, and persons over twenty-four, in eighteen Latin American countries. Table 5.5 shows that the total juvenile population in confinement is smaller than the total population in confinement of the other two age groups in these eighteen Latin American countries.

Figure 5.1 indicates the proportion of total secure confinement in juvenile and adult facilities that is occupied by persons under eighteen in these eighteen Latin American countries. In most countries, the confinement of youth accounts for only a very small share of total incarceration. Ten of the eighteen countries count fewer than 3% of those

TABLE 5.5. Population in Institutions of Secure Confinement by Age in Eighteen Latin American Countries

	Juveniles	Adults 18–24	Other adults
Argentina	1,375	14,071	60,789
Bolivia	1,874	n/a	13,489
Brazil	20,023	143,470	548,003
Chile	1,882	n/a	49,350
Colombia	3,300	n/a	113,884
Costa Rica	88	2,884	14,830
Dominican Republic	552	n/a	21,875
Ecuador	1,100	n/a	23,178
El Salvador	797	7,731	26,486
Guatemala	900	n/a	15,013
Honduras	278	n/a	11,879
Mexico	10,583	n/a	198,847
Nicaragua	153	n/a	7,200
Panama	428	5,231	14,593
Paraguay	256	n/a	7,924
Peru	1,558	10,526	61,390
Uruguay	500	3,707	9,418
Venezuela	887	n/a	24,069

Sources: Alertamerica, "Repositorio de datos," http://www.oas.org/dsp/Observatorio/database/countries.aspx? lang=es, for all countries except the data about Chile, which comes from Gendarmería de Chile, *Compendio estadístico penitenciario, 2010–2012*; and SENAME, *Boletín estadístico anual de los niños(as) y adolescentes vigentes en la red SENAME, 2003–2013*. All data are from between 2011 and 2013, with the exception of the data on Venezuela, which is from 2008.

locked up as under eighteen, with Costa Rica having fewer than 1% and Argentina fewer than 2%. Another seven countries have between 3% and 5.6% of total inmates under eighteen. Only Bolivia, with 12.2% of total confinement in the under-eighteen group, has relatively large concentrations, and the Bolivian data that were obtained report a total confined population under 15,370, for an adult confinement rate of 130 persons and a total confinement rate of 174 persons per 100,000.[53]

Table 5.6 and figure 5.2 compare adult and juvenile contact with the police—that is, people arrested, suspected, or cautioned by the police— with adult and juvenile confinement in twelve Latin American countries. The percentages of adult and juvenile formal contact with the police are a proxy for how many adult and juvenile cases get into the justice system in each of these countries. While the percentage of juvenile formal contact with police is *higher* than the percentage of juveniles in confinement, the adult percentage of formal contact with the police is *lower* than the percentage of adults in confinement out of the total confined population in ten out of twelve countries (table 5.6). This is

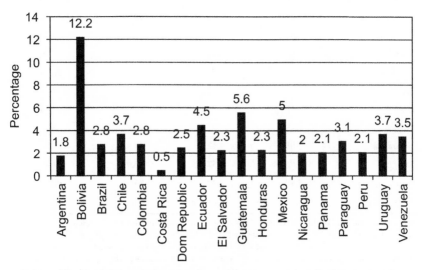

Figure 5.1. The percentage of persons under eighteen in institutions of secure confinement in eighteen Latin American nations. *Note:* The calculations shown are based on the data described in table 5.5. Under the definitions by Alertamerica, "juveniles" are persons under eighteen years, who are different from juveniles between eighteen and twenty-four years (whom we call "adults" in table 5.5, to use the category of juvenile consistently throughout this chapter), who are different from adults. However, to run the calculations of figure 5.1, we have assumed that those countries that did not report data for adults between eighteen and twenty-four years included any person eighteen years or older in their category of adults. Notice that if this assumption were not correct for one or more of these countries, the percentage of the juvenile population in confinement out of the total confined population would be even smaller. *Sources:* Alertamerica, "Repositorio de datos," http://www.oas.org/dsp/Observatorio/database/countries.aspx?lang=es, for all countries except the data from Chile, which come from Gendarmería de Chile, *Compendio estadístico penitenciario, 2010–2012;* and SENAME, *Boletín estadístico anual de los niños(as) y adolescentes vigentes en la red SENAME, 2003–2013.* The percentages are calculated based on the latest available data on each country. All data are from between 2011 and 2013, with the exception of the data on Venezuela, which is from 2008.

TABLE 5.6. Percentages of Adult and Juvenile Formal Contact with the Police and of Adult and Juvenile Confinement in Twelve Latin American Countries

	% of juvenile formal contact out of total formal contact with police	% of juvenile confinement out of total confinement	% of adult formal contact out of total formal contact with police	% of adult confinement out of total confinement
Chile	9.36	2.77	90.64	97.23
Colombia	10.24	1.84	89.76	98.16
Costa Rica	1.49	0.34	98.51	99.66
Ecuador	11.01	2.41	88.99	97.59
El Salvador	12.71	3.76	87.29	96.24
Guatemala	2.53	1.12	97.47	98.88
Honduras	8.10	2.26	91.90	97.74
Mexico	2.99	4.82	97.01	95.18
Nicaragua	6.08	1.12	93.92	98.88
Paraguay	11.96	2.57	88.04	97.43
Peru	4.19	4.49	95.81	95.51
Uruguay	14.74	3.67	85.26	96.33

Sources: Alertamerica, "Repositorio de datos," http://www.oas.org/dsp/Observatorio/database/countries.aspx?lang=es; United Nations Office on Drugs and Crime (UNODC), "Statistics on Criminal Justice," http://www.unodc.org/unodc/en/data-and-analysis/statistics/data.html. Comparison between the latest available data from the same year in the UNODC database on adult and juvenile formal contact with the police, and adult and juvenile confinement. When the UNODC database did not contain confinement data, we used data on confinement for the same year from the Alertamerica database. In the case of Mexico and Paraguay, we used data from two different years because data on these four variables for the same year were not available. Data on Ecuador is from 2004; Costa Rica and Guatemala from 2006; Paraguay from 2006 and 2007; Peru from 2009; Colombia and Nicaragua from 2010; Chile, El Salvador, and Honduras from 2011; and Mexico from 2011 and 2012.

an indication that juveniles are confined less often than adults in these countries. The two outliers are Peru and especially Mexico, where the percentage of juvenile formal contact with the police is lower than the percentage of juvenile confinement and the other way around for adults.[54] In the other ten countries, the percentage of juvenile contact with the police out of all contacts is substantially higher than the percentage of juveniles in confinement out of the total confined population. In these ten countries, the rate of juvenile contact with the police goes from being 2.3 times higher than the rate of juvenile secure confinement in Guatemala and 3.4 times higher in El Salvador to 5.7 times higher in Colombia (table 5.6).

We now analyze the ratio of adult and juvenile confinement to, respectively, adult and juvenile formal contact with the police in twelve Latin American countries. Comparing the ratio of adults in confinement to adults in formal contact with the police with the ratio of juveniles in confinement to juveniles in formal contact with the police gives us another indication of how often confinement is used for each of these two age groups. In ten out of the twelve countries for which data are available, the ratio of juvenile confinement to juvenile formal contact with the police is much lower than the ratio of adults in confinement to adults in formal contact with the police[55]—the two outliers are again

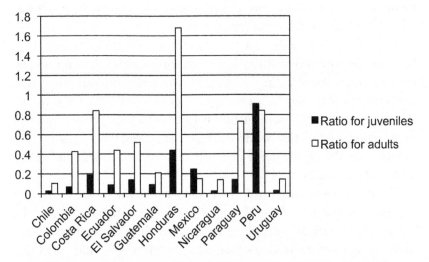

Figure 5.2. Ratio of adult confinement to adult formal contact with the police and of juvenile confinement to juvenile formal contact with the police in twelve Latin American nations. *Sources:* Alertamerica, Repositorio de datos, http://www.oas.org/dsp/Observatorio/database/countries.aspx?lang=es; United Nations Office on Drugs and Crime, "Statistics on Criminal Justice," http://www.unodc.org/unodc/en/data-and-analysis/statistics/data.html. Comparison between the latest available data from the same year in the UNODC database on adult and juvenile formal contact with the police, and adult and juvenile confinement. When the UNODC database did not contain confinement data, we used data on confinement on the same year from the Alertamerica database. In the case of Mexico and Paraguay, we used data from two different years because data on these four variables on the same year were not available. Data on Ecuador is from 2004; Costa Rica and Guatemala from 2006; Paraguay from 2006 and 2007; Peru from 2009; Colombia and Nicaragua from 2010; Chile, El Salvador, and Honduras from 2011; and Mexico from 2011 and 2012.

Peru and Mexico. In these ten countries, the ratio of adult confinement to adult formal contact with the police goes from being 2.3 times higher than the same ratio for juveniles in Guatemala to being 5.6 times higher in Nicaragua and 6.1 times higher in Colombia (figure 5.2). In other words, in Guatemala, there are 4.7 adults in formal contact with the police for each adult in confinement, while there are 10.8 juveniles in formal contact with the police for each juvenile in confinement. In Nicaragua, there are 7.1 adults in formal contact with the police for each adult in confinement, while there are 40.7 juveniles in formal contact with the police for each juvenile in confinement. In Colombia, there are 2.3 adults in formal contact with the police for each adult in confinement, while there are 14.2 juveniles in formal contact with the police for each juvenile in confinement (figure 5.2).

The overall picture that comes from these data indicates that confinement is used substantially less often for juveniles than for adults in most countries of Latin America. The data also provide some evidence of fewer or shorter punishments of incarceration for juvenile crimes. But we would need further data to draw stronger conclusions in this respect given that we do not have data about the length of confinement in the two systems or the balance between pre- and post-adjudication confinement.

The use of frequencies of formal contact with the police as a measure of adult and juvenile cases that come into the system (or of juvenile versus adult criminality) is imperfect because there are no indications of the severity of the offenses that led to this formal contact with the police. And the youngest offenders may be arrested more often in groups, which can overstate the proportion of crimes they represent. Despite these limitations, the large differences between the ratio of juvenile confinement to juvenile formal contact with the police and the ratio of adult confinement to adult formal contact with the police indicate that most systems of juvenile justice in Latin America follow through in practice with the emphasis on avoiding custodial confinement that is found in their laws on the books.

The same picture emerges from the time-series data that we have been able to collect on four Latin American jurisdictions—the state of Rio de Janeiro in Brazil, Colombia, Chile and El Salvador—as indicated in tables 5.7 to 5.10 and figures 5.3 to 5.6.

TABLE 5.7. Total Numbers and Percentages of Juveniles and Adults Arrests and in Confinement in the State of Rio de Janeiro (Brazil), 2007–2011

	2007	2008	2009	2010	2011
Arrested adults	14,355	15,508	18,468	19,877	23,090
Adults in secure confinement	22,393	21,306	22,443	24,867	27,685
Arrested juveniles	1,853	1,821	2,272	2,806	3,466
Juveniles in secure confinement	1,034	1,107	633	833	914
Percentage of adult arrests out of total arrests	88.57	89.49	89.05	87.63	86.95
Percentage of adult confinement out of total confined population	95.59	95.06	97.26	96.76	96.80
Percentage of juvenile arrests out of total arrests	11.43	10.51	10.95	12.37	13.05
Percentage of juvenile confinement out of total confined population	4.41	4.94	2.74	3.24	3.20

Sources: Secretaria de Estado de Segurança, Instituto de Segurança Pública, *Balanço de incidências criminais e administrativas.*

In the state of Rio de Janeiro, while the percentage of adult arrests was lower than the percentage of adult confinement, the percentage of juvenile arrests was higher than the percentage of juvenile confinement every year from 2007 to 2011 (table 5.7).[56]

In the state of Rio de Janeiro, the ratio of adult confinement to adult arrest was 2.80 times higher than the ratio of juvenile confinement to juvenile arrests in 2007 and 4.55 times higher in 2011, with a lowest difference between the two ratios being 2.26 times higher in 2008 (figure 5.3).

In Colombia, while the percentage of adult arrests was lower than the percentage of adult confinement, the percentage of juvenile arrests was higher than the percentage of juvenile confinement every year from 2007 to 2011 (table 5.8).

In Colombia, the ratio of adult confinement to adult arrests was 20.6 times higher than the ratio of juvenile confinement to juvenile arrests

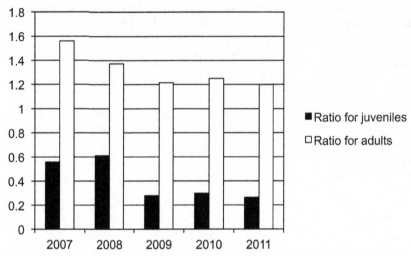

Figure 5.3. Ratio of adult confinement to adult arrests and ratio of juvenile confinement to juvenile arrests in the state of Rio de Janeiro (Brazil), 2007–2011. *Source*: Secretaria de Estado de Segurança, Instituto de Segurança Pública, *Balanço de incidências criminais e administrativas*.

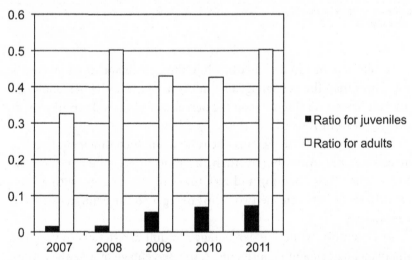

Figure 5.4. Ratio of adult confinement to adult arrests and ratio of juvenile confinement to juvenile arrests in Colombia, 2007–2011. *Sources*: Alertamerica, "Repositorio de datos," http://www.oas.org/dsp/Observatorio/database/countries.aspx?lang=es; Policía Nacional de Colombia, *Revista criminalidad* 45–56.

TABLE 5.8. Total Numbers and Percentages of Juveniles and Adults Arrests and in Confinement in Colombia, 2007–2011

	2007	2008	2009	2010	2011
Arrested adults	195,027	139,358	176,640	197,733	200,066
Adults in secure confinement	63,603	69,979	75,992	84,444	100,451
Arrested juveniles	32,894	26,685	21,501	22,552	24,661
Juveniles in secure confinement	519	462	1,219	1,584	1,805
Percentage of adult arrests out of total arrests	85.57	83.93	89.15	89.76	89.03
Percentage of adult confinement out of total confined population	99.09	99.34	98.45	98.16	98.23
Percentage of juvenile arrests out of total arrests	14.43	16.07	10.85	10.24	10.97
Percentage of juvenile confinement out of total confined population	0.81	0.66	1.58	1.84	1.77

Sources: Alertamerica, "Repositorio de datos," http://www.oas.org/dsp/Observatorio/database/countries.aspx?lang=es; Policía Nacional de Colombia, *Revista criminalidad* 45–56.

in 2007 and 6.86 times higher in 2011, with a lowest difference of 6.08 times higher in 2010 and a highest difference of 29.02 times higher in 2008. In other words, in 2007, there were 63.00 juvenile arrests for each juvenile in confinement, while there were 3.00 adult arrests for each adult in confinement. In 2008, there were 57.80 juvenile arrests for each juvenile in confinement, while there were 1.99 adult arrests for each adult in confinement. In 2010, there were 14.20 juvenile arrests for each juvenile in confinement, while there were 2.34 adult arrests for each adult in confinement. In 2011, there were 13.70 juvenile arrests for each juvenile in confinement, while there were 1.99 adult arrests for each adult in confinement (figure 5.4).

In Chile, while the percentage of adult arrests was lower than the percentage of adult confinement, the percentage of juvenile arrests was higher than the percentage of juvenile confinement every year from 2008 to 2012 (table 5.9).

TABLE 5.9. Total Numbers and Percentages of Adult and Juvenile Formal Contact with Police and Adult and Juvenile Confinement in Chile, 2008–2012

	2008	2009	2010	2011	2012
Adult formal contact with police	503,575	556,869	558,373	554,095	534,168
Adult confinement	48,824	52,947	54,628	53,606	49,350
Juvenile formal contact with police	53,386	51,448	48,033	57,227	54,932
Juvenile confinement	1,569	1,750	1,844	1,690	1,882
Percentage of adult formal contact out of total formal contact with the police	90.4	91.5	92.1	90.6	90.7
Percentage of adult confinement out of total confined population	96.9	96.8	97.7	96.9	96.3
Percentage of juvenile formal contact out of total formal contact with the police	9.6	8.5	7.9	9.4	9.3
Percentage of juvenile confinement out of total confined population	3.1	3.2	3.3	3.1	3.7

Sources: United Nations Office on Drugs and Crime, "Statistics on Criminal Justice," http://www.unodc.org/unodc/en/data-and-analysis/statistics/data.html; Gendarmería de Chile, Compendio estadístico penitenciario 2010–2012; SENAME, Boletín estadístico anual de los niños(as) y adolescentes vigentes en la red SENAME, 2003–2013.

From a different perspective, in this country, the ratio of adult confinement to adult formal contact with police was 3.30 times higher than the ratio of juvenile confinement to juvenile formal contact with the police in 2008 and 2.69 times higher in 2012, with a lowest difference of 2.55 times higher in 2010 (figure 5.5). In other words, in 2008, there were 10.3 adult arrests for each adult in confinement, while there were 34.0 juvenile arrests for each juvenile in confinement. In 2010, there were 10.3 adult arrests for each adult in confinement, while there were 33.9 juvenile arrests for each juvenile in confinement. In 2012, there were 10.8 adult arrests for each adult in confinement, while there were 29.1 juvenile arrests for each juvenile in confinement.

As in the other jurisdictions where these data are available, in El Salvador, the percentage of adult arrests was lower than the percentage of adult confinement, while the percentage of juvenile arrests was higher than the percentage of juvenile confinement every year from 2005 to 2012 (table 5.10).

In this country, the ratio of adult confinement to adult formal contact with the police was 2.68 times higher than the ratio of juvenile confinement to adult formal contact with the police in 2005 and 2.75 times higher in 2012, with a lowest difference of 2.62 times higher in 2006 and a highest difference of 4.67 times higher in 2009 (figure 5.6). In other words, in 2005, there were 7.3 adults in formal contact with the police for each adult in confinement, while there were 19.5 juveniles in formal contact with the police for every juvenile in confinement. In 2006, there were 8.6 adults in formal contact with the police for each adult in confinement, while there were 22.5 juveniles in formal contact with the police for every juvenile in confinement. In 2009, there were 2.4 adults

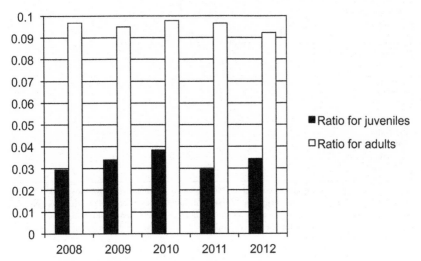

Figure 5.5. Ratio of adult confinement to adult arrests and ratio of juvenile confinement to juvenile arrests in Chile, 2008–2012. Sources: United Nations Office on Drugs and Crime, "Statistics on Criminal Justice," http://www.unodc.org/unodc/en/data-and-analysis/statistics/data.html; Gendarmería de Chile, Compendio estadístico penitenciario, 2010–2012; SENAME, Boletín estadístico anual de los niños(as) y adolescentes vigentes en la red SENAME, 2003–2013.

TABLE 5.10. Total Numbers and Percentages of Juvenile and Adult Formal Contact with Police and Confinement in El Salvador, 2005–2012

	2005	2006	2007	2008	2009	2010	2011	2012
Adult formal contact with police	90,574	123,604	58,243	55,790	51,213	55,549	48,885	47,718
Adult confinement	12,469	14,420	17,867	19,390	22,198	23,151	25,019	27,033
Juvenile formal contact with police	8,127	11,480	7,255	8,657	8,367	9,214	7,116	5,170
Juvenile confinement	417	511	630	701	776	836	971	1,064
Percentage of adult formal contact out of total formal contact with police	91.8	91.5	89.0	86.6	86.0	85.8	87.3	90.3
Percentage of adult confinement out of total confined population	96.8	96.6	96.6	96.5	96.6	96.5	96.3	96.2
Percentage of juvenile formal contact out of total formal contact with the police	8.2	8.5	11.0	13.4	14.0	14.2	12.7	9.7
Percentage of juvenile confinement out of total confined population	3.2	3.4	3.4	3.5	3.4	3.5	3.7	3.8

Sources: United Nations Office on Drugs and Crime, "Statistics on Criminal Justice," http://www.unodc.org/ unodc/en/data-and-analysis/statistics/data.html; Ministerio de Justicia y Seguridad Pública, "Dirección general de centros penales: Estadísticas penitenciarias," http://www.dgcp.gob.sv/index.php?option=com_content &view=article&id=123; Alertamerica, "Repositorio de datos," http://www.oas.org/dsp/Observatorio/database/ countries.aspx?lang=es.

in formal contact with the police for every adult in confinement, while there were 11.0 juveniles in formal contact with the police for every juvenile in confinement. In 2012, there were 1.8 adults in formal contact with the police for every adult n confinement, while there were 4.9 juveniles in formal contact with the police for every juvenile in confinement.

The overall picture that comes from the data presented is that there are large differences between the proportion of adults and juveniles who are confined after being arrested or in formal contact with the police. This section has shown that these differences stand in most of the region by using not only cross-country but also cross-temporal data from multiple sources. These differences provide important indications that systems of juvenile justice in Latin America follow through in practice with the emphasis on avoiding custodial confinement that is found in their law in the books and theoretical tracts.

It is not possible to know from these data to what extent this lower use of confinement for juveniles is the result of pretrial detention decisions or postadjudicatory measures and sanctions. It is also impossible to know from these data whether this lower use of confinement for juveniles is the result of lesser use or use of shorter terms of confinement for juveniles. We also cannot know from these data what specific mechanisms—such as the principle of using confinement as a

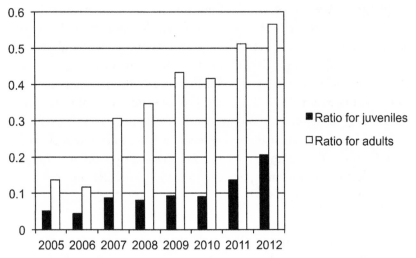

Figure 5.6. Ratio of adult confinement to adult arrests and ratio of juvenile confinement to juvenile arrests in El Salvador, 2005–2012. *Sources:* United Nations Office on Drugs and Crime, "Statistics on Criminal Justice," http://www.unodc.org/unodc/en/data -and-analysis/statistics/data.html; Ministerio de Justicia y Seguridad Pública, "Dirección general de centros penales: Estadísticas penitenciarias," http://www.dgcp.gob.sv/ index.php?option=com_content&view=article&id=123; Alertamerica, "Repositorio de datos," http://www.oas.org/dsp/Observatorio/database/countries.aspx?lang=es.

last resort, paternalistic sentiment toward juveniles, or the doctrine of diminished responsibility, to mention a few possibilities—explain this lower use of confinement.

But from these data, we can conclude that juvenile justice systems in most countries of Latin America are playing the function and goal of removing a substantial number of juveniles from criminal law by reducing the number of juveniles in conflict with the law who are subjected to confinement. Without denying the serious problems that juvenile justice systems in Latin America present, this is one stated goal of juvenile justice that a large proportion of Latin American juvenile justice systems seem to advance.

Future studies should further test whether these conclusions stand in individual countries and should reexamine these issues once better data are available about the functioning of juvenile justice systems in Latin America. Future studies could also deepen the approach taken in this chapter of making a double comparison between countries *and* between adult and juvenile systems in the region. In order to get a better picture of the law in action of juvenile justice in Latin America, it would be necessary to get cross-country and cross-temporal data on other variables, such as pretrial and posttrial confinement and pretrial and postconviction measures different from confinement, not only for offenses in the aggregate but also for individual offenses. More data on which actors within Latin American juvenile and criminal justice systems make the actual decisions on cases are also necessary. It would be ideal to obtain these data at the case level. In order to enable such studies, it is crucial that Latin American countries improve and widen their data collection on juvenile justice systems in particular and criminal justice more generally.

Evaluating the Recent Juvenile Justice Laws: The Chilean Law as a Case Study

As previously explained, Latin American countries have undergone a wave of reforms on juvenile justice in the past twenty-five years. Taking the CRC as one of their main models, Latin American countries have introduced reforms that have given more due process protections to juveniles and have established the principle that deprivation of liberty for juveniles should be used exceptionally and only in those cases when it is absolutely necessary.

Despite the importance of these reforms, there have been almost no qualitative or quantitative empirical evaluations of their results, even in Portuguese and Spanish.[57] This lack of empirical evaluations is itself the result of the unavailability of good data in most countries of the region on the functioning of juvenile justice systems before and after the introduction of the reforms, as well as the result of the small size of an empirically oriented sociolegal community in the region. This section tries to start filling this vacuum and prompting more empirical research in this area by analyzing the Chilean juvenile justice reform.

Our main conclusions are that while the new juvenile justice reform in Chile has improved due process for juveniles by diminishing the percentage of juveniles in pretrial detention, it has likely increased the absolute and relative levels of juvenile confinement in Chile. As the preceding section has shown, juveniles are confined at lower rates than are adults in Chile, as elsewhere in the region. But our data in this section show that after the introduction of the juvenile justice reform, juveniles are confined at higher rates than before the reform in Chile.

The Chilean reform was approved by the Chilean Congress in 2005 (Law 20.084) and came into effect on June 8, 2007.[58] The Chilean reform aimed at replacing the old "tutelary system," based on protective measures for non-criminally-liable youth, by a model in which children and adolescents are considered criminally responsible for their own acts but subjected to special regulations.[59] The goals of the new law were to ensure that the Chilean legislation met due process and constitutional standards as well as the standards established by the CRC.[60] The law's goals also included improving the efficiency of the juvenile justice system to protect the victims of juvenile crime.[61] There was thus a tension in the new law from its inception between its goals of protecting due process and the rights of children and adolescents in conflict with the law, on the one hand, and its crime control goals, on the other.[62]

The previous legislation considered all children and adolescents under sixteen years old and sixteen- and seventeen-year-olds who were declared without discernment by the court as not criminally liable and subject only to protective measures.[63] Special courts called "minor courts" had jurisdiction to make these discernment determinations and to take protective measures. If a sixteen- or seventeen-year-old juvenile was declared as having discernment, a regular criminal court would try his or her case under the same conditions as an adult, and the juvenile could be placed in an adult prison.

In contrast, the new Chilean juvenile law establishes the minimum age for criminal responsibility at fourteen years. Juveniles between fourteen and seventeen years are prosecuted under the same adversarial system implemented in Chile for adults between 2000 and 2005 but using the special regulations enacted for juvenile offenders.[64] The new legislation also abolishes the old minor courts and establishes that, as a general rule, the judges, public prosecutors, and public defenders who handle juvenile cases must be specialized in this area of law.[65] Though specialized in juvenile law, these judges do not sit in a separate juvenile court and may also intervene in adult cases.

The new legislation expressly states that authorities must consider all the rights and guarantees provided by the CRC and other international instruments that Chile has ratified.[66] The new legislation also determines that pretrial and postadjudication confinement of juveniles should be used only when there are no other available alternatives and never in cases in which it would not be appropriate for an adult.[67] The juvenile law also establishes precise sentencing rules in order to limit the use of arbitrary confinement, which was considered characteristic of the tutelary regime.[68]

The new law also establishes that people younger than eighteen years who are deprived of their liberty must be put in institutions of confinement that are different from adult prisons. The institution in charge of the enforcement of criminal court decisions under the new regime is the National Service of Minors (Servicio Nacional de Menores, or SENAME). The configuration of SENAME is very different from a typical penitentiary office because its goals include rehabilitation and protection of vulnerable children and adolescents—not just those who committed crimes—and because its administrators and staff tend to have a different professional background (e.g., as social workers) than do the administrators and staff of adult prisons.

There have been a few empirical studies on Chilean juvenile justice.[69] But these studies have only provided and analyzed data on the functioning of the juvenile justice system before or after the introduction of the

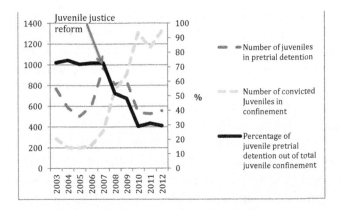

Figure 5.7. Number and percentage of juveniles in pretrial and postadjudication confinement in Chile, 2003–2012. *Note*: We have obtained the data on the number of juveniles in pretrial detention in the regular correctional system before the juvenile justice reform came into effect from the annual reports of Gendarmería, since the SENAME annual reports that we have used throughout the chapter as sources on the number of juveniles in confinement in Chile do not include such pretrial confinement data. As a consequence of using different sources, the numbers of total juveniles in confinement before the juvenile justice reform came into effect that figure 5.7 shows vary from the numbers we used in the rest of the chapter. However, the variation is not very significant (1,051 instead 927 juveniles in 2003, 784 instead of 799 individuals in 2004, 699 instead of 762 individuals in 2005, 827 instead of 848 juveniles in 2006, and 1,334 instead of 1,177 juveniles in 2007). And in any case, our analysis applies, since there is a substantial upward trajectory of juvenile confinement in Chile after the coming into effect of the juvenile justice reform. *Sources*: Gendarmería de Chile, *Compendio estadístico penitenciario, 2010–2012*; SENAME, *Boletín estadístico anual de los niños(as) y adolescentes vigentes en la red SENAME, 2003–2013*.

reform, rather than evaluating the reform.[70] Our strategy to make an evaluation of the reform is to include data before and after the juvenile justice reform and also data on adults that provide a point of comparison with the treatment of juveniles.

We start our assessment with figure 5.7, which shows the percentage and total levels of juvenile pretrial and postadjudication confinement. Figure 5.7 indicates that before the introduction of the juvenile justice reform (including the coming into effect of the adversarial procedure for juveniles), the levels of pretrial confinement were substantially higher than those of postadjudication confinement, being between 72.0% and 74.7% of the juvenile population in confinement from 2003 to 2006.

These high percentages of juvenile pretrial detention could be partially the product of inquisitorial proceedings that were written and very formalistic, and thus slow to reach the adjudicatory phase, and in which pretrial detention was the rule, rather than the exception, during the preadjudication stage. But since these percentages of juvenile pretrial confinement were much higher than for adults before the full coming into effect of the adversarial procedure for adults in 2005 (the adult pretrial detention was around 40%),[71] these high percentages of juvenile pretrial detention could also be partially the product of the tutelary system. Since the tutelary system conceived of confinement as a protective measure for juveniles, it was less important whether that protective measure was imposed before or after the formal adjudication of the juvenile case.

Since the entering into effect of the new juvenile justice reform in 2007, the distribution of juvenile pretrial and postadjudication confinement started to change dramatically. In this period, the percentage of juveniles in pretrial confinement went from 72.9% in 2007 to 29.6% in

TABLE 5.11. Total Number of Juveniles in Confinement and Percentage of Juvenile Confinement out of the Total Confined Population, Chile, 2003–2012

	2003	2004	2005	2006	2007	2008	2009	2010	2011	2012
Juveniles in confinement	927	799*	762	848	1,177	1,569	1,750	1,844	1,690	1,882
Percentage of juvenile confinement	2.5	2.2	2.0	2.1	2.6	3.1	3.2	3.3	3.1	3.7

Sources: Gendarmería de Chile, *Compendio estadístico penitenciario, 2010–2012*; SENAME, *Boletín estadístico anual de los niños(as) y adolescentes vigentes en la red SENAME, 2003–2013*.
* The annual human rights report by Universidad Diego Portales, *Facultad de derecho: Informe anual de derechos humanos 2006; Hechos de 2005* (Santiago, Chile, June 2006), shows a total juvenile population in confinement for 2004 that is close to 960 juveniles, instead of the 799 juveniles that we report (see pages 66 and 70–71 of the report). The difference may be (partially) explained by the fact that while we have used the annual reports of SENAME that consistently report the number of juveniles in confinement by December 31 of each year, the human rights report in question reports data on juveniles in "Centers of Observation and Diagnosis" and "Confined for Behavioral Rehabilitation" by September 30, 2004. In addition, it is possible that the number of juveniles in "Juvenile Sections of the Correctional System of Chile" indicated by the report refers to the total number of juveniles who were deprived of their liberty in those sections in the year 2004—though we cannot tell from the report if this was the case. Instead, the numbers that table 5.11 shows include the number of juveniles that were in the "Juvenile Sections" by December 31, 2004, as indicated by SENAME's annual report. In any case, the difference between our numbers and those of the human rights report for the year 2004 would not change the overall substantially upward trend of juvenile confinement in Chile before and after the juvenile justice reform.

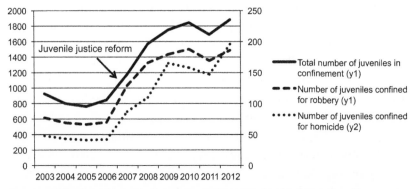

Figure 5.8. Number of juveniles in secure confinement for all crimes, for robbery, and for homicide, in Chile, 2003–2012. *Source*: SENAME, *Boletín estadístico anual de los niños(as) y adolescentes vigentes en la red SENAME, 2003–2013*.

2012. This result may be the product of the substantially shorter time to adjudication or the more liberal regulation of pretrial detention under the adversarial process, as has been the case with the application of the adversary process to adults.[72] This reduction in the percentage of juveniles in pretrial detention can be considered a due process improvement since now most of the juveniles in confinement have been found guilty beyond a reasonable doubt at trial or have pled guilty.[73] However, figure 5.7 shows that the number of juveniles in pretrial confinement has not gone down in comparison to 2005 and that the change in percentages of juvenile pretrial detention is also the result of a substantial increase in the number of convicted juveniles in confinement.

Table 5.11 and figure 5.8 show the number of juveniles in confinement in the aggregate and by the two most relevant crimes from 2003 to 2012.[74] Table 5.11 and figure 5.8 show that juvenile confinement increased substantially from 2003 to 2012. This upward trend in confinement levels of juveniles started in 2007, the year the juvenile justice reform came into effect, and substantially increased since then. The number of juveniles in confinement increased 103% from 2003 to 2012 and 121% from 2006 (the year before the coming into effect of the juvenile justice reform) to 2012. The percentage of juvenile confinement out of the total confined population (i.e., juvenile plus adult) also grew from 2.5% in 2003 or from 2.1% in 2006 to 3.7% in 2012.

Figure 5.8 also shows that the increase in juvenile confinement for robbery and homicide explains almost all of the increase in juvenile confinement. While the number of juveniles in confinement for robbery went from 556 juveniles in 2006 to 1,487 juveniles in 2012, the number of juveniles in confinement for homicide went from 42 in 2006 to 196 in 2012. These two categories represented 89% of the juvenile population in confinement in Chile in 2012.

Figure 5.9 suggests that the levels of juvenile crime or at least of the juvenile cases that reached the justice system do not explain the increase in juvenile confinement. The number of arrests of people younger than twenty years for robbery went down in the period in question. If we take 2006 as the starting year, total robbery arrests decreased 11.6%, robbery with force on things decreased 11.4%, and robbery with force on people decreased 11.8%.[75] As for homicide arrests, they increased 7.6% (from seventy-nine to eighty-five cases) from 2006 to 2011, but homicide arrests in 2005 were ninety-one.

Given that there are no indications of an increase in juvenile arrests in the period in question and the lack of other alternative explanations, it is reasonable to infer that aspects of the juvenile justice reform of 2007 contributed to an increase in juvenile confinement.[76]

In the remainder of this section, we argue that the procedural aspects of the juvenile justice reform cannot (fully) account for the increase in juvenile confinement. As already mentioned, the juvenile justice reform

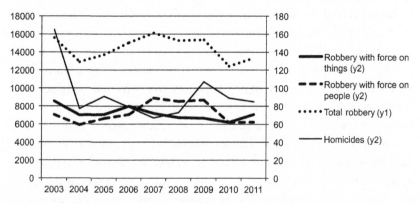

Figure 5.9. Robbery and homicide arrests for people younger than twenty years in Chile, 2003–2012. *Source*: Fundación Paz Ciudadana, *Anuario de estadísticas criminales, 2011*.

brought about deep procedural changes by making applicable to juveniles the adversarial reform that had come fully into effect for adults in 2005. This adversarial reform brought about not only due process rights to juvenile defendants but also other procedural and institutional features that could explain an increase in juvenile confinement. Empirical assessments of the adversarial reform regarding adults indicate that it has increased the efficiency of the Chilean administration of criminal justice by substantially reducing the time from arrest (or other ways of initiating a criminal process) to conviction through its deformalization of the pretrial phase and through the introduction of mechanisms such as guilty pleas and plea bargaining.[77] This time reduction would thus free resources and could enable the system to process more cases and enter more convictions—including convictions followed by confinement sentences. In addition, the adversarial reform strengthened the prosecuting institutions in Chile by creating an office of the prosecutor from scratch and by increasing police capacity.

The adversarial system was introduced for the adult population between 2000 and 2005 but only came into effect in Santiago (the largest region in the country in terms of population) in 2005. In the case of juveniles, the adversarial reform came into effect with the coming into effect of the new juvenile law in June 2007.

In order to evaluate whether the procedural aspects of the juvenile justice reform contributed to the increase of juvenile confinement, figure 5.10 indicates when the new adversarial criminal procedure system fully came into effect for adults and juveniles and presents data on the rate of adult and juvenile confinement between 2003 and 2012.

If we take the year 2003 as the baseline, with the full coming into force of the adversarial system for adults in 2005, the adult confined population increased 37% from 2003 to 2012. In the case of juveniles, taking again the year 2003 as the baseline, the juvenile confined population increased 103% during the same period. It is thus possible that the introduction of the adversarial criminal process was an intervening factor that has contributed to the increase of the adult and juvenile confinement population. However, the introduction of the same adversarial system for juveniles and adults could not explain why the juvenile confinement rate increased 2.78 times more than the adult confinement rate in this period, as shown by figure 5.10.

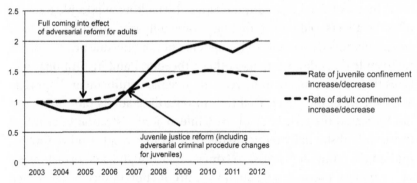

Figure 5.10. Rate of adult and juvenile confinement in Chile, 2003–2012, after the coming into effect of the adversarial system and the juvenile justice reform. *Sources:* Gendarmería de Chile, *Compendio estadístico penitenciario, 2010–2012*; SENAME, *Boletín estadístico anual de los niños(as) y adolescentes vigentes en la red SENAME, 2003–2013.*

In addition, this difference between the increase in adult and juvenile confinement is even more remarkable if we take into account that while the arrest rates do not seem to account for changes in juvenile confinement, changes in the rate of adult arrests may explain the increase in adult confinement, as figure 5.11 indicates. The upward part of the curve on arrests of people older than nineteen years track almost perfectly the upward curve on adult confinement. While total arrests of people older than nineteen years increased 47% (from 127,247 to 187,273 arrests) from 2004 to 2011, adult confinement increased 48% in the same period (from 36,123 to 53,606 cases).

If an increase in adult arrests may explain (a substantial share of) the increase in adult confinement, the adversarial reform would not explain such an increase. Unless the adversary system affected adult and juvenile cases in very different ways, the introduction of such a system would thus not (fully) explain the increase in juvenile confinement either.

However, it is possible that the adversary system affected adult and juvenile confinement differently given the different composition of the adult and juvenile docket. As we saw in figure 5.8, robbery, a crime that is comparatively easy to prosecute and try, accounts for 75% to 80% of juvenile confinement. In contrast, robbery and theft account for about 50% of adult confinement, and drug offenses—crimes that are generally more difficult to investigate, prosecute, and try than robbery—account for over 15%. Also, as figure 5.11 shows, while robbery arrests for adults increased 26%, drug offense arrests for adults increased 198% between 2003 and 2011. It is thus possible that the adversary system has contributed to (more of) an increase in juvenile confinement than in adult confinement because the adversary process has been particularly good at investigating, prosecuting, and trying crimes such as robbery, which is the crime that accounts for most of juvenile confinement.

But even if the adversary system affected adult and juvenile confinement differently, it is unlikely that it is the only aspect of the juvenile justice reform that accounts for the increase in juvenile confinement given how much higher it has been than the increase in adult confinement and given that arrests for people younger than twenty decreased, while arrests for people older than twenty went substantially up.

Other aspects of the juvenile justice reform could then partially explain the juvenile confinement increase. As already mentioned, the Chilean reform aimed at replacing the old "tutelary system," based on protective measures on non-criminally-liable youth, with a model in which youth are considered criminally responsible for their own acts, even if subject to special regulations. A number of the old "minor court" judges retired or were transferred to civil courts, and a new group of prosecutors and judges, trained and specialized in the new juvenile justice system, started to prosecute and adjudicate juvenile cases after the coming into effect of the juvenile justice reform in 2007. It is then

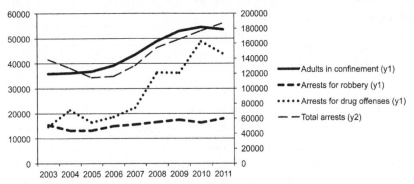

Figure 5.11. Adult confinement and arrests for people older than nineteen years in Chile, 2003–2011. Source: Fundación Paz Ciudadana, Anuario de estadísticas criminales 2011.

possible that the shift from a protective to a responsibility paradigm for juveniles has led to a higher use of confinement because it has left more room for decision makers to take into account retributive and incapacitation considerations that, as we mentioned, were one of the motivations or reasons for the introduction of the juvenile justice reform for a number of political actors. This may be particularly the case because the prosecutors and judges who try juvenile cases, though specialized in juvenile law, do not sit in a separate juvenile court and may also intervene in adult cases. Short of data at the case level on actual measures and sentences and other variables before and after the juvenile justice reform, which we do not have, the evidence to test this hypothesis can only be indirect.

In any case, whether there were particular interactions between the adversary system and the juvenile docket or whether the transition from a tutelary system to a criminal juvenile responsibility system left room to implement more punitive policies toward juveniles, our data suggest that the juvenile justice reform has contributed to higher confinement levels for juveniles.

As shown in table 5.9, juvenile confinement is only 3.7% of overall confinement, and confinement is used substantially less against juveniles than against adults in Chile. However, since the new juvenile justice system came into effect, juvenile confinement has doubled its absolute numbers and increased 2.78 times higher than adult confinement and represents a higher percentage of total confinement, without an increase in juvenile arrests. The new juvenile justice regime is likely responsible for this increase.

Conclusion

This chapter has provided an overview of the law in the books and the law in action of Latin American juvenile justice systems and has explored how much of a gap there is between the two. Latin American juvenile courts were created in the first half of the twentieth century under legal frameworks that conceived of youth in conflict with the law as subjects of protection and treatment. At the turn of the twenty-first century, there was a wave of juvenile justice laws that conceive of deviant youth as rights bearers who are protected by due process and are criminally responsible for their conduct.

In the two periods, Latin American juvenile justice laws have had as two of their stated goals rehabilitating these children and adolescents and removing them from criminal law and punishment. Without denying the serious problems that Latin American juvenile justice systems present, our analysis of Latin American juvenile justice systems suggests that the second goal is advanced by these systems since Latin American juvenile justice systems do remove a substantial number of these children and adolescents from criminal confinement.

Our analysis of the Chilean juvenile justice reform also suggests that the reform has likely brought about substantially higher levels of youth confinement. As in the rest of the region, juveniles are confined at a lower rate than are adults in Chile. But after the introduction of the juvenile justice reform, absolute and relative levels of juvenile confinement have gone up. Future studies should explore whether the Chilean reform is representative or an exception among the new juvenile justice reforms in the region.

NOTES

Mary Beloff wrote the first three (historical) sections of this chapter, on the basis of her works cited in note 2. She deeply thanks Máximo Langer for his attentive reading, lucid comments, and careful editing of these three sections. She also thanks E. O'Byrne and J. Hardwick for their assistance in her translation to English of her original essay. Máximo Langer did the research for and wrote sections "From Theory to Practice: Comparing Use of Confinement and Sanctioning Policies in Criminal and Juvenile Courts" and "Evaluating the Recent Juvenile Justice Laws: The Chilean Law as a Case Study" of this chapter. He thanks Ricardo Lillo for his outstanding research assistance. Both authors thank Marcelo Bergman, Jaime Couso, and Mauricio Duce for their excellent comments on an earlier draft and Frank Zimring for his insightful input. Unless otherwise indicated, all translations from Portuguese and Spanish are ours.

1. For instance, none of the main collections in English comparing juvenile justice systems include a chapter on a Latin American country or on Latin America as a region. See Frieder Dünkel, Joanna Grzywa, Philip Horsfield, and Ineke Pruin, eds., *Juvenile Justice Systems in Europe: Current Situation and Reform Developments*, 2nd ed., 4 vols. (Mönchengladbach, Germany: Forum Verlag Godesberg, 2011); Eric L. Jensen and Jorgen Jepsen, eds., *Juvenile Law Violators, Human Rights and the Development of New Juvenile Justice Systems* (Oxford, UK: Hart, 2006); Josine Junger-Tas and Scott H.

Decker, eds., *International Handbook of Juvenile Justice* (New York: Springer 2006); Jill Mehlbye and Lode Walgrave, eds., *Confronting Youth in Europe: Juvenile Crime and Juvenile Justice* (Copenhagen: AKF Forlaget, 1998); John Muncie and Barry Goldson, eds., *Comparative Youth Justice: Critical Issues* (London: Sage, 2006); Michael Tonry and Anthony Doob, eds., *Youth Crime and Youth Justice: Comparative and Cross-National Perspectives*, Crime and Justice 31 (Chicago: University of Chicago Press, 2004).

2. As indicated in the acknowledgment note, the historical sections of this chapter are mostly based on and follow the general historical account of the juvenile justice reforms provided in the following texts by Mary Beloff: "Sistema penal juvenil: ¿Garantías sin protección especial? La interpretación latinoamericana," in *Nova Criminis: Visiones criminológicas de la justicia penal* (Centro de investigaciones criminológicas de la justicia penal, Facultad de Ciencias Jurídicas y Sociales de la Universidad Central de Chile) 6 (December 2013): 63–118; "Medidas socio-educativas en la justicia juvenil: De la ley a la práctica," in *Un reto para la región: La aplicación de las medidas socio-educativas para adolescentes en conflicto con la ley penal* (Lima, Peru: ACCEDE/ BID, 2013), 21–44; "Quince años de vigencia de la Convención sobre Derechos del Niño en la Argentina," in *La familia en el nuevo derecho: Homenaje a Cecilia Grosman*, ed. Aída Kemelmajer de Carlucci (Santa Fe, Argentina: Rubinzal-Culzoni, 2009), 131–184; "Algunas confusiones en torno a las consecuencias jurídicas de la conducta transgresora de la ley penal en los nuevos sistemas de justicia juvenil latinoamericanos," in *Revista mexicana de Justicia: Los nuevos desafíos de la PGR* (México: Procuraduría General de la República, 2006), 105–140; and "Los sistemas de responsabilidad penal juvenil en América Latina," in *Derechos de la niñez y la adolescencia: Antología* (San José de Costa Rica: CONAMAJ/EJ/UNICEF, 2001).

3. Brazil was influenced by Lusitanian legislation that was similar to the Spanish one regarding youth deviant behavior.

4. See Luis Agote, Record of Sessions of the National Congress, Chamber of Deputies of the Nation, Argentina, Meeting no. 11, June 8, 1918, 262. The epigraph by Enoch Wines can be found in Anthony Platt, *The Child Savers: The Invention of Delinquency* (Chicago: University of Chicago Press, 1969), vi.

5. "Those articles . . . created bodies similar to the juvenile courts, as is expressly recognized by the Criminal Court of Appeals: 'The law for the welfare of minors, in its articles 14 et sequitur, is inspired by . . . North American laws and *in fact establishes the system of juvenile courts.*'" Leopoldo Lugones, Jr., *La menoría*, year 7, no. 82 (Buenos Aires: Biblioteca Policial, 1941), 74 (italics added).

6. Law 14.394, December 22, 1954 (Argentina).

7. See, e.g., Chilean Law of Minors 16.618 (1967).

8. See, e.g., Argentinian Law on Criminal Responsibility of Minors (1978); Code of Minors of Uruguay (1934); Criminal Code of Costa Rica (1941), art. 25.

9. See, e.g., *In Re Gault*, 387 U.S. 1, 16–17 (1967).

10. On the type of criminal process for adults that Latin American countries adopted between the second half of the nineteenth century and the early twentieth century, see Máximo Langer, "Revolution in Latin American Criminal Procedure:

Diffusion of Legal Ideas from the Periphery," *American Journal of Comparative Law* 55 (2007): 617–676.

11. While the U.S. Supreme Court ruled on whether the juvenile court was constitutional practically since its creation, the Supreme Court of Argentina began to consider only in the 1990s whether the proceedings to try juvenile criminal cases and making decisions on protective measures were constitutional. See, e.g., Supreme Court of Argentina, *Maldonado*, December 7, 2005.

12. On the broader criminal justice reforms in Latin America, see Langer, "Revolution in Latin American Criminal Procedure."

13. The Declaration was adopted by United Nations General Assembly Resolution 1386 (XIV) of 10 December 1959. On the influence of this declaration on article 227, see, e.g., Fernando Luiz Menezes Guiraud, "Atuação do Conselho Tutelar e a Questão das Drogas," *Igualdade* 41 (2008): 78–97, http://www.sociedadesemear.org.br/arquivos/20111024173251_ri_41_drogadicao.pdf.

14. See the English translation of Brazil's Constitution at http://www.stf.jus.br/repositorio/cms/portalStfInternacional/portalStfSobreCorte_en_us/anexo/constituicao_ingles_3ed2010.pdf (accessed July 15, 2014). On the Brazilian reform, see, e.g., *Ser niño en América Latina: De las necesidades a los derechos* (proceedings of Seminario Latinoamericano "Infancia, Situaciones de Riesgo y Políticas de Prevención en América Latina en el Marco de la Convención Internacional de los Derechos del Niño," Buenos Aires, September 10–14, 1990), 73–82, 227–230, 311–324.

15. See American Convention on Human Rights, art. 5.5: "Minors while subject to criminal proceedings shall be separated from adults and brought before specialized tribunals, as speedily as possible, so that they may be treated in accordance with their status as minors." Among the opinions and decisions issued by the Inter-American Court of Human Rights, see, e.g., Advisory Opinion OC-17/2002 of August 28, 2002, "Juridical Condition and the Human Rights of the Child"; and its decision in the case of the *"Juvenile Reeducation Institute" v. Paraguay*, Judgment of September 2, 2004.

16. For a critical analysis of the arguments and strategies that reformers articulated to advance these reforms, see Philippe de Dinechin, *La réinterprétation en droit interne des conventions internationales sur les droits de l'homme: Le cas de l'intégration de la Convention des droits de l'enfant dans les droits nationaux en Amérique latine* (Ph.D. diss., Paris III University, 2006), available at http://tel.archives-ouvertes.fr/docs/00/08/99/74/PDF/these_p_de_dinechin_515p_.pdf.

17. On criminal procedure reforms in Latin America, see, e.g., Langer, "Revolution in Latin American Criminal Procedure."

18. See, e.g., Message of the President of Chile, Law Number 20.084, in Biblioteca del Congreso Nacional de Chile, *Historia de la ley 20.084, Establece un Sistema de Responsabilidad de los Adolescentes por Infracciones a la Ley Penal* (2005), 6–7.

19. Argentina did not pass new juvenile justice laws in the period under analysis. Penal Regulations of Minority Law 22278 of 1980 are still the main substantive regulation of juvenile courts in Argentina, though provinces have approved new procedural regulations in the past twenty years to meet the standards of the CRC and other

human rights instruments. In October 2005, Law 26061, titled "Comprehensive Protection of the Rights of the Children and Adolescent Act" [Ley de Protección Integral de los Derechos de las Niñas, Niños y Adolescentes], was published. But this law only contains incidental regulations regarding juvenile justice.

20. These countries include Bolivia, Colombia, the Dominican Republic, Ecuador, Guatemala (although its first code passed never came into force), and Venezuela.

21. See, e.g., Message of the President of Chile, Law Number 20.084, 6 (explaining that meeting the principles and directives of the UN Convention on the Rights of the Child was one of the reasons for the adoption of the new juvenile law in Chile); Code of Childhood and Adolescence of Honduras, art. 2 (explicitly mentioning as general goals of the code the protection of the rights established in the Convention and the need to modernize the legal regime in this area).

22. See, e.g., Message of the President of Chile, Law Number 20.084, 7–8.

23. The exception is Costa Rica, where well-recognized jurists and criminal law scholars in particular took part in the legal reform process on child and youth matters.

24. The Brazilian statute is an example of poor legal drafting because the main drafters were activists, rather than jurists. Theoretical inconsistencies have come from the tension between the tutelary and criminal responsibility models. On this tension, see, e.g., Mary Beloff, "Algunas confusiones en torno a las consecuencias jurídicas de la conducta transgresora de la ley penal en los nuevos sistemas de justicia juvenil latinoamericanos," in *Revista mexicana de justicia: Los nuevos desafíos de la PGR* (México: Procuraduría General de la República, 2006), 105–140.

25. The Underage Offender Law of El Salvador was passed by Decree 863 on April 27, 1994, and had its name and some specific articles amended by Decree 395 on July 28, 2004. The Juvenile Criminal Justice Law, 7.576, of Costa Rica, was passed on March 8, 1996, and published on April 30 and has been in force since that date.

26. See, e.g., Code of Childhood and Adolescence of Honduras, art. 181; Dominican Republic, Law 136-06, art. 278.

27. See, e.g., Chile, Law 16.618 (Law of Minors), art. 32 (establishing that even when the judge reached the conclusion that the crime had not been committed or that the minor had not participated in it, he or she could still decide to apply any protection measure of those contemplated in that law in any case in which the minor was in material or moral risk).

28. See United Nations Standard Minimum Rules for the Administration of Juvenile Justice (Beijing Rules), Rule 3.

29. United Nations Assembly General Resolution, A/RES/45/112, sixty-eighth plenary meeting, December 14, 1990, Guidelines 5, 6, and 58.

30. See, e.g., Statute of Childhood and Adolescence of Brazil, arts. 99 et seq.

31. Remission is a mechanism adopted by most countries in the region.

32. See, e.g., Chile, Act 20.084, art. 27; Costa Rica, Act 7576, art. 9; Code of Childhood and Adolescence of Honduras, arts. 219 et seq.

33. On rehabilitation as one of the goals of the reforms, see, e.g., Chile, Law 20.084, art. 20; Ecuador, Code of the Childhood and Adolescence, Act 2002-100, arts. 307,

309. See also Mary Beloff, "¿Son posibles mejores prácticas en la justicia juvenil?," in *Derechos de niños, niñas y adolescentes: Seguimiento de la aplicación de la Convención sobre Derechos del Niño; Conceptos, debates y experiencias en justicia penal juvenil* (Buenos Aires: Ministerio de Justicia y Derechos Humanos, SENAF/UNICEF, 2007), 31–40.

34. See, e.g., Inter-American Commission of Human Rights, Rapporteurship on the Rights of the Child, *Juvenile Justice and Human Rights in the Americas*, OEA/Ser.L/V/ II. Doc. 78, pp. 39 (referring to the situation of Honduras), 126 (on El Salvador), 132 (referring to the lack of rehabilitation capabilities in drug-related cases in countries of the region); Committee on the Rights of the Child, comments to state reports: CRC/C/15/Add.241, November 3, 2004 (on the situation in Brazil); CRC/C/COL/CO/3, June 8, 2006 (on the situation in Colombia); CRC/C/15/Add.154, July 9, 2001 (on the situation in Guatemala). See also Beloff, "Sistema Penal Juvenil."

35. See Committee on the Rights of the Child, General Comment No. 10 (2007), on "Children's rights in juvenile justice," § 31.

36. See, e.g., Brazil, Statute of Child and Adolescent, art. 105; Guatemala, Law of Integral Protection of Childhood and Adolescence, art. 138; Peru, Code of Children and Adolescents, art. 242.

37. See, e.g., Ecuador, Code of the Childhood and Adolescence, Act 2002-100, art. 305.

38. See, e.g., United Nations Standard Minimum Rules for the Administration of Juvenile Justice (Beijing Rules), Rule 7; United Nations Rules for the Protection of Juveniles Deprived of Their Liberty, arts. 17, 18.

39. On due process regulations, see, e.g., Code of Childhood and Adolescence of Honduras, arts. 182, 183, 213, 226–229.

40. On this wave of criminal procedure reforms in Latin America, see Langer, "Revolution in Latin American Criminal Procedure."

41. See, e.g., Code of Childhood and Adolescence of Honduras, arts. 188–196.

42. See, e.g., Convention on the Rights of the Child, art. 40(2)(b)(v).

43. See, e.g., Code of Childhood and Adolescence of Honduras, art. 188.

44. See e.g. Chile, Act 20.084, art. 6.

45. See e.g. Chile, Act 20.084, art. 18.

46. See e.g. Chile, Act 20.084, art. 23.

47. See, e.g., Message of the President of Chile, Law Number 20.084, 13–14; Colombia, Code of Childhood and Adolescence, Act 1098, art. 178 (stating that the sanctions must have a protective, educative, and restorative purpose); Costa Rica, Act of the Juvenile Criminal Justice, Act Ley 7576, art. 123 (establishing that the sentence must have primarily an educative function); Ecuador, Code of the Childhood and the Adolescence, art. 369 (stating that the goal of the socioeducative measures are the social reintegration of and compensation for the damage caused by the juvenile); Code of Childhood and Adolescence of Honduras, art. 198 (stating that confinement should be limited to what is strictly necessary for rehabilitation purposes).

48. See sources cited in note 34.

49. See, e.g., Convention on the Rights of the Child, art. 37(b).

50. See, e.g., Beijing Rules, Rules 13 and 17; Rules for the Protection of Juveniles Deprived of Their Liberty, Rules 1, 2, and 17.

51. See, e.g., Colombia, Code of the Childhood and Adolescence, art. 181 (limited duration of the provisory internment or pretrial detention) and art. 187 (establishing limitations in the duration of the socioeducative measures); Code of Childhood and Adolescence of Honduras, art. 188 (stating that confinement is an exceptional measure that should be as brief as possible, limited to a maximum of eight years, and may only be taken in certain defined circumstances).

52. See, e.g., Code of Childhood and Adolescence of Honduras, art. 199.

53. There are also reasons to take the data on Bolivia with special caution given that this country reported data on juvenile confinement for only five years for the period 2000–2013. All the data about Bolivia, including the confinement rate per 100,000, are taken from the Alertamerica database available online and refer to the year 2012.

54. There are reasons to take some of these data on Mexico with special caution because Mexico has provided data to the United Nations Office on Drugs and Crime (UNODC) for only two years in the 2003–2012 period, which has required that we compare rates from different years in the case of this country (2011 and 2012). In addition, Mexico's total adult confinement levels reported in Alertamerica and in UNODC are suspiciously low because its rate of adult confinement for every one hundred thousand adults is much lower than this rate for Brazil. We thus wonder whether jails and other institutions of local government are counted in this analysis.

55. Honduras has an adult ratio of 1.6 because the reported number of adults in formal contact with the police is lower than the reported number of adults in confinement. As indicated by the source note to figure 5.2, these data refer to the year 2011 and come from the United Nations Office for Drugs and Crime.

56. Notice that while the number of adult arrests is normally higher than the number of adults in confinement, these data on Rio de Janeiro show a higher number of adults in confinement for every year reported. The data are taken from the single source indicated in table 5.7. We do not know what may explain this pattern.

57. The only possible exceptions are a few reports by governmental offices that have presented and analyzed data on juvenile justice systems. But such reports do not enable inferring conclusions about the results of the reforms because they have not considered the pre- and postreform periods or have only compared one year before and after the introduction of the reform or have not compared the adult and juvenile populations. See, e.g., Defensoría Penal Pública, Departamento de Estudios, *Informe estadístico: Primer año de vigencia; Ley de Responsabilidad Penal Adolescente (8 junio 2007 a 7 junio 2008)* (Santiago, Chile), available at http://www.dpp.cl/resources/upload/files/document o/8b1f1e8511e7dddb91209c4c6dac46ed.pdf; SENAME, *Informe de diagnóstico de la implementación de la ley 20.084: Junio 2007–Marzo 2010* (Santiago, Chile, 2010), available at http://www.sename.cl/wsename/otros/rpa/INFORME_LRPA_FINAL.pdf; Secretaria de Dereitos Humanos, *Atendimento socioeducativo ao adolescente em conflito com a lei: Levantamento nacional 2011* (Brasilia, Brazil, 2012), available at http://www.anajure.org. br/wp-content/uploads/2013/04/LEVANTAMENTO-NACIONAL-2011.pdf.

58. Act 20.084, December 2005.

59. Corporación Opción and UNICEF, ¡Conoce tus derechos! Manual sobre la Ley de Responsabilidad Penal de Adolescentes (Santiago, Chile, 2009).

60. See, e.g., Message of the President of Chile, Law Number 20.084, 5–7.

61. See, e.g., ibid., 7–8.

62. On this tension, see, e.g., Miguel Cillero y Martín Bernales, "Derechos humanos de la infancia/adolescencia en la justicia 'penal de menores' de Chile: Evaluación y perspectivas," Revista de Derechos del Niño (Universidad Diego Portales y UNICEF, Santiago, Chile) 1 (2002): 31–33; Mauricio Duce, "El proceso establecido en el proyecto de ley que crea un sistema de responsabilidad de los adolescentes por infracciones a la ley penal: Avances y problemas," Revista de Derechos del Niño (Universidad Diego Portales y UNICEF, Santiago, Chile) 2 (2004): 111–112.

63. Chile, Law 16.618, March 1967.

64. The Chilean adversarial reform was implemented gradually in different regions of the country. It came into effect in Santiago, the largest region in terms of its population, in 2005.

65. Chile, Law 20.084, art. 29.

66. Ibid., art. 2.

67. Ibid., art. 26 (confinement should be used as a last-resort measure and never in cases in which it would not be appropriate for an adult), art. 32 (pretrial confinement in a "closed regime" is applicable only for serious criminal offenses and when no alternative measure would be sufficient to meet the goals of pretrial detention). On these principles and the other principles that should guide the interpretation of the new Chilean law by courts and other actors of the system, see, e.g., Jaime Couso Salas and Mauricio Duce Julio, Juzgamiento penal de adolescentes (Santiago, Chile: LOM, 2013).

68. See, e.g., Chile, Law 20.084, art. 23.

69. See Defensoría Penal Pública, Informe estadístico; Defensoría Penal Pública, Unidad de Defensa Penal Juvenil, 3 años de vigencia Ley de Responsabilidad Penal del Adolescente 8 de Junio de 2007 a 7 de Junio de 2010 (Santiago, Chile, 2011); Gonzalo Berríos, "La Ley de Responsabilidad Penal del Adolescente como sistema de justicia: Análisis y propuestas," Política criminal 6, no. 11 (2011): 163–191; Couso and Duce, Juzgamiento penal de adolescentes; SENAME, Informe de diagnóstico.

70. The only exception is the report by Defensoría Penal Pública, Departamento de Estudios, Informe estadístico. But this report includes data about a short period that goes from one year before to one year after the juvenile justice reform entered into effect and does not compare total confinement levels, as we do in this section.

71. See Gendarmería de Chile, Departamento de Estudios, Compendio estadístico penitenciario 2010, 29.

72. For an analysis of the evolution of pretrial detention in Chile before and after the introduction of the more adversarial system there, see Mauricio Duce and Cristián Riego, La prisión preventiva en Chile: Análisis de los cambios legales y su impacto (Santiago, Chile: Ediciones Universidad Diego Portales, 2011).

73. This due process improvement would be in line with the U.S. case *In Re Winship*, 397 U.S. 358 (1970).

74. The annual reports by SENAME are the source of our numbers on juveniles in confinement or custodial or secure confinement—terms that we have used indistinctively throughout this chapter. The labels and types of categories of juveniles in confinement were different before and after the juvenile justice reform in Chile. We have included in the total number of juveniles in secure confinement before the reform those in "Centros de Observación y Diagnóstico" (COD, Centers of Observation and Diagnosis; measures that were equivalent to pretrial detention); in "Rehabilitación Conductual Internado" (Confined for Behavioral Rehabilitation; measures that applied to those who were considered guilty for a criminal offense who were younger than sixteen years or were sixteen or seventeen years without discernment); and "Secciones de Menores de Gendarmería de Chile" (Juvenile Sections of the Correctional System of Chile, where those who were sixteen or seventeen years with discernment were sent). After the introduction of the reform, we have included in the total number of juveniles in confinement those subjected to pretrial detention ("Internación Provisoria") and those convicted and deprived of their freedom by being subjected to the enclosed regime or the semienclosed regime ("Régimen Cerrado" or "Régimen Semicerrado," as defined by articles 16 and 17 of Act 20.084).

75. The data on juveniles from figure 5.9 are imperfect because they also include arrests of individuals who were eighteen and nineteen years. We still use them because they are the only data by crime that we have been able to obtain. An alternative would have been to use the data on juvenile formal contact with the police for all crimes in Chile in the same period from the United Nations Office for Drugs and Crime; these data go in the same direction as the reported data and show an 11% decrease.

76. Another hypothesis that we considered was that the Piñera administration that took office in March 2010 pushed for a change in criminal policy by articulating a law-and-order discourse that criticized courts for being soft on crime, thus informally indicating to criminal justice actors that they needed to increase the levels of confinement. See, e.g., "Piñera reitera críticas a acción de la justicia en caso del violador de Placilla," *La Tercera*, April 15, 2010, http://www.latercera.com/contenido/674_251648_9.shtml; Francisco Mendez Bernales, "Piñera y su curioso concepto de justicia," *El Quinto Poder*, March 3, 2014, http://www.elquintopoder.cl/politica/pinera-y-su-curioso-concepto-de-justicia/; "Presidente critica a fiscales, jueces de garantía y tribunales por seguridad ciudadana," *La Segunda*, February 26, 2014, http://www.lasegunda.com/Noticias/Politica/2014/02/917180/presidente-critica-a-fiscales-jueces-de-garantia-y-tribunales-por-seguridad-ciudadana. However, this hypothesis is not consistent with our data. As figures 5.8 indicates, the increase in the levels of juvenile confinement went up until 2010, the year that Piñera took office, and stalled or diminished after that. Available data thus indicate that the Piñera administration's law-and-order discourse on crime does not explain the increase in juvenile confinement that we are analyzing.

77. See, e.g., Duce and Riego, *La prisión preventiva en Chile*.

6

Juvenile Justice in Muslim-Majority States

LENA SALAYMEH

Is there an "Islamic juvenile justice"? This chapter provides overviews of laws relating to the crimes of minors in three distinct, legal-historical moments: in orthodox Islamic jurisprudence as developed in the late antique and medieval eras (roughly 610–ca. 1250 CE), in modern Islamic legal history (19th and 20th centuries), and in the legal systems of many contemporary Muslim-majority nation-states.[1] "Juvenile justice" is, of course, a modern category, and my objective is not to locate it in historical contexts but rather to understand how premodern Muslim jurists defined minors and dealt with their crimes. As will become apparent, many orthodox Islamic legal traditions on the treatment of children are not applied in contemporary Muslim-majority states.

A brief historical-jurisprudential exploration is necessary because Muslim jurists developed an orthodox methodology (*uṣūl al-fiqh*) and orthodox legal doctrines in the medieval period that remains relevant to contemporary laws in Muslim societies and to the daily life of Muslims globally. However, orthodox Islamic law is by no means the sole source in the legal life of Muslims today. This chapter is a broad-spectrum overview intended to explain that "Islamic jurisprudence" is not coterminous with "law in contemporary Muslim-majority states" (Salaymeh 2014).[2] Islamic jurisprudence is generated by an interpretive process anchored in canonical (and primarily late antique) Islamic texts, whereas law in contemporary Muslim-majority states is the product of legislative or other processes that often integrate colonial, international, customary, and Islamic laws (Salaymeh 2015a). This chapter responds to the question "is there an 'Islamic juvenile justice'?" by demonstrating that (a) most contemporary Muslim-majority states (rather than Muslim jurists trained in orthodox Islamic jurisprudence) determine juvenile laws with little recourse either to orthodox Islamic jurisprudence or to canonical Islamic legal texts; (b) for the most part, contemporary Muslim-majority states determine the content of juvenile justice laws in dialogue with international norms. Generally, colonial legal influences and international legal norms are more instrumental than orthodox Islamic jurisprudence in shaping juvenile law in most contemporary Muslim-majority states. Again, this is not surprising, since juvenile justice is a modern legal construct.

This chapter's recognition of the myriad historical, geographical, political, and legal-textual differences between "Islamic jurisprudence" and "law in Muslim-majority states" illustrates the variety, complexity, and diversity of law in contemporary Muslim societies. Contemporary Muslim-majority states include the following: Afghanistan, Albania, Algeria, Azerbaijan, Bahrain, Bangladesh, Brunei, Burkina Faso, Chad, Comoros, Djibouti, Egypt, Gambia, Guinea, Indonesia, Iran, Iraq, Jordan, Kazakhstan, Kosovo, Kuwait, Kyrgyzstan, Lebanon, Libya, Malaysia, Maldives, Mali, Mauritania, Morocco, Niger, Oman, Pakistan, Palestine, Qatar, Saudi Arabia, Senegal, Sierra Leone, Somalia, Sudan, Syria, Tajikistan, Tunisia, Turkey, Turkmenistan, United Arab Emirates, Uzbekistan, Western Sahara, and Yemen.[3] Of course, this chapter cannot comprehensively report on the juvenile justice systems in each of these states. Instead, I provide a broad overview of trends or patterns and highlight some exceptional cases.

Comparing historical and modern juvenile justice systems is not the objective of this chapter. Such an endeavor would likely be anachronistic and unproductive because the very meanings of childhood and crime are historically situated (Harlow et al. 2010). For example, in all parts of the premodern world, corporal punishment was normative. In the modern era, the bulk of criminal punishments globally are meted out through imprisonment; however, it appears that modern nation-states criminally punish a higher percentage of citizens than premodern states did (Cohen 1985). The modern elaboration and expansion of criminal law is related to the changing nature of the state and its use of violence (Friedman 1993) as well as privatization and expansion of social control (Feeley 2002). Modern legal responses to juvenile delinquents must be situated within broader trends in the modernization of law generally and in incarceration specifically (Dolovich 2009; Ferguson 2014). The contemporary expansion and intensification of the criminal legal system includes minors, who do not necessarily avoid adult punishments because of the existence of a complex juvenile justice system (Fagan 2010). Moreover, these changes in the type, frequency, and duration of punishment in the modern world have coincided with delayed adulthood, shrinking childhood, and the establishment of "emerging adulthood" as a new life stage (Arnett 2010). Childhood is a culturally specific creation that changes in response to a variety of sociopolitical and economic conditions, including literacy (Postman 1982). Put simply, criminal punishments of minors in the premodern and in the modern world are not easily compared because the meaning of "minor" and the effect of criminal punishments are historically and geographically situated.

Minors and Their Crimes in Orthodox Islamic Jurisprudence

This section provides a synopsis of the basic criminal legal categories and issues that are relevant to understanding criminal punishments of children under orthodox Islamic law. According to orthodox Islamic jurisprudence, which developed roughly between 610 and 1250 CE, there are two age categories for the purposes of criminal liability, "child" (or "minor") and "adult." In order to be subject to criminal punishments under Islamic law, an individual must be an adult, which is defined as having full mental and physical capacity (Ṣabāḥī 2008, 37).

Mental capacity is obtained gradually as a child matures. Medieval orthodox Muslim jurists identified three basic phases (or states) of legal competence: incompetent, semicompetent, and fully competent.[4] The phase of incompetency, during which one is not capable of distinguishing between right and wrong, lasts from birth until age seven; this is because children are instructed to begin praying at age seven, on the basis of a Prophetic tradition-report (ḥadīth) (Zaytūn 2001, 46–47).[5] The phase of semicompetence, during which one is only partially capable of recognizing immoral acts, lasts from the age of seven to puberty (Zaytūn 2001, 47). Full competence coincides with puberty, which Muslim jurists often defined in terms of physical manifestations (Zaytūn 2001, 48). While this three-stage competency process was reflected in rulings on conversion, taxation, and commercial dealings, by and large, it was not applied for criminal punishments (Ṣabāḥī

2008, 39–73)—except to determine if a child had sufficient competence to warrant a disciplinary punishment (Ṣabāhī 2008, 555). In addition, orthodox Muslim jurists considered a child's "mistake" and "intention" to be equivalent, such that a child lacks the capacity for criminal intent that an adult has (Ṣabāhī 2008, 174).

Medieval jurists defined physical capacity as resulting from the onset of puberty and identified puberty on the basis of physical signs. If the physical signs were not discernible or were ambiguous, jurists delineated a default (maximum) age of puberty (Peters 2005, 21). However, there is juristic disagreement on this default age: the majority of orthodox jurists (Shāfiʿīs, Ḥanbalīs, some Ḥanafīs, and some Imāmī Shīʿīs) identified it as 15 years old for both male and female persons; in contrast, Abū Ḥanīfah (d. 767; Iraq) considered puberty to be 18 years for males and 17 years for females; Mālikīs considered puberty to be 18 years old for both males and females (Ṣabāhī 2008, 76; Ustarūshanī 1997, 119; Zaytūn 2001, 49). While the majority of orthodox jurists identified 15 as the maximum age of puberty, they also recognized that puberty may occur at a later age (Ṣabāhī 2008, 81). In short, the majority of Muslim jurists did not hold children under the age of puberty liable for adult crimes and imposed distinctly lesser punishments for crimes of minors (aḥdāth).

There are two identified categories of crimes in orthodox Islamic jurisprudence: fixed crimes (ḥudūd), which have binding penalties, and discretionary crimes (taʿzīr), the penalties for which are determined by a judge or a state. Fixed crimes include theft (punished by amputation of the right hand), robbery (yearlong banishment or cross-amputation),[6] unlawful sexual intercourse (100 lashes or stoning), falsely accusing someone of unlawful sexual intercourse (80 lashes), drinking alcohol (40 or 80 lashes), and apostasy (execution). Some crimes overlap with the category of retribution torts (qiṣāṣ) and therefore can generate both criminal punishment and tort compensation (i.e., financial or physical retribution).[7] However, the victim or his or her next of kin can waive retribution by accepting financial compensation or by forgiveness. Retribution torts include murder, quasi-intentional murder, unintentional murder, and intentional and unintentional physical injury.

The majority of Muslim jurists identified both puberty and full mental competency as a prerequisite for legal responsibility (taklīf). Consequently, children lack legal responsibility and are not punished like adults. The main legal evidence that jurists cite to support minors being immune from adult punishments is a Prophetic report that exempts three categories of people: the mentally insane, the unconscious, and children—until they reach the age of puberty. Generally, children who commit fixed crimes (including adultery, falsely accusing someone of committing adultery, consuming alcohol, theft, and brigandage) are not subject to the binding punishments (Ṣabāḥī 2008, 251, 275, 287, 317, 349). Instead of the binding physical punishments imposed for fixed crimes, children may be subject to disciplinary (*tā'dīb*) punishments that differ from those meted out to adults or be forced to pay compensation (Ṣabāḥī 2008, 273, 277, 292, 298, 323). In the case of discretionary crimes, orthodox Muslim jurists disagreed on the issue of punishing children: Ḥanafīs, some Shāfiʿīs, and Imāmī Shīʿīs asserted that children are punished; Mālikīs, some Shāfiʿīs, Ḥanbalīs, and Ẓāhirīs do not punish children. Disciplinary punishments are determined on a case-by-case basis but may not cause serious physical harm and are not intended to punish minors (Ṣabāḥī 2008, 355, 550). Moreover, disciplinary punishments are set by parents or by judges in extreme cases (Ṣabāḥī 2008, 563). In addition, children are not subject to physical retributions because they lack full legal competence (Ṣabāḥī 2008, 158–159, 237, 242). Instead, families are responsible for paying financial compensation to the victim(s) of a child's retribution tort (Ṣabāḥī 2008, 164).

To summarize, under orthodox Islamic law, an individual must have full mental and physical capacity to be subject to adult criminal punishment. These legal opinions on the type of punishment meted out to minors must be balanced against the frequency of convictions. Strict Islamic evidentiary rules and flexible criminal procedural rules create formidable barriers to sentencing; for example, fixed crimes require two eyewitnesses, with the exception of unlawful sexual intercourse, which necessitates four eyewitnesses (Peters 2005, 13–14). In addition, there is a general legal principle of uncertainty in law or in facts that can result in avoidance of fixed punishments (Peters 2005, 21–23). Moreover, jurisprudential discussions on determining capacity and evaluating the child's situation imply considerable judicial discretion in dealing with the crimes of minors. Indeed, the extent to which these criminal punishments were actually meted out in the diverse parts of the premodern Muslim world is difficult to determine.

Islamic jurisprudential attention to the legal status of minors has a long history (Hashemi 2007, 225). Two of the earliest surviving Islamic monographs dedicated to the rights of the child are *Aḥkām al-ṣighār* (*Rulings on Minors*) by the Ḥanafī jurist Ustarūshanī (d. 1234/1235; Samarqand) and *Tuḥfat al-mawdūd bi-āḥkām al-mawlūd* (*Magnum Opus on Children's Rulings*) by the Ḥanbalī jurist Ibn Qayyim al-Jawzīyah (d. 1350; Syria). al-Jawzīyah's text devotes little attention to a child's criminal responsibility, focusing instead on the rights of and rituals around children (Ibn Qayyim al-Jawzīyah 1977, 235–236). Ustarūshanī's text has a more extensive discussion of the criminal liability of minors and provides insights into how 13th-century orthodox Muslim jurists viewed the criminal liability of children (i.e., those who have not reached puberty) and adolescents (i.e., those past puberty). According to Ustarūshanī, children are not punished for engaging in illicit sex (1997, 131–132). Children and their adolescent or adult comalefactors are not subject to the penalties for some fixed crimes—such as theft and brigandage (Ustarūshanī 1997, 134–135). Overall, however, the text imagines the child as the victim of crimes, rather than as a perpetrator. This reflects a general assumption, prevalent in many medieval Islamic legal texts, that children who commit crimes are coerced to do so by adults. These two medieval texts indicate that premodern Muslim jurists situated the crimes of minors within all-encompassing discussions of children's legal protections. This contrasts with modern practices of isolating juvenile criminality from the rights of minors.

Ottoman Legal History: Modern Precedents for Dealing with Minors and Their Crimes

Since many (though not all) parts of the Muslim world were under Ottoman sovereignty (1299–1923 CE), Ottoman law provides a window into legal modernization processes that gradually transformed the orthodox Islamic jurisprudential tradition. In the mid-19th century, the Ottoman Empire pursued a reorganization process (*tanzīmāt*) that generated administrative and legal reform, with some implications for children (Inalcik 1976). The 1858 Ottoman penal code (modified in 1863) absolves youth (past the age of puberty) from severe punishments by reducing death or life sentences to imprisonment of five to

10 years (Ottoman Empire 1888, 16–17). Similarly, in 1883 (soon after British occupation), Egypt established a penal code for juvenile offenders that discharged children under seven from criminal punishments and gave children under 17 either a reduced penalty or other form of punishment (Abiad and Mansoor 2010, 102). On the basis of orthodox Islamic jurisprudence, a youth passed the age of puberty would receive lesser punishments than those prescribed by Islamic law only if a judge viewed his or her capacity to commit the crime as diminished in some way. In contrast, modern Ottoman and Egyptian laws suggest an integration of a modern conceptualization of youth as a middle category between child and adult. While this modification in the understanding of childhood may have occurred prior to the 19th century, it was clearly and explicitly delineated in 20th-century Ottoman law: the 1911 Ottoman criminal code identifies the age of majority as 18 and stratifies punishments on the basis of age. Instead of treating puberty as the pivotal point for criminal liability, Ottoman law identified four age categories: under 13, between 13 and 15, between 15 and 18, and over 18 (Ottoman Empire 1913, 29–30). The guardians of children under the age of 13 who committed crimes were responsible for damages, and the child could be sent to rehabilitation. An adolescent between the ages of 13 and 15 years old could be imprisoned for between five and 10 years for major crimes (e.g., felonies) and could receive between one-fourth and one-third of an adult's punishment for minor crimes (e.g., misdemeanors). Adolescents between the ages of 15 and 18 years old could be imprisoned between seven and 15 years for major crimes and receive one-half to two-thirds of an adult's punishment for a minor crime. Consequently, minors were excluded from the death penalty and life imprisonment under early 20th-century Ottoman law.

In the post-Ottoman era, juvenile justice systems in Muslim-majority areas were elaborated under colonial rule and postcolonial nation-states. Whether through direct occupation or indirect political and economic pressure, Western colonial interventions in the Muslim world provoked a variety of legal reforms and legal innovations (Salaymeh 2015a). During and after colonization, many Muslim-majority states merged civil or common law traditions from the West with Islamic legal traditions (Salaymeh 2015b). Some of these changes were prompted by the needs of modern nation-states and modern administrative practices; other changes were triggered by socioeconomic and political pressures. As a result, the legal systems of Muslim-majority states fall into three nearly equal categories: hybrid legal systems that integrate common law, civil law, and Islamic law; a predominantly "secular" legal system (primarily civil law); or a predominantly Islamic legal system. In any Muslim-majority state, laws pertaining to juvenile justice reflect complex relationships between orthodox Islamic legal traditions and colonial or customary laws.

Juvenile Justice in Contemporary Muslim-Majority States

For the most part, contemporary Muslim-majority states have largely integrated and adapted global trends in juvenile justice. The legal status of juvenile offenders in these states generally shifts in response to changing understandings of childhood and evolving trends in criminal punishment. Still, despite general legal transformations, a state's juvenile justice system cannot be isolated from broader sociopolitical and economic factors—including the state's economic conditions and the efficacy of the rule of law. In many authoritarian states, legal institutions lack sufficient oversight and tend to operate at the discretion of institutional actors. Consequently, a particular state's official laws—on the treatment of juveniles or any number of legal issues—may not be implemented by local actors (Zalkind and Simon 2004, 101). In addition, establishing a separate and effective juvenile justice system necessitates the dedication of financial and human resources that are not universally available (UNICEF 1998). Thus, while the majority of contemporary Muslim-majority states have specific juvenile legislation, they do not necessarily have the financial means to realize their official objectives (Zalkind and Simon 2004, 103). Problems within a juvenile system are often pervasive to the criminal legal system as a whole. For example, abuse and torture of prisoners, including juveniles, is not uncommon in Egypt (Abiad and Mansoor 2010, 115; Zalkind and Simon 2004, 103). Some states have specific regulations intended to deal with problems that contribute to juvenile delinquency. For example, in 2003, Egypt initiated a project known as the National Strategy for the Rehabilitation and Reintegration of Street Children (Abiad and Mansoor 2010, 105).

But Egypt's deep problems of poverty, homelessness, and authoritarian rule remain unsolved, disproportionately disadvantaging children. Thus, formal legal structures neither reflect nor resolve the situation of juvenile offenders.

UN Convention on the Rights of the Child

Every Muslim-majority state is a signatory to the 1989 UN Convention on the Rights of the Child (CRC), with the specific exceptions of Kosovo (declared independence in 2008), Palestine (UN observer status granted in 2012), and Western Sahara (not recognized by the UN as an independent state) (United Nations 1989). However, Somalia signed the CRC in 2002 but did not ratify or accept it (United Nations 1989). A minority of Muslim-majority states submitted general reservations to the CRC on the basis of the state's interest in implementing only those aspects of the CRC that do not conflict with orthodox Islamic laws; these states include Afghanistan, Algeria, Iran, Iraq, Jordan, Kuwait, Maldives, Mauritania, Oman, Qatar, Saudi Arabia, Syria, and United Arab Emirates (United Nations 1989). In general, these states did not object to specific provisions of the CRC, but rather indicated that their compliance would be limited by their constitutional or other legal obligation to abide by Islamic law. Still, there are states that officially recognize Islamic law as a source of legislation or as a state religion but did not submit reservations to the CRC.[8]

For most Muslim-majority states, the CRC does not pose a conflict. Indeed, Saudi Arabia and Oman have both claimed that the CRC is entirely consistent with Islamic law (Hashemi 2007, 201). But one aspect of the CRC that generally conflicts with orthodox Islamic jurisprudence and is relevant for issues of juvenile justice is the age of majority; the CRC defines a child as any individual under the age of 18, which seems to conflict with Islamic legal traditions that define puberty as the age of adulthood (Hashemi 2007, 199). However, this "conflict" is a matter of interpretation that reflects the complexity of translating orthodox Islamic legal doctrines into the modern, civil legal system of a nation-state. As previously noted, some orthodox jurists set the default age of puberty at 18, thereby corresponding to the CRC's age of majority. To understand how Muslim-majority states have implemented the CRC, it is necessary to isolate and to survey specific legal questions, as will be explored here.

It should be noted that conflicts between international legal norms and Islamic legal traditions have prompted some scholars and activists in the Muslim world to adopt defensive stances. Some claim that modern legal systems exacerbate problems of juvenile justice that could be minimized by the implementation of orthodox Islamic law (Ṣabāḥī 2008, 21). But the primary response of Muslim-majority states to international norms on the child has been accommodation. The Organisation of Islamic Cooperation (OIC; formerly Organisation of the Islamic Conference) adopted a covenant on the rights of the child in Islam (2005). This covenant recommends separate juvenile detention facilities, specialized juvenile courts, a right to counsel, an opportunity for appeal, the banning of forced testimony or guilty pleas, and rehabilitation. In other words, the OIC's covenant by and large implements the CRC.

Minimum Age of Penal Capacity (MAPC)

Muslim-majority states differ widely in how they define the minimum age of penal capacity (MAPC), as demonstrated in table 6.1. According to modern international legal definitions, the MAPC "is the lowest age upon which children may potentially be judged delinquent or held liable" according to a state's penal laws (Cipriani 2009, 157). The global median MAPC is 12 years old; actors dominant in prescribing international legal norms advocate that this age be established as an international MAPC (Cipriani 2009, 160). However, "academic evidence to date is not sufficiently compelling to recommend one optimal" MAPC for all states (Cipriani 2009, 159). Individual states understand the purpose of the MAPC in dissimilar ways. Moreover, the formal MAPC can be quite misleading: in some states, children younger than the MAPC may be tried in a juvenile court; in other states, children at or above the MAPC receive behavioral measures, rather than punishments (UNICEF 1998, 4). Regardless of the official MAPC, juvenile judges determine if children have sufficient maturity, knowledge of their acts, and legal knowledge to warrant punishment. It is important to recognize that the

TABLE 6.1. The MAPC in Muslim-Majority States

Muslim-majority state	Minimum age of penal capacity	Potential or probable corresponding orthodox Islamic principle or other legal source[a]
Afghanistan	12	Islamic jurisprudence: minimum age of puberty according to Ḥanafī school
Albania	14	Soviet law
Algeria	13	French law
Azerbaijan	14	Soviet law
Bahrain	7	Islamic jurisprudence: maximum age of puberty according to majority opinion
Bangladesh	9	Islamic jurisprudence: minimum age of puberty according to majority of Sunnī legal schools
Brunei	7	Islamic jurisprudence: age of legal semicompetence
Burkina Faso	13	French law
Chad	13	French law
Comoros	13 or puberty	French law and Islamic jurisprudence: majority = puberty
Djibouti	13	French law
Egypt	7	Islamic jurisprudence: age of legal semicompetence
Gambia	12	unclear; Mālikī school is most influential in this state, so minimum age of puberty according to Ḥanafī school probably does not explain this MAPC
Guinea	13	French law
Indonesia	8	possibly Islamic jurisprudence: in between age of legal semicompetence (7 years) and minimum age of puberty according to majority of Sunnī legal schools (9 years)
Iran	9 female 15 male	Islamic jurisprudence: maximum age of puberty according to Imāmī Shīʿī school
Iraq	9	Islamic jurisprudence: minimum age of puberty according to majority of Sunnī legal schools
Jordan	7	Islamic jurisprudence: age of legal semicompetence
Kazakhstan	14	Soviet law
Kosovo	unknown	
Kuwait	7	Islamic jurisprudence: age of legal semicompetence
Kyrgyzstan	14	Soviet law
Lebanon	7	Islamic jurisprudence: age of legal semicompetence
Libya	7/14[b]	Islamic jurisprudence (age of legal semicompetence) and possibly Soviet law
Malaysia	10[c]	possibly English common law
Maldives	puberty	Islamic jurisprudence: age of majority = puberty
Mali	13	French law

(continued)

TABLE 6.1 (*continued*)

Muslim-majority state	Minimum age of penal capacity	Potential or probable corresponding orthodox Islamic principle or other legal source[a]
Mauritania	7	Islamic jurisprudence: age of legal semicompetence
Morocco	12	unclear; Mālikī school is most influential in this state, so minimum age of puberty according to Ḥanafī school probably does not explain this MAPC
Niger	13	French law
Oman	9	Islamic jurisprudence: minimum age of puberty according to majority of Sunnī legal schools
Pakistan	7	Islamic jurisprudence: age of legal semicompetence
Palestine	9	Islamic jurisprudence: minimum age of puberty according to majority of Sunnī legal schools
Qatar	7	Islamic jurisprudence: age of legal semicompetence
Saudi Arabia	7/puberty	Islamic jurisprudence: age of legal semicompetence and majority = puberty
Senegal	13	French law
Sierra Leone	14	Unclear
Somalia	15	Islamic jurisprudence: maximum age of puberty according to majority opinion
Sudan	7/15	Islamic jurisprudence: age of legal semicompetence and maximum age of puberty according to majority opinion
Syria	10	possibly Islamic jurisprudence: minimum age of puberty according to Ḥanbalī school
Tajikistan	14	Soviet law
Tunisia	13	French law
Turkey	12	possibly Islamic jurisprudence: minimum age of puberty according to Ḥanafī school
Turkmenistan	14	Soviet law
United Arab Emirates	7	Islamic jurisprudence: age of legal semicompetence
Uzbekistan	13	unclear
Western Sahara	12	this state is under Moroccan rule
Yemen	7	Islamic jurisprudence: age of legal semicompetence

Note: This table is based on the information provided in Cipriani 2009, 98–108, table 5.1, but modifies the information on the basis of my additional research.

[a] I could not verify all of these classifications, so many of them are hypotheses based on the information provided in Cipriani 2009, 109.

[b] While Libyan law subjects children between seven and 14 to optional, disciplinary punishments, this likely reflects the orthodox Islamic legal treatment of children with legal semicompetence and is not equivalent to a MAPC. Here I differ with Cipriani (2009, 102).

[c] While Malaysian law subjects children under 10 to optional disciplinary punishments, this may reflect the orthodox Islamic legal treatment of children with legal semicompetence and is not equivalent to a MAPC. Here I differ with Cipriani (2009, 102).

official MAPC is not conclusive as to the treatment of a minor in the juvenile system. Thus, international organizations (such as UNICEF) may be misguided when they criticize the MAPC in various states for being lower than international norms because they focus on form rather than substance.

Additionally, the MAPC is a relatively modern concept, and there is no clear equivalent in orthodox Islamic jurisprudence; many states have defined it in reference to four distinct categories in orthodox Islamic jurisprudence: (1) the minimum age of legal competence (which is seven), (2) the minimum age at which puberty may occur (which is nine), (3) the maximum age at which puberty is assumed to have occurred (which varies, but most jurists identify as 15), and (4) physical signs of puberty. First, as previously mentioned, orthodox Muslim jurists identified a phase of semicompetence from age seven to puberty; during this phase, a child could receive flexible disciplinary punishments but not criminal punishments. Several contemporary Muslim-majority states appear to use the minimum age of legal competence in orthodox Islamic legal jurisprudence as their MAPC. As indicated in table 6.1, states that define the MAPC as seven years old include Brunei, Egypt, Jordan, Kuwait, Lebanon, Libya, Mauritania, Pakistan, Qatar, Saudi Arabia, Sudan, United Arab Emirates, and Yemen. Saudi Arabia raised the age of penal capacity for boys from seven to 12 in 2006, but there is reason to believe that it is not being enforced in practice (Human Rights Watch 2008a, 2). Second, orthodox Muslim jurists identified a minimum age for puberty, which is nine for both boys and girls according to the majority of jurists (Peters 2005, 21).[9] As indicated in table 6.1, states that define the MAPC as nine years old include Bangladesh, Iraq, Oman, and Palestine. Some states may be applying the minimum age of puberty of specific legal schools: 10 years of age is the MAPC in Syria and the minimum age of puberty according to the Ḥanbalī school; 12 is the MAPC in Afghanistan and Turkey and the minimum age of puberty according to the Ḥanafī school. Third, the maximum age of puberty (15 according to the majority orthodox Islamic opinion) influences the MAPC in Bahrain, Iran (where the maximum age of puberty is nine for girls), and Somalia. Fourth, physical signs of puberty define the MAPC in the Maldives and play some role in determining penal capacity in Comoros and Saudi Arabia. What these variations demonstrate is that contemporary Muslim-majority states interpret, translate, and implement orthodox Islamic jurisprudence in dissimilar ways.

At the same time, it must also be noted that non-Islamic principles influence the MAPC in many Muslim-majority states. French colonial law may have influenced the MAPC of 13 in the following states: Algeria, Burkina Faso, Chad, Djibouti, Guinea, Mali, Niger, Senegal, and Tunisia. In addition, Soviet law may have influenced the MAPC of 14 in the following states: Albania, Azerbaijan, Kazakhstan, Kyrgyzstan, Tajikistan, and Turkmenistan. The integration of Soviet and western European legal systems into many Muslim-majority states is a legacy of colonialism and the USSR that has unsystematic consequences: Islamic laws may or may not influence a particular area of legal doctrine. Moreover, there does not appear to be a correlation between a low MAPC and low ages of majority or of minimum ages of marriage (see table 6.2). Indeed, most Muslim-majority states define the age of majority and the minimum age of marriage in line with international norms.

Some scholars and activists claim that Muslim-majority countries who follow the orthodox Islamic jurisprudential tradition in defining majority as equivalent to puberty engage in "gender discrimination" because girls experience puberty before boys and are therefore subject to criminal punishments at a younger age (Cipriani 2009, 82). First, it should be emphasized that only the Maldives defines the MAPC as based on physical signs of puberty (rather than specifying an age); Comoros, Iran, and Saudi Arabia are the only other states that appear to permit the gender differences in puberty to have legal effect. Thus, very few Muslim-majority states actually implement gender differences in their penal system. Second, there is little evidence that recognizing gender differences in puberty actually results in girls being punished at younger ages than boys—especially considering that significantly fewer girls (as compared to boys) commit crimes. Third, the allegation of "gender discrimination" is an oversimplification of the complications that occur when various modern nation-states seek to implement the orthodox Islamic legal tradition in their legal systems. The critique of gender bias misrepresents how the age of puberty functions in premodern, orthodox Islamic law: for boys, it is the age at which they can be enlisted in warfare and become financially responsible for their families—two responsibilities that do not fall on girls. Consequently, medieval orthodox jurists constructed legal consequences around a boy's puberty that were not motivated by making girls liable for criminal punishment at a younger age; instead, they were most probably motivated by an interest in delaying the distinct socioeconomic burdens placed on boys in premodern societies. In other words, it may be the case that the orthodox Islamic definition of a minor (and its gender distinctions) "cannot be translated into a liberal language" (Kayaoglu 2014, 89). Fourth, this claim is part of a broader and more complicated debate about the colonial underpinnings of international law (Rajagopal 2006). International organizations often criticize states in the global south for not meeting legal standards that are, in actuality, not implemented in the global north or that are difficult to implement in the global south because of political, economic, and cultural conditions. Ultimately, since there is no correlation between the MAPC and severity of punishment (UNICEF 1998, 5), international advocacy pertaining to the MAPC is misguided in focusing on the formal MAPC.

Defining the Age of Majority and Stratifying Juvenile Punishments

Muslim-majority states differ widely in how they define a child or a young person for the purpose of juvenile punishments. Yet most Muslim-majority states have set 18 as the age of majority, following the Ottoman precedent (Ottoman Empire 1913, 29–30) and in line with the CRC (Hashemi 2007, 200); only a few define the age of majority as equivalent to puberty or as younger than 18 (see table 6.2). The age of majority is 18 (or older) in every Muslim-majority state with the following exceptions: the age of majority is 15 in Bahrain (Amnesty International 2013a, 6), Somalia (African Child Policy Forum 2013a), and Yemen (Human Rights Watch 2013, 22); 16 in Bangladesh (UNICEF 2006, 39) and Qatar (al-Meezan 2014); and puberty in Iran and Saudi Arabia. In Iran, puberty is officially defined as 15 years old for boys and nine years old for girls—although, in practice, Iranian judges do not always implement these distinctions or apply these ages (Abiad and Mansoor 2010, 139; Zalkind and Simon 2004, 104). While Saudi law recognizes a fixed age of majority, in practice, the majority age is flexibly based on physical and mental signs that result in a range between 12 and

TABLE 6.2. Comparing Laws Defining Childhood in Muslim-Majority States

Muslim-majority state	Minimum age of penal capacity (MAPC)[a]	Majority age (i.e., age at which one is considered an adult and will be tried in adult court)	Minimum legal age for marriage[b]	Voting age[c] (legal exceptions not provided)
Afghanistan	12	18 (UNICEF 2006, 3)	16 female; 18 male (YouthPolicy.org 2013)	18
Albania	14	18 (UNICEF 2009a, 9)	not available	18
Algeria	13	19 (African Child Policy Forum 2013a)	19 female; 19 male (African Child Policy Forum 2013b)	18
Azerbaijan	14	18 (UNICEF 2009b, 21)	17 female; 18 male (United Nations 2008)	18
Bahrain	7	15 (Amnesty International 2013a, 6)	not available	18
Bangladesh	9	16 (UNICEF 2006, 39)	18 female; 21 male (United Nations 2008)	18
Brunei	7	18 (YouthPolicy.org 2014a)	none (Emory Law 2002)	not applicable
Burkina Faso	13	20 (African Child Policy Forum 2013a)	17 female; 20 male (African Child Policy Forum 2013b)	18
Chad	13	18 (African Child Policy Forum 2013a)	17 female; 18 male (African Child Policy Forum 2013b)	18
Comoros	13 or puberty	18 (African Child Policy Forum 2013a)	18 female; 18 male (African Child Policy Forum 2013b)	18
Djibouti	13	18 (African Child Policy Forum 2013a)	18 female; 18 male (African Child Policy Forum 2013b)	18
Egypt	7	21 (African Child Policy Forum 2013a)	18 female; 18 male (African Child Policy Forum 2013b)	18
Gambia	12	18 (African Child Policy Forum 2013a)	18 female; 18 male (African Child Policy Forum 2013b)	18
Guinea	13	21 (African Child Policy Forum 2013a)	18 female; 18 male (African Child Policy Forum 2013b)	18
Indonesia	8	18 (UNICEF 2011b, 7)	16 female; 19 male (United Nations 2008)	17
Iran	9 female 15 male	9 female; 15 male (Abiad and Mansoor 2010, 139)	15 female; none male (United Nations 2008)	18

264

TABLE 6.2 (*continued*)

Muslim-majority state	Minimum age of penal capacity (MAPC)[a]	Majority age (i.e., age at which one is considered an adult and will be tried in adult court)	Minimum legal age for marriage[b]	Voting age[c] (legal exceptions not provided)
Iraq	9	18 (El Aougi 1965, 6)	18 female; 18 male (United Nations 2008)	18
Jordan	7	18 (El Aougi 1965, 6)	18 female; 18 male (United Nations 2008)	18
Kazakhstan	14	18 (UNICEF 2012c)	18 female; 18 male (United Nations 2008)	18
Kosovo	unknown	21 (UNICEF 2010c, 3)	not available	18
Kuwait	7	18 (UNICEF 1996a)	15 female; 17 male (United Nations 2008)	21
Kyrgyzstan	14	18 (UNICEF 2012c)	18 female; 18 male (United Nations 2008)	18
Lebanon	7	18 (Abiad and Mansoor 2010, 177)	17 female; 18 male (Emory Law 2002)	21
Libya	7/14	18 (African Child Policy Forum 2013a)	20 female; 20 male (African Child Policy Forum 2013b)	18
Malaysia	10	18 (Abiad and Mansoor 2010, 198)	18 female; 18 male (United Nations 2008)	21
Maldives	puberty	18 (UNICEF 2006, 3)	15 female; 15 male (Emory Law 2002)	18
Mali	13	18 (African Child Policy Forum 2013a)	16 female; 18 male (African Child Policy Forum 2013b)	18
Mauritania	7	18 (African Child Policy Forum 2013a)	18 female; 18 male (African Child Policy Forum 2013b)	18
Morocco	12	20 (African Child Policy Forum 2013a)	18 female; 18 male (African Child Policy Forum 2013b)	18
Niger	13	21 (African Child Policy Forum 2013a)	15 female; 18 male (African Child Policy Forum 2013b)	18
Oman	9	18 (OmanLegal.net 2014)	18 female; 18 male (United Nations 2008)	21
Pakistan	7	18 (UNICEF 2006, 3)	16 female; 18 male (United Nations 2008)	18
Palestine	9	18 (YouthPolicy.org 2014b)	15 female; 16 male (YouthPolicy.org 2014b)	18

(*continued*)

TABLE 6.2 *(continued)*

Muslim-majority state	Minimum age of penal capacity (MAPC)[a]	Majority age (i.e., age at which one is considered an adult and will be tried in adult court)	Minimum legal age for marriage[b]	Voting age[c] (legal exceptions not provided)
Qatar	7	16 (al-Meezan 2014)	not available	18
Saudi Arabia	7/puberty	puberty (Human Rights Watch 2008b, 11)	17 female; 20 male (United Nations 2008)	21 (males only)
Senegal	13	18 (African Child Policy Forum 2013a)	16 female; 18 male (African Child Policy Forum 2013b)	18
Sierra Leone	14	21 (African Child Policy Forum 2013a)	18 female; 18 male (African Child Policy Forum 2013b)	18
Somalia	15	15 (African Child Policy Forum 2013a)	18 female; 18 male (African Child Policy Forum 2013b)	18
Sudan	7/15	18 (African Child Policy Forum 2013a)	puberty female; 10 male (African Child Policy Forum 2013b)	17
Syria	10	18 (El Aougi 1965, 6)	17 female; 18 male (Emory Law 2002)	18
Tajikistan	14	18 (UNICEF 2012c)	18 female; 18 male (YouthPolicy.org 2014c)	18
Tunisia	13	18 (African Child Policy Forum 2013a)	18 female; 18 male (African Child Policy Forum 2013b)	18
Turkey	12	18 (Abiad and Mansoor 2010, 288)	17 female; 17 male (United Nations 2008)	18
Turkmenistan	14	18 (UNICEF 2012c)	16 female; 16 male (YouthPolicy.org 2014d)	18
United Arab Emirates	7	18 (Abiad and Mansoor 2010, 306)	not available	not applicable
Uzbekistan	13	18 (UNICEF 2012c)	17 female; 18 male (United Nations 2008)	18
Yemen	7	15 (Human Rights Watch 2013, 22)	15 female; 15 male (United Nations 2008)	18

[a] This column is based on table 6.1.
[b] Nearly all states provide judicial discretion for marriages at younger ages.
[c] All voting-age information provided by the CIA website (CIA 2014).

15 years (Gilani 2006, 149; El Aougi 1965, 6–8). The age of majority is a modern classification that does not correspond neatly to age categories (specifically, the age of legal competence or the age of puberty discussed earlier) elaborated by orthodox Muslim jurists in the medieval era. However, some Ḥanafīs and Mālikīs defined the maximum age of puberty as 18; this could partially explain the prevalence or general lack of resistance to having 18 be the majority age. By way of comparison, the equally modern legal category of voting age is also 18 (or older) in most Muslim-majority states (see table 6.2).

Regardless of the MAPC or the age of majority, most Muslim-majority states stratify juvenile punishments by assigning particular penalties for certain age groups. This also appears to be a continuation of the Ottoman precedent (Ottoman Empire 1913, 29–30). Afghanistan limits juvenile punishments to one-third of adult punishments for juveniles between 12 and 16 and to one-half of adult punishments for those between 16 and 18 (UNICEF 2006, 35). Algeria subjects children under 13 to rehabilitation but not punishment; minors between 13 and 16 receive mitigated punishments, and minors between 13 and 18 may be sentenced to imprisonment in juvenile detention centers (Kebir 1999–2000, 161). In Egypt, children between the ages of seven and 12 may be tried at the discretion of the Child Court; there are special penalties for minors between the ages of 12 and 15 and reduced penalties for minors between 15 and 18 (Abiad and Mansoor 2010, 112–133). In Iran, there are also three age groups for minors: minors from age nine to 12 are referred to social workers, while those ages 12 to 15 and 15 to 18 receive punishments (Abiad and Mansoor 2010, 137). Jordanian law defines four phases of legal competence and liability, each with its own specific legal consequences: (1) from birth to age seven, (2) from age seven to age 12, (3) from age 12 to 15, (4) from age 15 to 18 (Zaytūn 2001, 49). Lebanese law identifies three age groups of juvenile offenders: between seven and 12, between 12 and 15 (sentenced to various forms of rehabilitation), and between 15 and 18 (can receive rehabilitation and reduced prison sentences) (Abiad and Mansoor 2010, 177). Malaysia's Child Act of 2001 absolved children under 10 of criminal liability, granted children ages 10 to 12 partial immunity, identified children over 12 as having full penal capacity, and defined minors as under the age of 18 (Abiad and Mansoor 2010, 190, 196). Nigerian law identifies two phases of penal capacity and punishment: from age 12 to age 14 and from age 14 to age 18 (Abiad and Mansoor 2010, 212–133). In general, age stratifications for criminal punishment imply recognition that juvenile crimes should be treated distinctly, primarily through reduced punishments.

Independent Juvenile Courts

In line with the global trends identified in this volume's introduction, most Muslim-majority states have independent juvenile courts that have been functioning for several decades (see table 6.3). In general, these courts appear to have been based on Western models or international legal norms (UNICEF 1998, 10). It is difficult, however, to identify the precise source of influence or history of juvenile courts in each and every Muslim-majority state. Afghanistan's 1976 criminal law regulated separate juvenile courts, which may have been functioning prior to this date (Lau 2001–2002, 41). Rules for separate juvenile courts were promulgated in 1950 in Egypt (Abiad and Mansoor 2010) and in 1953 in Syria (El Aougi 1965, 40), but both Egypt and Syria may have established separate juvenile courts in 1905 (El Aougi 1965, 39). A 1962 law regulated Iraq's juvenile courts (El Aougi 1965, 41). Lebanon passed a law in 2002 that regulates juvenile courts (Abiad and Mansoor 2010, 183), but separate juvenile courts have been operating since 1948 (El Aougi 1965, 40). By the 1960s, most states in the "Middle East" appear to have established separate juvenile courts (El Aougi 1965, 42). Malaysia established its separate juvenile court system in 1947 and renamed it the Court for Children in 2001 (Abiad and Mansoor 2010, 190, 198). Pakistan's juvenile courts were established in 1955 (Abiad and Mansoor 2010, 234). Yemen's juvenile courts were established in 1995 (Shamiri 1997–1998, 395). A few Muslim-majority states do not appear to have separate juvenile courts or specialized juvenile judges, including Azerbaijan, Brunei, Chad, Kosovo, Kyrgyzstan, Palestine, Turkmenistan, and Uzbekistan. These states likely lack the necessary financial resources to establish separate juvenile courts. Of course, the absence of a separate juvenile court does not mean that a state lacks an effective juvenile justice system (UNICEF 1998, 10). A variety of alternatives to juvenile courts have been recognized for their efficacy in dealing with juvenile crimes (UNICEF 1998, 11). Without systematic comparative studies, it is

TABLE 6.3. Independent Juvenile Courts in Muslim-Majority States

Muslim-majority state	Does the state have a separate juvenile court? (This column records the existence of the institution, not its quantity, quality, or efficacy.)
Afghanistan	Yes (Gholami 2007; UNICEF 2006, 8, 34).
Albania	No, Albania does not have a separate juvenile court but does have specialized judges and prosecutors (UNICEF 2009a, 19).
Algeria	Yes (Qawāsimīyah 1992).
Azerbaijan	No (UNICEF 2009b, 4).
Bahrain	Yes (Amnesty International 2013a, 6).
Bangladesh	Yes, but many children are sent to adult courts (UNICEF 2006, 43–44).
Brunei	No (CRIN 2014).
Burkina Faso	Yes, being established by UNICEF (UNICEF 2014a).
Chad	No, but likely recently been established because information is outdated (UNICEF 1997).
Comoros	Yes (UNICEF 2011a, 15).
Djibouti	Yes (UNICEF 2012d, 4).
Egypt	Yes (Abiad and Mansoor 2010, 110)
Gambia	Yes (Gambia 1949).
Guinea	Unknown
Indonesia	Yes (UNICEF 2011b, 10).
Iran	Yes (UNICEF 2012a, 13; Abiad and Mansoor 2010, 135).
Iraq	Yes (El Aougi 1965, 43).
Jordan	Yes (El Aougi 1965, 43).
Kazakhstan	Yes, and it covers criminal, family, and child protection matters (UNICEF 2012c, 15, 27).
Kosovo	No (UNICEF 2010c, 23).
Kuwait	Yes (UNICEF 1996a).
Kyrgyzstan	No (UNICEF 2012c, 27).
Lebanon	Yes (Abiad and Mansoor 2010, 183)
Libya	Yes (UNICEF 1996b).
Malaysia	Yes (Abiad and Mansoor 2010, 190, 198).
Maldives	Yes (UNICEF 2006, 8, 77).
Mali	Yes (UNICEF 2014b).
Mauritania	Yes (UNICEF 2010a, 1).
Morocco	Yes (Sharādī 2002).
Niger	Yes (UNICEF 2008, 5).
Oman	Yes (OmanLegal.net 2014).
Pakistan	Yes (Abiad and Mansoor 2010, 246; UNICEF 2006, 96).

(continued)

TABLE 6.3 (*continued*)

Muslim-majority state	Does the state have a separate juvenile court? (This column records the existence of the institution, not its quantity, quality, or efficacy.)
Palestine	No (Qafisheh 2011).
Qatar	Yes (al-Meezan 1994).
Saudi Arabia	Yes (Human Rights Watch 2008a, 1).
Senegal	Yes (UNICEF 2010b, 11).
Sierra Leone	Yes (Adala 2009).
Somalia	Yes (UNICEF 2012b, 36).
Sudan	Yes (Human Rights Watch 2008b, 15).
Syria	Yes (Zalkind and Simon 2004, 109).
Tajikistan	No, but some judges are designated to handle juvenile cases (UNICEF 2012c, 27).
Tunisia	Yes (Gaïgi 2000–2001, 306).
Turkey	Yes (Abiad and Mansoor 2010, 292).
Turkmenistan	No (UNICEF 2012c, 27).
United Arab Emirates	No, does not have a separate juvenile court but does have specialized judges (Abiad and Mansoor 2010, 313).
Uzbekistan	No (UNICEF 2012c, 27).
Yemen	Yes (Human Rights Watch 2013, 22).

not possible to presume a correlation between the existence of separate juvenile courts and the treatment of juvenile offenders.

Death Penalty

In most Muslim-majority states, individuals under the age of 18 (hereafter, used interchangeably with "youth") are not subject to the death penalty or other harsh penalties. There is a long history of minors not being subject to the death penalty in Muslim-majority areas. Youth have not been subject to the death penalty in Egypt since the 1883 Penal Code, if not earlier (Abiad and Mansoor 2010, 102; Zalkind and Simon 2004, 103). Article 40 of the 1911 Ottoman Penal Code specified that minors under the age of 18 would be punished by imprisonment rather than being subject to the death penalty (Ottoman Empire 1913, 30). Modern Muslim-majority states that were previously under Ottoman sovereignty may have continued the Ottoman practice of absolving minors under 18 of the death penalty; by the 1960s, most states in the broader "Middle East" had excluded minors under 18 from the death penalty (El Aougi 1965, 63–65). Afghanistan prohibits punishing juveniles with either the death penalty or life imprisonment (UNICEF 2006, 35). Lebanon does not apply capital punishment to anyone under 18 (Abiad and Mansoor 2010, 178–179). Pakistan's 1955 Children's Act excluded minors under the age of 16 from the death penalty, and a 2000 law banned the death penalty for minors under 18; but the law is not being implemented consistently (Abiad and Mansoor 2010, 234, 252). Turkey does not subject anyone under 18 to the death penalty (Abiad and Mansoor 2010, 300). A 1976 law exempted minors from the death penalty in the United Arab Emirates (Abiad and Mansoor 2010, 307). While it is difficult to determine precisely when Muslim-majority states began to abolish the death penalty for juveniles, this matter should be connected to death penalty abolition for adults. As outlined in table 6.4, several Muslim-majority states (Albania, Azerbaijan, Dijibouti, Kyrgyzstan, Senegal, Turkey, Turkmenistan, and Uzbekistan) have abolished the death penalty completely, while many others (Algeria, Brunei, Burkina Faso, Maldives, Mali, Mauritania, Morocco, Niger, Sierra Leone, Tajikistan, and Tunisia) have not implemented the death penalty in many years.

There are a few exceptional Muslim-majority states that continue to subject juveniles to the death penalty (see table 6.4). Iran subjects any criminal past puberty to the death penalty, which includes youth (Abiad and Mansoor 2010, 140; Zalkind and Simon 2004, 106–107); there are known cases of the Iranian government executing persons under the age of 18 (Human Rights Watch 2008b). Nigeria applies the death penalty to anyone over the age of 17 (Abiad and Mansoor 2010, 224). A 2000 Pakistani law prohibits the death penalty as a punishment for anyone under 18, but a youth was executed in 2006 (Human Rights Watch 2008b, 13–15). As for Saudi Arabia, Human Rights Watch is "aware of at least 12 cases of persons sentenced to death for offenses committed while under age 18, including three cases of juvenile offenders who were executed in 2007"; however, there may be more youth sentenced to the death penalty because the Saudi government does not publish this information (Human Rights Watch 2008a, 2). In recent decades, several youth have been executed in Yemen, despite the state's 1994 Penal Code abolishing the death penalty for anyone under 18 (and imposing

TABLE 6.4. The Death Penalty in Muslim-Majority States

Muslim-majority state	Death penalty abolition or retention for adults (and juveniles)	Date of abolition for all crimes (A) or ordinary crimes (O)	Date of last adult execution (E); date of last known juvenile execution (JE)
Albania	abolitionist for all crimes	2007 (A); 2000 (O)	
Algeria	abolitionist in practice		1993 (E)
Azerbaijan	abolitionist for all crimes	1998 (A)	1993 (E)
Brunei	abolitionist in practice		1957 (E)
Burkina Faso	abolitionist in practice		1988 (E)
Djibouti	abolitionist for all crimes	1995 (A)	
Iran	imposes death penalty on juveniles		2011 (JE)
Kazakhstan	abolitionist for ordinary crimes only	2007 (O)	
Kyrgyzstan	abolitionist for all crimes	2007 (A)	
Maldives	abolitionist in practice		1952 (E)
Mali	abolitionist in practice		1980 (E)
Mauritania	abolitionist in practice		1987 (E)
Morocco	abolitionist in practice		1993 (E)
Niger	abolitionist in practice		1976 (E)
Pakistan	imposes death penalty on juveniles in practice (not legal)		2006 (JE)
Saudi Arabia	imposes death penalty on juveniles		2013 (JE)
Senegal	abolitionist for all crimes	2004 (A)	1967 (E)
Sierra Leone	abolitionist in practice		1998 (E)
Sudan	imposes death penalty on juveniles		2005 (JE)
Tajikistan	abolitionist in practice		2004 (E)
Tunisia	abolitionist in practice		1991 (E)
Turkey	abolitionist for all crimes	2004 (A); 2002 (O)	1984 (E)
Turkmenistan	abolitionist for all crimes	1999 (A)	
Uzbekistan	abolitionist for all crimes	2008 (A)	2005 (E)
Yemen	imposes death penalty on juveniles		2011 (JE)

Note: This table is based on two Amnesty International reports (2013b, 2014).

a 10-year maximum sentence) and its ratification of the Convention on the Rights of the Child and other international legal agreements that prohibit capital punishment for minors (defined as under the age of 18) (Human Rights Watch 2013, 1, 20). Yemen may be an example of a state where local courts have the power to disregard national laws, which could result in the uneven application of juvenile laws in the state. Sudan is the only signatory to the CRC that has expressed reservations about absolving individuals under the age of 18 from the death penalty, citing Islamic criminal punishments and Islamic legal definitions of adulthood (Hashemi 2007, 205). While Iran, Pakistan, Saudi Arabia, and Sudan subject individuals under 18 to the death penalty, these states are not representative of Muslim-majority states. Indeed, they are not representative of global trends: Amnesty International has, since 1990, documented executions of youth in only nine states: China, the Democratic Republic of Congo, Iran, Nigeria, Pakistan, Saudi Arabia, Sudan, the United States, and Yemen (2014). This means that every other Muslim-majority state has not executed a minor (under the age of 18) since 1990, if not earlier. Still, the application of the death penalty to youth is not, in and of itself, indicative of how minors are treated under a state's legal system. More broadly, the application of the death penalty to youth does not, in and of itself, define a state's legal system as illegitimate (or, more problematically, illiberal).

Conclusion

To return to our question: Is there an "Islamic juvenile justice"? The simple answer is no. Every Muslim-majority state translates or adapts orthodox Islamic jurisprudence distinctly and, in some cases, not at all. There are multiple approaches to juvenile justice that are enacted by Muslim-majority states, but these diverse trends do not form a systematic body of "modern Islamic juvenile justice" that is anchored in Islamic jurisprudence.

Because juvenile justice is a modern legal development, contemporary Muslim-majority states have applied Islamic legal traditions in ways that are neither unified nor consistent. Indeed, there are aspects of orthodox Islamic jurisprudence that may not be translatable to modern nation-states. It is important to recognize that there are no precise orthodox Islamic jurisprudential rules for defining the modern legal categories of minimum age of penal capacity, majority age, minimum legal age for marriage, or voting age—as amply illustrated by the variability in table 6.2. There are orthodox Islamic legal traditions pertaining to the criminal liability and punishment of children that define the age of criminal responsibility and adulthood; but these traditions are understood and applied in wide-ranging ways. Not surprisingly, the majority of contemporary Muslim-majority states have ratified and implemented international legal norms on the rights of the child; for the most part, these states do not perceive their legislation on juvenile justice as contradicting orthodox Islamic jurisprudence. (Those states that contravene international norms by defining the age of majority as less than 18 or subjecting minors to the death penalty are exceptional.) Yet this broad-scale implementation of international (or, more accurately, Western) juvenile justice structures in Muslim-majority states raises several concerns: why and to what end? Undoubtedly, UNICEF and other international organizations have placed considerable pressure on states to develop separate juvenile justice systems. But are they necessary or effective? Imposing a particular minimum age of penal capacity or age of majority, establishing separate juvenile courts, and abolishing the death penalty do not guarantee juvenile rehabilitation. If the objective of juvenile justice is rehabilitation, then it is the legal infrastructure for rehabilitation that should be scrutinized. And then there is the matter of prevention: a legal system's protection of juveniles is only marginally effective so long as it does not also provide a framework for preventing juveniles from resorting to crimes. In other words, juvenile criminal punishment should be analyzed in conjunction with broader children's rights. It may be the case that there is no direct correlation between a robust juvenile justice system and fundamental legal protections for children.

Appendix: Brief Country Summaries

Afghanistan

Afghanistan promulgated a juvenile code in 2005 (UNICEF 2006, 33).[10] As is the case for all Afghans accused of crimes, a slow justice system keeps juveniles in detention for extended periods of time (UNICEF 2006, 34). Juvenile court sessions are private, and children have a right to an attorney (UNICEF 2006, 34). Most juvenile boys are detained in separate facilities within adult male prisons, while girls are not separated from women (UNICEF 2006, 35). Conditions within detention centers are poor, and there are insufficient rehabilitative programs (UNICEF 2006, 36). Local dispute resolution can be beneficial in helping juveniles avoid formal criminal punishments (UNICEF 2006, 36).

Bangladesh

Bangladesh promulgated juvenile laws in the 1970s, but many of these laws are not actually implemented (UNICEF 2006, 39, 41). Youth between 16 and 18 receive adult criminal punishments (UNICEF 2006, 39), and youth under 16 can receive a sentence of life imprisonment (UNICEF 2006, 45). Police, who are not specialized to deal with juveniles, have excessive discretion to arrest and to detain minors; there are reports of children being abused while in custody (UNICEF 2006, 40). Most juveniles are not placed in separate detention facilities (UNICEF 2006, 42). Juveniles are not afforded a right to legal representation (UNICEF 2006, 44). There are specialized juvenile detention centers, but they lack rehabilitative resources and conditions are poor (UNICEF 2006, 46).

Egypt

Egypt's first juvenile penal code was established in 1883 and was applied to children ages seven to 17, who were punished with social measures or reduced penalties (Abiad and Mansoor 2010, 102). The UN Convention on the Rights of the Child was implemented most closely through Egypt's Child's Law 126/2008 (Abiad and Mansoor 2010, 105). In addition to a juvenile police unit, Egypt has a juvenile criminal procedure (El Aougi 1965, 49). Egypt's "child courts" provide social workers, involve parents, hold private sessions, permit appeal, promote rehabilitative measures, and consider the socioeconomic circumstances of juvenile offenders; at least one female expert is required to participate in every juvenile trial (Zalkind and Simon 2004, 100). In 2002, Egypt pursued a "National Strategy for the Rehabilitation and Reintegration of Street Children" to deal with its particularly large population of impoverished street children (Abiad and Mansoor 2010, 105). Egypt imposes a variety of rehabilitative measures and reduced penalties for juveniles; while the death penalty cannot be imposed on juveniles, life imprisonment can (Zalkind and Simon 2004, 102). Despite this legal infrastructure, juveniles are abused (physically or sexually), sometimes tortured, and denied basic needs (Abiad and Mansoor 2010, 116–123). Egypt claims that a lack of financial resources is to blame for the gap between legislation and implementation (Zalkind and Simon 2004, 103). In accordance with Juvenile Law 31 (of 1974), juveniles under the age of 17 can be subjected to hard labor but not life imprisonment (or the death penalty) (Abiad and Mansoor 2010, 4).

Indonesia

Indonesia's juvenile justice system has been characterized as relatively punitive, rather than rehabilitative. According to research from 2006, approximately "96 per cent of child cases that came to court resulted in custodial sentences," and "60 per cent of these sentences exceeded one year" (UNICEF 2011b, 157). A 2009 survey suggests that "approximately 7.5 per cent of children aged 10–18 years old" have been imprisoned (UNICEF 2011b, 157). For the most part, legal representation is not provided to or obtainable by juveniles (UNICEF 2011b, 158). While separate juvenile detention facilities exist, most juveniles are detained with adults, exposing them to abuse and exploitation (UNICEF 2011b, 158).

Iran

Iran's recently revised Penal Procedure Code improves the operations of juvenile courts and creates juvenile police units (UNICEF 2012a, 13). The revised penal code also instructs juvenile judges to consider a child's mental maturity and legal understanding of a prohibited act in order to facilitate alternative punishments (UNICEF 2012a, 13). Juveniles have a right to legal representation (Zalkind and Simon 2004, 105). Juvenile detention centers are organized by age, gender, and severity of crime; the facilities provide therapy, education, vocational training, and moral teachings with the goal of rehabilitation (Zalkind and Simon 2004, 108). There are some incidents of abuse (physical and sexual) and other forms of mistreatment during incarceration (Abiad and Mansoor 2010, 147; Zalkind and Simon 2004, 106).

Iraq

Iraq established a juvenile justice system with its 1955 Act on Juvenile Offenders (El Aougi 1965, 3–6). Its 1983 Juvenile Care Law established juvenile rehabilitation schools and specialized procedural rules for juvenile cases (Catlett 2010). As the result of foreign occupation and destruction of Iraq's infrastructure, the juvenile justice system is outdated and deprived of necessary resources. Iraq has specialized juvenile judges, courts, police, and rehabilitation centers (El Aougi 1965, 43, 54–57). The state recognizes phases prior to adulthood, with the first being from the minimum age of penal capacity to 15 and the second from 15 to 18 (El Aougi 1965, 6).

Kazakhstan

In 2008, Kazakhstan pursued a "Juvenile Justice System Development Concept and Plan of Action" (UNICEF 2012c, 11). Juveniles have a right to legal representation (UNICEF 2012c, 28), and there are specialized juvenile detention centers (UNICEF 2012c, 38).

Kyrgyzstan

Juveniles have a right to legal representation (UNICEF 2012c, 28), and there are specialized juvenile detention centers (UNICEF 2012c, 38). Kyrgyzstan has a specialized juvenile police unit dedicated to investigating juvenile crimes (UNICEF 2012c, 56).

Lebanon

Lebanon's Law 422 of 2002 legislates all juvenile justice matters, including the state's juvenile courts (Abiad and Mansoor 2010, 177). Lebanon established specialized juvenile courts in 1948 (El Aougi 1965, 3, 40).

The state has separate juvenile detention centers (Abiad and Mansoor 2010, 183), and judges often rely on the UN Convention on the Rights of the Child in implementing national laws (Abiad and Mansoor 2010, 185).

Malaysia

Malaysia has developed and expanded its juvenile justice system through various legislation in 2001 and 2009 (Abiad and Mansoor 2010, 188–190). In 2011, Malaysia passed a Child Act with the objective of further improving its juvenile justice system, but internal critics argue that even with this new law, the state's system is punitive and focused on deterrence, rather than rehabilitation (Samuri et al. 2012). Juveniles are provided with rehabilitation services, counseling, and probation officers (Abiad and Mansoor 2010, 191–194). In addition to a juvenile judge, Malaysian law requires at least one of two juvenile court advisers to be a woman (Abiad and Mansoor 2010, 199). Malaysian juveniles are not subject to the death penalty (Abiad and Mansoor 2010, 196).

Maldives

The Maldives' 1991 laws protecting children defines minors as under the age of 18 (UNICEF 2006, 75). There is a specialized juvenile police unit (UNICEF 2006, 76). Juvenile court sessions are private (UNICEF 2006, 77.) Youth who have reached puberty may be subject to orthodox Islamic criminal punishments for certain crimes (UNICEF 2006, 78). Maldives places significant emphasis on "diversion and restorative justice" and provides minors with significant protections in its juvenile justice system (UNICEF 2006, 81).

Pakistan

Pakistan has inconsistent legal definitions for juveniles (Abiad and Mansoor 2010, 235–237, 246–248). The 2000 Juvenile Justice System Ordinance was intended to systematize the state's juvenile laws, but aspects of it conflict with (and do not supersede) Pakistan's implementation of orthodox Islamic criminal laws (UNICEF 2006, 93–94). Generally, Pakistan's juvenile justice system "draws heavily from outdated British legislation and places primacy on formal court structures and institutional-based responses" (UNICEF 2006, 102). There are reports of police abusing children, as well as generally not implementing juvenile legal protections (UNICEF 2006, 94). Observers claim that Pakistani courts impose punishments—including corporal—that are not proportionate to the crime committed (UNICEF 2006, 11). Pakistan's juvenile detention centers do not provide sufficient facilities or rehabilitation resources and are overcrowded and unsafe (UNICEF 2006, 13, 99). The Juvenile Justice System Ordinance of 2000 forbids the death penalty for juveniles, but it is not implemented (Human Rights Watch 2008b). So-called antiterrorism legislation is one of the means by which Pakistan subjects juveniles to the death penalty (UNICEF 2006, 11–12, 97).

Saudi Arabia

Saudi Arabia has separate juvenile courts and detention facilities (Human Rights Watch 2008a, 1), but the country lacks published codes—including for criminal law and criminal procedure (Gilani 2006, 150). Judges consider mental capacity and psychological state when evaluating the age of a child (Gilani 2006, 149). Juveniles are subjected to corporal punishments and to the death penalty (Human Rights Watch 2008a, 1). Juveniles commonly do not have legal representation, and judges have broad discretion (Human Rights Watch 2008a, 11).

Syria

Syria established specialized juvenile courts in 1953 (El Aougi 1965, 3, 40). Juveniles have the right to an attorney, private court sessions, sealed records, and access to juvenile detention centers (Zalkind and Simon 2004, 110–122). In addition to rehabilitation, juveniles are punished with reduced detention sentences, which can include forced labor (Zalkind and Simon 2004, 112). Juveniles are officially not subject to execution or life imprisonment, but in practice this restriction has occasionally not been implemented (Zalkind and Simon 2004, 112).

Tajikistan

Tajikistan passed a "National Plan of Action for Juvenile Justice System Reform" in 2009 (UNICEF 2012c, 11). Its criminal code prohibits punishing juveniles with the death penalty or life imprisonment and provides juveniles with the right to legal representation (UNICEF 2012c, 16). There are specialized juvenile detention centers (UNICEF 2012c, 38).

Turkey

Turkey's constitution includes special provisions for juveniles (Abiad and Mansoor 2010, 287). Motivated by an interest in joining the European Union, Turkey established a new Child Protection Law in 2005 (Abiad and Mansoor 2010, 281), and among other protections, it guarantees a right to an attorney and to privacy (Abiad and Mansoor 2010, 297). Juveniles are processed through specialized police units that conduct investigations (Abiad and Mansoor 2010, 294), and juveniles receive a variety of services (including counseling, education, health care, and housing) (Abiad and Mansoor 2010, 282).

United Arab Emirates

The United Arab Emirates (UAE) has specialized juvenile judges, not juvenile courts (Abiad and Mansoor 2010, 313). The state provides juveniles with separate rehabilitation institutions, private hearings, counseling, expunged records, and significantly reduced penalties (Abiad and Mansoor 2010, 313–317). Judges have complete discretion in determining punishments for juveniles between the ages of seven and 16 and partial discretion for juveniles between 16 and 18 (Abiad and Mansoor 2010, 307). Recently, the UAE has been attempting to implement the UN Convention on the Rights of the Child in its national laws (Abiad and Mansoor 2010, 306). Police officials, public prosecutors, and government officials who interact with juveniles need further training (Abiad and Mansoor 2010, 317).

Uzbekistan

Uzbekistan's criminal laws provide juveniles with a right to legal representation and requires separate detention from adults (UNICEF 2012c, 16).

Yemen

Yemen's 1994 Penal Code abolished the death penalty for juveniles; but Yemeni law is applied inconsistently, and consequently, juveniles are subject to greater punishments than provided by law (Human Rights Watch 2013, 3, 20). Yemen's juvenile court system is only available to juveniles under the age of 15 (Human Rights Watch 2013, 3). Juvenile detainees report torture by police and mismanagement of their cases (Human Rights Watch 2013, 3). Yemen's low rate of birth registration and a general social disregard for recording exact birthdates makes it difficult to determine a juvenile's exact age (Human Rights Watch 2013, 8).

NOTES

1. For feedback and engagement with this chapter, I thank Mohammad Fadel, Rhiannon Graybill, Máximo Langer, Ira Lapidus, and Frank Zimring. I thank my research assistants, Kenna Nicole Falk and Jennifer Yuan Pierson, for their valuable contributions to this project. I thank Keramet Reiter and Ashley Rubin for references to various background sources.

2. Since both the objective and coverage are broad, rather than exhaustive, this chapter provides an introductory survey, relying primarily on secondary sources—in English, for the benefit of the nonspecialist reader.

3. There are additional states with large Muslim populations, but I have focused here on the 48 states with a Muslim-majority population. Thus, for example, Nigeria is not included—despite the implementation of Islamic law in some regions—because the state's population is nearly evenly split between Christians and Muslims; on occasion, however, I will refer to Nigerian laws. By comparison, there are 57 member states in the Organisation of Islamic Cooperation (see http://www.oic-oci.org/oicv2/states/).

4. The term "orthodox Muslim jurists" refers to those jurists who founded or followed one of the orthodox schools of legal interpretation. Both Sunni (Ḥanafī, Ḥanbalī, Mālikī, and Shāfiʿī) and Shīʿī (Imāmī, Ismāʿīlī, and Zaydī) legal schools have contemporary followers (Salaymeh 2015a).

5. *Ḥadīth* is a tradition-report of the sayings and acts of Muḥammad and some of his early companions; tradition-reports were compiled in canonical collections in the medieval era, and they have precedential value in Islamic jurisprudence.

6. Cross-amputation is the amputation of the right arm and left leg or left arm and right leg.

7. Many premodern societies recognized this legal category. William Ian Miller (2006) explores the relationship between retributive justice and modern criminal legal systems.

8. Muslim-majority states that are members of the United Nations include 11 that have Islamic law as a primary source of legislation, 15 in which Islam is the state religion, and 20 that are not explicitly identified with Islam (Kayaoglu 2014, 66).

9. To be more precise, Imāmī Shī'īs do not identify a minimum age of puberty for either girls or boys; they only identify a maximum age of puberty. By comparison, Ḥanbalīs define the minimum age of puberty for boys as 10, and Ḥanafīs set it at 12 (Peters 2005, 21).

10. The summaries in this section are not intended to be comprehensive but rather provide a general synopsis of some juvenile justice issues in select states.

REFERENCES

Abiad, Nisrine, and Farkhanda Zia Mansoor. 2010. *Criminal law and the rights of the child in Muslim states: A comparative and analytical perspective.* London: British Institute of International and Comparative Law.

Adala, Ochieng. 2009. *Sierra Leone: A country review of crime and criminal justice, 2008.* Institute for Security Studies Monographs 160. Institute for Security Studies. http://www.issafrica.org/uploads/M160CHAP7.PDF.

African Child Policy Forum. 2013a. *Age of majority.* http://www.africanchildforum .org/clr/Harmonisation%20of%20Laws%20in%20Africa/other-documents -harmonisation_2_en.pdf.

African Child Policy Forum. 2013b. *Minimum age of marriage in Africa.* http://www .girlsnotbrides.org/wp-content/uploads/2013/04/Minimum-age-of-marriage -in-Africa-March-2013.pdf?utm_source=GNB+Members+Newsletter+English& utm_campaign=bae7fef4ff-GNB_Members_Newsletter_April20134_26_2013&utm_ medium=email.

al-Meezan: Qatar Legal Portal. 2014. Article 20 of Law No. 11 of 2004 Issuing the Penal Code 11/2004. http://www.almeezan.qa/LawArticles.aspx?LawTreeSectionID=163& lawId=26&language=en (accessed 11 December 2014).

Amnesty International. 2013a. *Bahrain: Children in a maze of injustice.* http://www .amnesty.org/en/library/asset/MDE11/057/2013/en/80b7e23b-1296-4620-b66c -a1ee5fec94d8/mde110572013en.pdf.

Amnesty International. 2013b. *Death penalty: Abolitionist and retentionist countries.* http://www.amnesty.org/en/death-penalty/abolitionist-and-retentionist-countries.

Amnesty International. 2014. *Executions of juveniles since 1990.* http://www.amnesty
.org/en/death-penalty/executions-of-child-offenders-since-1990.

Arnett, Jeffrey Jensen. 2010. "Oh, grow up! Generational grumbling and the new life
stage of emerging adulthood—Commentary on Trzesniewski and Donnellan
(2010)." *Perspectives on Psychological Science* 5 (1): 89–92. doi: 10.2307/41613313.

Catlett, Ian. 2010. "Juvenile justice in transition: Past challenges and new opportunities
in post-conflict Iraq." *Journal of Humanitarian Assistance,* 14 October. http://sites
.tufts.edu/jha/archives/787.

CIA. 2014. "Suffrage." CIA World Factbook. https://www.cia.gov/library/publications/
the-world-factbook/fields/2123.html (accessed 18 April 2014).

Cipriani, Don. 2009. *Children's rights and the minimum age of criminal responsibility:
A global perspective.* Aldershot, UK: Ashgate. Available online at http://public.eblib
.com/EBLPublic/PublicView.do?ptiID=438593.

Cohen, Stanley. 1985. *Visions of social control: Crime, punishment, and classification.*
Cambridge, UK: Polity.

CRIN (Child Rights International Network). 2014. *Brunei Darussalam: National laws.*
https://www.crin.org/en/library/publications/brunei-darussalam-national-laws.

Dolovich, Sharon. 2009. "Foreword: Incarceration American-style." *Harvard Law and
Policy Review* 3 (2): 237–259.

El Aougi, Mustafa. 1965. *Comparative survey of juvenile delinquency, part five: Middle
East.* New York: United Nations Bureau of Social Affairs.

Emory Law, Islamic Family Law. 2002. "Islamic family law: Legal profiles." http://
aannaim.law.emory.edu/ifl/index2.html.

Fagan, Jeffrey. 2010. "The contradictions of juvenile crime and punishment." *Daedalus*
139 (3): 43–61. doi: 10.2307/20749841.

Feeley, Malcolm M. 2002. "Entrepreneurs of punishment: The legacy of privatization."
Punishment and Society 4 (3): 321–344.

Ferguson, Robert A. 2014. *Inferno: An anatomy of American punishment.* Cambridge:
Harvard University Press.

Friedman, Lawrence M. 1993. *Crime and punishment in American history.* New York:
Basic Books.

Gaïgi, Afif. 2000–2001. "Country survey: Tunisia." In *Yearbook of Islamic and Middle
Eastern law,* vol. 7, edited by Eugene Cotran, 301–311. London: Kluwer Law Inter-
national; Centre of Islamic and Middle Eastern Law at the School of Oriental and
African Studies, University of London.

Gambia. 1949. *Children and young persons act, chapter 45 of the laws of the Gambia.*
African Child Forum. Available online at http://www.africanchildforum.org/clr/
Legislation%20Per%20Country/Gambia/gambia_children&youth_1949_en.pdf
(accessed 20 April 2014).

Gholami, Hossein. 2007. *Basics of Afghan law and criminal justice.* Translated by Bashir
Tanin and Valey Arya. Edited by Ebrahim Afsah. The German Federal Government; Germany Deutsche Gesellschaft für Technische Zusammenarbeit. Available

online at http://www.auswaertiges-amt.de/cae/servlet/contentblob/343976/ publicationFile/3727/Polizei-Legal-Manual.pdf.

Gilani, Syed Nazir. 2006. "Juvenile justice in Saudi Arabia." In *Delinquency and juvenile justice systems in the non-Western world*, edited by Paul C. Friday and Xin Ren, 145–162. Monsey, NY: Criminal Justice Press.

Harlow, Mary, Ray Laurence, Louise J. Wilkinson, Sandra Cavallo, Silvia Evangelisti, Elizabeth A. Foyster, James Marten, Colin Heywood, Joseph M. Hawes, and N. Ray Hiner, eds. 2010. *A cultural history of childhood and family*. 6 vols. Oxford, UK: Berg.

Hashemi, Kamran. 2007. "Religious legal traditions, Muslim states and the Convention on the Rights of the Child: An essay on the relevant UN documentation." *Human Rights Quarterly* 29 (1): 194–227. doi: 10.2307/20072793.

Human Rights Watch. 2008a. *Adults before their time: Children in Saudi Arabia's criminal justice system*. New York: Human Rights Watch.

Human Rights Watch. 2008b. *The last holdouts: Ending the juvenile death penalty in Iran, Saudi Arabia, Sudan, Pakistan, and Yemen*. New York: Human Rights Watch.

Human Rights Watch. 2013. *"Look at us with a merciful eye": Juvenile offenders awaiting execution in Yemen*. New York: Human Rights Watch.

Ibn Qayyim al-Jawzīyah, Muḥammad ibn Abī Bakr. 1977. *Tuḥfat al-mawdūd bi-āḥkām al-mawlūd*. Cairo: al-Maktabah al-Qayyimah.

Inalcik, Halil. 1976. *Application of the Tanzimat and its social effects*. Lisse, the Netherlands: Peter de Ridder.

Kayaoglu, Turan. 2014. "Giving an inch only to lose a mile: Muslim states, liberalism, and human rights in the United Nations." *Human Rights Quarterly* 36 (1): 61–89.

Kebir, Yamina. 1999–2000. "The status of children and their protection in Algerian Law (part II)." In *Yearbook of Islamic and Middle Eastern law*, vol. 6, edited by Eugene Cotran, 156–162. London: Kluwer Law International; Centre of Islamic and Middle Eastern Law at the School of Oriental and African Studies, University of London.

Lau, Martin. 2001–2002. "Introduction to Afghanistan's legal system." In *Yearbook of Islamic and Middle Eastern law*, vol. 8, edited by Eugene Cotran and Martin Lau, 27–44. London: Kluwer Law International; Centre of Islamic and Middle Eastern law at the School of Oriental and African Studies, University of London.

Miller, William Ian. 2006. *Eye for an eye*. Cambridge: Cambridge University Press.

OmanLegal.net. 2014. *Juvenile crimes law*. http://www.omanlegal.net/vb/showthread .php?t=6717 (accessed 20 April 2014).

Organisation of the Islamic Conference. 2005. *Covenant on the rights of the child in Islam*. http://www.oicun.org/uploads/files/convenion/Rights%20of%20the%20Child %20In%20Islam%20E.pdf.

Ottoman Empire. 1888. *The Ottoman penal code, 28 zilhijeh 1274 [1858]*. Translated by Charles George Walpole. London: W. Clowes and Sons.

Ottoman Empire. 1913. *The imperial Ottoman penal code: A translation from the Turkish text, with latest additions and amendments together with annotations and explanatory commentaries upon the text and containing an appendix dealing with the* special amendments in force in Cyprus and the judicial decisions of the Cyprus courts. Translated by John A. S. Bucknill and Haig Apisoghom S. Utidjian. London: H. Milford, Oxford University Press.

Peters, Rudolph. 2005. *Crime and punishment in Islamic law: Theory and practice from the sixteenth to the twenty-first century.* Themes in Islamic law 2. Cambridge: Cambridge University.

Postman, Neil. 1982. *The disappearance of childhood.* New York: Delacorte.

Qafisheh, Mutaz M. 2011. "Juvenile justice system in Palestine: Current situation and reform prospects." *International Journal of Law, Policy and the Family* 25 (3): 365–397.

Qawāsimīyah, Muḥammad ʿAbd al-Qādir. 1992. *Junūḥ al-aḥdāth fī al-tashrīʿ al-Jazāʾirī.* Algeria: l-Muʾassasah al-Waṭanīyah lil-Kitāb.

Rajagopal, Balakrishnan. 2006. "Counter-hegemonic international law: Rethinking human rights and development as a Third World strategy." *Third World Quarterly* 27 (5): 767–783. doi: 10.2307/4017777.

Ṣabāḥī, Muḥammad Rabīʿ. 2008. *Jarāʾim al-aḥdāth fī al-sharīʿah al-islāmīyah: Al-mushkilah wa-al-ʿilāj: dirāsah fiqhīyah tarbawīyah.* Beirut: Dār al-Nawādir.

Salaymeh, Lena. 2014. "Commodifying 'Islamic law' in the U.S. legal academy." *Journal of Legal Education* 63 (4): 640–646.

Salaymeh, Lena. 2015a. "Islamic law." In *The international encyclopedia of social and behavioral sciences,* edited by James D. Wright. Oxford, UK: Elsevier.

Salaymeh, Lena. 2015b. "Middle Eastern and North African legal traditions." In *The international encyclopedia of social and behavioral sciences,* edited by James D. Wright. Oxford, UK: Elsevier.

Samuri, Mohd Al-Adib, Zuliza Mohd Kusrin, Anwar Fakhri Omar, Noor Aziah Mohd Awal, and Fariza Md. Sham. 2012. "Legal issues in sentencing child offenders in Malaysia." *Advances in Natural and Applied Sciences* 6 (7): 1093–1098.

Shamiri, Nageeb. 1997–1998. "Country survey: Yemen." In *Yearbook of Islamic and Middle Eastern law,* vol. 4, edited by Eugene Cotran and Chibli Mallat, 386–416. London: Kluwer Law International; Centre of Islamic and Middle Eastern law at the School of Oriental and African Studies, University of London.

Sharādī, ʿAbd al-Raḥmān Muṣliḥ. 2002. *Inḥirāf al-aḥdāth fī al-tashrīʿ al-maghribī wa-al-qānūn al-muqāran.* Rabat: Maṭbaʿat al-Amnīyah.

UNICEF. 1996a *State party report: Kuwait.* http://www.unicef-irc.org/portfolios/documents/403_kuwait.htm.

UNICEF. 1996b *State party report: Libya.* http://www.unicef-irc.org/portfolios/documents/406_libyan-aj.htm.

UNICEF. 1997 *State party report: Chad.* http://www.unicef-irc.org/portfolios/documents/366_chad.htm.

UNICEF. 1998. *Innocenti digest 3: Juvenile justice.* International Child Development Centre. http://www.unicef-irc.org/publications/pdf/digest3e.pdf.

UNICEF. 2006. *Juvenile justice in South Asia: Improving protection for children in conflict with the law.* UNICEF Regional Office for South Asia. http://www.unicef.org/rosa/Juvenile_Justice_in_South_Asia.pdf.

UNICEF. 2008. *Niger: Country programme document, 2009–2013*. http://www.unicef
.org/about/execboard/files/Niger_final_approved_18_Septembe_2008.pdf.

UNICEF. 2009a. *Assessment of juvenile justice reform achievements in Albania*. UNICEF Regional Office for CEE/CIS. http://www.unicef.org/ceecis/UNICEF_JJ Albania08.pdf.

UNICEF. 2009b. *Assessment of juvenile justice reform achievements in Azerbaijan*. UNICEF Regional Office for CEE/CIS. July. http://www.unicef.org/ceecis/ UNICEF_JJAzerbaijan08.pdf.

UNICEF. 2010a. *Annual report for Mauritania*. http://www.unicef.org/about/annual report/files/Mauritania_COAR_2010.pdf.

UNICEF. 2010b. *Annual report for Senegal*. http://www.unicef.org/about/annualreport/ files/Senegal_COAR_2010.pdf.

UNICEF. 2010c. *Assessment of juvenile justice reform achievements in Kosovo*. UNICEF Regional Office for CEE/CIS. January. http://www.unicef.org/ceecis/UNICEF_JJ_ Kosovo_web.pdf.

UNICEF. 2011a. *Annual report 2011 for Comoros*. http://www.unicef.org/about/annual report/files/Comoros_COAR_2011.pdf.

UNICEF. 2011b. *The situation of children and women in Indonesia, 2000–2010*. Centre for Population and Policy Studies, Gajah Mada University. http://www.unicef.org/ sitan/files/Indonesia_SitAn_2010.pdf.

UNICEF. 2012a. *Annual report 2012 for Iran (Islamic Republic of)*, MENA. http://www .unicef.org/about/annualreport/files/Iran_COAR_2012.pdf.

UNICEF. 2012b. *Annual report 2012 for Somalia*, ESARO. http://www.unicef.org/about/ annualreport/files/Somalia_COAR_2012.pdf.

UNICEF. 2012c. *Juvenile justice in Central Asia: Reform achievements and challenges in Kazakhstan, Kyrgyzstan, Tajikistan, Turkmenistan and Uzbekistan*. UNICEF Regional Office for Central and Eastern Europe and the Commonwealth of Independent States. April. http://www.unicef.org/ceecis/UNICEF_JJ_Synthesis_2012_ Web.pdf.

UNICEF. 2012d. *Republic of Djibouti: Country programme document, 2013–2017*. http://www.unicef.org/about/execboard/files/Djibouti-2013–2017-final_approved -English-14Sept2012.pdf.

UNICEF. 2014a. *Burkina Faso: Child protection*. http://www.unicef.org/bfa/english/ protection.html (accessed 20 April 2014).

UNICEF. 2014b. *Mali: child protection*. http://www.unicef.org/mali/3934_4096.html (accessed 20 April 2014).

United Nations. 1989. *Convention on the Rights of the Child*. 20 November. https:// treaties.un.org/pages/ViewDetails.aspx?src=TREATYandmtdsg_no=IV-11and chapter=4andlang=en#EndDec.

United Nations. 2008. *Minimum legal age for marriage without consent*. United Nations Statistics Division. http://data.un.org/Data.aspx?d=GenderStat&f=inID:19&c=1,2,3,4,5,6&s=crEngName: asc,sgvEngName:asc,timeEngName:desc&v=1.

Ustarūshanī, Muḥammad ibn Maḥmūd. 1997. *Aḥkām al-ṣighār*. Beirut: Dār al-Kutub al-'Ilmīyah.

YouthPolicy.org. 2013. *Afghanistan factsheet*. 13 December. http://www.youthpolicy.org/ factsheets/country/afghanistan/.

YouthPolicy.org. 2014a. *Brunei factsheet*. 6 February. http://www.youthpolicy.org/ factsheets/country/brunei/.

YouthPolicy.org. 2014b. *Palestine factsheet*. 5 February [cited 20 April 2014. Available from http://www.youthpolicy.org/factsheets/country/palestine/.

YouthPolicy.org. 2014c. *Tajikistan factsheet*. 5 February. http://www.youthpolicy.org/ factsheets/country/tajikistan/.

YouthPolicy.org. 2014d. *Turkmenistan factsheet*. 4 February. http://www.youthpolicy .org/factsheets/country/turkmenistan/.

Zalkind, Paola, and Rita J. Simon. 2004. *Global perspectives on social issues: Juvenile justice systems*. Lanham, MD: Lexington Books.

Zaytūn, Mundhir 'Arafāt. 2001. *al-Aḥdāth, mas'ūlīyatuhum wa-ri'āyatuhum fī al-sharī'ah al-islāmīyah*. Amman: Majdalāwī.

PART III

The Relationship between Political Change and Juvenile Justice

Three Case Studies

The special focus of the three chapters in this part is how major political changes influence the principles and practices of juvenile justice. In chapter 7, Barbara Stańdo-Kawecka provides a history of the development of juvenile justice in Poland and also considers the influence of the transition away from Soviet influence on criminal and juvenile justice. In chapter 8, Ann Skelton provides a history of juvenile justice in South Africa and explores the impact of the transition from apartheid to multiracial democracy in the 1990s on the principles and outcomes in the juvenile justice system. Both the Polish and South African studies combine comprehensive histories of the evolution of juvenile justice in the 20th century with a special focus on the impact of political change. In chapter 9, Jae-Joon Chung presents data on the impact of legal change in juvenile and criminal justice in Japan and compares the recent Japanese experience with the large shifts in policy that happened in South Korea without any specific legislation during its transition to vibrant two-party democracy.

7

Juvenile Justice in Poland

BARBARA STAŃDO-KAWECKA

Development of a Separate Juvenile Justice System

A juvenile justice system distinct from the adult criminal law was shaped in Poland for the first time in the 1920s and 1930s. The 1928 Code of Criminal Procedure provided for separate juvenile courts as well as specific rules of proceedings in cases concerning juvenile offenders. Substantive provisions on the criminal responsibility of juvenile offenders were included in the 1932 Criminal Code.

Due to political reasons, discussions on a separate juvenile justice system started in Poland slightly later than in other European countries, such as Belgium, France, Germany, and Switzerland. In those countries, the Youth Court Movement emerged at the very beginning of the twentieth century. It relied on the North American "Child-Saver" movement as well as the North American concept of a juvenile court. The emergence of that movement in Europe coincided with the development of the "modern school of criminal law," which stressed utilitarian goals of punishment, such as deterrence, rehabilitation, and incapacitation. In comparison with the classical doctrine of punishment, it was focused not on retributive penalties strictly proportionate to the gravity of the offense but on the personality of the offender, individual and social factors contributing to crime, and penal sanctions aiming at prevention of reoffending. The Youth Court Movement was a part of that modern approach to crime, criminals, and criminal law. It emphasized the importance of removing juveniles from the adult criminal justice system and rehabilitating them within a separate system according to their personal circumstances and needs (Albrecht 2013, 646).

At the very beginning of the twentieth century, when the movement toward separate juvenile justice systems emerged in Europe, Poland did not exist as an independent country. At that time, its territory was divided between Austria, Prussia, and Russia. It regained its independence in 1918. After having regained independence, one of the most important tasks of the government was to unify legal provisions because different areas of the country applied former Austrian, Prussian, or Russian law. In 1919, a legislative commission was set up in Poland in order to prepare drafts of both the criminal and civil law. Issues related to juvenile offenders were disputed in a subdivision of the legislative commission for the reform of the criminal law. Members of that commission commonly shared the opinion that juveniles who had violated the criminal law should not be treated as "little adults" and that they should not receive the same penalties as adult offenders. The matter of controversy, however, was if penalties should be completely abandoned in cases concerning juvenile offenders.

Thus, from the very beginning of work on a separate juvenile justice system in Poland, there was a dispute between supporters of the "pure" welfare approach and those who preferred the justice approach modified by some welfare elements. The first group advocated for a juvenile court dealing with both juvenile offenders and juveniles who showed other problematic behaviors in order to apply to them protective and educational measures focused exclusively on their needs. Supporters of a more moderate approach proposed the separation of juvenile offenders from otherwise endangered children. In their opinion, children who were "in danger of becoming offenders" because of begging, vagrancy, prostitution, and other immoral behaviors (predelinquent children) should not be dealt with within the juvenile justice system. Instead, they should be supported in the same way as children who did not display problematic behaviors but were in need of care because of the lack of proper parental care. The scope of the juvenile justice system should be limited to persons who violated the criminal law before reaching the age of criminal majority. The catalogue of responses to juvenile offending should include protective and educational measures; however, the possibility to impose penalties should also be retained for youth who committed offences with discernment (*rozeznanie*), that is, with the ability to understand the meaning of their acts and direct their behaviors (Komisja Kodyfikacyjna Rzeczypospolitej Polskiej 1921, 11–12).

The first draft of an act regulating the separate juvenile justice system was prepared by a legislative commission in 1921. It was named as the draft of an act on juvenile courts. Despite its name, it contained provisions that related not only to the organization of juvenile courts but also to measures applied to juveniles as well as procedural issues in juvenile proceedings. Generally, the draft constituted a kind of compromise between supporters of the radical "pure" welfare orientation and those more moderate scholars willing to retain penalties for older juveniles who acted with discernment. The age of criminal majority was set at 17 years. "Juveniles" as defined in the draft were persons who infringed the criminal law below the age of 17 as well as persons below the same age who displayed other problematic or immoral behaviors, such as begging, vagrancy, and prostitution. Juvenile offenders below 13 years of age were considered not criminally responsible. They could not be punished for offenses, and only educational measures were applied to them. Among educational measures, the draft enumerated reprimand and supervision of parents, guardians, a trustworthy person, or institution, as well as placement in an educational institution. The same educational measures applied to older juveniles who committed offenses without discernment as well as to persons below 17 years of age who displayed problematic or immoral behaviors other than violation of the criminal law. All educational measures were imposed on juveniles for an unspecified period and might be enforced until they reached the age of 21.

According to the draft, juveniles who were at least 13 years of age who committed an offense as a rule were to be sentenced to placement in a correctional institution, provided that they acted with discernment. When the juvenile court sentenced a juvenile to placement in a correctional institution, it did not specify the length of stay. Instead, it determined only the minimum and maximum length of stay in such an institution. The juvenile might be released after the minimum length of stay depending on his or her progress in rehabilitation. The placement of a juvenile in a correctional institution constituted a kind of a specific penalty provided for older juveniles that replaced "ordinary" prison sentences imposed on adult offenders. Due to financial reasons, the 1921 draft of an act on juvenile courts was not enacted. Most of its provisions were finally included in the 1928 Code of Criminal Procedure as well as in the 1932 Criminal Code.

The 1928 Code of Criminal Procedure contained provisions on separate juvenile courts; however, in practice, before World War II, juvenile courts were set up only in some of the biggest cities (Korcyl-Wolska 2004, 30). Proceedings in juvenile cases regulated by the Code differed significantly from adult criminal proceedings. The most important feature of proceedings in juvenile cases was the dominant role of the juvenile judge. During the preparatory proceedings in juvenile cases, the juvenile judge served as an investigating judge who subsequently took part in adjudicating the same case at the court stage. Hearings were closed to the public; features of adversarial trial were strongly limited, as were the powers of the prosecution service. The same judge specializing in juvenile cases was to deal with the case at its different stages in order to establish contact with the juvenile and his or her parents or caregivers, to obtain extensive knowledge on his or her personality and family circumstances, and to respond to juvenile crime with the most adequate measure or sanction. Thus, in 1928, in cases concerning juvenile offenders, the legislature chose the inquisitorial process in order to enable juvenile judges to focus on juveniles' needs and to give dispositions most likely to achieve the educational and correctional goals of juvenile proceedings (Taracha 1988, 118–119).

Substantive provisions concerning the criminal responsibility of juvenile offenders were contained in a special chapter of the 1932 Criminal Code. Generally, the Code was based on a balanced compromise between the ideas of the classical and positivist (sociological) schools in the criminal law. The impact of the latter school was even more evident in provisions concerning juvenile offenders than in those regulating the criminal responsibility of adults because retributive penalties proportional to the gravity of the offense were almost totally excluded from the catalogue of responses to juvenile crime (Marek 1988, 42–43). The age of criminal majority according to the 1932 Criminal Code was 17 years, the same as was suggested in the 1921 draft of an act on juvenile courts. As defined in the Code, a "juvenile" was a person who committed an act prohibited by the criminal law while being below the age of 17. Unlike the 1921 draft, the legislature decided not to include in the juvenile justice system predelinquent children who displayed problematic or immoral behaviors. The division of juveniles suggested in the

1921 draft to those acting with and without discernment was retained in 1932. Juveniles who committed an offense below 13 years of age as well as those who committed an offense after the 13th birthday but prior to the 17th without discernment were treated as not criminally responsible. Only educational measures—that is, reprimand; supervision of parents, other trustworthy persons, or institutions, and placement in a state or private educational institution—could be imposed on them. Juveniles aged 13 to 16 who had committed an offense with discernment as a rule were sentenced to placement in a correctional institution (*zakład poprawczy*). It was possible, however, to impose educational measures on such juveniles as well, if the court found placing them in a correctional institution useless on the basis of the circumstances of the offense or the juvenile's character or conditions of his or her life and environment. The enforcement of the placement in a correctional institution could also be conditionally suspended by the court.

According to the 1932 Criminal Code, the juvenile court did not determine even the shortest or longest period of stay in a correctional institution; juveniles could be institutionalized until the age of 21. However, they might be granted conditional release earlier. In the doctrine of the criminal law, the legal nature of the placement of a juvenile in a correctional institution under the 1932 Criminal Code was controversial. According to some lawyers, such placement constituted a special preventive measure, different from educational measures envisaged in the Code. According to the prevailing opinion of scholars, it was a specific penalty, quasi-penalty, or educational penalty that replaced "ordinary" prison sentences provided for adult offenders and combined some retributive elements and a predominant rehabilitative goal (Stańdo-Kawecka 1993, 10–15). The basic prerequisite for sentencing a juvenile to placement in a correctional institution was committing of an offense with discernment, which corresponded to culpability as defined in the adult criminal law. The length of stay, however, was detached from the seriousness of the offense and depended on the progress of a juvenile in his or her reformation. Thus, indefinite length of stay in correctional institutions was in line with the primary aim of rehabilitation. It should be added that in certain cases specified in the 1932 Criminal Code, the placement in a correctional institution might be replaced by an "ordinary" prison sentence, particularly in cases concerning juvenile offenders who during court proceedings were above 17 years of age (Stańdo-Kawecka 2007, 280–282).

The Juvenile Justice System under the 1982 Juvenile Act

Currently, the juvenile justice system in Poland is regulated by the 1982 Juvenile Act (*ustawa o postępowaniu w sprawach nieletnich*). Provisions on dealing with juvenile offenders included in the 1928 Code of Criminal Procedure and 1932 Criminal Code remained in force until May 1983, when the 1982 Juvenile Act (JA) entered into force. However, in the first years after World War II, several repressive provisions were introduced into the criminal law, including the juvenile criminal law, by means of special acts on crimes against the interests of the communist state (Grześkowiak 2009, 29). In the 1950s, during work on new criminal codification, it was decided to regulate all matters relating to juvenile delinquents in a separate act. Preparation of a draft of such an act turned out to be very difficult because of different views presented by lawyers, teachers, psychologists, and criminologists. As a result, the Criminal Code, the Code of Criminal Procedure, and the Code of Execution of Penalties passed in 1969 did not introduce new provisions concerning juvenile offenders. The adoption of the 1982 JA was preceded by many years of discussions among scholars and practitioners on the best approach to prevent and combat juvenile delinquency. In the 1960s and 1970s, a dozen or so projects of separate laws on juveniles were prepared not only within the Ministry of Justice but also in the Ministry of Education (Rdzanek-Piwowar 1993, 207–220).

In comparison with the 1932 Criminal Code, the 1982 JA introduced a significantly more welfare-oriented, paternalistic, and protective approach. First of all, in 1982, the legislature returned to the idea included in the 1921 draft of an act on juvenile courts that the juvenile justice system should cover not only juveniles who committed an act prohibited by the criminal law but also children who were "in danger of becoming offenders" because of displaying other problematic or immoral behaviors. As a result, "juveniles" as defined in the 1982 JA are not only perpetrators of "punishable acts" committed after having reached 13 but before 17 years of age but also minors under 18 who show problematic behaviors not prohibited by the criminal law, referred to by the legislature as signs of "demoralization."

According to the criminal law, offenders are punished for offenses (*przestępstwo*), including fiscal offenses (*przestępstwo skarbowe*).[1] Under the 1982 JA, juveniles are not punished, but measures are imposed on them for "punishable acts" and/or signs of "demoralization." "Punishable acts" mean acts prohibited by the criminal law as offenses and certain petty crimes (contraventions). In 1982, the legislature chose a different terminology in order to stress that it was no longer the subject of proceedings in juvenile cases to establish the culpability of a juvenile. The criterion of a juvenile's acting with or without discernment was abandoned because it was found irrelevant for the choice of the most adequate measures. As for "demoralization," the JA has not defined this notion. Article 4 of the act only enumerates some examples of behavior types or circumstances that are treated as signs of "demoralization": violation of the principles of community life, commission of a prohibited act, truancy, use of alcohol or drugs, running away from home, prostitution, and association with criminal groups. It should be noted that there is no minimum age limit for juveniles who show signs of "demoralization." At least theoretically, it is possible to institute proceedings due to signs of "demoralization" in cases concerning very young children who behave in an unacceptable way. The commission of an act prohibited by the criminal law by a child who is less than 13 years of age is considered to be a sign of "demoralization" and does not constitute a "punishable act" under the JA. Provisions on juveniles who show signs of "demoralization" are in line with the protective and paternalistic ideology according to which judges dealing with juvenile cases should be provided with broad discretion in initiating state intervention in order to protect predelinquent children before they violate the criminal law (Krajewski 2006, 159).

The next important change introduced by the 1982 JA consisted in the creation of family courts. The 1928 Code of Criminal Procedure provided for special juvenile courts dealing exclusively with children and youth who violated the criminal law. After World War II, the jurisdiction of those special courts was gradually extended, and cases concerning the deprivation of parents of their parental responsibility or limitation of that responsibility were transferred to these special courts from civil courts. In 1982, the legislature decided to establish family courts as special units of district courts and to entrust them with a broad category of different cases concerning families, including interventions in parental responsibility and proceedings in juvenile cases due to "punishable acts" and signs of "demoralization."

The underlying assumption of the reform was that the same family court, and also the same family judge, should deal with cases related to different problems faced by the same family in order to give consistent judgments based on his or her extensive knowledge of this family. As was stressed in publications shortly after the adoption of the 1982 JA, the functions of the family judge in juvenile cases were not limited to adjudication but also included organizing and inspiring the juvenile's educational and rehabilitative activities (Patulski 1985, 18). Thus, the 1982 JA assigned the tasks concerning the prevention of offending and reoffending by juveniles to family courts. At the same time, the family court dealing with juvenile cases has been recognized rather as a welfare agency and not as a criminal court. Its tasks, at least theoretically, are not to punish juveniles but to protect, help, educate, and rehabilitate children in danger of becoming adult criminals. It should be noted, however, that the family court has the authority to apply to juveniles compulsory educational and correctional measures, including placement in closed residential institutions. In line with the welfare approach, all measures are to be imposed on juveniles not in the name of punishment but in the name of their protection and rehabilitation.

The revised concept of courts dealing with juvenile cases resulted in changes to procedures. Under the 1928 Code of the Criminal Procedure, the procedure in juvenile cases differed from adult criminal procedure,[2] but as a matter of fact, it was a modified criminal procedure. In 1982, the legislature introduced a "hybrid" procedure in juvenile cases that combined procedural provisions contained in the JA with elements of both the civil and criminal procedure (Stańdo-Kawecka 2010, 1008–1013). The preparatory stage of proceedings in juvenile cases was governed as a rule by the civil procedure. The same procedure (with certain changes introduced by the JA) was applied at the court stage in cases concerning signs of "demoralization." In juvenile cases regarding "punishable acts," the family judge after completion of the preparatory stage would decide that the proceedings at the court stage should be conducted according to the civil or criminal procedure on a basis of his or her opinion on measures that should be applied to the juvenile. The civil procedure was used if in the opinion of the family judge educational or medical measures were sufficient. If the family judge was of the opinion that the placement of a juvenile in a correctional institution should be applied, he or she would choose "correctional proceedings" (*postępowanie poprawcze*), which were governed by the criminal procedure. Different procedures used in juvenile cases regarding "punishable acts" at the court stage were justified by the legislature with the aim of providing older juveniles, on whom the most serious measure of placement in a correctional institution might be imposed, with better procedural safeguards, as would not be possible under the civil procedure. Additionally, in the course of correctional proceedings, the family court could exceptionally impose a penalty provided for adults instead of placement in a correctional institution if the juvenile was at least 18 years of age at the time of giving sentence and the court considered such placement inadvisable. The exceptional possibility to replace the correctional measure with a penalty also supported the need to provide juveniles with better procedural safeguards (Patulski 1985, 24). In practice, the creation of a kind of conglomerate of civil procedure (nonlitigious proceeding), criminal procedure, and procedural provisions contained in the JA turned out to be difficult to apply and resulted in serious problems.[3]

It should be added that one of basic ideas of the Polish juvenile justice system established in 1982, according to which the same family judge should deal with the juvenile case at its every stage, was found by the European Court of Human Rights to be contrary to the right to impartial tribunal that is provided for by the European Human Rights Convention. In the case *Adamkiewicz v. Poland*, the European Court of Human Rights found a violation of article 6, § 1, of this convention in a situation in which the same family judge conducted at first the evidence-gathering procedure, then decided to refer the case to the stage of adjudication, and then ruled in the same case as president of the trial bench.[4] In order to implement this judgment, an amendment to the 1982 JA was adopted by the parliament on 30 August 2013. Generally, the legislature abandoned the division of juvenile proceedings into preparatory and court stages. According to the amended JA, juvenile cases are dealt with by a family court in a unified court proceeding that does not distinguish the preparatory stage. As a rule, proceedings in juvenile cases are regulated by the Code of Civil Procedure, but there are also exceptions when provisions of the Code of Criminal Procedure apply, for example, in matters related to the collection and preservation of evidence by the police as well as the appointment and functions of a defense lawyer. The 2013 amendment did not alter the dominant role of the same family judge during the whole proceedings in juvenile cases. It is still possible that the same family judge, who functions as family court composed of a single judge, at first gathers and preserves evidence of a "punishable act" and then, on the basis of evidence gathered by him- or herself, adjudicates the case. In such cases, the impartiality of the family court may still be questioned.

The Minimum Age of Criminal Responsibility

Under the Polish criminal law since the 1930s, the age of criminal majority has been 17 years at the time of the offense. According to article 10, § 1, of the currently binding Criminal Code of 1997, rules on criminal responsibility determined by the Code apply to perpetrators who committed an offense while being at least 17 years of age. The Code does not apply to juveniles, that is, persons who committed an act prohibited by the criminal law below the age of 17. Instead, provisions of the JA apply. However, the age limit of 17 years at the time of the offense is not rigid, and some exceptions are provided for by the Code. Pursuant to article 10, § 2, of the Code, a juvenile may be exceptionally criminally responsible provided that he or she committed one of the most serious crimes enumerated in this article while being 15 or 16 and that the circumstances of the offense and the offender, the level of his or her maturity, and the ineffectiveness of educational or correctional measures justify directing the case to an adult criminal court. In cases in which juveniles of 15 or 16 years old are exceptionally criminally responsible on a basis of article 10, § 2, of the Criminal Code, they are tried by a criminal court according to provisions of the criminal procedure. Penalties provided for by the Code apply to them with the exception of life imprisonment; however, maximum penalties are lower than those that may be imposed on adult offenders, that is, perpetrators at least 17 years old at the time of the offense who are sentenced for the same offense.

Perpetrators who committed an offense while being 17 years of age are "adults" as defined in Polish criminal law. They are dealt with by common criminal courts according to provisions of the criminal procedure even if they are still under 18 at the time of the trial. The minimum age of criminal majority being set at 17 years raises concerns about compliance of the criminal law with the UN Convention on the Rights of the Child, which states in article 1 that a child means every human being below the age of 18 years, unless under the law applicable to the child, majority is attained earlier. The Committee on the Rights of the Child in General Comment No. 10 informed the states parties that the upper age limit for the application of the rules of special juvenile justice—both in terms of special procedural rules and in terms of rules for diversion and special dispositions—should apply for all children who at the time of an offense had not reach the age of 18 years (Committee on the Rights of the Child 2007, 11–12).

Measures Applied to Juveniles

As was mentioned earlier, with a few exceptions, no penalties provided for adults may be imposed on juvenile lawbreakers. The catalogue of sanctions applied to juveniles contains a wide range of educational, medical, and correctional measures. All educational and medical measures may be applied both to juveniles who have committed "punishable acts" while between 13 and 16 years of age and to juveniles less than 18 years of age displaying problematic behaviors (signs of "demoralization"). Correctional measures, that is, suspended or unsuspended placement of a juvenile in a correctional institution, may be imposed only on juveniles who have committed "punishable acts" prohibited by the criminal law as offenses or fiscal offenses after the 13th birthday but prior to the 17th.

While choosing between educational, medical, and correctional measures, the family court must take into account the interests of the juvenile concerned, the need to achieve positive changes in his or her personality and behavior, and the need to encourage and support proper fulfillment of duties by the juvenile's parents or guardians. As regards correctional measures, some additional factors should be taken into account, such as a high degree of the perpetrator's "demoralization" and the circumstances and the nature of the act committed as well as ineffectiveness of educational measures that have proved not to or are not likely to lead to rehabilitation of the offender. The JA does not require the establishment of the culpability of the juvenile with regard to his or her ability to act with discernment at the time of the "punishable act." It also does not provide the principle of proportionality in reactions to the circumstances of the offense.

The catalogue of educational measures has changed since 1982 to a limited extent. Currently, article 6 of the JA enumerates the following educational measures:

a. A reprimand
b. Supervision by parents, a guardian, a youth or other social organization, a workplace, a trustworthy person, or a probation officer
c. Application of special conditions, such as redressing the damage, making an apology to the victim, performing unpaid work for the benefit of the victim or local community, taking up school education or a job, taking part in educational or therapeutic training, avoiding specific locations, refraining from the use of alcohol and other intoxicants
d. A ban on driving
e. Forfeiture of objects gained through the commission of a punishable act
f. Placement of a juvenile in a youth probation center in which he or she spends a couple of hours daily
g. Placement of a juvenile in a professional foster family
h. Placement of a juvenile in a suitable institution or organization providing education, therapy, or vocational training
i. Placement of a juvenile in a residential youth educational center

The vast majority of educational measures do not change the place of residence of the juvenile, who stays with his or her family during the enforcement of imposed measures. Among measures resulting in the change of the former place of residence may be mentioned the placement of a juvenile in a professional foster family as well as in a youth educational center. Unlike the original catalogue of educational measures introduced by the 1982 JA, currently binding provisions do not include the possibility to place a juvenile in a child care institution, such as a children's home or family foster children's home.

Medical measures may be applied to juveniles who are suffering from mental deficiency, mental disease, some kind of mental disorder, or alcohol and drug addiction. These measures imply placing juveniles in a psychiatric hospital, other suitable health care institutions, a social welfare institution, or a suitable youth educational center. Both educational and medical measures are applied to juveniles for an indeterminate period of time. As a rule, these measures terminate when a juvenile reaches the age of 18, but in some cases, their duration may be extended to his or her 21st birthday. The family court that executes the measures may change, revise, or repeal them at any time if it is advisable for educational reasons.

Correctional measures consist in suspended or unsuspended placement of a juvenile in a correctional institution. Such institutions are subordinated to the Ministry of Justice; however, they do not form any part of the prison system. Similar to other categories of measures, correctional measures are also applied for an indeterminate period of time. The juvenile placed in a correctional institution can stay there no longer than up to 21 years of age, although he or she may be granted conditional release earlier. Provisions governing the enforcement of the placement of juveniles in correctional institutions emphasize the need to prepare an individual treatment plan for each juvenile and to provide him or her with a broad range of therapeutic, educational, and vocational activities in order to achieve the goal of rehabilitation. It should be added that in 2012 the Constitutional Court ruled that several provisions on correctional institutions and youth detention centers issued by the Minister of Justice were unconstitutional,[5] because they regulated matters related to limitation of personal liberty, which required a statutory basis.[6] The prosecutor general, while outlining his position, stated that the legislature provided adult offenders serving prison sentences with a significantly higher standard of protection of their rights and freedoms than it provided juveniles placed in correctional institutions.

Educational, medical, and correctional measures are applied by family courts if it is established that a juvenile committed a "punishable act" or displayed signs of "demoralization." During the course of proceedings, the family court may apply temporary (provisionally) measures that are much the same as educational and medical measures imposed on juveniles after adjudicating their cases. The legislature prefers temporary measures that are not connected with the change of the place of residence of a juvenile, such as placement of a juvenile under supervision of a probation officer, a trustworthy person, or an organization. Only if such measures are found insufficient, the family court may place a juvenile temporarily in a professional foster family or a youth educational center as well as apply provisionally medical measures. A distinct temporary measure has been provided for juveniles if in the course of the proceedings circumstances emerge in favor of placement in a correctional institution and there is justified fear that the juvenile may escape or destroy evidence. In such a case, the placement of a juvenile in a youth detention center (*schronisko dla nieletnich*) may be ordered as a provisional measure. The latter centers are under the authority of the Ministry of Justice. As a rule, juveniles cannot be detained in remand prisons for adults suspected of committing offenses. Under article 18, § 2, of the JA, however, in exceptional cases, a juvenile of at least 15 years at the time of the offense may be temporarily placed in a remand prison provided that there are grounds for sentencing him or her to a penalty under article 10, § 2, of the Criminal Code and placement in a youth detention center would not be sufficient. According to prison statistics, on 31 December 2012, there were six persons aged 15–16 who were detained on remand in detention facilities for adults (Central Administration of the Prison Service 2013, 14).

Juvenile Crime According to Police Statistics

Statistical data on crime and criminal justice, in the form of police statistics, court statistics, and prison statistics, were published in Poland in the communist period, at least after 1956. However, police statistics published before 1990 were unreliable because both the reporting of offenses by victims and the recording of them by the police were influenced by organizational, ideological, and political factors (Krajewski 2004, 383). According to police statistics published after the political, economic, and social change that took place in 1989, the overall crime rate was relatively stable during the first half of the 1990s (figure 7.1). During

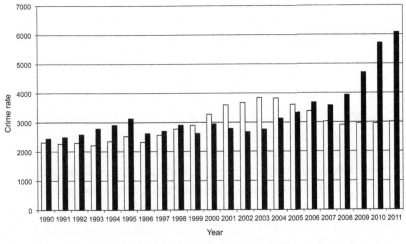

Figure 7.1. Overall crime rate and juvenile crime rate in the years 1990–2011. *Sources:* Data for the years 1990–2007 come from Habzda-Siwek 2009, 48; data for the years 2008–2011 were calculated on the basis of police statistics available online (http://www .policja gov.pl) and data on population in Poland according to age categories published yearly in *Statistical Yearbook of the Republic of Poland*.

the second half of the decade and in the first years of the new millennium, it was increasing; however, in 2004, this trend reversed. Finally, in the years 2007–2011, the overall crime rate stabilized at around 3,000 offenses per 100,000 population. In comparison with the overall crime rates, the development of juvenile crime has differed. What is most striking is the sharp increase in the juvenile crime rate in the past few years. In 2007, the number of juvenile offenses per 100,000 young people aged 13 to 16 amounted to 3,574, while in 2011 it grew to 6,075.

"Juvenile crimes" as defined in police statistics are acts prohibited by the criminal law as offenses or fiscal offenses committed by perpetrators who were at the time of the offense at least 13 but under 17 years of age. The police may treat recorded crime as juvenile crime only if they know the age of the perpetrator. The changes in the number of recorded juvenile crimes may arise not only from the actual growth in juvenile delinquency but also from other factors, such as the changing concentration of police work on juvenile lawbreakers. Unfortunately, in

Poland, police statistics have been the only source of systematic data on juvenile crime rates. The lack of other sources of data, including systematic self-reported data, makes it impossible to reveal trends in juvenile crime more precisely.

In the years 1990–2011, the proportion of juvenile crimes among all recorded crimes oscillated between 4.3% and 8.5%. At the same time, the percentage of juvenile suspects among all suspects amounted to 8.4%– 16.1%. As may be seen from figure 7.2, the number of juvenile offenses grew significantly in the years 2008–2012, while at the same time, the number of juvenile suspects remained stable or even slightly diminished. Explanation of those opposite trends in the numbers of juvenile crimes and juvenile offenders may be possible only on the basis of empirical research. Unfortunately, there is no such research in Poland, and it is difficult to say if in the past few years a similar number of juveniles committed many more offenses than previously or if there were other factors contributing to the rising number of juvenile offenses, such as changes in police activity or in the manner of collecting data.

Structure of Measures Imposed on Juveniles by Family Courts

Court statistics published in the *Statistical Yearbook of the Republic of Poland* include data on the total number of juveniles on whom family courts have imposed educational, medical, or correctional measures or penalties.[7] Pursuant to the JA, penalties provided for by the Criminal Code can be imposed by family courts on juvenile perpetrators of "punishable acts" only exceptionally if the juvenile offender at the time of adjudication is older than 18 and the court is of the opinion that the placement in a correctional institution would be inadvisable. This possibility was repealed by the 2013 amendment to the JA. As a result, family courts are no longer able to impose penalties on juvenile offenders even if they are 18 or older at the time of adjudication. According to court statistics, in previous years, provisions repealed by the 2013 amendment were used by family courts extremely rarely, if at all. In the years 1984– 2011, the number of juveniles sentenced by family courts to imprisonment did not exceed 12 in any year.

Pursuant to the 1982 JA, juveniles may be dealt with by family courts in proceedings instituted due to signs of "demoralization" as well as

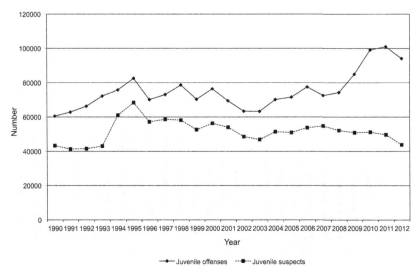

Figure 7.2. Juvenile crime and juvenile suspects in the years 1990–2012. *Source:* Police statistics available online: http://www.policja.gov.pl.

"punishable acts." In the mid-1980s, shortly after the entry into force of the JA in May 1983, family courts adjudicated yearly about 3,000–4,000 juveniles due to signs of "demoralization" and 8,000–9,500 juveniles who committed "punishable acts" (figure 7.3). In subsequent years, until the end of the last century, there was an increase in numbers of both categories of juveniles. Different trends may be observed in the period of from 2000 to 2008, in which the number of juveniles on whom measures were imposed due to "punishable acts" was more or less stable but the number of juveniles found to show signs of "demoralization" grew from 8,878 in 2000 to 20,089 in 2008. Since 2008, there has been a decrease in the numbers of juveniles adjudicated in proceedings due to signs of "demoralization" as well as "punishable acts." Generally, under the 1982 JA, which introduced proceedings in juvenile cases concerning signs of "demoralization," the number of juveniles adjudicated in such proceedings has increased fivefold (from 3,072 in 1984 to 15,670 in 2011). At the same time, the number of juvenile offenders, that is, perpetrators of "punishable acts," adjudicated by family courts has grown at a much slower rate (from 9,260 in 1984 to 22,807 in 2011).

In proceedings concerning signs of "demoralization," only educational or medical measures may be applied to juveniles. In the years

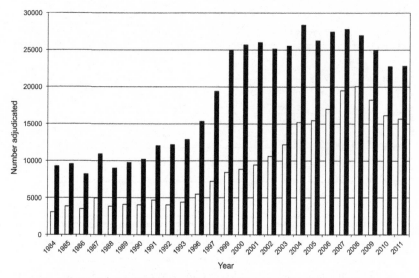

Year

□Juveniles adjudicated due to signs of demoralization ■Juveniles adjudicated due to punishable acts

Figure 7.3. Juveniles adjudicated by family courts in the years 1984–2011. *Source: Statistical Yearbooks*; data for the years 1994, 1995, and 1998 are not available.

1984–2011, such measures were applied mainly as supervision by a probation officer or parents, reprimand, and application of special conditions. Educational measures depriving juveniles of their liberty, that is, placement in a youth educational center or youth sociotherapeutic center, have been recently imposed on about 6% of those showing signs of "demoralization" (Czarnecka-Dzialuk and Wójcik 2011, 882–883). It should be added that proceedings due to signs of "demoralization" have been strongly supported by some scholars and practitioners, who have emphasized that interventions taken by the family court would be able to stop unacceptable behaviors displayed by children in "danger of becoming offenders" (Grześkowiak et al. 1991, 8–9; Bojarski 2009, 273–274). This opinion, however, has not been commonly shared. Shortly after the entry of the JA into force, interventions of the family court due to signs of "demoralization" were criticized by some scholars because of their potentially stigmatizing effects (Kowalska-Ehrlich 1988, 120–121). No empirical research meeting high methodological standards has been conducted in order to assess the effectiveness of measures applied by family courts to juveniles showing problematic behaviors. Unlike Western countries, in Poland, the empirical basis for assessing the effectiveness of strategies of early intervention has been extremely limited.

Juveniles who commit one of the most serious offenses while being at least 15 or 16 years of age may be tried by common criminal courts and receive penalties provided for adults. The proceedings in such cases are criminal proceedings, and they are not included in family court statistics on responses to "punishable acts" committed by juveniles. In proceedings concerning "punishable acts," family courts may impose educational, medical, or correctional measures. Prior to January 2014, when the 2013 amendment to the JA came into force, family courts were also authorized to apply penalties provided for adults, but it was possible only exceptionally if the juvenile was older than 18 at the time of the court decision and correctional measures were inadvisable. As was mentioned previously, in the years 1984–2011, penalties were imposed by family courts a few times a year, and in some years, penalties were not used at all. During the same period, the total number of juvenile perpetrators of "punishable acts" adjudicated by family courts oscillated between 8,199 in 1986 and 28,342 in 2004.

Family court dispositions in proceedings concerning "punishable acts" mainly imposed educational measures, including supervision by a probation officer or parents, reprimand, and application of special conditions (figure 7.4). Since the mid-1990s, there has been a significant increase in numbers and proportions of juvenile offenders to whom reprimand as well as special conditions were applied. In 2011, about one in three adjudicated juveniles was given reprimand, while in 1984, it was about one in ten. Special conditions were applied to about 6% of juvenile offenders adjudicated in 1984; in 2011, the percentage was 26%. At the same time, the proportion of supervision by a probation officer has been decreasing (from 44% to 32%). In recent years, educational measures consisting of placement in residential educational institutions have been applied to around 5% of juveniles adjudicated due to "punishable acts." Detailed analysis of trends in the application of residential educational measures since 1984 has not been possible because types of such institutions and rules governing placement in them were changing in that period.

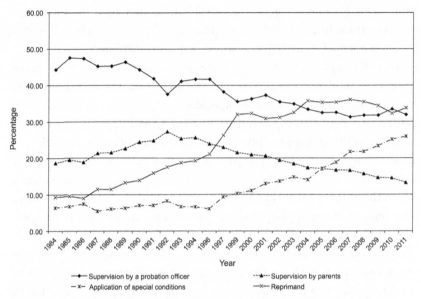

Figure 7.4. Prevalence of educational measures imposed on juvenile offenders in the years 1984–2011. *Note*: Not all cases have educational measures, and some have more than one. *Source*: *Statistical Yearbooks*; data for the years 1995 and 1998 are not available.

As regards correctional measures, these are the most severe measures provided by the JA for juvenile offenders; they have been used by family courts less and less frequently (table 7.1). In 1984, family courts decided to impose placement in a correctional institution (suspended and unsuspended) on about one in five juveniles adjudicated due to "punishable acts." As a result of a steady decline in the use of correctional measures, in 2011, they were imposed on 3% of juvenile offenders. As figure 7.5 indicates, the drop in the use of correctional measures since 1984 related to both suspended and unsuspended placement of a juvenile in a correctional institution. In 1984, 513 out of 9,260 juveniles adjudicated due to "punishable acts" (5.5%) received unsuspended placement in a correctional institution. In 2011, 259 juvenile perpetrators of "punishable acts," or 1.1% of all adjudicated juvenile offenders, were immediately placed in a correctional institution.

A decreasing number of juveniles placed by family courts in correctional institutions resulted in the decline in the population of such

TABLE 7.1. Number and Proportion of Correctional Measures Imposed on Juvenile Offenders in the Years 1984–2011

Year	Total number of juveniles adjudicated due to "punishable acts"	Juveniles on whom correctional measures (suspended and unsuspended) were imposed	
		Number	Percentage
1984	9,260	1,968	21.3
1985	9,545	1,531	16.0
1986	8,199	1,398	17.1
1987	10,895	1,553	14.3
1988	9,000	1,122	12.5
1989	9,750	1,082	11.1
1990	10,200	1,107	10.9
1991	12,050	1,287	10.7
1992	12,200	1,242	10.2
1993	12,900	1,168	9.1
1994	15,650	1,167	7.5
1996	15,350	1,176	7.7
1997	19,387	1,891	9.8
1999	24,909	1,345	5.4
2000	25,667	1,173	4.6
2001	25,976	1,144	4.4
2002	25,111	1,280	5.1
2003	25,521	1,259	4.9
2004	28,342	1,322	4.7
2005	26,228	1,158	4.4
2006	27,419	1,075	3.9
2007	27,790	1,026	3.7
2008	26,957	927	3.4
2009	24,953	870	3.5
2010	22,758	882	3.9
2011	22,807	691	3.0

Source: Statistical Yearbooks; data for the years 1995 and 1998 are not available.

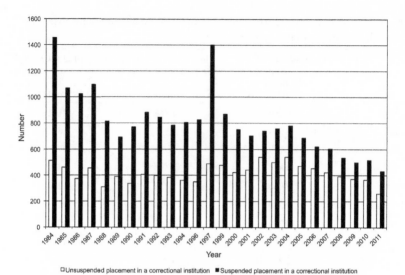

Figure 7.5. Number of suspended and unsuspended placements in a correctional institution imposed in the years 1984–2011. *Source: Statistical Yearbooks*; data for the years 1995 and 1998 are not available.

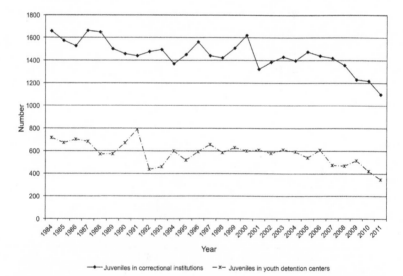

Figure 7.6. Number of juveniles in correctional institutions and youth detention centers in the years 1984–2011 (on 31 December). Source: *Statistical Yearbooks*; data for the years 1984–1994 include juveniles placed in correctional institutions who stayed in so-called semiliberty groups organized as branches of correctional institutions; in that period, up to 122 juveniles participated in such groups.

institutions (figure 7.6). On 31 December 2011, there were 1,100 juveniles in 27 correctional institutions. On the same day in 1984, there were 29 correctional institutions that housed 1,658 juveniles. A similar trend may be observed in relation to the temporary placement of juveniles in youth detention centers, which correspond to remand prisons for adult suspects. At the end of 1984, there were 716 juveniles in such detention centers. In 2011, this number dropped to 348, a decrease of over 50%.

Generally, responses to juvenile crime in the whole period after the 1982 JA came into force were based mainly on educational measures implemented in the community. The number and proportion of juveniles on whom correctional measures, that is, the most severe measures provided for by the JA, were imposed by family courts have been decreasing. As a result, the population of juveniles deprived of their liberty in correctional institutions has dropped significantly. The vast majority of educational measures applied to juvenile offenders consisted in leaving them in their families while giving them a reprimand, imposing certain obligations on them, or placing them under the supervision of parents or a probation officer. Unlike the adult criminal justice system, the juvenile justice system has not experienced an increase in the repressiveness of responses to juvenile crimes.

Prison Population in the Years 1984–2012

In Poland, the prison population includes three categories of prisoners (figure 7.7):

a. Persons remanded in custody (pretrial detention)
b. Prisoners sentenced to imprisonment for offenses or fiscal offenses under the Criminal Code or Code on Fiscal Offences
c. Persons on whom the penalty of arrest has been imposed for petty crimes (contraventions) under the Code on Petty Crimes

The total population of Poland since 1984 has not changed significantly, and that is why the prison population rate per 100,000 inhabitants has followed much the same patterns as the number of prisoners (figure 7.8). In December 2012, there were 220 prisoners per 100,000 population.

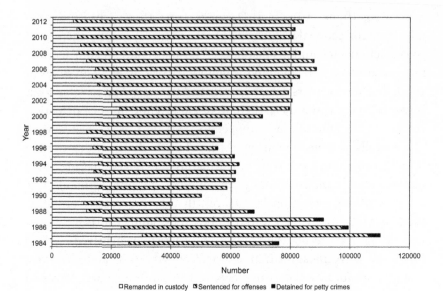

Figure 7.7. Prison population in Poland in the years 1984–2012 (on 31 December). *Source*: Data for the years 1984–2010 come from *Statistical Yearbooks*; data for the years 2011–2012 come from prison statistics published online by the Central Administration of the Prison Service (http://www.sw.gov.pl).

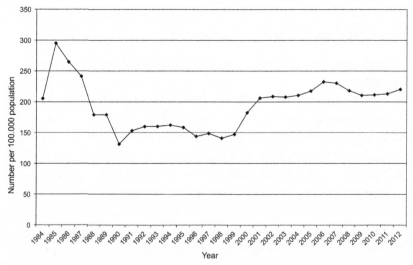

Figure 7.8. Prison population rate per 100 thousand inhabitants in the years 1984–2012 (on 31 December). *Source*: Migdał and Szymanowski 2014, 269–270.

314

As can be seen in figure 7.7, in the mid-1980s, the number of prisoners in Poland was extremely large. It oscillated around 90,000–110,000 persons, with the exception of the years when it slightly diminished as a result of amnesty statutes passed in 1984 and 1986. In 1989, however, the prison population dropped to 40,321, which represented a decrease of 41% in comparison to the previous year. This sudden decrease in the number of prisoners in 1989 resulted to a large extent from the two amnesty statutes (Melezini 2003, 495). In the following years, the number of prisoners grew, and in the early and mid-1990s, it stabilized at the level of 55,000–60,000.

This stabilization of the prison population in the mid- and late 1990s can be explained to a large extent by changes both in the criminal law and in sanctioning practice. Another factor of considerable importance was the "penal climate" in the first years after the 1989 transformation. Many members of the parliament, chosen in 1989 in partly free election, were involved in opposition activities in communist times and were detained by communist authorities as political prisoners. They personally experienced unfair trials, repressive penalties, and inhuman conditions in prisons. Undoubtedly, their experience concerning the criminal justice system contributed to a broad political consensus on the need for liberalization of criminal policy that was reached in Poland at the beginning of the 1990s. Independent of the work done on the draft of the new criminal code, after 1989, numerous changes to the 1969 Criminal Code were passed in order to adjust the criminal law to international standards as well as to make it more humane, liberal, and rational.[8] At the same time, significant changes were made in the jurisprudence of courts. The stabilization of the prison population at a relatively low level in the mid- and late 1990s took place despite the fact that the number of recorded crimes, including violent crimes, was significantly higher than before the 1989 transformation (Stańdo-Kawecka and Krajewski 2010, 700; Siemaszko 2000, 17). In the mid-1990s, however, the political consensus on the liberalization of criminal policy started to diminish.

As A. Šelih has noted in her article on crime in the period of transformation, changes made after 1989 in central and eastern European countries, arising from the transition from communism to capitalism and liberal democracy, were so large, multidimensional, and unique that it is very difficult, if possible at all, to explain crime rates by means of one theoretical model. Additionally, postcommunist countries do not constitute a homogeneous group. There were significant differences between them before the collapse of the communist system, and the political and economic transformation even deepened some of these differences (Šelih 2012–2013, 8). What was common for central and eastern European countries after the transformation was a sudden increase in the number of recorded crimes in comparison with crime rates before 1989. This phenomenon seemed contrary to expectations that in societies that regained freedom, the crime level should not increase. Possible explanations for the rise in recorded crimes refer to different theories and factors, such as disintegration of social bonds, increase in opportunities to commit crimes, weakening of self-control, changing patterns of activity of the police, or increasing willingness of citizens to inform police about being the victim of a crime. The same can be said about trends in criminal policy and prison population; there were many factors contributing to changes in these areas in particular postcommunist countries (Šelih 2012–2013, 8; Krajewski 2012a, 1414–1416).

In Poland, in 1997, new criminal codification was enacted (Criminal Code, Code of Criminal Procedure, and Code of Execution of Penalties), which came into force in September 1998. Although the 1997 Criminal Code was based on the assumptions of humanization, liberalization, and rationalization of criminal policy, it was under this Code when the prison population in Poland started to rise again in 1999–2001. The growing number of prisoners in that time as well as the large prison population in the subsequent years cannot be explained simply by increasing crime rates. The main factor contributing to the high number of prisoners seems to lie in the changing social and political climate around issues of crime. The "penal climate" was changing parallel to growing unemployment, falling enthusiasm about economic reforms among people most seriously affected by them, and rising feelings of both social insecurity and fear of crime. The latter was to a large extent generated by extensive media coverage on rare but outrageous violent or sexual offenses. Social and media pressure for tougher punishment for perpetrators encouraged politicians to seek the support of voters by making criminal policy more repressive through legislative changes but also by influencing the practice of criminal justice agencies. The latter efforts were particularly visible in the first years of the new millennium in the activity of the prosecution service, governed at that time by the minister of justice acting also as the prosecutor general. The politicization of criminal policy was manifest in media campaigns organized by the minister of justice, who involved other public prosecutors to promote his achievements. As stressed by K. Krajewski, "Investigations appear to have often been conducted and arranged to produce the best possible media effects and political impact" (2012b, 97). This activity of the prosecution service was not without influence on the large number of persons detained on remand at the beginning of the new century.

The decisive factor that in recent years has inhibited reforms aimed at making the policies of temporary detention and punishment more repressive seems to be the jurisprudence of the European Court of Human Rights in cases concerning too long periods of detention on remand as well as violation of the ban on inhuman and degrading treatment or punishment because of overcrowding in Polish penitentiaries. In 2009, the European Court of Human Rights found that overcrowding in Polish prisons had revealed a structural problem.[9] Additionally, in 2008, the Constitutional Court passed a judgment concerning the unconstitutionality of article 248(1) of the 1997 Code of Execution of Penalties. The latter article had allowed for the placement of prisoners in a cell in which the area was smaller than the statutory size (three square meters) for an indefinite period of time and did not set a minimum permissible area.[10] The lack of resources necessary to build new prisons and maintain a large number of prisoners in human conditions contributed to such recent reforms in the field of criminal policy as the introduction of electronic monitoring as an alternative way of serving prison sentences up to one year, liberalization of formal premises for early conditional release, or changes to provisions regulating the enforcement of the penalty of liberty limitation[11] in order to broaden the scope of application of noncustodial penalties. So far, these reforms focused mainly on the elimination of prison overcrowding and did not bring with them profound changes in the whole system of punishment or significant decline in the size of the prison population.

Figure 7.9 indicates that among offenders deprived of their liberty on the basis of a court judgment given in 2012, the largest group constituted those who initially were sentenced to suspended imprisonment, which was subsequently revoked because of violations of imposed conditions

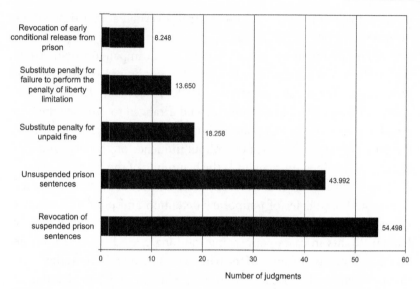

Figure 7.9. Court judgments resulting in offenders' deprivation of liberty in 2012. Source: *Justification of the Government's Draft of an Act Amending the Criminal Code and Some Other Acts*, submitted to the parliament on 15 May 2014 (form No. 2393), 127, available online at http://www.sejm.gov.pl/sejm7.nsf/druk.xsp?nr=2393.

and obligations. It seems that currently the large number of prisoners stems not so much from longer prison sentences or a high proportion of imprisonment in the structure of imposed penalties but rather from a restrictive policy of early conditional release and a considerable number of offenders who finally enter prisons although they initially received noncustodial penalties, such as a fine, the penalty of liberty limitation, or suspended imprisonment. In order to reduce the number of prisoners, it is necessary to carry out reforms in the field of enforcement of noncustodial sanctions, including reforms concerning both the probation service and cooperation between different services targeting offenders' criminogenic needs.

Trends in Juvenile and Criminal Policy after Transformation

In the first years after the political, economic, and social change in 1989, there was in Poland a broad political consensus on the need to make criminal policy more human, liberal, and rational. As this consensus broke down in the late 1990s, the prison population started to grow. The relative stabilization of the prison population in Poland in recent years has resulted mainly from judgments of the European Court of Human Rights as well as the Polish Constitutional Court concerning prison overcrowding.

As in other central and eastern European countries, in Poland after transformation, the crime problem came to be perceived as a serious social problem that was very difficult to control. Such views have not been supported by statistical data concerning rates of recorded crimes in Europe. According to these data, central and eastern Europe during the past twenty years have been characterized by a significantly lower level of recorded crimes than in western European countries. Despite victimization surveys, it is still not entirely clear what is the relationship between the number of recorded and actually committed crimes (Siemaszko 2009, 180–186); however, only recorded crimes are dealt with by the criminal justice system and influence the prison population. The prison population has been much higher in central and eastern European countries than in western Europe in the whole period after the 1989 transformation. Taking into account lower levels of recorded crimes and higher rates of persons deprived of their liberty per 100,000 population, it must be stated that postcommunist countries have not been able to change their criminal policy in such a way as to make the level of incarceration closer to that in western Europe. As a result, despite the trend toward integration in many areas, Europe has still been divided into two "penal climate" zones. Unlike western European countries, characterized by mild a "penal climate," Poland and other postcommunist countries belong to the zone of a much more severe "penal climate" (Krajewski 2012a, 1426).

In contrast to criminal policy concerning adult offenders, the juvenile justice policy did not experience an increase in the severity of responses to juvenile offending after the 1989 transformation, which might be explained by several factors. The 1982 JA was drafted with active participation of criminologists working in the Polish Academy of Sciences who in the 1960s and 1970s carried out extensive empirical research on juvenile delinquency as well as "morally neglected" and socially maladjusted children. Results of the research revealed a number of family and school factors contributing to juvenile problematic behaviors.

They also pointed to the need for early intervention and differentiation of measures applied to juveniles according to their family and school situation (Buczkowski, Klaus, and Woźniakowska-Fajst 2009, 54–58). The approach to juveniles built into the 1982 JA was in accordance with this research. Although repressive adult criminal law was strongly criticized by scholars long before the 1989 transformation, the educational and rehabilitative aims of the 1982 JA were commonly accepted by criminologists and justice practitioners in the period of transition to a liberal and democratic state. In later years, family courts dealing with juveniles were not influenced by the changing "penal climate." On the contrary, the limited use of correctional measures seems to indicate that they were guided rather by skepticism about the possibility of achieving rehabilitative aims by means of deprivation of juveniles' liberty. It is also possible that recently the decreasing number of juveniles placed in correctional institutions is connected with the judgment given in 2010 by the European Court of Human Rights in the case *Adamkiewicz v. Poland*. The correctional proceeding conducted in this case was deemed a violation of the right to impartial tribunal and fair trial. It cannot be excluded that as a result of this judgment, family courts have avoided correctional proceedings because they did not want to have their sentences quashed in appellate courts.

In the past decade, different drafts of new juvenile acts have been prepared by different commissions set up by the Ministry of Justice, but they have been met with criticism. A draft juvenile act prepared in the years 2003–2006 was criticized mainly because of proposing too formalized procedural provisions based on criminal procedure, while the draft prepared in the years 2006–2007 was met with criticism for being too repressive (Marek 2009, 389–390). The 2013 amendment to the JA still raises concerns about whether it actually provides juveniles with the right to impartial tribunal and procedural safeguards. Although the juvenile justice system has not evolved in the direction of increasing repressiveness, there is still the question of whether it is effective in dealing with children in conflict with the law. Available empirical studies on the rate of juvenile reoffending are rather pessimistic and indicate that over 50% of juvenile offenders commit crimes also as adults, that is, after reaching the age of criminal majority (Rzeplińska 2013, 284). In contrast to Western countries, in Poland, there is little discussion on the need for a holistic approach to juveniles and programs that "work." It is also very difficult to change the juvenile justice system in such a way as to balance the discretionary powers of family courts with the basic procedural rights of juveniles, because so far the proponents of these two values have not been able to work out a compromise.

Conclusions

The 1982 JA was based on the Belgian Youth Protection Act of 1965, and as was also the case of the Belgian juvenile law, it presented one of the most welfare-oriented juvenile laws in Europe (Christiaens, Dumortier, and Nuytiens 2010, 99). As a result of regulations included in the 1982 JA, the Polish juvenile justice system ceased to be a juvenile criminal justice system and was remodeled in the direction of a modified version of a youth protection system. Family courts dealing with both delinquent and "problematic" but nondelinquent juveniles were granted large discretionary powers, and juveniles were treated generally not as persons responsible for their behaviors but rather as objects of protective, educational, and rehabilitative efforts made by family judges in cooperation with probation officers and diagnostic, educational, or correctional institutions. In the 1980s, juvenile justice systems based so strongly on a protective and paternalistic philosophy were rather unique in western European countries, which mostly chose a more moderate approach combining elements of justice and welfare in dealing with juvenile offenders. At the same time, such a system was also exceptional in communist countries, in which issues concerning criminal liability of juvenile offenders were usually regulated in criminal codes and constituted modified versions of adult criminal law, while delinquent children under the minimum age of criminal responsibility were dealt with by "commissions for minors" having broad powers to control juvenile behaviors (Pruin 2010, 1515–1516).

The Belgian Youth Protection Act of 1965, which strongly influenced the Polish 1982 JA, was in 2006 modernized into "a hybrid model of welfare, restorative justice and 'just deserts'" (Christiaens, Dumortier, and Nuytiens 2010, 125). In Poland, the paternalistic and protective approach to juveniles introduced by the 1982 JA has been preserved also after the transformation of 1989. There have been no significant changes to the philosophy of dealing with juvenile offenders and pre-delinquent children despite changes in the "penal climate" concerning adult offenders. Proposals that aimed to make the juvenile law more punitive were opposed by most criminologists and did not obtain the sufficient support of politicians and public opinion to adopt a new juvenile law. Family courts proved to be resistant to trends to expand the scope of incarceration. Undoubtedly, the juvenile justice system in Poland, when compared with other European countries, has not been marked by repressiveness. However, it has been marked by a significantly lower level of protection of juveniles' procedural rights in juvenile proceedings. This problem may be illustrated by the statement of a defense lawyer interviewed recently during research conducted for the project "Protecting Young Suspects in Interrogations: A Study on Safeguards and Best Practice";[12] the lawyer stated that if he had committed a crime and had a choice, he would prefer to be dealt with in adult criminal proceedings and not in juvenile proceedings. He explained his views with the argument that there are significantly greater procedural restrictions on the use and duration of pretrial detention of adult suspects in comparison with juveniles. He added that in juvenile proceedings conducted by family courts, such procedural safeguards as the right of the suspect to remain silent are not respected in practice even if they are provided for by the JA. What makes the matter even worse, in his opinion, is the amount of interinmate violence experienced by juveniles in educational and correctional institutions, which is higher than in detention institutions for adults.

One of the most important questions concerning the juvenile justice system in Poland seems to be whether the system, which is not repressive, at the same time provides juveniles with child-friendly justice. In the past few years, the protection of rights of children who come into contact with judicial or nonjudicial proceedings in many ways (for example, as suspects, victims, or witnesses) has been a priority for the Council of Europe.[13] The same could be said about the European Union; in November 2013, the European Commission presented a proposal of a directive of the European Parliament and of the Council on procedural safeguards for children suspected or accused in criminal proceedings (COM(2013) 822/2);[14] the proposal aims, among other things, at ensuring a more homogeneous protection of children's rights within the European Union. It would be interesting to continue research on the juvenile justice system in Poland in order to determine if the current European discussion on both the notion of "criminal proceedings" in juvenile cases and children's rights in different types of proceedings will influence the welfare-paternalistic approach. It would also be valuable to carry out comparative research on the influence of European legislation on juvenile justice systems in countries that had a communist or socialist regime after World War II, particularly because these countries are usually underrepresented in international comparisons (Pruin 2010, 1517).

NOTES

1. In Poland, criminal responsibility for fiscal offenses, such as tax offenses, has been regulated by the separate Code on Fiscal Offenses of 1999.

2. As was mentioned earlier, the same juvenile judge served as an investigating and adjudicating judge. Additionally, court sittings were less formal than in cases concerning adult offenders and were closed to the public.

3. As an example of the lack of synchronization of procedural rules, it was indicated that the family judge applied provisions of the Code of Civil Procedure (nonlitigious proceeding) during the explanatory (preparatory) proceeding in juvenile cases, while the police acted pursuant to provisions of the Code of Criminal Procedure when collecting and preserving evidence. As a result, the rights of interrogated juveniles as well as witnesses were narrower or wider at different stages of the same case, depending on whether the interrogation was conducted by a family judge or the police.

4. ECtHR 2 March 2010, *Adamkiewicz v. Poland*, no. 54729/00, paras. 93, 94.

5. *Rozporządzenie Ministra Sprawiedliwości w sprawie zakładów poprawczych i schronisk dla nieletnich*, issued on 17 October 2001 with subsequent amendments.

6. Judgment of Constitutional Court U 1/12, issued on 2 October 2012.

7. The *Statistical Yearbook of the Republic of Poland* (*Rocznik Statystyczny Rzeczypospolitej Polskiej*; before 1990: *Rocznik Statystyczny*) is published by the Central Statistical Office (Główny Urząd Statystyczny). In this chapter, statistical data on enforceable court decisions given in juvenile cases have been used consistently. Data on family court decisions given in the first instance differ significantly from data on enforceable court decisions, which is difficult to explain without empirical research, as has been stressed by Czarnecka-Dzialuk and Wójcik 2011, 873–875.

8. Major changes introduced in 1990 and 1995 consisted of the repeal of regulations on the obligatory tightening of penalties imposed on recidivists, the passing of a statutory moratorium on capital punishment, the reintroduction of life imprisonment, and the introduction of unpaid work for public purposes with the consent of the offender as a substitute penalty for a fine.

9. See ECtHR 22 October 2009, *Orchowski v. Poland*, no. 17885/04; ECtHR 22 October 2009, *Norbert Sikorski v. Poland*, no. 17599/05.

10. Judgment of Constitutional Court SK 25/07, issued on 26 May 2008.

11. The penalty of liberty limitation involves allowing the offender to remain in the community while imposing on him or her the obligation to fulfill unpaid work for public purposes in the amount of from 20 to 40 hours monthly; this penalty is to some extent similar to the community sentence known in western Europe. The maximum duration of the penalty of liberty limitation is one year and, exceptionally, two years. In some cases, the obligation to fulfill unpaid work for public purposes can be replaced with deduction from the remuneration received by an employed offender for his or her job.

12. The project "Protecting Young Suspects in Interrogations: A Study on Safeguards and Best Practice" has been carried out in Belgium, England and Wales, Italy, Poland, and the Netherlands. It has been funded by a Criminal Justice Action Grant of the European Commission (JUST/2011/JPEN/AG2909). Results will be published in 2015.

13. In 2010, the Council of Europe adopted "Guidelines of the Committee of Ministers of the Council of Europe" on child-friendly justice. Text of the guidelines is available online: http://www.coe.int/t/dghl/standardsetting/childjustice/default_en.asp (accessed 10 April 2014).

14. The proposal is available online: http://www.ecba.org/extdocserv/projects/ps/20131127_PropEC_Children.pdf (accessed 10 April 2014).

REFERENCES

Albrecht, H. J. (2013). "Juvenile Criminal Law and Justice in Germany: Accounting for Trends in the German Juvenile Criminal Law System." In: Sözüer, A. (ed.), *3rd International Crime and Punishment Film Festival: Juvenile Justice: Academic Papers*, 643–686. Istanbul.

Bojarski, T. (2009). "Nieletni przed sądem: Uwagi o niektórych założeniach ogólnych oraz praktyce." *Archiwum Kryminologii* 29–30:269–285.

Buczkowski, K., Klaus, W., and Woźniakowska-Fajst, D. (2009). "Zakład Kryminologii INP PAN z perspektywy współczesnej." *Archiwum Kryminologii* 29–30:49–63.

Central Administration of the Prison Service. (2013). *Roczna informacja statystyczna za rok 2012*. http://sw.gov.pl/Data/Files/001c169lidz/rok-2012.pdf.

Christiaens, J., Dumortier, E., and Nuytiens, A. (2010). "Belgium." In: Dünkel, F., Grzywa, J., Horsfield, P., and Pruin, I. (eds.), *Juvenile Justice Systems in Europe: Current Situation and Reform Developments*, vol. 1, 99–129. Mönchengladbach, Germany: Forum Verlag Godesberg.

Committee on the Rights of the Child. (2007). *General Comment No. 10 (2007), Children's Rights in Juvenile Justice*. http://www.crin.org/docs/CRC_GeneralComment10 .pdf.

Czarnecka-Dzialuk, B., and Wójcik, D. (2011). "Reagowanie na czyny karalne i demoralizację nieletnich—koncepcje teoretyczne, statystyki i opinie sędziów rodzinnych." In: Siemaszko, A. (ed.), *Stosowanie prawa: Księga jubileuszowa z okazji XX-lecia*. Instytut Wymiaru Sprawiedliwości, 868–922. Warsaw: Wolters Kluwer.

Grześkowiak, A. (2009). "Funkcje prawa nieletnich." In: Hofmański, P., and Waltoś, S. (eds.), *W kręgu prawa nieletnich: Księga pamiątkowa ku czci Profesor Marianny Korcyl-Wolskiej*, 21–42. Warsaw: Wolters Kluwer.

Grześkowiak, K., Krukowski, A., Patulski, W., and Warzocha, E. (1991). *Ustawa o postępowaniu w sprawach nieletnich. Komentarz*. Warsaw: Wydawnictwo Prawnicze.

Habzda-Siwek, E. (2009). "Aktualne trendy przestępczości nieletnich w Polsce w świetle danych ze statystyk policyjnych." In: Hofmański, P., and Waltoś, S. (eds.), *W kręgu prawa nieletnich. Księga pamiątkowa ku czci Profesor Marianny Korcyl-Wolskiej*, 43–64. Warsaw: Wolters Kluwer.

Komisja Kodyfikacyjna Rzeczypospolitej Polskiej. (1921). *Projekt ustawy o sądach dla nieletnich uchwalony przez Komisję Kodyfikacyjną Rzeczypospolitej Polskiej w dniu 7 grudnia 1921*. Warsaw.

Korcyl-Wolska, M. (2004). *Postępowanie w sprawach nieletnich*. Zakamycze: Kantor Wydawniczy Zakamycze.

Kowalska-Ehrlich, B. (1988). *Młodzież nieprzystosowana społecznie a prawo*. Warsaw: Wydawnictwo Prawnicze.

Krajewski, K. (2004). "Crime and Criminal Justice in Poland." *European Journal of Criminology* 1 (3): 377–407.

Krajewski, K. (2006). "The Juvenile Justice System in Poland." In: Jensen, E. L, and Jepsen, J. (eds.), *Juvenile Law Violators, Human Rights, and the Development of New Juvenile Justice Systems*, 155–186. Oxford, UK: Hart.

Krajewski, K. (2012a). "Czy w Europie istnieją dwie odrębne strefy 'klimatu penalnego.'" In: Kardas, P., Sroka, T., and Wróbel, W. (eds.), *Państwo prawa i prawo karne: Księga jubileuszowa Profesora Andrzeja Zolla*, vol. 2, 1413–1429. Warsaw: Wolters Kluwer.

Krajewski, K. (2012b). "Prosecution and Prosecutors in Poland: In Quest of Independence," *Crime and Justice: A Review of Research* 41:75–116.

Marek, A. (1988). "Sądownictwo dla nieletnich w Polsce na tle porównawczym." In: Bojarski, T. (ed.), *Postępowanie z nieletnimi: Orzekanie i wykonywanie środków wychowawczych i poprawczych*, 38–54. Lublin: Uniwersytet Marii Curie-Skłodowskiej.

Marek, A. (2009). "Uwagi o reformie prawa dotyczącego nieletnich." *Archiwum Kryminologii* 29–30:383–391.

Melezini, M. (2003). *Punitywność wymiaru sprawiedliwości karnej w Polsce w XX w.* Białystok: Temida 2.

Migdał, J., and Szymanowski, T. (2014). *Prawo karne wykonawcze i polityka penitencjarna*. Warsaw: Wolters Kluwer.

Patulski, W. (1985). "Rola i zadania sądów rodzinnych w wypełnianiu wskazań ustawy o postępowaniu w sprawach nieletnich." *Zeszyty Naukowe Instytutu Badania Prawa Sądowego* 23:16–37.

Pruin, I. (2010). "The Scope of Juvenile Justice Systems in Europe." In: Dünkel, F., Grzywa, J., Horsfield, P., and Pruin, I. (eds.), *Juvenile Justice Systems in Europe: Current Situation and Reform Developments*, vol. 4, 1513–1555. Mönchengladbach, Germany: Forum Verlag Godesberg.

Rdzanek-Piwowar, G. (1993). "Granice nieletniości w polskim prawie karnym." *Archiwum Kryminologii* 19:191–231.

Rzeplińska, I. (2013). "Polityka karna sądów wobec dawnych nieletnich sprawców przestępstw." In: Górowski, W., Kardas, P., Sroka, T., and Wróbel, W. (eds.), *Zagadnienia teorii i nauczania prawa karnego. Kara łączna. Księga Jubileuszowa Profesor Marii Szewczyk*, 283–288. Warsaw: Wolters Kluwer.

Šelih, A. (2012–2013). "Teoretyczne wyjaśnienia przestępczości w okresie transformacji." *Biuletyn Polskiego Towarzystwa Kryminologicznego im. profesora Stanisława Batawii* 20:7–13. Available online at http://www.inp.pan.pl/towa/Biuletyn_Nr_20_1 .pdf.

Siemaszko, A. (2000). "Crime and Criminal Policy in Poland: A Look Back and into the Future." In: Siemaszko, A. (ed.), *Crime and Law Enforcement in Poland on the Threshold of the 21st century*, 15–25. Warsaw: Oficyna Naukowa.

Siemaszko, A. (2009). "International Crime Victim Survey '04/05: Polska na tle wybranych krajów Unii Europejskiej." *Archiwum Kryminologii* 29–30:169–192.

Stańdo-Kawecka, B. (1993). "Charakter prawny zakładu poprawczego w kodeksie karnym z 1932 r." *Przegląd Więziennictwa Polskiego* 4–5:10–15.

Stańdo-Kawecka, B. (2007). *Prawo karne nieletnich: Od opieki do odpowiedzialności.* Warsaw: Wolters Kluwer.

Stańdo-Kawecka, B. (2010). "Poland." In: Dünkel, F., Grzywa, J., Horsfield, P., and Pruin, I. (eds.), *Juvenile Justice Systems in Europe: Current Situation and Reform Developments*, vol. 2, 991–1026. Mönchengladbach, Germany: Forum Verlag Godesberg.

Stańdo-Kawecka, B., and Krajewski, K. (2010). "Polen." In: Dünkel, F., Lappi-Seppälä, T., Morgenstern, C., and van Zyl Smit, D. (eds.), *Kriminalität, Kriminalpolitik, strafrechtliche Sanktionspraxis und Gefangenenraten im europäischen Vergleich*, vol. 2, 691–733. Mönchengladbach, Germany: Forum Verlag Godesberg.

Taracha, A. (1988). "Udział organów ścigania w postępowaniu w sprawach nieletnich (w postępowaniu przygotowawczym)." In: Bojarski, T. (ed.), *Postępowanie z nieletnimi: Orzekanie i wykonywanie środków wychowawczych i poprawczych*, 118–129. Lublin: Uniwersytet Marii Curie-Skłodowskiej.

8

Freedom in the Making

Juvenile Justice in South Africa

ANN SKELTON

This account of the story of juvenile justice in South Africa begins in precolonial times. Prior to the colonization of South Africa, a child who had offended against customary norms appeared before a traditional court, the purpose of which was to solve the problem, to provide restitution or compensation, and to reconcile the families concerned. Once the "civilized" laws of Europe arrived, these processes were largely swept aside in favor of a punitive criminal justice system based on imprisonment, deportation, and corporal punishment.

It would be a gross oversimplification to depict South Africa's subsequent history of children in the criminal justice system as entirely unenlightened, however. This chapter demonstrates that the child-saving movement had its followers in colonial South Africa. It recounts valiant reform efforts in the Union era, followed by the bleak downward spiral of the apartheid years. It depicts the struggle for justice by children in the Soweto uprising, later continued by activists as South Africa was preparing for the first democratic elections in 1994. The Bill of Rights contained in the South African Constitution (1996) has given rise to important judgments confirming the rights of children in the criminal justice system. In 2010, the Child Justice Act of 2008 came into operation. This chapter describes its aims and mechanisms and offers an early analysis of its operation. The picture is sketched against the broader canvas of South Africa's harsh current realities as a country that emerged strongly from its transition but is currently laboring under immense poverty and inequality, as well as failures in education and other systemic failures. But I remain cautiously optimistic about a future in which socioeconomic circumstances cause fewer children to come into conflict with the law.

Before and After Colonization

During the precolonial era, under African customary law, childhood was not defined by age but rather by other defining characteristics such as male circumcision or setting up a separate household (Maithufi 2000). Welfare of children was interwoven with the communal welfare of the extended family, tribe, or group (Bennett 1999).

Offenses were dealt with by the traditional courts. Chief Mwelo Non-kanyana (1997) describes how a child accused of an offense would have been summoned together with his or her father, or other male elder, to answer the charge or charges against him or her. The involvement of the elderly man, usually the family head, helped to maintain the family unit and to ensure that any decision for restitution would be effected. The adults of the child's family were considered vicariously liable to compensate the victim so as to help the community in maintaining respect of societal norms and values.

Prior to colonization, there was no imprisonment or institutionalization. Crimes were treated as wrongs between individuals and families, to be solved in ways that promoted harmony and well-being in society. Harsher punishment such as corporal punishment or banishment was meted out for serious crimes (Koyana and Bekker 2002).

Colonization caused the customary law system to be overlaid by the Roman-Dutch and English legal systems. Corporal punishment, deportation (to Robben Island), and imprisonment for crimes became commonplace (Saffy 2003). It is therefore apparent that the African customary approach to children's wrongdoing was replaced by a far more punitive form of justice (Skelton and Tshehla 2008). At the time that Roman-Dutch law was adopted, the approach to criminal justice was retributive. The laws were inherited prior to the period of enlightenment that typified European discussions about punishment in the 1800s. Ronald Graser (1982, 69) records that by the time the British occupied the Cape in 1795, "the penal philosophy in Europe and Britain had started to take a more humanitarian turn." Justice Albie Sachs, in

S v. Makwanyane (1995, at par. 384), makes a similar point, describing the penal system at the Cape prior to the British occupation as being "as yet unaffected by the changes sweeping across Europe." During the eight years of the first period of British rule, several of the harsher punishments, such as breaking on the wheel, were discontinued (Venter 1959). Only hanging and imprisonment were to remain. Justice Sachs recounts the mood: "The incumbent judges protested. . . . The public executioner was so distressed he hanged himself" (*Makwanyane* 1995, par. 385). Imprisonment became a popular solution, as it was considered more humane than the punishment practices that had preceded it (Venter 1959).

General Approach to Child Offenders during the Colonial Period and the Union

The Colonies and the Boer Republics

From 1602, the courts established by the Dutch East India Company at the Cape of Good Hope used the common law of the Province of Holland (Geffen 1928). At the Cape, criminal cases were dealt with by the "Raad van Justitie" (Council of Justice). Children could be brought before that body for criminal matters and also in cases in which they were described as "onbeheerbaar" (incorrigible) (De Villiers 1988). Sentences handed down on children for misbehavior seem startlingly harsh from a modern viewpoint: a boy who refused to attend church and swore at his parents was sentenced by the Raad to a month in detention on a diet of bread and water, with an additional order that he be conscripted into the army at the end of his sentence (Midgley 1975; Saffy 2003). For other offenses, children could be whipped or branded, put in stocks, or deported to Robben Island. Herman Venter (1959) also records that those found guilty of sodomy, whether the convicted were young boys or men, were rowed out to sea and thrown overboard, with weights tied to their legs, to drown.

The British colonial administration did away with some of these harsh punishments and showed some sympathy for the idea that children who were dependent or destitute should be protected, but it was not until 1895 that the Destitute Children's Relief Act of 1895 provided a legal basis for children needing care to be placed in children's homes and hostels.

John Eekelaar (2002) has observed that the early law of English child welfare is to be found within the practice of apprenticeship, an idea that found its way into South Africa through the Masters and Servants Act and continued to be a sentencing option for children under the Prisons and Reformatories Act of 1911 and under the Children's Protection Act of 1913. Linda Chisolm (1989) has argued that the aim of apprenticeship schemes linked to the criminal justice system was largely to feed employers' demands for indentured labor.

There is probably no better evidence that news of the child-saving efforts that were happening elsewhere in the world drifted across the Atlantic than the establishment of reform schools and, later, industrial schools. William Porter, the attorney general of the Cape Colony, left 20,000 pounds in his will for the establishment of "a reformatory for juvenile offenders" (Saffy 2003). This led to the Reformatory Institutions Act in 1879 and the subsequent establishment of Porter Reformatory in Cape Town. Porter strongly believed (along with other social reformers in England and America at that time) that character was shaped by environmental influences. The Porter Reformatory was modeled on British reformatories such as Redhill and Parkhurst, and a strict regime of work and discipline was observed. Apprenticeship was an integral part of the operation of the institution, providing domestic and agricultural labor for local farmers (Chisolm 1989). Initially, Porter Reformatory was for all races (Sloth-Nielsen 2001), though by 1909 the dormitories were segregated by race (Chisolm 1989). In the same year, Houtpoort Reformatory was established at Heidelberg in the Transvaal.

The Union Years Prior to 1948

Following the second Anglo-Boer war (1899–1902, also known as the South African war), the Boer Republics fell under the control of the British colonial powers. South Africa became a Union in 1910, and this appears to have led to a flurry of lawmaking as laws of the colonies and republics had to be harmonized, and the earlier developments in the Cape Colony (such as the establishment of reformatories) now had to be extended to the country as a whole, albeit on a limited scale (Midgley 1975). It was an opportunity for reformers to ensure that the new laws were imbued with modern penological ideas (Chisolm 1987; Van Zyl Smit 1990; Van der Spuy, Schärf, and Lever 2004).

Prisons and Reformatories Act of 1911

An important piece of legislation reflecting the ideas of the reformers was the Prisons and Reformatories Act of 1911. James Midgley (1975) makes the important observation that while the 1911 act relied heavily on institutional care, as a remedy for both crime and for children in need of care, it was also the first piece of legislation to establish the principle that children and young adults should not be imprisoned. This may not have meant much in practice, because there were very few alternative facilities available, and those available also operated under harsh regimes.

Children's Protection Act of 1913

Elrena Van der Spuy et al. have commented that "through this Act child-saving ideas, very much in vogue in the international community at the time, were imported into South Africa" (2004, 172). An important innovation of the 1913 act was that it introduced the idea of a "place of detention" as an alternative to prison. Midgley (1975) underscores the fact that this reflected concern over child imprisonment, as while sentenced children could be sent to reformatories, children who were on remand were usually detained in the police cells or in the remand sections of adult prisons. "In an effort to modify this situation, the Act allowed that children could be detained in a place of safety while an investigation was being pursued. This referred not only to children who had broken the law but children deemed to be in need of care" (Midgley 1975, 57). However, this may have been more of a theoretical option than a real one—fifteen years after the act was passed, Irene Geffen observed that "not many special places of detention have been established, however" (1928, 245).

Section 34(1)(i) of the 1913 act allowed a court to decline to proceed with a trial upon any charge of a child, and after an inquiry, the court was empowered to commit a child to a government industrial school or other "certified institution." This clause came up for scrutiny in two important cases in the early 1920s, which give enormous insight into the judicial thinking of the time about the policy approach to children committing crimes. The first was *R. v. Smith* (1922). In this case, a ten-year-old boy, who was described by the court as having been allowed to "run wild," was tried for stealing a bicycle, and the magistrate had convicted him and ordered him to be detained in an industrial school for five years in terms of section 34(1)(i) and then apprenticed in terms of section 350(2) of the Children's Protection Act of 1917 until he reached the age of eighteen years. This decision was appealed, the point being raised that a conviction should not have been made, as the magistrate was empowered to stop the proceedings and make the order that he did. The court was of the view that while a ten-year-old boy might be found to be *doli capax*, the "modern" view had to take into account newly understood factors. Judge President John Wessels explained it thus:

> This ancient view was based upon philosophical theories established by *a priori* reasoning rather than upon the psychology of childhood. Modern psychologists do not consider that children of tender years are to be regarded as capable of appreciating the exact moral or legal import of the acts they do. Children imitate the acts of the persons in whose *milieu* they live. In other words, the child of tender years is very much the creature of environment. Now this is the view that has gradually been adopted by the great European nations and has been followed by us in our Act No. 25 of 1913, called the Children's Protection Act. (201)

The last sentence gives a very clear indication that in the early years of the Union, the legislature and the judiciary were fully aware of the developments in other parts of the world, and their thinking was accordingly influenced. The judge went on to say that the legislature had "set its face against sending children of tender years to gaol, to herd with hardened criminals, and has provided institutions for their welfare and betterment" (202). The conviction was set aside, as was the sentence to apprenticeship, and the child was ordered to be sent to a reformatory until he reached the age of eighteen years.

The second matter was *Attorney General of the Transvaal v. Additional Magistrate for Johannesburg* (1924). The facts of the case involved an Indian boy (fifteen years old) and a coloured boy (twelve years old) who were arrested for housebreaking. This is significant as it does indicate that children of all races could be referred to industrial schools, although they were racially segregated. The additional magistrate had stopped the prosecution of the two children and, following an inquiry, had referred them to an industrial school. The case provides a window on the enlightened thinking of the time. Chief Justice James Rose-Innes reflects as follows on the Children's Protection Act: "The object of the Act is sufficiently indicated by its title. Among other things it provides machinery for the special treatment of children who have fallen into crime by removing them from their old environment and placing them amid surroundings conducive to reformation" (425).

However, while there was an interconnection between the criminal justice and welfare systems in relation to children being able to be placed in an industrial school or certified institution, "South African policy makers separated the jurisdictions of welfare and criminal justice by creating two distinct judicial institutions" (Midgley 1975, 45). The choice of whether to channel children through the welfare system of the children's court or through the criminal courts lay with officials in the system: prosecutors could decide whether to charge the child, and magistrates could decide whether to stop the proceedings and proceed in terms of section 34(1)(i).

The conclusion to be drawn is that despite the influence of the "child-saving" movement, the majority of South African children remained in a punitive criminal justice system that paid minimal attention to their special needs as children. Van der Spuy et al. describe the divided approach thus: "The legal regime for the care and control of juveniles was bifurcated from the beginning of a unified South Africa" (2004, 171). Although the possibility existed since 1911 that criminal proceedings may be stopped and the matter referred to the children's court, this was generally underutilized. The majority of child offenders appearing before the court between 1911 and 1939 were whipped, fined, or given suspended sentences, and more of them were sent to prison than to reformatory (Chisolm 1998). Even prior to apartheid, during the Union years, "white offenders were much more likely to be diverted into reeducation and reintegration efforts than their black counterparts" (Van der Spuy et al. 2004, 173). The left-wing scholar Jack Simons observed that the enlightened provisions of the 1913 act were "largely inoperative in the case of black and coloured juveniles and [were] mainly for the benefit of the white children" (1931, 147).

Whipping as a Sentence

Whipping as a sentence for children and young people does not fit neatly into any period of South African history because it unfortunately straddles all eras until its abolition by the Constitutional Court in 1995 (*S. v. Williams* 1995). Whipping as a sentence was brought to South Africa by the Dutch colonizers. Midgley records that "even the enlightened Roman-Dutch jurist, Van der Linden, who condemned torture saw the usefulness of corporal punishment in the penal process" (1975, 62). The whippings in colonial days were very severe—sometimes consisting of several hundred lashes (Venter 1959). In the later period of the colonial era, the number of lashes was reduced, and whipping was seen as a lenient sentence, articulated in the 1870s in the phrase that "children should be birched and not branded as criminals" (Saffy 2003, 18). H. C. Nicholas (1975) recorded that at the time of the Union, fifty strokes was the legal maximum in the Cape, Natal, and Transvaal, and the maximum was twenty-four in the Orange Free State; but in 1917, the law set a new maximum of fifteen strokes. This was later reduced to ten and then again (in 1977) to seven strokes, which was the maximum number of strokes that a child could receive until abolition of the penalty.

Lashes were always meted out to African offenders more than to any other race group (Pete 1986). In the 1882 case of *Q. v. George* (1882), children as young as seven and nine years were sentenced to fifteen strokes with a light cane, and a five-year-old was sentenced to six strokes. Though the High Court set aside the conviction of the five-year-old, no comment was made about the sentence of the other three children, which indicates that fifteen strokes for such young children was considered to be appropriate.

Writing in 1928, Geffen recorded without adverse comment the fact that any male child below sixteen years could receive a "moderate correction" of whipping, not exceeding fifteen cuts, or six cuts in the case of children below the age of twelve years. Although Geffen was a reformer and advocate for the rights of women and children, she apparently did not see anything to criticize in a law that permitted corporal punishment on child offenders, giving some indication of how acceptable it was to the general public at that time. Alan Paton, a social reformer who had detested being physically punished himself as a child, nevertheless continued to use corporal punishment as a method of control at Diepkloof Reformatory, where he was principal, an approach quite at odds with his other reformist approaches (Paton 1980). As will be described shortly, the infliction of corporal punishment was used even more frequently during the apartheid years.

The Young Offender's Bill

In 1934, the government appointed an Inter-Departmental Committee on Destitute, Neglected and Delinquent Children and Young Persons. The committee's terms of reference included the instruction to "consider whether it is desirable and practicable to dispense with criminal procedure in dealing with juvenile and/or juvenile-adult delinquents, and instead to deal with them paternally, on the lines of the procedure adopted in administering the Children's Protection Act" (Union Government 1937, 5). The committee followed a highly consultative approach, visiting numerous sites around the county and taking written and verbal evidence from informed individuals representing public and private bodies. After considering various examples, the committee concluded that the creation of a noncriminal court to deal with young offenders would "involve radical changes in our whole organization of child welfare and would give rise to too many fundamental legal questions" (13). The committee found that the consensus of opinion in South Africa favored "a modification of present practice with a view to the application of educational measures within the framework of the administration of justice" (13). The committee's recommendations were set out in three bills: the Children's Protection Bill, the Young Offender's Bill, and the Maintenance of Relatives Bill. Midgley observes that, had these bills been passed, they would have "comprehensively restructured child welfare and juvenile justice legislation in South Africa" (1975, 62). Sadly, this was not to be.

The committee submitted its report and the draft bills to the minister of education, J. H. Hofmeyr, early in 1937. The minister, however, asked the committee to modify the Children's Protection Bill by adding to it a number of provisions dealing with committal to reform school. In his view, this would solve the immediate needs relating to child offenders, and the Young Offender's Bill could be considered at a later stage. The frustration of the committee regarding this request is apparent in the introductory remarks of the report made to the minister of education: "At your request (made for reasons of expediency which you explained at the time) the Committee undertook the preparation of a consolidated measure which is entitled 'The Children's Bill'" (Union Government 1937, 6). The committee went on to say that some of the most important of its recommendations, regarding the trial of "juvenile delinquents," had been omitted from the consolidated bill. The committee urged that the Young Offender's Bill should be looked on as being of primary importance: "It should be enacted at an early date if South Africa is to have the full benefit of comprehensive legislation covering the whole field of child and juvenile welfare" (6).

It is clear from the report that one of the difficulties the committee faced was resistance to the idea that young offenders should be taken out of the purview of the Criminal Procedure Act. In this regard, the committee made the following cautious observation: "The Committee's proposal that a separate enactment is preferable is dictated by no want of appreciation of the Criminal Procedure Act" (Union Government 1937, 6). However, the committee pointed out that that act had already attained "unusually large proportions" and would become unwieldy if the new provisions were added. A further important point was made: "Moreover, the enactment of a separate statute has some effect, slight as it may be, in emphasising the essential difference between child and adult delinquency" (6).

The consolidated bill was supposed to be a temporary measure until it was possible for the Young Offender's Bill to be fully implemented, but in fact the Young Offender's Bill was never passed. Midgley (1975) observed that the committee was not forceful enough. This bill, if enacted, would have made sweeping changes to the way in which children in the criminal justice system would have been dealt with.

Important changes proposed by the bill included raising the minimum age of criminal capacity from seven to ten years (and the upper limit of *doli incapax* from fourteen to sixteen years), a ban on imprisonment for children below the age of sixteen years, and the abolition of the death penalty for children. This bill was published at the same time as the Children's Bill. The then minister for education decided that the Children's Bill should be promulgated, with the addition of a few provisions relating to child offenders—such as provisions relating to the power of referral of cases to the children's court and reform schools as a sentencing option. Once the consolidated bill had been passed into law as the Children's Act of 1937, the Young Offenders' Bill faded into obscurity.

Would the Young Offender's Bill, had it become an act, have benefited children of all races equally? The committee was certainly concerned about this issue, and its report concluded with some interesting remarks in this regard. First, it made the following point: "The draft bills submitted by the Committee make no distinction on racial grounds. The principles underlying the treatment of children 'in need of care' or of delinquents are of equal validity whether the children to whom they apply are of one race or another" (Union Government 1937, 52). The committee went on to reveal that the services made available to "non-European" children at that time were unequal to services offered to white children. It also pointed out inequities in the staffing of the system. The committee sounded the following note of warning: "It is a wrong policy to adopt a two-fold standard with regard to the problem of dependency and delinquency, one for Europeans and one for non-Europeans, for a community is vulnerable if it neglects to deal in an effective way with maladjustment in its midst on the part of one section of its population. Yet this is the effect, though probably not the intention of the present system" (53).

The liberal views of the committee notwithstanding, it appears that inequality of resource allocation would probably have limited access to services for black, coloured, and Indian children. Nevertheless, there is no doubt that the Young Offender's Bill, had it been passed, would have provided legal protection to all children. The bill represented a state-of-the-art approach and would have placed South Africa among leading nations of the world in relation to child justice.

Reform of the Reformatories

A positive feature of the 1937 Children's Act was that it stressed that the treatment of child offenders was an educational rather than a penal problem. In 1934, reformatories and industrial schools were transferred from the Department of Prisons to the Department of Education (Paton 1993). When the Children's Act came into force on 18 May 1937, responsibility for its administration was given the Union Department of Education. In the same year, the first Department of Social Welfare was established, and the administration of the act was handed over to that department. The Education Department retained responsibility for the administration of the industrial schools and reform schools, as the government felt these were essentially educational institutions (Midgley 1975). In line with this thinking, school principals were appointed to transform these institutions from prisons to schools. Two of these principals took their mandate very seriously and managed to make significant changes. W. D. Marais, who was appointed at the reform school at Tokai, which housed white boys, and Alan Paton, who was to become more famous for his novel *Cry the Beloved Country*, took the post at Diepkloof, which was for African boys.

Paton was a passionate reformer. He believed that beyond the two general approaches to punishment—retributive and deterrent—there were two further views of punishment. The third view of punishment was "reformatory," in which the word "punishment" would be replaced with "treatment." The fourth view of punishment explored by Paton was a radical one: that there need be none at all. According to this view, steps are taken against the offender for the sole reason to protect society. If society does not need protection, then the person need not be punished (Paton 1993). Paton experimented with his ideas at Diepkloof, with a system of the boys being encouraged to take personal responsibility and being granted rewards and "graduated freedom." A unique feature of Paton's approach was the importance he placed on public ritual and ceremony. The receipt of a *vakasha* (meaning "go for a walk") badge was done at a public ceremony with a ritual promise not to go beyond the boundaries of the farm. The idea was to shift control from physical containment to each boy taking personal responsibility for his own behavior (Paton 1980). Paton caused some consternation when he took down the fences at the reformatory school (Sargeant 1997; Paton 1993). However, while the fences at Diepkloof were coming down, the political walls were going up—the National Party came to power in 1948, and the apartheid years began.

The Apartheid Years

The Union period in South Africa continued until 1961, when South Africa declared itself to be a republic. However, from the late 1940s, the approach to governing the country, and to managing crime, underwent a dramatic change in direction. It thus makes sense to write about "the apartheid years," which include both the later period of the Union and those years of the Republic from 1961 to 1994.

The Use of Whipping Extended

The Penal and Prison Reform Commission, generally known as the Lansdown Commission, was established in 1945 and submitted a report to Parliament in 1947, just a year before the National Party came to power. The commission had inquired, among many other matters, into the desirability of corporal punishment for children and adults. The commission was ambivalent about the use of whippings as a sentence for children. The commission observed that there were relatively few alternatives available (Union Government 1947), and as a result it recommended that corporal punishment as a sentence for children should be retained. However, the commission was of the view that the circumstances and conditions of corporal punishment should be carefully regulated. The commission stressed that the sentence of corporal punishment could be used in order to express the court's disapproval of the child's actions but that "those sitting in judgment should deliberate long before ordering the infliction of corporal punishment" (Union Government 1947, sec. 491).

The measured, dispassionate arguments of the Lansdown Commission belonged to an era that was rapidly disappearing. The National Party approach to managing crime is characterized by Van der Spuy et al. as "a counter-discourse of repressive crime control" (2004, 167). The cane became the major solution to crimes committed by children, as "the South African magistrates *corps* attempted to lash recalcitrant youth into submission" (Van der Spuy et al. 2004, 167). The Lansdown Commission's recommendations on whipping were largely ignored, and for the first time in 1952, courts were compelled to impose corporal punishment of up to ten strokes for certain crimes (Criminal Sentences Amendment Act of 1952). Ellison Kahn (1960) demonstrates the effect of mandatory whipping: in 1940, the total number of offenders sentenced to a whipping was 1,864. By 1954, it had risen to an annual total of 13,879. By 1957, the number was 18,442. The enthusiasm for the sentence was not to ebb, despite the fact that it did not bring about any reduction in the commission of serious crimes (Khan 1960). The Criminal Procedure Act of 1977 merely reduced the maximum number of strokes from ten to seven. Despite strident criticisms of the continued use of corporal punishment over the years (Hunt 1968; Midgley 1974, 1975; Van Zyl Smit and Offen 1984; Roberts and Sloth-Nielsen 1986; Sloth-Nielsen 1990), whipping of young offenders remained shockingly popular over the next forty years, and by the early 1990s, the state was carrying out more than 32,000 whippings on young people per year (Pinnock 1997; Sloth-Nielsen 2001).

A Fallow Period for Child Justice

After the demise of the liberal groups that were committed to the improvement of the system for young offenders during the 1930s, the field of child justice fell into a fallow period from the late 1940s to the 1980s. A handful of legal academics continued to write, rather abstractly, about legalistic questions pertaining to children in the criminal justice system (Hunt 1968; Midgley 1974; Labuschagne 1978; Van Rooyen 1978; Steytler 1984; Milton 1988). Studies of children committing crime became polarized into evaluations of different race groups (Venter and Retief 1960). Dirk Van Zyl Smit (1989) explains how academic criminology in South Africa reflected Afrikaner national ideology through racial stereotyping and by involving itself in tactics to ensure the survival of the apartheid system. It was not until the 1980s that a new generation of South African criminologists began to draw the links between crime and the exercise of power and to build a vision for a role for criminology in a democratic South Africa (Davis and Slabbert 1985; McLachlan 1984).

Calls for reform prior to the 1980s were few—the government's disposition toward youth and crime was well known, and little was likely to change. Midgley's 1975 publication titled *Children on Trial: A Study of Juvenile Justice* was the first thorough exposition of the situation of children in the criminal justice system. It provided a detailed history, as well as the results of a study on children in the juvenile court in Cape Town. Midgley did provide some statistical information regarding children and young people.

Midgley concluded with an impassioned call for the government to opt for a welfare-centered system based on community-based preventive and remedial programs, the diversion of children away from adjudication, and the establishment of a nonformalistic court outside the criminal justice system. The publication made little more than a stir beyond academic circles and organizations such as National Institute for Crime Prevention and Reintegration of Offenders (NICRO). The government was not listening. It was, after all, 1975—the Soweto uprising was only a year ahead. The youth were seen as a burgeoning problem: teargas, *sjamboks* (rubber whips), and detention, rather than prevention and welfare, were to be the favored solutions.

Children at the Forefront of the Struggle against Apartheid

In 1976, a group of schoolchildren in Soweto took to the streets to voice their objections to being taught key subjects in Afrikaans. Francis Wilson and Mamphela Ramphele describe the situation thus: "In the end, the children won that battle but in the process of doing so they brought down upon their heads the armed wrath of the State which, in reacting to the protests, escalated the confrontation to an entirely new level" (1987, 57).

The march turned into a violent crisis, and so began a series of events, which the U.S.-based organization Lawyers Committee for Human Rights later described as "a war against children" (Cooke 1986). By 1985, approximately 200 children had died in political township violence, nineteen of whom were below the age of ten years. Official state figures revealed that 102 children had been shot dead by police during 1985. Many thousands of children were detained without trial during the late 1970s and the 1980s, some for several months (Wilson and Ramphele 1987; Skelton 1993c).

Following the declaration of a state of emergency in June 1986, the situation escalated. The Detainees' Parents Support Committee issued a dossier on the suffering of children under the state of emergency as part of a "Free the Children Campaign," in which they claimed that 8,800 children had been detained between June and November 1986 (McCurdle 1989). The report also gave details of brutalization and torture, resulting in some children needing psychiatric treatment after their release (Ransome 1987; Marcus 1988). Children became perpetrators of violence, too, many of them taking part in "necklace" killings of people thought to be informers or traitors (Skelton 1993c). "Necklace" killings involved putting a car tire filled with petrol around the victim's neck and then setting him or her alight. Wilson and Ramphele record that Bishop Desmond Tutu was and outspoken critic of the practice of necklacing for the following reasons: "This growing concern is not only directed at the barbaric nature of the deaths suffered by the victims of the necklaces but more at the long-term consequences of these acts on the children who are the executioners. Their psyches run the risk of permanent damage. The loss of innocence that flows from these acts is a human tragedy whose full cost remains to be counted" (1987, 60). Wilson and Ramphele went on to point out that white children, too, were being brutalized through conscription into the military and by being made to be part of the machinery of oppression.

Political organizations, human rights lawyers, and detainee support groups rallied to the assistance of many of these children (Thomas 1990). There was also evidence of grave concern at an international level (Sloth-Nielsen 2001). In January 1989, an interdisciplinary group of experts from Switzerland and Germany came to South Africa to carry out an investigation into the situation of children in prison in South Africa (Interdisciplinary Group 1989). At the time of their arrival, there were forty-two detainees below the age of eighteen years, but by 18 April 1989, there was only one detainee below eighteen years of age. By 1990, political detentions of children had ceased. The reality then became apparent to activists that there were substantial numbers of children awaiting trial on crimes that were nonpolitical in nature but that could invariably be traced to the prevailing socioeconomic ills caused by apartheid (McQuoid Mason 1987; Sediti 1991).

In 1989, the African National Congress, then in exile, organized a conference in Harare titled "Children, Repression and the Law in South Africa." According to Vivienne Taylor, "The poignant stories of children and the extent of the brutality they experienced shocked the world" (1997, 169). This conference is widely recognized as "having heralded the birth of the children's rights movement in South Africa" (Sloth-Nielsen 2001, 18). Following the conference, the National Children's Rights Committee (NCRC) was established, which aimed to bring together a coalition of organizations working on children's rights issues. The NCRC established a legal committee, which was influential in ensuring the inclusion of a children's rights section in the interim constitution of 1993 (Sloth-Nielsen 2001).

Toward Reform

Because of the focus on the struggle to achieve basic human rights in South Africa, the call for a fair and equitable child justice system emerged somewhat later than in many comparable countries (Skelton 2002). The first intensive calls for such reforms came about in the early 1990s and emanated from a group of nongovernmental organizations (NGOs) that went into courts, police cells, and prisons to provide assistance to children who were appearing in courts or awaiting trial (Community Law Centre et al. 1992).

An initiative was launched in 1992 by NICRO that was an important milestone in South African child justice history. NICRO established a program aimed at the diversion of children away from the formal court system. With no enabling legislation in place, the diversion programs began when NICRO personnel negotiated directly with public prosecutors to allow for cases to be withdrawn on condition that child offenders complete a program organized by NICRO. Near the end of 1992, programs with small groups of young offenders were established. From the outset, these programs were framed within a restorative justice paradigm: the earliest booklet issued by NICRO (Muntingh and Shapiro 1993) explained diversion within the context of restorative justice as described in Howard Zehr's *Changing Lenses* (1990).

The death of Neville Snyman in 1992 was a watershed moment for the movement working toward the reform of South Africa's child justice system (Skelton 2003). Neville was only thirteen years old when he and a group of friends broke into the local shop in Robertson and stole sweets. Neville was detained in police cells with other offenders under the age of twenty-one. He was beaten to death by his cellmates. Nongovernmental organizations had been raising the issue of children in the criminal justice system and calling for law reform (Community Law Centre et al. 1992). Until this time, however, their calls had fallen on deaf ears. Neville's tragic death led to a public outcry, and the government took action by setting up a national working committee on children in detention.

In the meanwhile, nongovernmental organizations redoubled their efforts. Lawyers for Human Rights (LHR) ran a campaign called "Free a Child for Christmas," which resulted in the release of 260 children who had been awaiting trial in prison by 25 December 1992. It also raised awareness and forged linkages between nongovernmental organizations working throughout the country, due to the fact that it aimed to cover all the prisons in the country.

In 1992, the Community Law Centre (CLC), LHR, and NICRO initiated a campaign to raise national and international awareness about young people in trouble with the law. The organizations issued a report (Community Law Centre et al. 1992) that called for the creation of a comprehensive juvenile justice system, for humane treatment of young people in conflict with the law, for diversion of minor offenses away from the criminal justice system, and for systems that humanized rather than brutalized young offenders.

In 1993, at an international seminar titled "Children in Trouble with the Law," a paper was presented that called for a comprehensive juvenile justice system (Skelton 1993). A drafting committee (the Juvenile Justice Drafting Consultancy) was set up following the conference, which led to the publication of *Juvenile Justice for South Africa: Proposals for Policy and Legislative Change* in 1994. The new vision encompassed the charging, arresting, diverting, trying, and sentencing of young offenders in a system that would affirm the child's sense of dignity and worth and clearly define the role and responsibility of the police, prosecutors, probation officers, and judicial officers with due regard to the rights of victims.

With the coming into power of the new democratic government in 1994, the stage was set for transformation of the way that children were dealt with by the criminal justice system. The newly appointed minister of justice in the Mandela cabinet requested the South African Law Commission (now known as the South African Law Reform Commission—the SALRC) to include an investigation regarding juvenile justice in its program, which led to the appointment of a project committee.

The committee commenced its work in the beginning of 1997. A consultative process was followed, and a report accompanied by a proposed draft Child Justice Bill was handed to the minister for justice and constitutional development in August 2000. The bill was introduced into Parliament toward the end of 2002 and, after a series of public hearings, was deliberated on by the Portfolio Committee on Justice and Constitutional Development during 2003. These hearings have been described by James Maguire as pushing the bill into "a distinctly more punitive direction" (2012, 92). This punitive movement was being driven by the new government's increasing worry about the crime rate and its law-and-order response in which it was influenced by "zero tolerance" thinking (Dixon 2000, 30).

Deliberations on the Child Justice Bill came to a halt because of the general elections in 2004, and the bill, although still appearing on the parliamentary agenda, remained in limbo for almost four years. Discussions on the bill resumed in the Portfolio Committee in February 2008, starting off with another round of public hearings. A host of NGOs seized the opportunity to make new submissions to the committee on the basis of what were widely perceived as major flaws in the last official version of the bill and called for amendments to bring the bill closer to its original objectives (Skelton and Gallinetti 2008).

The Child Justice Bill, after thorough and at times even fierce debate (Skelton and Tshehla 2008), was approved by Parliament on 7 May 2009 and came into operation on 1 April 2010. Ann Skelton and Jacqui Gallinetti (2008) observe that although civil society participants in the parliamentary process did not win every point that they argued, the final product is a "fairly balanced" piece of legislation. Maguire takes the view that while the Child Justice Bill is, for a large number of South African children, "clearly a good thing," he sketches many examples of how the final version of the act is more punitive than the original conceptualization (2012, 117).

Influences on the New Approach to Child Justice

Before discussing the provisions of the Child Justice Act, it is important to consider two very important international movements that strongly influenced its development. The first of these was children's rights, and the second was the international trend toward increased use of restorative justice.

International Children's Rights and the South African Constitution

In November 1989, the Convention on the Rights of the Child (CRC) was adopted by the UN General Assembly. Already, the United Nations Rules for the Administration of Juvenile Justice had been adopted by the UN General Assembly in November 1985, and in 1990, the UN Rules for the Protection of Juveniles Deprived of their Liberty and the UN Guidelines for the Prevention of Juvenile Delinquency were also adopted. Together these international instruments set out a framework of the principle that a good juvenile justice system should embrace.

The timing of this international groundswell of children's rights application to juvenile justice was very positive for South Africa. A conference held in Harare, Zimbabwe, referred to earlier, had been a springboard for a children's rights movement in South Africa, spearheaded to a great extent by the National Children's Rights Committee, which played the role of coordinating body for a range of children's rights organizations that were working on the ground. In February 1990, Nelson Mandela was released from prison, and South African civil society, together with returning exiles and local African National Congress members, began to plan a new vision for a future, postapartheid South Africa (Sachs 1990). A key feature of that vision was a new constitution containing a justiciable Bill of Rights. The constitutionalization of children's rights was included in this early thinking, and the CRC provided inspiration. Albie Sachs pointed this out in his inimitable style:

> For lawyers to whom the right to sue your neighbour is the basis of all legal rights, the idea of a charter of children's rights might seem more like poetry than law. The problem really lies with the lawyers, and not with the charter; they must open their eyes to the new range of legal strategies developed in recent decades in various parts of the world. In particular, the adoption by the United Nations of the International Convention on the Rights of the Child, provides a secure foundation for legislation in all countries. (1990, 87)

The Interim Constitution

In 1993, an "interim" constitution was passed to set the stage for the first democratic elections in 1994. Only a year later, South Africa ratified the CRC on 16 June 1995, the nineteenth anniversary of the Soweto uprising. The interim constitution contained a specific children's rights section. A "child" was expressly defined as a person below the age of eighteen years. Julia Sloth-Nielsen has related the story about the development of the children's rights clause, which was supported by all parties. Indeed, the head of the opposition party said of children's rights that "like chicken soup, they did no harm" (1996, 9). In fact, children's rights have subsequently proved to be a powerful force in constitutional jurisprudence (Sloth-Nielsen and Mezmur 2008). The South African Constitution requires the courts, when interpreting the Bill of Rights provisions, to consider international law. Thus, the CRC, soft law instruments, and General Comments of the Committee on the Rights of the Child, together with the African Charter on the Rights and Welfare of the Child, have all frequently been referred in the Constitutional Courts judgments (Sloth-Nielsen and Mezmur, 2008; Skelton 2013).

An important juvenile justice case that was decided by the Constitutional Court while the interim constitution was in place was *S. v. Williams* (1995). The court considered international law (including the CRC) and foreign law and declared the sentence of juvenile whipping to be unconstitutional on the grounds that it exposed young offenders to cruel, degrading, and inhuman treatment and infringed their right to dignity. Having done so, the court decided it was not necessary to decide on the question of whether it also infringed children's rights to be protected from abuse and to have their best interests considered. Nevertheless, the judgment by Justice Pius Langa showed considerable concern for the child offender.

Langa stated that our society should be laying a strong foundation for the values of the constitution in young people, as they were the future custodians of the new democratic order (para. 63). The judgment traversed the argument put forward by the state that there were differences between adults and juveniles, the latter's character and personality being still in formation. Thus, juveniles would be susceptible to this type of correction (para. 46). This argument was rejected by Langa:

> I do not agree. One would have thought that it is precisely because a juvenile is of a more impressionable and sensitive nature that he should be protected from experiences which may cause him to be coarsened or hardened. If the state, as role model *par excellence*, treats the weakest and the most vulnerable among us in a manner which diminishes rather than enhances their self-esteem and human dignity, the danger increases that their regard for a culture of decency and respect for the rights of others will be diminished. (*S. v. Williams* 1995, para. 46)

He also observed that there was "a growing interest in moves to develop a new juvenile justice system" in South Africa. He referred to the hope that these processes, still in their infancy, could be developed through the involvement of the state and nongovernmental organizations that were involved in juvenile justice projects. His remarks were prescient—those fledgling attempts eventually resulted in the Child Justice Act (2008).

The Final Constitution

Following the first democratic elections in 1994, and during the era of the Mandela government, the final constitution was drafted. This time there was an organized lobby to ensure greater protection for child offenders. The interim constitution stated that every child who was in detention, in addition to the rights that all offenders have, shall "have the right to be detained under conditions and to be treated in a manner that takes account of his or her age" (sec. 30(2)). This was positive, but in the opinion of child rights activists, it did not go far enough. Submissions were made to the Constitutional Assembly, and the final constitution included section 28(1)(g), which reads as follows:

> Every child has the right not to be detained except as a measure of last resort, in which case, in addition to the rights a child enjoys under sections 12 and 35, the child may be detained only for the shortest appropriate period of time, and has the right to be—
> (i) kept separately from detained persons over the age of 18 years; and
> (ii) treated in a manner and kept in conditions, that take account of the child's age.

This was an important development in the field of juvenile justice, and it had a significant influence on the Child Justice Act, which contains many provisions to avoid or reduce custodial treatment, particularly imprisonment. Long before the Child Justice Act was promulgated, however, the new government introduced new minimum sentences legislation as a populist move to woo voters who were angry about high crime rates. The law excluded persons below sixteen years of age but included sixteen- and seventeen-year-olds within its ambit.

A challenge to the constitutionality of the minimum sentences law, insofar as it applied to sixteen- and seventeen-year-olds, was launched in the case of *Centre for Child Law v. Minister of Justice and Constitutional Development* (2009). The Constitutional Court held that the minimum sentencing legislation should not apply to children aged sixteen and seventeen years old. The majority of the Constitutional Court found that the minimum sentencing legislation limited the discretion of sentencing officers by directing them to hand down long sentences (including life imprisonment) as a first resort. Furthermore, the legislation discouraged the use of noncustodial options, it prevented courts from individualizing sentences, and it was likely to cause longer prison sentences. All of these features of the law amounted to an infringement of child offenders' rights in terms of section 28(1)(g), and the court found that no adequate justification had been provided for the limitation. The court found that children should be treated differently from adults not for sentimental reasons but because of their greater physical and psychological vulnerability and the fact that they were more open to influence and pressure from others. The court observed that child offenders are generally more capable of rehabilitation than adults are. These are the premises on which the constitution requires the courts and Parliament to differentiate child offenders from adults. The court went on to explain, "We distinguish them because we recognise that children's crimes may stem from immature judgment, from as yet unformed character, from youthful vulnerability to error, to impulse, and to influence. We recognise that exacting full moral accountability for a misdeed might be too harsh because they are not yet adults. Hence we afford children some leeway of hope and possibility" (*Centre for Child Law* 2009, para. 28).

The court went on to acknowledge that children can and do commit very serious crimes and that the legislature has legitimate concerns about violent crimes committed by people below the age of eighteen years. The court pointed out that the constitution does not prohibit Parliament from dealing effectively with such offenders—the fact that detention must be used only as a last resort in itself implies that imprisonment is sometimes necessary. However, the Bill of Rights mitigates the circumstances in which such imprisonment can happen. It must be a last (not first or intermediate) resort, and it must be for the shortest appropriate period. If there is an appropriate option other than imprisonment, the Bill of Rights requires that it be chosen. In this sense, incarceration must be the sole appropriate option. But if incarceration is unavoidable, its form and duration must also be tempered, so as to ensure detention for the shortest possible period of time (*Centre for Child Law* 2009, para. 31). The order declared section 51(1) and (2) invalid to the extent that they refer to sixteen- and seventeen-year-olds.

It is interesting to note that although the litigation team was aware of the brain science findings in the US and the use of that evidence in prominent juvenile justice cases there, a conscious decision not to rely on this evidence was made. It was referred to obliquely in papers that drew the court's attention to *Roper v. Simmons*, but limited reliance was placed on it. This was because the Centre for Child Law was already planning to challenge a law that criminalized consensual sex between adolescents (between twelve and sixteen years of age). First, precedents from South African courts over many decades had shown that the judiciary already fully appreciated that children were different from adults and lacked full culpability. Second, it was considered risky to rely on evidence that seemed to suggest that adolescents are incapable of making good decisions when it would not be long before a case would be heard that would ask the court to respect adolescents' right to make decisions in the exercise of their sexual autonomy. The decision not to rely on the brain science appears to have garnered good results. Both cases were won, and the court recognized the need to protect children from the harsh aspects of the criminal justice system, while recognizing their right to develop through participating in developmentally normative sexual behavior (*Teddy Bear Clinic v. Minister of Justice and Constitutional Development* 2013).

The constitutional provisions and the two cases dealt with here in which the Constitutional Court made decisions about child offenders indicate the strength of a rights-based approach to child justice in South Africa. It is important to note that even if political expediency might in the future lead to an erosion of rights in legislation, any changes will have to be tested by the standards set in the Bill of Rights, interpreted within the broader framework of internationally and regionally recognized children's rights.

Restorative Justice

Restorative justice was a powerful influence on South Africa's child justice system. It is significant that the Child Justice Bill was in development as South Africa was going through its extraordinary transition from apartheid state to progressive democracy. That transition provided an opportunity to transform laws, policies, and systems. It encouraged a new way of thinking about almost everything. A new way of thinking about justice was writ large on the contemporary canvas as South Africa's Truth and Reconciliation Commission (TRC) found a way to transcend hatred, fear, guilt, and revenge. The postamble to the interim constitution said, "These can now be addressed on the basis that there

is a need for understanding but not for vengeance, a need for reparation but not for retaliation, a need for *ubuntu* but not for victimisa-
tion." *Ubuntu* is an African philosophy that, broadly stated, means "a
person is a person through other people." Bishop Desmond Tutu has
explained that it was this approach that animated the TRC (1999, 34–
35). So although South Africa retained its Roman-Dutch law base for
the law, the lawmakers were encouraged to broaden their approach to
include more restorative, more *ubuntu*-oriented ways of thinking about
justice. Restorative concepts and procedures were thus included in the
Child Justice Bill. Despite the fact that during the bill's sometimes rocky
ride through Parliament there was a wave of popular punitiveness, the
restorative justice elements of the bill largely weathered that storm and
were retained in the final version of the act (Skelton 2005, 490–492).

Overview of the Child Justice Act (2008)

Child law specialists decided to opt for the term "child justice" because
there was a feeling that the term "juvenile" was slightly pejorative. The
term "youth," on the other hand, was politically loaded and included
persons up to the age of thirty-five years. As the constitution called
everyone below the age of eighteen years "a child" and as this usage
accords with African conceptions of childhood, it seemed like a good
idea to capitalize on this.

The act takes a justice-oriented (rather than a welfare-oriented)
approach. However, it offers many special features and opportunities
that aim to divert children away from courts and custodial options
toward restorative, community-based options as far as possible. Children are to be held accountable but in ways that try to link them with
pathways to a crime-free life.

In a rather unusual preamble, the act roots its genesis in the historical
past by recognizing that "before 1994, South Africa, as a country, had
not given many of its children, particularly black children, the opportunity to live and act like children, and also that some children, as a
result of the circumstances in which they find themselves, have come
into conflict with the law." The preamble goes on to explain that the
act takes into account "the past and sometimes unduly harsh measures

taken against some of these children" and "the long-term benefits of a less rigid criminal justice process that suits the needs of children . . . in appropriate cases" (Child Justice Act 2008, preamble).

The act applies to any person under the age of eighteen years who is alleged to have committed an offense. The minimum age of criminal capacity is raised from seven to ten years. It is presumed that children between the ages of ten and fourteen years lack criminal capacity, but the state may prove such capacity beyond reasonable doubt.

In order to keep children out of police cells and prisons, the act encourages the release of children into the care of their parents or other suitable adults and entrenches the constitutional requirement that detention should be a measure of last resort for a child. A probation officer will assess every child who is alleged to have committed an offense, irrespective of the child's age. A preliminary inquiry is held in respect of every child within forty-eight hours of arrest and is presided over by a magistrate, referred to as the "inquiry magistrate." Prosecutors may, however, divert children who have committed Schedule 1 (less serious) offenses before a child's appearance at a preliminary inquiry. Decisions to divert the child away from the formal court procedure to a suitable program may be taken at the preliminary inquiry stage, if the prosecutor indicates that the matter may be diverted. Diversion is a central feature of the new system, and the act sets out a range of diversion options.

Those children who are not diverted (because they indicate that they intend to plead not guilty to the charge or because the prosecutor or director of public prosecutions refuses to divert the matter) will proceed to plea and trial in the child justice court. The envisaged child justice court is not a completely specialized or separate court. In urban areas, where there are sufficient cases to warrant it, full-time child justice courts with specially selected and trained personnel will be set aside, in the manner of the current juvenile courts. In rural areas, the court will simply constitute itself as a child justice court, following the procedures set out in the legislation. This arrangement existed prior to the act in some of the bigger towns and cities but has never previously been legislated for. Furthermore, the act makes it clear that the superior courts are bound by the special provisions for children set out in the draft Child Justice Act.

The act includes a wide range of sentencing options, including non-residential or community-based sentences, sentencing involving restorative justice concepts such as restitution and compensation to the victim, and finally, sentences involving compulsory residence in a child and youth care center. The act makes it clear that imprisonment should only be used as a measure of last resort and then for the shortest possible period of time. A prohibition is placed on imprisonment as a sentence with respect to children who are under the age of fourteen years at the time of being sentenced, and certain criteria that are linked to the severity of the offense are laid down with respect to children who are fourteen years or older. The maximum sentence of imprisonment is twenty-five years (eligible for parole after serving half of that period), and there is no life imprisonment for persons who committed a crime while below the age of eighteen years.

The act also proposes monitoring mechanisms to ensure the effective operation of this legislation and promotes cooperation between all government departments and other organizations and agencies involved in implementing an effective child justice system.

Implementation of the Child Justice Act and Trends since 1994

Act Put to the Test Soon after Its Commencement

The Child Justice Act had a baptism of fire when, within days of its commencement on 1 April 2010, a sixteen-year-old was charged (together with an adult) for the murder of the white right-wing leader Eugene Terre-Blanche. There was some confusion about how the sixteen-year-old should be dealt with, and the enormous media interest in the case led to a court application for the media to sit in on the case. This was vigorously opposed by the civil society organization Media Monitoring Africa, which entered as a friend of the court, legally represented by the Centre for Child Law. The court ruled that the media should not be permitted to sit in the court and that the identity of the child offender was not to be revealed. However, arrangements were made for the media to watch the trial via CCTV linkup, provided that the child offender's face was blurred (*Media 24 Limited v. National Prosecuting Authority* 2011). The act passed its first test.

Decline in Numbers of Children Entering the System since Act Commenced

A concern has been expressed that there has been a sharp decline in the numbers of children coming through the child justice system. According to the government's *Annual Report on the Implementation of the Child Justice Act* (Department of Justice and Constitutional Development 2011), 73,435 children were "charged" by the South African Police Service (SAPS) in the first year of implementation. This translates roughly to about 6,286 children per month. And yet, in 2008, the government had reported to Parliament that approximately 10,000 children were charged every month (Badenhorst 2011). This downward trend in numbers continued in the second year of implementation, down to 57,592 children charged by SAPS (or approximately 4,799 children per month). This amounts to a decrease of 23% from the previous year and an overall decrease of approximately 52% since 2008. The 2008 figures may have been overestimated, but the drop in numbers is also confirmed by the fact that diversion numbers have also dropped significantly—and this is verified by nongovernment service providers. Charmain Badenhorst (2012) has offered the most plausible explanation for the drop. She points out that police officials, who are the gatekeepers of the system, have been inadequately trained. It seems that SAPS members, unsure of their new duties under the act, are erring on the side of caution, and in their zeal not to arrest, they fail to use the alternative measures provided by the act to secure a child's attendance at a preliminary inquiry. Thus, it seems that police are conducting their own unofficial diversion practice. While a drop in numbers of children coming into the system is certainly less alarming than the opposite would be, it was not the intention of the system to have informal diversion by the police, and some observers believe that children who get into trouble are losing the opportunity to be linked with the necessary services and that this will "catch up" with them later (Wakefield 2011; Badenhorst 2012).

Continuing Downward Trend in the Use of Pretrial Imprisonment

Another area in which there has been a drop in numbers is the pretrial imprisonment of children. This, however, is the continuation of a trend that started prior to the Child Justice Act and is definitely a positive picture. Unfortunately, South African prison statistics regarding pretrial imprisonment of children below eighteen years prior to 1994 are difficult to obtain. However, the Department of Correctional Services has provided a consistent set of data since 1995. In the year 1994–1995, when the first democratic government came to power, there were 1,359 children (below the age of eighteen years) in prison. One of the first policy steps taken by the Mandela government was a legislative ban on the pretrial detention of children in prison or police cells (Sloth-Nielsen 1995) and thus the numbers of children in prison dipped down in the 1995–1996 year to 871. However, this drop was short-lived, because little had been done to provide alternatives to prison for children. The government thus changed tack, and a new law was passed that allowed children to be held in prison awaiting trial in certain circumstances (Sloth-Nielsen 1996). Despite the fact that the law limited pretrial detention by age and by offense type, the numbers of children quickly climbed to a higher number than in 1994 and continued to climb until it reached an alarmingly high figure of 4,141 in 2002–2003.

Table 8.1, drawn from Lukas Muntingh and Claire Ballard (2012, 17), provides not only the overall figures for pretrial imprisonment but also the number of detentions by the type of offense. From 2003 onward, the numbers began to drop steadily, and by 2010, when the Child Justice Act came into operation, that number had come down dramatically to 979 (Muntingh and Ballard 2012). This success story began when a United Nations technical assistance project, located in the Department of Justice, established an "inter-sectoral committee for child justice," which met monthly to discuss solutions to the problem of children in prison awaiting trial. A protocol for the management of children awaiting trial was issued in 2002. Government departments worked together, ensured legal representation, and got the message out to magistrates and prosecutors. Another important development was the establishment of "secure care" facilities in all provinces. As these came into being, children who could not be released to their parents were placed there instead of prisons (Sloth-Nielsen 2013). Some commentators have warned that we may simply be transferring children from one form of pretrial detention to another (Skelton 2011; Sloth-Nielsen 2013).

TABLE 8.1. Number of Pretrial Detentions

Year	Economic	Aggressive	Sexual	Narcotics	Other	Total
1994–1995	734	443	103	21	58	1,359
1995–1996	436	289	99	10	37	871
1996–1997	768	518	196	18	64	1,564
1997–1998	1,232	803	353	31	76	2,495
1988–1999	1,244	944	449	27	73	2,737
1999–2000	1,788	1,364	557	30	127	3,866
2000–2001	1,627	1,451	534	30	113	3,755
2001–2002	1,709	1,511	521	28	118	3,887
2002–2003	1,804	1,641	536	35	125	4,141
2003–2004	1,705	1,690	501	34	126	4,056
2004–2005	1,346	1,484	436	33	115	3,414
2005–2006	809	1,147	344	21	78	2,399
2006–2007	720	1,020	289	21	99	2,149
2007–2008	714	965	280	27	90	2,076
2008–2009	552	788	284	20	75	1,719
2009–2010	462	668	257	19	69	1,475
2010–2011	287	451	199	11	31	979

However, detailed data about children in child and youth care centers are not easy to obtain and impossible to make effective comparisons with. The government has reported that during 2011, there were 8,879 admissions to child and youth care centers, of which 110 were sentenced children (Department of Justice and Constitutional Development 2011). However, the prison figures represent a snapshot taken on a particular day, while the admissions to child and youth care centers reflects an annual total of admissions—thus thwarting effective comparisons. Taking both types of pretrial detention into account, Muntingh and Ballard (2012) estimate the overall number, expressed as the number per 100,000 people, as 1.67, on the basis of 2009–2010 figures. The length of time in pretrial custody is estimated to be an average of 120 days, or a median of 70 days—and this is differentiated depending on the offense, with more serious crimes such as attempted murder, murder, and rape (but also housebreaking) attracting longer periods of pretrial custody

(Muntingh and Ballard 2012). In the first two years of the act's life, a further reduction in children awaiting trial has been noted. According to Muntingh and Ballard (2012), there were 196 children awaiting trial in prison on 14 August 2011. On December 2012, the total of children awaiting trial was only 178 (Government of South Africa 2013). This continuing reduction is linked to the general drop in the number of children coming into the system but may also be indicative of the awareness of magistrates and judges to limit detention as required by the act.

Another trend that can be observed from table 8.1 is the shift in the type of charges on which children are being held. Pretrial detention for economic crimes has waned, while detentions for aggressive and sexual crimes have risen. Muntingh and Ballard (2013, 342) interpret this as a positive development, indicating that courts are less likely to detain children in prison for economic crimes and reserve this option for more serious offenses.

Trends in the Sentencing of Children

Muntingh and Ballard provide a detailed breakdown of sentences from 1995 to 2011. The total average number of children serving sentences in each year is reflected in table 8.2. These figures follow roughly the same pattern as the statistics for children awaiting trial, starting off at a low base in 1995 and rising to a high in 2004, then reducing annually since then. It is difficult to provide a coherent explanation for the rise in numbers during the second half of the 1990s. It may have been the courts' response to popular punitiveness that drove public debates about crime during those years (Dixon and Van der Spuy 2004). The steady reduction since then has probably been influenced by case law. Superior court

TABLE 8.2. Average Number of Children Serving Prison Sentences

	1995	1996	1997	1998	1999	2000	2001	2002	2003
Average	677	841	1,202	1,261	1,558	1,697	1720	1,806	1,817

	2004	2005	2006	2007	2008	2009	2010	2011
Average	1,823	1,245	1,105	898	872	854	709	559

judgments such as *Brandt v. S.* (2005) and *Centre for Child Law v. Minister of Justice and Constitutional Development* (2009) have provided a clear precedent to the lower courts that the principles of last resort and shortest appropriate period of time must be upheld in sentencing. Since the introduction of the act, the numbers of children serving sentences in prison have continued to drop. Only 287 children were recorded as serving prison sentences on 31 December 2012. Muntingh and Ballard's 2012 analysis of the detailed sentencing statistics since 1995 indicates that, with regard to the length of sentences, there was a slight upward trend in the use of longer sentences, which mirrors the pattern in the adult criminal justice system, where the increase is more pronounced and has been driven by the introduction of minimum sentences (Muntingh and Giffard 2006). Somewhat surprisingly, Muntingh and Ballard (2012) show that while prison sentences have been dropping, so has the use of "correctional supervision"—a community-based sentence monitored by the Department of Correctional Services. This poses a question as to what kind of sentences children are actually receiving. The Department of Social Development reported that during the period April 2010 to March 2011, 110 children were sentenced to child and youth care centers, but this figure is difficult to compare with the average annual figures for prison sentences, and a lack of historical data makes it difficult to know if that figure is going up or down. Lack of reliable information about the number of trials and the range of sentences being utilized makes it difficult to get an accurate picture of precisely what is happening, and there have been calls for an improvement of data collection and analysis by the government departments concerned (Wakefield 2011; Courtenay and Hansungule 2014)

Issues for Review and Reflection

Despite the fact that the Child Justice Act is relatively new, the need for reflection and review is already apparent. The first issue is the minimum age of criminal capacity—indeed the architecture of the act requires a review of this issue within five years of the act coming into operation. The second issue is an apparent collision between the aims of the Child Justice Act and the aims of the Sexual Offences Act, which was passed by Parliament in 2007 and was incrementally implemented around the same time as the Child Justice Act. This issue has already come to the attention of the courts.

Age and Criminal Capacity

As explained earlier in this chapter, the Child Justice Act raised the minimum age of criminal responsibility from seven to ten years of age and retained a rebuttable presumption that a child who is ten years or older but under the age of eighteen years lacks criminal capacity. When the bill was being debated in Parliament, there were submissions from various civil society organizations urging a higher age than ten years, particularly in the light of the UN Committee on the Rights of the Child's General Comment No. 10 (2007), in which states were urged to set a minimum age of no less than twelve years of age. Parliament stopped short of doing that but nevertheless included an unusual clause in the act. Section 8 provides that in order to determine whether or not the age of capacity should be raised, the minister of justice must submit a report to Parliament within five years of the act coming into operation (in 2015). The report will include information about the nature and prevalence of crimes committed by children between the ages of ten and fourteen years. Skelton and Badenhorst (2011) have pointed to various practical difficulties in the individual assessment of children, especially in the light of South Africa's limited number of qualified professionals who can assess capacity. They promote the introduction of a single age of criminal capacity—twelve years—to replace the current system, which is based on the *doli incapax* approach. This accords with UN Committee on the Rights of the Child's General Comment No. 10. Internationally, there is a call to move away from replacing one arbitrary age limit with another and to opt instead for an approach that replaces the concept of "criminal" responsibility with a more general idea of responsibility (CRIN 2012). In other words, children should be held responsible for their crimes but not criminally responsible. While recognizing these approaches, it is necessary to seize the opportunity to raise the age that the Child Justice Act offers. Indeed, the UN Committee has stated that states should continually raise the minimum age, incrementally, toward eighteen years. Given the constraints of any criminal law reform process, one small step will be a positive start on that journey.

The Child Justice Act and the Sexual Offences Act: A Clash of Paradigms

The Criminal Law (Sexual Offences and Related Matters) Amendment Act 32 of 2007 (hereafter Sexual Offences Act) was passed shortly before Child Justice Act (2008). This comprehensive piece of legislation broadened the common law concept of rape to "penetrative sexual violation," which is now gender neutral and includes a wide range of penetrative acts into any orifice, with various parts of the body or with objects. A central aim of the act is to protect children from sexual offenses, but an unforeseen consequence of the law has been to draw child "offenders," particularly adolescents, within its ambit. It is a fact that many sexual offenses against children are committed by other children.

Internationally, concern has been expressed about how new, tough laws on sexual offenses have a disproportionately harsh impact on child offenders (Zimring 2004; Human Rights Watch 2013). Most modern juvenile justice or youth justice systems focus on early intervention measures such as diversion and emphasize treatment-based approaches to young sex offenders. However, new sexual offenses legislation tends to be punitive and exclusionary and draws young offenders within its net. Many such laws expand the definitions of sexual offenses, which, in some instances, criminalize behavior that is not harmful. Practices such as taking a picture of oneself naked on a cell phone camera and sending it via SMS to a girlfriend or boyfriend has suddenly become "manufacturing and distributing child pornography." Legislators appear to overlook the fact that while it is wrong for adults to be sexually interested in children, children and adolescents being sexually interested in one another is normal. Of course, an unwanted sexual act is an offense, whether between children or adults, but many of these sexual offenses laws also criminalize consensual sexual activity between children and adolescents.

As mentioned earlier in the chapter, a constitutional challenge has declared unconstitutional a section of the Sexual Offences Act that included a requirement that when two children who are both between the ages of twelve and sixteen years indulge in any consensual sexual act (penetrative or nonpenetrative) and a decision is taken to prosecute, then both children must be prosecuted. In the case of *Teddy Bear Clinic v. Minister of Justice and Constitutional Development* (2013), the Constitutional Court handed down a unanimous judgment that found that the impugned provisions infringed adolescents' rights of dignity and privacy and further violated the principle of the best interests of the child. The judgment underlined the dignity of children, describing the law as having placed youthful transgressors in "a state of disgrace" for behavior that was developmentally normative.

The Sexual Offences Act also introduced a sex offender register aimed at preventing persons convicted of sexual offenses from being permitted to work with children. This aspect of the law is also under constitutional scrutiny insofar as it relates to child offenders. The Constitutional Court heard argument in February 2014 on whether the automatic inclusion of persons on the register who were below the age of eighteen at the time of the commission of the offense is constitutionally permissible. Judgment is awaited.

Conclusion

This chapter has charted a long journey of how the law in South Africa has dealt with child offenders, starting in precolonial times, through the colonies and Boer Republics, the South African Union, the apartheid years, and the post-1994 era of constitutional democracy.

The Roman-Dutch law superimposed a harsh retributive system over a customary law system that sought reconciliation and restitution. Although "child-saving" influences can be seen in the smatterings of legal provisions and judgments that recognized children should be treated differently from adults, the opportunity to introduce a separate act for child offenders in the 1930s failed, despite the enthusiasm of its reformist drafters. From 1948, apartheid crime-control measures attempted to lash South African youth into submission, but their rebellion in the 1970s and their suffering in detention did eventually bear fruit, as the baton of their struggle was taken forward by activists who fought for a new child justice system within a progressive constitutional order. The journey is not complete and probably never will be. Three years after commencement, there are already issues up for review and reflection, but the success of the act will rest on proper implementation by the government, as well as constant vigilance and scrutiny by civil society.

The law reform process has succeeded is in ensuring that everyone below the age of eighteen years is considered a child and that the constitutional protections apply to him or her. No person below the age of eighteen years is tried as an adult. Attempts by the government to draw sixteen- and seventeen-year-olds into the minimum sentencing regime have been trounced by the Constitutional Court. That attempt—heralded by the new, not the old, government—may have come as a surprise to some observers. However, it is important to note that crime levels in South Africa are indeed high and that the efforts for more progressive laws for dealing with child offenders have been debated against a backdrop of considerable concern about violent crime. Thus, the Child Justice Act seems to be somewhat schizophrenic. On the one hand, it promotes alternatives to arrest and detention, and yet on the other hand, it retains a maximum sentence of twenty-five years in prison. Writing a journal editorial in 2009, I posed the question of whether the South African public was afraid for children or was afraid of children (Skelton 2009b). James Maguire (2012) has recently taken up the same theme. In the South African rhetoric about children and youth, he sees them depicted alternatively as victims of circumstance and threats to society. He is of the view that the Child Justice Act does not resolve this tension but has found ways of subverting it through a new vocabulary of governance and social management. In my 2009 editorial, I posited that the Child Justice Act does in fact straddle the divide, and four years after the commencement of the act, I remain optimistic that it does. It does so, first, by giving the majority of children opportunities to be linked to diversion and restorative justice options and keeping most of them out of custody. Second, it simultaneously deals with public concerns about crime through allowing the minority of those who commit serious offenses to be dealt with in a manner that promotes public safety through detention. Third, it tempers the sentencing options by forcing them to be applied through a prism shaped by the principles of last resort and shortest appropriate time.

The structural causes of crime in South Africa, however, show few signs of abating. The Gini coefficient stands at 0.7, meaning that probably nowhere else in the world are there so many desperately poor people living in close proximity to comfortable, wealthy people (World Bank 2012). Although the Mandela government understood the challenges and vowed to tackle poverty and deprivation through a reconstruction and development plan, the country has subsequently lost its way. The education system is in crisis, with the vast majority of South African scholars performing well below their counterparts in other African countries (Spaull 2013). The youth unemployment rate has been found by the World Economic Forum's *Global Risks 2014* report to be the third highest in the world. It is evident, therefore, that the Child Justice Act can do little in the way of prevention or effective reintegration, despite the aspiration in its preamble to "break the cycle of crime."

The South African National Planning Commission in the Presidency has issued an ambitious National Development Plan (NDP). It aims to build consensus about the key obstacles to the country's achievement of its goals and what needs to be done to overcome them, to provide a shared long-term strategic framework within which more detailed planning can take place in order to advance the goals set in the NDP, and to make choices about how best to use limited resources. If all South Africans—particularly its leaders—heed this call, the country may get firmly back onto the path of sustainable development. The National Development Plan sets out a strikingly optimistic vision for 2030, some might say a naïve one. I cannot resist ending the chapter by quoting a small slice of it: "South Africa belongs to all its peoples. We, the people, belong to one another. We live the rainbow. Our homes, neighbourhoods, villages, towns and cities are safe and filled with laughter. Through our institutions, we order our lives. The faces of our children tell of the future we have crafted" (National Planning Commission 2013, 23).

REFERENCES

Attorney General of the Transvaal v. Additional Magistrate for Johannesburg. 1924.
    AD 421.
Badenhorst, Charmain. 2011. *Overview of the Implementation of the Child Justice Act,*

2008 (*Act 75 of 2008*): *Good Intentions: Questionable Outcomes*. Cape Town: Open Society Foundation.

———. 2012. *Second Year of the Child Justice Act's Implementation: Dwindling Numbers*. Cape Town: Open Society Foundation.

Bennett, Tom. 1999. *Human Rights and African Customary Law*. Cape Town: Juta.

Brandt v. S. 2005. All SA 1 (SCA).

Centre for Child Law v. Minister of Justice and Constitutional Development. 2009. (6) SA 632 (CC).

Chisolm, Linda. 1987. "Crime, Class and Nationalism: The Criminology of Jacob de Villiers Roos 1869–1918." *Social Dynamics: A Journal of African Studies* 13 (2): 46–59.

———. 1989. "Reformatories and Industrial Schools in South Africa: A Study in Class, Colour and Gender, 1882–1939." PhD diss., University of Witwatersrand.

Community Law Centre, NICRO, and Lawyers for Human Rights. 1992. *Justice for the Children: No Child Should Be Caged*.

Cooke, Helena. 1986. *The War against Children: South Africa's Youngest Victims*. New York: Lawyers Committee for Human Rights.

Courtenay, Morgan, and Zita Hansungule. 2014. "Protecting the Rights of Children in Conflict with the Law: A Review of the South Africa's Child Justice Act." In *South Africa's Progress in Realising Children's Rights: A Law Review*, edited by Paula Proudlock, 153–165. Cape Town: Children's Institute and Save the Children.

CRIN. 2012. "Stop Making Children Criminals." http://www.crin.org/en/library/publications/stop-making-children-criminals.

Davis, Dennis, and Mana Slabbert, eds. 1985. *Crime and Power in South Africa: Critical Studies in Criminology*. Cape Town: David Philip.

Department of Justice and Constitutional Development. 2011. *Annual Report on the Implementation of the Child Justice Act*.

De Villiers, Dawid. 1988. "Die Strafregtelike Verantwoordelikheid van Kinders." LLD thesis, University of Pretoria.

Dixon, Bill. 2000. *The Globalisation of Democratic Policy Sector Policing and Zero Tolerance in the New South Africa*. Cape Town: Institute of Criminology, University of Cape Town.

Dixon, Bill, and Elrena Van der Spuy, eds. 2004. *Justice Gained? Crime and Crime Control in South Africa's Transition*. Lansdowne, South Africa: University of Cape Town Press / Willan.

Eekelaar, John. 2002. "Child Endangerment and Child Protection in England and Wales." In *A Century of Juvenile Justice*, edited by Margaret K. Rosenheim, Franklin E. Zimring, David S. Tanenhaus, and Bernardine Dohrn, 381–412. Chicago: University of Chicago Press.

Geffen, Irene A. 1928. *The Laws of South Africa Affecting Women and Children*. Johannesburg: R. L. Esson.

Government of South Africa. 2013. *Initial Country Report on the African Charter on the Rights and Welfare of the Child*. Reporting period June 2000 to April 2013.

Graser, Roland R. 1982. "Parole in South Africa." PhD diss., University of Durban-Westville.

Human Rights Watch. 2013. *Raised on the Registry: The Irreparable Harm of Placing Children on the Sex Offender Registries in the US*. http://www.hrw.org/reports/2013/05/01/raised-registry.

Hunt, Peter. 1968. "Corporal Punishment: Juveniles." *South African Law Journal* 2:243.

Interdisciplinary Group from Switzerland and Germany. 1989. *Children and Juveniles in the Prisons of South Africa: Detainees, Awaiting-Trial and Sentenced Prisoners.*

Khan, Ellison. 1960. "Crime and Punishment 1910–1960: Reflections on Changes since Union in the Law of Criminal Punishment and its Application." *Acta Juridica* 1960:191–222.

Koyana, D. S., and J. C. Bekker. 2002. "The Courts." In *Introduction to Legal Pluralism in South Africa*, edited by J. C. Bekker, J. M. T. Labuschagne, and L. P. Vorster, 141–153. Durban, South Africa: LexisNexis Butterworths.

Labuschagne, Johan. 1978. "Strafreglike Aanspreesklikheid van Kinders." *De Jure* 310.

Maguire, James. 2012. "Children of the Abyss: Permutations of Childhood in South Africa's Child Justice Act." *New Criminal Law Review* 15 (1): 68–121.

Maithufi, Ignatius. 2000. "The Best Interests of the Child and African Customary Law." In *Introduction to Child Law in South Africa*, edited by C. J. Davel, 137–149. Lansdowne, South Africa: Juta.

Marcus, Gilbert. 1988. "Liability for the Health of Detainees." *South African Medical Journal* 74 (9): 456–459.

McCurdle, Janet. 1989. "Their Only Right a Name: Children under the State Emergency." Western Cape Free the Children Alliance.

McLachlan, Fiona. 1984. *Children in Prison in South Africa*. Cape Town: Institute of Criminology, University of Cape Town.

McQuoid Mason, David. 1987. "Children in the Dock." Unpublished paper.

Media 24 Limited v. National Prosecuting Authority in re: S. v. Mhlangu. 2011. (2) SACR 321 (GNP).

Midgley, James. 1974. "Sentencing in the Juvenile Court." *South African Law Journal* 91:451–466.

———. 1975. *Children on Trial: A Study of Juvenile Justice*. Cape Town: NICRO.

Milton, John. 1988. "Law Reform: The Demise of Impunity of Pre-pubescent Rapists." *South African Journal of Criminal Justice* 1:123–126.

Muntingh, Lukas, and Claire Ballard. 2012. *Children in Prison in South Africa*. Cape Town: Community Law Centre.

———. 2013. "Are the Rights of Children Paramount in Prison Legislation?" *South African Journal of Criminal Justice* 3:337–353.

Muntingh, Lukas, and Chris Giffard. 2006. *The Effect of Sentencing on the Size of the South African Prison Population*. Cape Town: Open Society Foundation.

Muntingh, Lukas, and Rosemary Shapiro. 1993. *Diversions: An Introduction to Diversion from the Criminal Justice System*. Cape Town: NICRO.

National Planning Commission. 2013. *National Development Plan 2030: Our Future—Make It Work.* The Presidency, Republic of South Africa.

Nicholas, H. C. 1975. "Consistency and Discretion in Sentencing in the Courts" in *Crime and Punishment in South Africa*, edited by J. Midgley, J. H. Steyn and R. Graser, 153–167. Johannesburg: McGraw-Hill.

Nonkanyana, Mwelo. 1997. "The Role of Culture and Tradition in Justice for Young People." Unpublished paper.

Paton, Alan. 1980. *Towards the Mountain: An Autobiography.* Cape Town: David Philip.

———. 1993. *Diepkloof: Reflections on Diepkloof Reformatory.* Compiled and edited by Clyde Broster. Cape Town: David Philip.

Pete, Steve. 1986. "Punishment and Race: The Emergence of Racially Defined Punishment in Colonial Natal." *Natal University Law Review* 1 (2): 99–114.

Pinnock, Don. 1997. *Gangs, Rituals and Rites of Passage.* Cape Town: Africa Sun Press / Institute of Criminology, University of Cape Town.

Q. v. George. 1882. 2 EDC 392.

R. v. Smith. 1922. TPD 199.

Ransome, Oliver. 1987. "Children in Places of Detention: A Code for Their Handling." *South African Medical Journal* 71: S1–8.

Roberts, Angela, and Julia Sloth-Nielsen. 1986. "Whippings, the Courts, the Legislature and the Unrest." *South African Journal of Human Rights* 2:224–229.

S. v. Makwanyane. 1995. (2) SACR 1 (CC).

S. v. Williams. 1995. BCLR 861 (CC).

Sachs, Albie. 1990. *Protecting Human Rights in a New South Africa.* Cape Town: Oxford University Press.

Saffy, Jacky. 2003. "A Historical Perspective of the Youthful Offender." In *Child and Youth Misbehaviour in South Africa*, edited by Chris Bezuidenhout and Sandra Joubert, 12–22. Pretoria: Van Schaik.

Sargeant, Roy. 1997. *The Principal: Alan Paton's Years at Diepkloof Reformatory.* Johannesburg: Penguin.

Sediti, Dawn. 1991. "Social Work and the Administration of Juvenile Justice." Pretoria: NICRO.

Simons, H. Jack. 1931. "Crime and Punishment with Reference to the Native Population of South Africa." Master's thesis, University of South Africa.

———. 1993. "Violence against Rural and Urban Children in South Africa." Unpublished paper.

———. 2002. "Restorative Justice as a Framework for Juvenile Justice Reform: A South African Perspective." *British Journal of Criminology* 42:496–513.

———. 2003. "Current Policy and Practice, and Future Prospects." In *Child and Youth Misbehaviour in South Africa: A Holistic View*, edited by Chris Bezuidenhout and Sandra Joubert, 185–194. Pretoria: Van Schaik.

———. 2005. "The Influence of the Theory and Practice of Restorative Justice in South Africa with Special Reference to Child Justice." LLD thesis, University of Pretoria.

Simons, H. Jack. 2009. "Fear for Children or Fear of Children? Child Justice Bill Breaches the Divide." *Acta Criminologica* 22 (1).

———. 2011. "Children Locked Up: Towards Detention as a Measure of Last Resort." In *Law Order and Liberty*, edited by Marita Carnelley and Shannon Hoctor, 207–236. Pietermaritzburg, South Africa: University of Kwa Zulu Natal Press.

———. 2013. "South Africa." In *Litigating the Rights of the Child: The UN Convention on the Rights of the Child in Domestic and International Jurisprudence*, edited by T. Liefaard and J. Doek, 13–30. Dordrecht, Netherlands: Springer.

Skelton, Ann, and Charmain Badenhorst. 2011. *The Criminal Capacity of Children in South Africa: International Developments and Considerations for a Review*. Cape Town: Child Justice Alliance.

Skelton, Ann, and Jacqui Gallinetti. 2008. "A Long and Winding Road: The Child Justice Bill and Civil Society Advocacy." *SA Crime Quarterly* 15:3–10.

Skelton, Ann, and Boyane Tshehla. 2008. *Child Justice in South Africa*. Monograph 150. Pretoria: Institute for Security Studies.

Sloth-Nielsen, Julia. 1990. "Corporal Punishment: Acceptable State Violence?" In *Towards Justice? Crime and State Control in South Africa*, edited by Desirée Hansson and Dirk Van Zyl Smit, 195–208. Cape Town: Oxford University Press.

———. 1995. "1994–1995 Juvenile Justice Review." *South African Journal of Criminal Justice* 8:331–343.

———. 1996. "Chicken Soup or Chainsaws: Some Implications of the Constitutionalisation of Children's Rights in South Africa." *Acta Juridica* 1996:6–27.

———. 2001. "The Role of International Law in Juvenile Justice Reform in South Africa." LLD thesis, University of the Western Cape.

———. 2013. "Deprivation of Children's Liberty 'as a Last Resort' and 'for the Shortest Period of Time': How Far Have We Come? And Can We Do Better?" *South African Journal of Criminal Justice* 3:316–336.

Sloth-Nielsen, Julia, and Benyam Mezmur. 2008. "2 + 2 = 5? Exploring the Domestication of the CRC in the South African Courts (2002–2006)." *International Journal of Children's Rights* 16 (1): 1–28.

Spaull, Nicholas. 2013. *South Africa's Education Crisis: The Quality of Education in South Africa 1994–2011*. Stellenbosch, South Africa: Stellenbosch University.

Steytler, Nico. 1984. "Shoplifting by Juveniles—A Case for Diversion." *South African Journal of Criminal Law and Criminology* 8 (2):107.

Taylor, Vivienne. 1997. *Social Mobilisation: Lessons Learned from the Mass Democratic Movement*. Cape Town: UNICEF and SADEP.

Teddy Bear Clinic v. Minister of Justice and Constitutional Development. 2013. Case CCT 12/13. Available at http://www.constitutionalcourt.org.za.

Thomas, Adelle. 1990. "Violence and Child Detainees." In *People and Violence in South Africa*, edited by Brian McKendrick and Wilma Hoffman, 185–194. Cape Town: Oxford University Press.

Tutu, Desmond. 1999. *No Future without Forgiveness*. London: Rider.

Union Government. 1937. *Report of the Inter-Departmental Committee on Destitute, Neglected, Maladjusted and Delinquent Children and Young Persons 1934–1937.* Pretoria.

———. 1947. *Report of the Penal and Reform Commission.* Pretoria.

Van der Spuy, Elrena, Wilfried Schärf, and Jeffrey Lever. 2004. "The Politics of Youth Crime and Justice in South Africa." In *The Blackwell Companion to Criminology,* edited by Colin Sumner, 162–179. Oxford, UK: Blackwell.

Van Rooyen, K. 1978. "Juveniles: What Alternatives?" *South African Journal of Criminal Law and Criminology* 98.

Van Zyl Smit, Dirk. 1989. "Adopting and Adapting Criminological Ideas: Criminology and Afrikaner Nationalism." *Contemporary Crises* 13:227–251.

———. 1990. "Introduction: Contextualising Criminology in Contemporary South Africa." In *Towards Justice? Crime and State Control in South Africa,* edited by Desirée Hansson and Dirk Van Zyl Smit, 5–6. Cape Town: Oxford University Press.

Van Zyl Smit, Dirk, and Liz Offen. 1984. "Corporal Punishment: Joining Issue." *South African Journal of Criminal Law and Criminology* 8:69–74.

Venter, Herman J. 1959. *Die Geskiedenis van die Suid Afrikaanse Gevangenisstelsel: 1652–1958.* Pretoria: HAUM.

Venter, Herman J., and Gerhard M. Retief. 1960. *Bantoejeugmisdaad.* Cape Town: HAUM.

Wakefield, Lorenzo. 2011. "Is the Act Working for Children? The First Year of Implementation of the Child Justice Act." *South African Crime Quarterly* 38:45–50.

Wilson, Francis, and Mamphela Ramphele. 1987. *Children on the Frontline: The Impact of Apartheid, Destabilization and Warfare on Children in Southern and South Africa.* New York: UNICEF.

World Bank. 2012. "GINI Index." http://data.worldbank.org/indicator/SI.POV.GINI (accessed 20 April 2014).

World Economic Forum. 2014. *Global Risks 2014.* http://www.weforum.org/reports/global-risks-2014-report.

Zehr, Howard. 1990. *Changing Lenses: A New Focus for Crime and Justice.* Scottdale, PA: Herald.

Zimring, Franklin E. 2004. *An American Travesty: Legal Responses to Adolescent Sex Offending.* Chicago: University of Chicago Press.

9

Legislative Impact, Political Change, and Juvenile Detention

Comparing South Korea and Japan

JAE-JOON CHUNG

This chapter reports on my effort to assess the impact of legislative change and political change on juvenile justice policy in two neighboring Asian nations, Japan and South Korea. The two nations are close geographically and have legal systems more remarkable for their similarities than their differences. Japan is the larger nation, a dominant regional power until the end of the Second World War and a fully developed economic power in the world by 1985. South Korea has about one-third the population of Japan and did not begin its rapid economic development until around 1960. Japan has been a functioning democracy since 1946, while South Korea transitioned from dictatorship to a competitive two-party democratic system only in the 1980s and 1990s.

The changes that invite analysis in Japan are legislation that shifted policies and procedures in criminal justice and in juvenile justice over the period after the mid-1990s. This was an era of economic recession and modestly expanding crime in Japan. The ruling political party had been consistently in power for decades but was under pressure as the economic decline continued and public dissatisfaction with the government grew. One result of this situation was a series of legislative measures to facilitate criminal prosecution and to increase punishments. The primary focus of these efforts was the criminal courts, but twice in the period after 1998, there were significant "get tough" measures directed at juvenile crime and its punishments in 2000 and 2007. Crime and punishment was not a major element in national politics, but the ruling Labor Democratic Party (LDP) hoped for modest political advantage from the new laws.

The major shift I examine in South Korea was the replacement of a long-serving series of right-wing political presidents with popularly elected presidents from left-leaning political parties in the decade after 1997. The right governed postwar South Korea first with authoritarian controls close to dictatorship that were followed in 1988 and 1993 with elected presidents of the right. The election of Kim Dae Jung in 1997 and his succession by Roh Moo Hyun from 2003 to 2007 produced substantial changes in both the personnel and the policies of the national government. Crime policy was not a significant issue in the 1997 campaign except for the history of using criminal law as an instrument of political repression. While there were no major legislative changes in either criminal or juvenile justice, there was ample room for discretionary powers of judges, prosecutors, and administrator to make changes in practice that did not require any shift in formal statutory law.

Measuring the Impact of Legal Change in Japan

A series of legal changes in Japan that are perceived as a "get tough" campaign may have both direct and indirect influence on penal policy. What I call "direct effects" in this context are whatever effects the specific changes made will be expected to produce on conviction rates and penal sanctions. What I mean by "indirect effects" includes all of the ways that "get tough" policies send messages to prosecutors and judges to encourage more punitive use of the wide discretion available to these officials. One dramatic example of the extent of indirect effects comes from the "strike hard" era in mainland China. When the PRC announced in 1983 that as part of its "strike hard" campaign against crime, the Supreme People's Court would no longer routinely review death-sentence convictions, a direct effect of such a change on the number of capital sentences and executions is the number of capital cases that prosecutors decided to bring only because the costs and risks of appeal had been reduced. That number was probably modest and a vast understatement of the actual impact of the announcements. The central government was also sending a message to prosecutors and judges to produce harsh punishments, and the local authorities quickly responded with tens of thousands of death sentences and at least 5,000 executions (Johnson and Zimring 2009, 264–268). The first lesson from this historical example is that "indirect effects" on criminal law enforcement of such campaigns may be much more substantial than direct effects. The second lesson from this example is that the best measure of the impact of such campaigns is trends in criminal sanctions. The best measures of the total effects of the "strike hard" campaign were trends in executions and death sentences. So careful study of overall punishment trends over time is necessary to evaluate changes.

Incidentally, when the national government of the PRC wished to "reform" the death-penalty system after 2005, it again appears that the indirect effect of sending a message (of restraint this time) was again much more substantial than the proposals for appellate review and guidelines would have produced on their own terms. The best measure of total effects here again is estimating the reduction in death sentences and executions (Johnson and Zimring 2009, 270–286).

The Direct and Indirect Effects of Japanese Legislation

The most efficient way to test both the direct and indirect effects of the Japanese campaign on criminal court offenders is to assess trends in penal confinement. Figure 9.1 provides prison population trends for persons aged 20–40 in Japan for the 19 years after 1988. Incarceration for persons aged 20–40 falls from 38.3 per 100,000 population in that age group to 32 per 100,000 from 1989 to 1995 and then begins to climb significantly after 1998. The period associated with the crackdown produces a significant jump, from 34 per 100,000 in 1998 to an average rate of 47.6 for the three years after 2003. While Japanese imprisonment is still quite low by international standards, the 38% jump in the rate in four years represents a very substantial impact on total imprisonment. The discretionary actors in Japanese criminal justice got the message.

The impact of the juvenile justice changes in 2000 over time are harder to locate. Figure 9.2 reports the rate of confined juveniles per 100,000 juveniles confined in detention facilities, training schools, prisons, and other public facilities. Figure 9.2 shows an increase in rates of juvenile confinement during 1977–2001 in Japan with most of that increase evident before the legal change in 2000. But rates then drop after 2003 and are lower for every year after that than at the year 2000 starting point for the first wave of juvenile legislation. By contrast, the

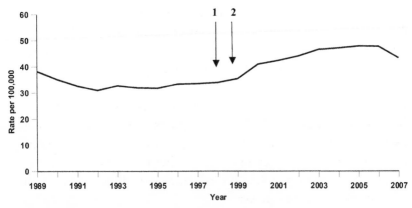

Figure 9.1. Incarceration rate of persons aged 20–40, Japan, 1989–2007. *Notes*: The rate of incarceration was calculated using the reported number in prison and the total population aged 20–40; 1 = wiretapping and child pornography laws; 2 = law concerning the punishment of organized crime (Law 136 of 1999). *Sources*: population, Japanese census; imprisonment, Ministry of Justice of Japan, "White Paper on Crime," 1990–2008, cited in Chung 2010, 167.

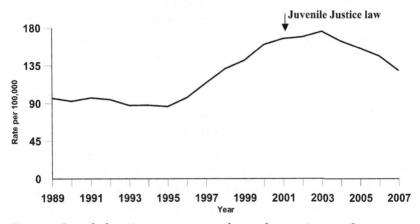

Figure 9.2. Juvenile detention rate, persons aged 12–19, Japan, 1989–2007. *Sources*: Population, Japanese census; imprisonment, Ministry of Justice of Japan, "White Paper on Crime," 1990–2008, cited in Chung 2010, 170.

rate of incarceration for adults in 2007 is 20% higher than in 2000. Why this divergence? No definitive answer to this question can be provided from an analysis of the available data, but one plausible theory might stress the different attitudes and priorities of the powerful actors in Japanese criminal and juvenile justice. The most powerful actors in Japanese criminal justice are prosecutors, and prosecutors are usually a very receptive audience when government sends out "get tough" messages. But both juvenile court judges and administrative actors in probation and social services are much more powerful in the juvenile than in the criminal system. And these officials might be more resistant to "get tough" messages for two reasons: because they are skeptical of the benefits of locking up juvenile offenders and because they might resent the government's attempt to limit their own discretionary authority. Criminal court prosecutors, on the other hand, may see hard-line changes in government policy as a validation of their preferences rather than a challenge to their power.

While conclusive proof of what caused the different impact of "get tough" policies cannot be established, three preliminary conclusions do seem clear from the Japanese case study. First, it is unwise to assume that similar legal changes will produce effects of the same kind and same magnitude in juvenile and criminal systems. A second finding is that the indirect effects of legal changes seem to be more important than the direct influence of newly established procedures when modest legal changes are instituted. That must be why confinement rates can go up in criminal justice but down in juvenile justice, because any direct effects would lead to increases in both cases.

The third conclusion that comes from the juvenile justice changes in Japan is that even obvious attempts to "get tough" are not a sufficient condition for increasing the severity of sanctions in juvenile justice systems that are not dominated by prosecutors. When policy is made by officials with extensive discretion and these decisions are not visible in ordinary circumstances, changing legal standards is far from a guarantee of significant impact in levels of punitive sanction.

The Influence of Political Change on Criminal and Juvenile Justice in South Korea

The 70-year history of Korea after 1945 was both more volatile and more variable than for government and politics in Japan. Japan's involvement in a massive shooting war ended in 1945, while South Korea was at war on its home territory until 1954. Japan was a political democracy shortly after World War II, while the South Korean government was nondemocratic and authoritarian well into the 1980s. Japan was a low-crime-rate nation by the 1950s, while crime and punishment levels in South Korea were and are much higher than in Japan.

The primary influences on juvenile justice in Korea were foreign models imposed first by the Japanese in the early 1940s and then by the Americans after 1945. The first "homegrown" Korean juvenile justice legislation was adopted in 1958, and a reform (including a training school act) was instituted in 1988. But there were no major changes in the legal framework of juvenile justice between 1988 and 2007. But while legislation did not change, the political environment in South Korea shifted importantly.

The increasing degree of democratic processes in South Korean politics was important throughout the 1990s, but there was a great deal of continuity in the people who were employed in governmental jobs. The election of Kim Dae Jung in 1997 was a dramatic point of inflection in South Korean politics and government. The Kim Dae Jung transition was far more than simply a shift from one democratically elected president to another; it was also the end of a continuous, almost half century of authoritarian governance. A substantial fraction of the administrative staff in South Korean national government had been put in place by dictators of the right. The presidential election of 1997 was therefore a signal of substantial changes in personnel as well as polices in the national government of South Korea.

One clear indication of how important the transition was felt to be concerned the abrupt shift in death-penalty policies. On December 30, 1997, after the presidential election that brought Kim Dae Jung to power and two months before the presidential succession, the departing government conducted 23 executions in a single day, more than twice the number that regime had previously executed in an average year during Kim Young Sam's presidency. (These were South Korea's last executions to date; Johnson and Zimring 2009, 172).

So the political transition in 1998 was highly visible and also marked a significant shift from right to center-left that lasted for a decade. But this decade was not an era when major legislation relating to crime and punishment was proposed or enacted. So government changed but not penal law. In the language of my previous discussion of Japan, the absence of new law meant that there were no direct effects to measure during the decade after 2008, only indirect effects. But the sharp changes in the orientation of the national administration were consistent with substantial indirect effects as new governmental actors with different ideologies replaced the administrators of the 1970s and 1980s.

Figure 9.3 shows trends by year in the prison population in South Korea. The rate of imprisonment per 100,000 persons aged 20–40 was much higher throughout the period than in low-crime Japan. The rate was increasing slightly in the decade after 1989 and did not show any immediate response to the change of regime in 1998. The four years after the 1997 elections produced rates of imprisonment that averaged just over 150 per 100,000. But the five years after 2001 produced a steady and accelerating downward trend from 149 per 100,000 at the beginning of the period to 102 five year years later in 2006. The cumulative effect of this downturn was substantial—a 32% drop in the total rate of imprisonment. So the decline after 2001, which took place with no change in penal law, was as substantial as the increase in the imprisonment of persons aged 20–40 that we observed in Japan. If the entire post-2001 change was an indirect impact of new presidential leadership and changes in personnel and philosophy, a drop of nearly one-third in carceral population would be remarkable. The stability just after the election and the accelerating drop after 2002 would suggest that changing personnel associated with the new political leadership was a major influence in the downturn. The delayed-reaction decline could be expected if new administrators, prosecutors, and judges were the moving parts in the reduction in imprisonment. There is, however, no conclusive proof that all of the decline was attributable to political change.

The pattern over time for juvenile arrests and detention is more dramatic than the prison trends for adults and also was more immediate in reflecting the 1997 elections, as shown in figure 9.4, which show trends over time in total juvenile incarceration per 100,000 population in detention, training schools, or prisons.

One reason changes in the total number of children locked up can happen faster than changes in the total rate of adult incarceration is because adult sentences are much longer. The faster turnover in detained and sentenced youth means that shifts in the sentences of new cohorts of offenders will have a larger impact on the total population locked up. But the drop in the number of juveniles behind bars was very large very

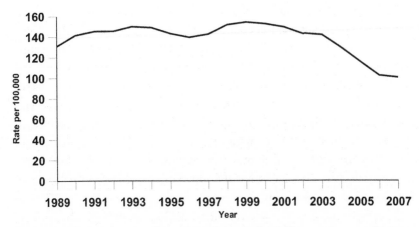

Figure 9.3. Incarceration rate of persons aged 20–40, South Korea, 1989–2007. *Sources:* Population, Korean census; imprisonment, Ministry of Justice of South Korea, "White Paper on Crime," 2008, cited in Chung 2010, 152.

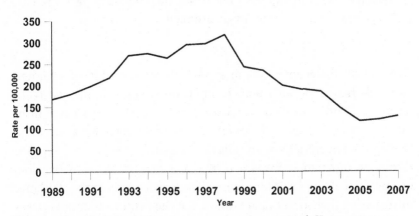

Figure 9.4. Juvenile incarceration rates, persons aged 12–19, South Korea, 1989–2007. Sources: Population, South Korean census; imprisonment, Ministry of Justice of South Korea, "White Paper on Crime," 1990–2008, cited in Chung 2010, 154.

quickly, so the pattern in figure 9.4 does not look like the cumulative effects of new juvenile administrators and judges. The more rapid drop suggests that whatever "message" the change in the presidency sent to the juvenile justice system was welcomed by many of the existing staff in the juvenile system. The statistical evidence for this assessment is circumstantial and inconclusive, but the theory seems plausible.

The almost two-thirds decline in juvenile incarceration in seven years is the most substantial change noted in either nation in this study, yet there was no legislative change to explain it. This very large shift puts observers on notice that there are occasions when major changes in the policies delivered in juvenile justice need not have legislative causes. It should also be said, however, that the transition in 1998 was about as large a shift as can be experienced in democratic government. Indeed, the scale of the change of governance in 1998 went beyond the boundaries of plural democracy because the Kim Dae Jung election was also the decisive move of South Korea away from the legacy of authoritarian dictatorship.

There is evidence in more recent South Korean history that transitions between parties holding the presidency are no longer of such profound impact on the government. The two presidencies of the left were followed, beginning in 2009, with two elections won by center-right leadership. This shift appears to have had no obvious impact on penal policy or many other aspects of government.

* * *

The aim of this chapter was to explore the relationship of legal and political change to penal policies in criminal and juvenile courts. In Japan, legislation intended to increase criminal convictions and punishments appears to have had that effect in the criminal courts but not in the reported operations of juvenile justice system. Those who exercised discretion in Japanese juvenile justice may have doubted the wisdom of a new penal emphasis for young offenders or resented the legislative intrusion on their traditional powers. But the contrast in trends warns us to pay close attention to the indirect effects of legislative change and not to assume that similar changes in procedures or legislated penalties will have the same effect in juvenile and criminal justice systems. Legislation is an important first step in changing the conditions of criminal and juvenile justice, but the contingencies and complications that stand between a legislative pronouncement and a penal result are considerable.

Since wide discretion is a universal feature of juvenile court dispositional decisions, observers can expect that shifts in attitude can have extensive influence on the sanctions delivered to the system even without legislative change. And because the training and attitudes of professional actors in juvenile justice systems are frequently different from that of those who hold power in the criminal courts, the same sorts of legislative action may have different impacts in the operation of juvenile and criminal courts.

REFERENCES

Chung, Jae-Joon. 2010. "Politics, Ideology and Juvenile Justice Policy in South Korea and Japan." J.S.D. dissertation, University of California, Berkeley.
Johnson, David T., and Franklin E. Zimring. 2009. *The Next Frontier: National Development, Political Change, and the Death Penalty in Asia.* New York: Oxford University Press.

PART IV

Some Theoretical Implications

Almost all of the nations that have developed specialized legal policies toward young offenders have created separate judicial institutions
to process and sanction young persons charged with law violations.
Why? In this final part, we consider whether the patterns of organization and disposition reviewed in previous chapters might suggest why
separate courts are so nearly universal. The usual explanation of the
special character of juvenile courts involves theories of rehabilitation,
but the facilities and policies of modern courts do not fit a rehabilitative
model. The actual operations of modern juvenile court are most closely
connected to avoiding incarceration and thus keeping juvenile offenders in the schools and community settings when their eventual maturity provides a long-term social defense. This "maturational" theory of
juvenile courts explains the emphasis on diversion and limited doses of
custodial control.

10

One Theme or Many?

The Search for a Deep Structure in Global Juvenile Justice

FRANKLIN E. ZIMRING AND MÁXIMO LANGER

The ambition of this chapter is to use the global portrait of juvenile courts found in the volume to address a central and essential question: why is it almost universal in our contemporary world that special policies toward young offenders have come hand in hand with separate judicial institutions? The historical pattern is that dissatisfaction with the outcomes that young persons faced in criminal courts led to not merely different policies toward young offenders but different judicial institutions to generate case outcomes. This imperative for institutional separation almost always goes beyond the practical safeguards of separate institutions of confinement and separate types and intensities of sanctions. What young offenders are thought to need is instead an entirely separate set of institutions and decision makers to dispose of and adjudicate their cases. And the strong commitment to institutional separation of young offenders is not confined to juvenile courts created at the turn of the 20th century. The new juvenile policies in the People's Republic of China (PRC) in the 1980s were just as firmly committed to a separate court and separate judges for juveniles as the Illinois reformers of 1899 were. And once a separate juvenile court is established in a modern state, its separate structure and operations are almost never undone.

In this final chapter, we discuss possible explanations for the almost ubiquitous existence of separate juvenile courts around the world. After briefly analyzing the role that power, emulation, and structural factors have played in the global diffusion of the juvenile court, we discuss what theory of juvenile courts may underlie their actual practices. We argue that the main function that juvenile courts have performed has been letting juvenile offenders grow up out of crime and that such a function also provides the best justification for the continuing existence of these courts.

Theories on Institutional Diffusion and the Insufficiency of Power and Emulation Explanations

According to existing understandings that our chapters have not disputed, the first juvenile court was created in Chicago in 1899 and spread from there to the rest of the world.[1] The literature on the diffusion of institutional innovations among states has articulated different types of theories to explain these diffusion processes. A first set of theories emphasizes power, in the form of military occupation, threats, or material incentives by states.[2] This group of explanations helps to explain the diffusion or transplantation of juvenile courts to some countries, such as India and a number of Muslim-majority countries,[3] and to East Asian countries, such as South Korea, which was subjected to Japanese and American influence and occupation before and after World War II.[4]

However, power did not seem to play a role in the diffusion of juvenile courts from the United States to Europe and to peripheral countries such as those of Latin America.[5] There are no indications that in these cases the United States or any other state encouraged or facilitated the diffusion of juvenile courts in the first half of the 20th century. It should also be noted that the United States was not a world superpower at the time. In this sense, the global diffusion of juvenile courts does not fit into a flow of diffusion from central to central or from central to peripheral or semiperipheral countries that is typical in these power explanations.[6] In addition, even countries that initially adopted juvenile courts during colonial or occupation times kept and expanded the use of juvenile courts after independence and political transitions.[7]

In recent times, power may have played an explanation in the European context, given the incentives that countries that wanted to enter or stay in the European Union or the European system of human rights have had to adopt certain regional juvenile law standards.[8] But this trend took place after (most of) these very countries had already adopted juvenile courts.

A second set of explanations emphasizes processes of emulation as a cause for the diffusion of policies or institutions. In these accounts, policies or institutions are adopted due to nonrational or semirational phenomena, such as the reputation of the originating jurisdiction, the creation of a new international social norm, or a fashion in a certain policy area.[9] Jurisdictions adopt the new policy or institution not because they have material incentives to do so but because it is simply what others are doing or is the appropriate thing to do.

The chapters in this volume provide some support for this sort of explanation on the global diffusion of juvenile courts. In a real sense, the process that generated the worldwide growth of juvenile courts in the 20th century was the international prominence of a U.S. court that inspired domestic imitations in many different nations.[10] This leadership by example may not have been an original priority of the U.S. reformers, but it was welcomed and soon became an objective of those who were interested in the international aspects of children's welfare. The high positive status and frequent emulation of juvenile courts in other nations soon became an important element of what political scientists call the "soft power" of admirable examples that invite emulation.[11] The way that the new court spread to new places was to provide domestic advocates with both positive and negative examples to use— the negatives were the jailing and criminal justice processing of young offenders, and the positive was the new court for children. All of this contagion was informal in the early 20th century.

Even if emulation plays a role in explaining the global diffusion of juvenile courts, the chapters in this volume and other available data indicate that emulation does not fully explain such a process. Emulation or acculturation processes tend to take place within a relatively short span of time, especially after they reach a tipping point. Even if juvenile courts arguably reached a tipping point in the first half of the 20th century with their spread to a substantial number of countries, the span of time in the diffusion of these courts was long. For instance, as Weijian Gao's chapter on China indicates, that country only adopted juvenile courts in the1980s.[12]

In addition, at the time of the adoption of the Chicago juvenile court in 1899, the United States as a country and legal system had not become a global model and one of the main producers of international norms. Also, processes of emulation often take place among countries with a common language or cultural or political background that places them within a group of peers that pay attention to what other members of the group are doing in different policy areas. In contrast, juvenile courts have spread across world regions, languages, cultures, and political regimes.

Furthermore, once a separate juvenile court is established in a modern state, its separate structure and operations are almost never undone.[13] This continuing existence of juvenile courts suggests that there may be characteristics of young offenders that help explain the reproduction of this type of court over time.

We are thus going to spend most of the rest of this chapter exploring a third type of theories on the global diffusion of policies and institutions. These theories can be called functionalist or structural. The idea behind this third set of explanations is that the diffusion of institutions among states is triggered, facilitated, or brought about by structural background conditions or by the need to have institutions or policies perform certain functions.

In this regard, some of the chapters in this volume suggest that there may have been a relationship between the creation and diffusion of juvenile courts and processes of industrialization and urbanization in specific countries and around the world.[14] These processes of industrialization and urbanization contributed to concern for children and adolescents who were in conflict with the law and in a vulnerable situation and thus opened windows of opportunity for reformers to introduce juvenile courts. In addition, some of the chapters in this volume also describe the role that the juvenile justice system has had, together with other state institutions, in the reproduction of social, racial, and ethnic inequalities and oppression.[15]

However, without discarding these possible structural factors as part of the explanation for the spread of juvenile courts to many countries as well as the reproduction of these courts over time, in the following sections, we concentrate on the analysis of possible penological reasons for the creation, diffusion, and reproduction of juvenile courts around the world. We argue that an analysis of these penological reasons or functions are central to understanding not only why juvenile courts have spread around the world but also what role they perform once adopted by individual jurisdictions. We also maintain that one of these penological theories, maturation, provides an appealing rationale for the continuing existence of juvenile courts.

Juvenile Courts and Diminished Responsibility

There are a number of penological explanations for separate policies toward young offenders that do not fully justify a separate court for young offenders. At times, the rhetoric of reform comes close to denying that youth can be criminal, but as a technical matter, that notion is contradicted both by the technical definition of delinquency (requiring the commission of a crime) and by the legal potential for trying juveniles who have been transferred from juvenile court to criminal courts. But there is a deeper reason why juvenile justice is closely linked to the special character of criminality by the young. It is law violation by the young that was always the principal element that triggered the jurisdiction of the juvenile court and that is now frequently the only behavior that invites the court's concern.

That said, the capacity of young persons to commit crimes does not mean that they are as blameworthy as older offenders and should be punished as harshly. Diminished capacity by reason of immaturity is an obvious dimension of youth crime and one that legal systems have acknowledged for centuries.[16] But this lack of full blameworthiness is not a basis for excluding criminal court jurisdiction for intellectually handicapped or mistaken criminal defendants. Criminal courts have a long tradition of considering diminished capacity in measuring just punishments. Why not for kids who offend? The issue of diminished penal capacity is a part of determining just punishments in a retributive system. An agency that is dedicated to determining just punishment would have the comparative advantage in adjusting the punitive price tag for youthful offending. Creating a separate institution in these circumstances to deal with juvenile offenders is a clear signal that something very different from just punishments must be the objective of the special institutions for the young who offend. But what might that be?

The Myth and Reality of Juvenile Court Rehabilitation

From the very beginning of juvenile justice in Illinois, the official rationale for the new institution was not the downward adjustment of punitive consequences (the metric of diminished capacity because of immaturity) but rather a totally distinct basis for imposing consequences and measuring the justness of outcomes. Here is Judge Julian Mack writing the famous prospectus for the Illinois Juvenile Court in the *Harvard Law Review* of 1909, declaring that the purpose of the new judicial institution was "not so much to punish as to reform, not to degrade but to uplift, not to crush but to develop, not to make him a criminal but a worthy citizen."[17]

And the rhetorical case for juvenile justice was quite clear on how the new system could accomplish the tasks of uplifting and reforming—the process was called rehabilitation. Rehabilitation also played such a rhetorical role in the adoption of juvenile courts in the first half of the 20th century in different corners of the world.[18]

Penal rehabilitation is a process of trying to change offenders by external programs of education or therapy or drug treatment. This was to be compulsory but beneficent state intervention in the lives of young offenders, similar in its combination of forceful methods and good intentions to other state programs for the young, such as compulsory education.

Belief in what Francis Allen came to characterize as "the rehabilitative ideal" was not confined to juvenile courts in the first two-thirds of the 20th century, but there was probably no other institution of social control whose announced ambitions fit more perfectly with rehabilitation as a state objective than the delinquency jurisdiction of the juvenile court.[19] The fact of criminal offending manifested a need for programs of attitudinal and behavioral change. The youth of the court's clientele provided the court with the clear analogy of compulsory public education and also supported the assumption that young delinquents were malleable and could be changed in the direction that rehabilitation programs and juvenile court officials desired.

One other feature of rehabilitation as a penal purpose is of particular importance when searching for the justification of the need to create a juvenile court separated from criminal courts. The commitment to selecting interventions on the basis of the need for rehabilitation is *not* a complement to retributive justice and the search for deserved punishments; it is an antagonistic alternative to a jurisprudence of just deserts. If the same court were trying to make retributive punishment decisions for adults and rehabilitative choices for youth, the clash of antagonistic principles would prove painful and confusing to the decision maker.[20] With a separate system for distinct priorities, the new court for young offenders could function most harmoniously. As a wholly separate institution, it would not face the conflict between punishment and rehabilitation because its only operating logic is rehabilitation.

So rehabilitation as a dominant, indeed exclusive, basis for choosing interventions when delinquency was established became the orthodox jurisprudence of juvenile courts in Anglo-American law at least through the first two-thirds of the 20th century, and rehabilitative sentiment may to this day continue as the distinguishing rhetoric of some juvenile courts. The chapters in this volume indicate that this rehabilitation rhetoric is still alive also around the world.[21]

But the programs and logic of penal rehabilitation were *never* dominant parts of the real world of juvenile courts, not in 1899, not in 1970, and not in 2015. The real contrast between penal sanctions in criminal courts and delinquency dispositions in juvenile courts is not the richer variety of programs that juvenile courts send young offenders to join. The real contrast is that secure confinement is used less in juvenile court and terms of confinement, when given, are much shorter. The strong preference in modern juvenile courts is to keep kids in community settings, on probation rather than in jails or training schools. The virtues of the modern juvenile court are almost all passive virtues. The use of intensive programs and special residential programs is rare.

And this was also the pattern from the very beginning of juvenile courts. The early Illinois court kept 75% of its delinquents in their homes and communities despite the fact that all the new court's probation officers were unpaid volunteers (typically off-duty police). The training schools that were the court's most serious placement option were not well regarded by the court or by the ardent supporters of juvenile justice in the community—they were a last resort rather than a hope of carefully programmed methods of changing troubled youth. The training school's only virtue was that it was not as bad as a prison. The occasional efforts to scientifically access the impact of intensive supervision and counseling were disappointingly bereft of evidence that programs changed behavior. In the famous Cambridge-Somerville experiments, the kids with more treatment did worse than the controls.[22]

And by the 1960s, the constitutional courts reviewing procedures in juvenile courts did not extend any special leeway to juvenile courts because they were engaged in a helping enterprise. The key constitutional decision on this matter was *In the Matter of Winship*,[23] in which a state juvenile court act had only required that delinquency be established by a preponderance of the evidence rather than the much more restrictive criminal conviction standard of proof beyond a reasonable doubt. New York argued that the state's more beneficent objective in juvenile versus criminal courts justified a lower, essentially civil standard of proof. But the U.S. Supreme Court rejected this argument, imposing instead as a constitutional minimum proof beyond a reasonable doubt.

Reaching this kind of decision *must* undermine the rehabilitative logic of juvenile justice. The justification for the criminal standard of proof beyond a reasonable doubt is that conviction of the innocent carries a larger social cost than acquittal of the guilty. The Law Day speeches proclaim that "it is better that ten guilty men go free than for one innocent man to get convicted." But was the court in *Winship* saying, "it is better that ten kids who need help don't get it than for one kid who doesn't need help to receive it"? Or was the court unwilling to assume that the street-level reality of juvenile justice in the United States was a rehabilitative enterprise?

And many of the patterns long noted in the United States are documented in this volume in a very wide variety of different systems. There is a strong preference in both the theory and practice of juvenile courts to keep young offenders in their home and community settings in all the major juvenile systems studied. Probation and community supervision are the first resort of the vast majority of juvenile courts from Poland to Pretoria and from Brussels to Rio de Janeiro.[24] In practice, all of the modern juvenile court's advantages over criminal justice seem to be the passive virtues of intervening less. But isn't this quite far from the profile of a muscular penal rehabilitation regime?

There is another striking feature in this book's global profile that undermines a rehabilitative theory of juvenile courts. The one region that operates *without* a separate set of judicial institutions for juvenile offenders is Scandinavia—a group of nations as dedicated to government programs for the improvement of citizens as anywhere on earth.[25] If the true distinguishing feature of juvenile courts were an emphasis on rehabilitative interventions, Norway, Sweden, Denmark, and Finland should be the first in line to create such a court rather than the only advanced nations without juvenile courts.

And a large number of the nations that embrace separate institutions for young offenders include many with no facilities for interventions. What, if anything, is the particular promise of juvenile courts in Tajikistan in 2012? Rehabilitation?

The more recent history of juvenile justice in the United States provides one further reason to doubt the dominance of belief in rehabilitation for the strong commitment to separate juvenile courts. In the generation after *In Re Gault* and *In Re Winship* were decided, after the Supreme Court had forcefully disconnected juvenile justice from its claims of rehabilitation, there was no retreat from the jurisdictional reach and autonomous status of juvenile courts in the 50 U.S. states.

Whatever justified a wholly separate court for young offenders in 1915 seemed fully in place a century later. But what was that animating theory or function?

In the past few decades, restoration has been proposed as a new goal of the juvenile court.[26] Restorative justice refers to victim-offender reconciliation, mediation, or mechanisms that would require reparation or apology to the victim by the youth or his or her family.[27] But as a recent theory on the goals of juvenile justice, restorative justice could not provide a rationale for the establishment of independent juvenile courts for most of the 20th century. In addition, even in those jurisdictions where restorative justice programs have been implemented, these programs cover only a fraction of the reactions of the juvenile justice system.[28] In other words, we do not dispute the value of restorative justice as a possible goal of juvenile courts, but this goal could provide, at best, a partial explanation and justification for the existence of these courts.

Two Meanings of Malleability

There are two different theories of malleability that distinguish the aspects of adolescence that lie at the heart of separate policies of juvenile justice. The notion that young offenders are easier to change was the battle cry for programmatic rehabilitation and for an active and powerful juvenile court system that would intervene forcefully in the lives of young offenders to bend their wills toward appropriate behavior and social ambitions. This was the active mode of juvenile justice decisively rejected in the era of *Gault* and *Winship*.

But the same young persons who might be hard to change programmatically are in the midst of a period of very rapid social, economic, and educational change. They are growing up. And this dynamic progress of maturation provides another basic approach to state policy toward adolescent crime. Rather than active intervention, why not keep the offending young in community and home settings where a normal maturation process will reduce the propensity to offend as they grow up? The policies based on this theory of juvenile malleability and of juvenile justice are passive rather than active. The court should be restrained in its punishments and careful not to interrupt a normal maturation process that is the best hope for the eventual reduction of social risk. In this policy approach, the best cure for youth crime is growing up. This is a juvenile court that aims, at almost all costs, to facilitate a normal maturation.

Both the rehabilitative and maturational theories of juvenile justice are deeply invested in the unique character of adolescence as a period of development, and both theories hope to exploit the changeability of young persons to create a specific jurisprudence of youth crime. But the two theories differ almost to the point of contradiction in both their philosophies and modes of practice. After making the case for the dominance of the maturational perspective in the practice of modern juvenile justice, we will return to the striking contrasts between maturational and rehabilitative theories of juvenile justice and show that maturational strategies are the heart of progressive juvenile justice globally.

A Separate Court to Facilitate Maturation

The maturational juvenile court understands high rates of adolescent law violation as a usually transitional phenomenon. Whenever possible, the court's task is to balance the need to condemn harmful acts and to create some punitive consequences for them with continuity in the offender's home life and in the community-based educational and work experiences of normal maturation. The strategic ambition is to wait out a difficult transitional period with the minimum necessary intervention. So the strong preference of this kind of court is for informal and nondisruptive reactions to law violation. All over the developed world, juvenile misbehavior results in "station adjustments" by police, as well as diversionary adjustments by probation screeners at the front door of the juvenile court for the young offenders who make it to the front door as well as prehearing diversion to counseling or community resources with no court proceedings. For the cases that survive these diversionary screenings, three-quarters of the offenders adjudicated are assigned to probationary supervision or other orders that keep them in the community. When secure confinement is used, it is most often short term and frankly punitive detention that its architects hope does not last long enough to disrupt the youth's normal living situation.

This long list of minimal interventions, and the very few longer custodial sentences issued by juvenile courts, are the result of a delicate balancing act between the punitive and incapacitation sentiments that serious law violations provoke and the court's reluctance to interrupt normal maturation. Young offenders do commit crimes with very harmful consequences. A car theft or burglary can lead to probation in a maturational juvenile court, but what if the car injured or killed a pedestrian, or what if someone was shot? The retributive and incapacitation pressures that serious offending generates are relevant to the calculus of a maturational court's consideration of sanctions, as they may have to be. But the balance between the pressure for punishment that interrupts normal development and the young offender's prospects for growth is not the typical calculus of just deserts. And the prospect of natural maturation also affects incapacitation calculations in particular ways.

Why a Separate Court?

If the penal requirements of youth crime are considered by the maturational juvenile court, what elements of such a court's jurisprudence
make a separate court for juvenile offenders a necessity? There are two
reasons why the policies and the dispositions of this kind of court cannot be seamlessly blended into the usual business of criminal courts.
The first problem is that youth welfare interests will trump the usual
demands of penal justice in most cases. This kind of court will choose
probation in a large number of cases in which the seriousness of the
offense might generate a short prison sentence in a criminal court.
And the scales of maturational juvenile justice only produce long penal
confinement outcomes when the harm and guilt are overwhelming. So
the biases that are designed into a maturational juvenile court would
clash with the just deserts and the incapacitation calculus of the modern criminal court. The strong preference for noncustodial outcomes
contradicts the preferred outcome in criminal courts. And this contrast
in outcomes is not an idiosyncratic feature of the incarceration-heavy
U.S. system so much as a general distinction between penal and juvenile
courts in most countries.

The second element of the workload of the "maturational" juvenile
court that requires a separate court is the need to design even punitive dispositional sanctions around the specific developmental needs
of young offenders. Young offenders must be the center of attention
and regard in the maturational juvenile court, as they never were in the
criminal courts of most developed nations. Of course, the best interests
of the young offender has never been the only interest to be balanced in
juvenile court, but it must be a major concern at every stage and a particular priority when dispositional sanctions are at issue. So one simi-
larity between a juvenile justice system organized around rehabilitation
and what we have termed the "maturational" court is that both require
a separate juvenile court system to function properly. But even though
both types of court are organized around the changeability and developmental needs of young offenders, they are as different as night and day
in most other respects.

The rehabilitative court uses state programs to interrupt the development of young offenders to change their behavior. It is an active and

aggressive form of government intervention. The maturational court hopes to wait out a normal developmental process in most cases. It is a passive program when pursuing its priority, considering restraint to be a judicial virtue. The principle of minimum intervention is one of its guiding maxims.

The two systems are also in stark contrast in their sentiments about both adolescents and state programs. The believer in penal rehabilitation is a pessimist about the future prospects of young offenders left without major intervention. That must be the reason heavy intervention is necessary. But this pessimism about the kids is combined with an optimism about the ability of state intervention to create positive change.

The proponents of a maturational policy are usually pessimistic about the ability of compulsory programs to generate positive change in youth behavior. But this pessimism about state intervention is balanced by an optimistic assessment of the capacity for kids to grow up and grow out of delinquent lifestyles. The maturational judge is optimistic about kids and pessimistic about programs. The rehabilitative judge is optimistic about programs and pessimistic about kids.

One other important contrast between maturational and rehabilitative theories of juvenile justice concerns the timing of expected crime-prevention benefits. The impact of an intervention program should be relatively soon after the program has been experienced by its subjects. So the search for program impacts is a short-term expectation of relative improvement if rehabilitative programs are effective. But keeping young offenders in community settings while expecting them to grow up is a much longer-term investment, and continued offending in the short term is not necessarily a sign of failure. A maturation strategy can look past rearrests after earlier court processing without admitting failure. This long-term hope for a law-abiding adulthood is reminiscent of Mark Twain's observation, "It's easy to quit smoking. I've done it hundreds of times." Just as with people who keep trying to quit smoking, it is not so much the outcome of individual attempts that is important but whether repeated efforts produce eventual success. While any focus on short-term rearrest chances will be frustrated by the ironically high rearrest propensities of young offenders, a policy that can successfully shift the focus to eventual success can tolerate short-term frustration.

Maturation theories could also accommodate easily the due process demands brought by the civil rights revolution in the United States and by the human rights revolution at a global level. We already explained the tension between the rehabilitative ideal and due process demands. Instead, from the perspective of maturation, "it is better that ten guilty kids who will likely mature naturally go free than one innocent kid who will also mature naturally be unnecessarily convicted." In fact, from the perspective of maturational theory, it does not make much sense to convict (almost) any of them.

Unity and Diversity in the Practice of Juvenile Justice

The major focus of this volume has been describing and analyzing the treatment of young offenders in a wide variety of different settings. The vast majority of systems studied use separate juvenile courts for young offenders, but there are substantial variations in types and intensities of sanctions and some variance as well in the ages that serve as a transition from juvenile to criminal court jurisdiction. In other words, even if the chapters show that the juvenile court is an almost global phenomenon, individual jurisdictions have translated or adopted this institution in different fashions.[29] How deep are the similarities between the juvenile justice systems found in Europe and Asia and Latin America and South Africa, and how great are the differences? And what would explain these differences?

With very few exceptions, one characteristic of most juvenile courts everywhere is a lack of explicit discourse about priorities and the reasons for case outcomes. Even after the procedural changes brought about since *In Re Gault* and the inclusion of due process provisions in the UN Convention on the Rights of the Child and other international instruments, in many places, trial courts exercise huge discretion, they rarely issue detailed explanations of dispositional decisions, and their dispositions are rarely appealed.[30] And the ambiguous phrases and general sentiments of statutory law are almost never tested against decisions about dispositions in individual cases. For juvenile justice systems all over the world, the only path to knowledge is to watch what they do rather than to listen carefully to the announced justifications for decisions. In this sense, careful observation of the statistics on case processing, secure confinement, and sanctioning does provide important indications of the real priorities in juvenile court polices. If we do a good job of observing what juvenile courts do, we can learn a great deal about them. And the authors who have built this volume have done a good job of learning from the statistics as well as from the rhetoric of their national systems.

This section summarizes our view of the common trends and noted differences in the national systems covered in the first nine chapters of the book. The following section will consider the current and potential role of international standards influencing the principles and practice of juvenile courts.

The nations examined in this book have a lot in common in their legal policies toward young offenders. The notion that immaturity by reason of youth should reduce maximum deserved punishment is universally accepted in both juvenile and criminal courts. While some Muslim nations use a religiously based reduced age boundary for the end of a period of protected immaturity,[31] the 18th birthday is a nearly universal boundary for protected youthful status, perhaps because secondary education typically ends about then. While both the idea of diminished responsibility and the 18th-birthday boundary are the subject of consensus, different systems seem to have very different standards of appropriate levels of punishment. The only place where diminished responsibility is the only major influence on different punishments for youth is with very serious crimes where an offender has been transferred out of juvenile court jurisdiction.[32]

A second pattern to be discovered in the previous chapters is the absence of aggressive interventions based on penal rehabilitation without concern for the severity of the offense or the wishes of the family.[33] In every system observed in this book, the real contrast between juvenile and criminal court is that the juvenile court does less when dealing with its clients than would a criminal court for the same offense.

The mechanisms used to reduce the confinement of young offenders vary widely and do not always reflect the statutory framework of juvenile justice. Different degrees of economic and human resources in developed and developing countries may contribute to explaining the gap between legal regulations and the law in action of juvenile justice in this regard.[34] However, the interactions between the levels of confinement according to the juvenile law on the books and the juvenile law in action are complex and go in multiple directions. In India, for example, Ved Kumari shows a statutory framework that emphasizes noncustodial sanctions after adjudication, and the rate of juvenile confinement in India is also quite low. But the main reason detention rates per 100,000 kids is low in India is a lack of arrests. And patchy statistics on custody in "special homes" show substantial use when young offenders do penetrate the system. In Scandinavia, the arrests of 15- to 17-year-olds are processed by a criminal court with no special rules for separate treatment, but penal confinement rates are much lower in such courts than for the next youngest group of defendants in three of the four Scandinavian nations.

A different degree of economic and human resources in different countries may also account for how much of a gap there is between the promises of juvenile policies and the actual practice beyond confinement, such as, for instance, whether states provide social programs to juveniles in conflict with the law.[35] Religious influence may also explain certain differences among juvenile systems. For instance, among Muslim-majority countries, we find differences in the minimum age of penal responsibility that may be partially explained by the French colonial, Islamic, or Soviet origin of the regulation.[36]

While detailed profiles of juvenile court sanctions are not available for many nations, there are enough statistics on case outcomes in various systems to demonstrate substantial differences in the penalties imposed in different juvenile court systems. The data that Weijian Gao obtained about theft adjudications in the PRC shows that a majority of such cases lead to confinement in juvenile court, a much higher percentage than would happen in most other systems. No data come from case outcomes in places such as Saudi Arabia and Iran, but the assumption of informed observers is that confinement is common and the terms of confinement can be expected to be longer than in most other places.

Do such contrasts in outcome in different juvenile systems result from different philosophies of juvenile justice? The question is an important one, and the apparent answer is yes, with important qualifications. The different outcomes reflect a real contrast in the mix of philosophies in different systems, but this is not a result of different philosophies of juvenile justice as much as the different power in different systems of retributive or incapacitation priorities of the same kind that govern dispositions in criminal courts. In the PRC, the relatively new juvenile courts operate under the same penal code as criminal courts but with somewhat different patterns of emphasis. So it is not a competition between maturational and rehabilitative theories of juvenile justice that produces more custody and longer terms in the PRC so much as the conflict between conventional retributive or incapacitation priorities and maturational concepts of juvenile justice. Whether the overlap between criminal and juvenile sanctions will diminish in China as the juvenile courts develop further is yet to be seen. But what China has now is a weaker form of juvenile courts, rather than a different philosophy of juvenile justice. The same seems to be true in many Middle Eastern nations, although the empirical foundations for any firm conclusions there are lacking.

The passive and reactive preferences in juvenile courts are widespread, but they compete with the retributive or incapacitation pressures of conventional criminal justice with varying degrees of success in different places. This overlap with retributive pressures is most evident in younger systems and where the institutions of juvenile justice still depend on the punishments provided in a penal code.

Most of the variations we observe in juvenile sanctions are then a function not of different philosophies of juvenile justice but rather of the continued power of conventional retributive or incapacitation pressures from criminal justice that still compete with the standard maturational priorities of juvenile court. The conflicts that are observed in 2015 are not that far removed from those in the early years of juvenile courts in the Western world.

Our chapters suggest that politics, the degree of autonomy of juvenile judges and other officials, and the penological preferences of the operators of the juvenile system are three crucial variables in explaining the extent to which a maturational policy of juvenile justice has the upper hand over a retributive emphasis in a given situation.[37] The transitions from authoritarian to democratic rule in central and eastern Europe, Latin America, South Africa, and South Korea opened up policy windows for the introduction of less punitive and more due-process-oriented rhetoric or legal regulations on juvenile courts.[38] In the case of

Poland, these regulations resulted in a less punitive legal regime. In the case of the South Korean transition to democracy, a less punitive turn in juvenile justice took place without a need for formal reform, as the operators of the juvenile justice system supported or accepted the winds of political reform.[39]

Political agendas that created, responded, or channeled concerns about crime have pushed juvenile justice in the opposite direction, as indicated by the chapters in this volume on China, Europe, Japan, India, Latin America, Poland, and South Africa.[40] In some cases, these concerns have brought an increase in the use of punitive rhetoric or measures on juveniles.[41] However, in Japan, the degree of autonomy of the juvenile justice system seemed to have neutralized the effect of formal "tough-on-crime" changes on the levels of sanctions for juveniles.[42] The fact that prosecutors do not dominate the Japanese juvenile justice system may have enabled such an autonomy from and neutralization of "tough-on-crime" policies.[43] (In fact, we have not received indications from the chapters in this volume that prosecutors' pressures on the juvenile justice system, which has become a central characteristic of the U.S. system in the past few decades, has spread around the world.)[44]

Political regimes that torture or otherwise abuse prisoners may also abuse juveniles under detention.[45] In addition, institutional weakness and insufficient penetration of national laws may help explain why some countries have still executed juveniles despite national policies prohibiting such a practice.[46]

But despite these different trends in different countries, it is remarkable that juveniles accused of the commission of crime are thought to require a different set of adjudicatory institutions and less or nonpunitive measures. In any case, as we already mentioned, any conclusion about the current circumstances of juvenile justice must be qualified by the substantial limits on information available on juvenile and criminal case outcome. The comparative study of juvenile justice is still too much a guessing game for important systems in Asia, Latin America, and Africa. And one of the larger dangers of limited data is that observers are tempted to see what they want to see. So most of our conclusions should be regarded as tentative, subject to corrections in the face of better data. We hope that our efforts and opinions about current circumstances will provoke more careful statistical profiles that can test and may supplant the findings in this volume.

International Standards as an Influence on National Systems

In the previous sections, we have analyzed the global spread of juvenile courts around the world. Such a spread took place in a decentralized way, with the Chicago juvenile court being the first model for reform that was then followed by other possible reform models in Europe, Latin America, and elsewhere. The United States has still been influential in this area in the past few decades with the trend of due process requirements brought about or highlighted by *In Re Gault* and with new scientific studies on the adolescent brain that have been brought to the foreground by decisions such as *Roper v. Simmons* and *Graham v. Florida*.[47] But many juvenile justice advocates and scholars have also considered the United States a problematic case not to be followed due to its more punitive approach to juvenile cases in the past few decades.[48]

Simultaneously, the last few decades of the twentieth century brought global standards in this area, with the articulation of international legal documents on juveniles and juvenile justice, such as the United Nations Standard Minimum Rules for the Administration of Juvenile Justice (also known as the "Beijing Rules"), the United Nations Rules for the Protection of Juveniles Deprived of Their Liberty (the "Havana Rules"), the United Nations Guidelines for the Prevention of Juvenile Delinquency (the "Riyadh Guidelines"), and the United Nations Convention on the Rights of the Child.

In addition, bodies such as the European Court of Human Rights started to develop a line of cases on juvenile justice, interpreting the European Convention on Human Rights and Freedoms to protect juveniles' rights.[49] Decisions made by that body are enforced in Europe by monetary damages, have contributed to the arguments of advocates in Europe and elsewhere, and have led to legislative changes in a number of countries.[50]

These international developments do not seem to have played a role in the introduction of separate juvenile courts, partially because by the time the specific international regulations on children and juveniles were passed, most countries had already adopted separate juvenile courts. But these international instruments and developments have played a role in and had an impact on juvenile policies in many countries.[51]

The central document concerning a global policy relating to juvenile justice is the United Nations Convention on the Rights of the Child, adopted in 1989 and ratified at last count by 193 nations. The Committee on the Rights of the Child, composed of 18 independent experts appointed by state parties, monitors the implementation of the Convention through country reports.[52] Country reports and other documents issued by the committee have had an influence on specific countries, as the chapters in this volume on India, Poland, and South Africa indicate.[53] By the end of 2011, the United Nations General Assembly approved an optional protocol to the Convention on a communications procedure, which allows individual children to submit complaints regarding specific violations of their rights under the Convention. This protocol entered into force upon ratification by 10 United Nations Member States in April 2014.[54]

In addition, depending on the relationship of individual legal systems to international law and human rights treaties, the Convention may be self-executing and have a legal status superior to regular laws and even a constitutional status in some states.[55] These standards have also provided rhetorical and normative support for children's advocates in legislative and judicial discussion about juvenile justice policy, even in one of the very few countries of the world that has not ratified the Convention, the United States.[56]

In the spirit of the earlier Universal Declaration of Human Rights, the Convention seeks to prohibit a wide range of abusive and neglectful threats to child development and to generate positive rights to support, education, family life, and privacy. The document is concerned with the treatment of young offenders both in its positive aspirations and in the harmful state policies it seeks to prohibit. The positive ambitions include a qualified right to the status of childhood ("A child means a human being below the age of eighteen years unless under the law applicable to the child majority is attained earlier" under article 1) and the apparent prohibitions of solely punitive state interventions ("In all actions concerning children . . . the best interests of children shall be a primary consideration" under article 3.1). Positive aspirations have also included, among other rights, the right of the child to the enjoyment of the highest attainable standard of health and to facilities for the treatment of illness (article 24), the right to benefit from social security (article 26), and the right to a standard of living adequate for the child's physical, mental, spiritual, moral, and social development (article 27). Domestic laws implementing the Convention have thus included similar rights that have also been seen as crime-preventive measures.[57] However, often no programs or adequate programs for the implementation of these rights have actually been adopted.[58]

The practices that article 37 of the Convention seeks to prohibit are more limited: "No child shall be subjected to torture or other cruel, inhuman or degrading treatment or punishment. Neither capital punishment nor life imprisonment without possibility of release shall be imposed for offenses committed by persons below eighteen years of age." Article 37's limit on incarceration is more qualified: "The arrest, detention or imprisonment of a child shall be used only as a last resort and for the shortest appropriate period of time."

The two specific and unqualified prohibitions in article 37 have probably had more impact on domestic policy than the general standard about the "shortest appropriate period of time" for confinement has, at least among states that could still apply the death penalty and life without parole on juveniles, such as the United States. While the general definition of childhood's boundary at 18 is qualified so that an earlier age of majority is allowed, the prohibition of both state execution and life without the possibility of release for acts committed under age 18 are unqualified. Whether the general acceptance of these exclusions is a product of their widespread popularity independent of the Convention or in part a result of the article 37 condemnation should be explored further in future studies.

As a literal matter, it may be fanciful to ask what theory or theories of juvenile justice are favored by the Convention on the Rights of the Child. In relation to juvenile justice, the Committee on the Rights of the Child issued General Comment No. 10 (2007) on "children's rights in juvenile justice" in order "to provide the States parties with more elaborated guidance and recommendations for their efforts to establish an administration of juvenile justice in compliance with the Convention on the Rights of the Child" (§ 3). On theories of juvenile justice, Comment No. 10 says,

> Children differ from adults in their physical and psychological develop-
> ment, and their emotional and educational needs. Such differences con-
> stitute the basis for the lesser culpability of children in conflict with the
> law. These and other differences are the reasons for a separate juvenile
> justice system and require a different treatment for children. The protec-
> tion of the best interests of the child means, for instance, that the tradi-
> tional objectives of criminal justice, such as repression/retribution, must
> give way to rehabilitation and restorative justice objectives in dealing
> with child offenders. (§ 10)

A number of countries that have introduced new juvenile justice acts after ratifying the Convention also mention rehabilitation as a rationale for the reforms.[59]

Despite the Comment No. 10's reference to rehabilitation as one of the theories underlying juvenile justice, there are three sets of provi-sions in the Convention and in Comment No. 10 that instead point collectively toward a maturational philosophy. The first is that the Con-vention establishes that "the child, for the full and harmonious develop-ment of his or her personality, should grow up in a family environment, in an atmosphere of happiness, love and understanding" (preamble) and that "States Parties shall ensure to the maximum extent possible the . . . development of the child" (art. 6). According to Comment No. 10, this right to development "should result in a policy of responding to juvenile delinquency in ways that support the child's development" (§ 11). In addition, article 40.1 of the Convention establishes that "States Parties recognize the right of every child alleged as, accused of, or rec-ognized as having infringed the penal law to be treated in a manner consistent with the promotion of the child's sense of dignity and worth, . . . which takes into account the child's age and the desirability of pro-moting the child's reintegration and the child's assuming a constructive role in society."

The second set of provisions that point toward a maturational phi-losophy is the clear downgrading of punitive sanctions including confinement "except as a last resort" (article 37(b)) and the requirement that in all state actions concerning children, "the best interests of the child shall be a primary consideration" (article 3.1). Article 40.3(b) of the Convention also establishes, "States Parties shall seek to promote the establishment of laws, procedures, authorities and institutions specifically applicable to children alleged as, accused of, or recognized as having infringed the penal law, and, in particular: . . . Whenever appropriate and desirable, measures for dealing with such children without resorting to judicial proceedings, providing that human rights and legal safeguards are fully respected." The preference for passive over active state programs can be seen not only in the rejection of confinement and formal judicial proceedings but also in the right of the child to preserve family relations (article 8) and the restriction of separation from family to circumstances in which separation is "necessary for the best interests of the child" (article 9). The emphasis on the rights of the child is one of family and child choices and state responsibility.

The third set of provisions is the explicit rejection of status offenses and the imposition of criminal justice due process standards, in article 40, that can be considered inconsistent with rehabilitative theories of state involvement. In relation to status offenses, article 40.2(a) says that no "child shall be alleged as, be accused of, or recognized as having infringed the penal law by reason of acts or omissions that were not prohibited by national or international law at the time they were committed." And General Comment No. 10 says,

> It is quite common that criminal codes contain provisions criminalizing behavioural problems of children, such as vagrancy, truancy, runaways and other acts. . . . These acts, also known as Status Offences, are not considered to be such if committed by adults. The Committee recommends that the States parties abolish the provisions on status offenses in order to establish an equal treatment under the law for children and adults. In this regard, the Committee also refers to article 56 of the Riyadh Guidelines which reads: "In order to prevent further stigmatization, victimization and criminalization of young persons, legislation should be enacted to ensure that any conduct not considered an offence or not penalized if committed by an adult is not considered an offence and not penalized if committed by a young person."

As for due process protections, article 40 of the Convention provides for a wide variety of rights, including the presumption of innocence, the right to proper legal assistance, and the right against compulsory self-incrimination. As pointed out previously, these types of due process protections are in tension with the rehabilitative ideal.

Juvenile courts are only one of the domains of concern to authors and interpreters of the Convention on the Rights of the Child. But their general conceptions of childhood, state responsibility, and juvenile justice are compatible with and even closely linked to the passive virtues of a maturational juvenile court policy.

Conclusion

The aim of this chapter was to test theories of the objectives of juvenile court against the data reported on the actual operations of juvenile courts in many countries. There is a relatively small literature on theories of juvenile justice, and there is also a growing number of empirical profiles of juvenile courts, for the most part concerning North America and Europe. But these two developing literatures have often been isolated from each other rather than combined. This chapter is one preliminary attempt to use the operational reality of modern juvenile courts to observe what must have been the priorities being served.

The major contrast operationally between criminal and juvenile courts is that juvenile courts use much lower levels of confinement and shorter durations of confinement for juvenile offenders. The juvenile offender is far more likely to remain in the community while the system waits out the process of his or her growing up. There is not now, nor was there ever, substantial investment in relocation and indoctrination of young offenders. Instead, the court for young offenders hopes to do less harm than long-term incarceration would produce. Most of the virtues of what we have called a maturational strategy of juvenile justice are passive virtues.

This strategy has special appeal for the treatment of youthful offenders because they do grow up. The dynamic processes that go with the adolescent years promise not an instant reformation of kids who offend but a relatively swift transition for most kids into adult roles and reductions in offending.

NOTES

We would like to thank Frieder Dünkel, Ved Kumari, Tapio Lappi-Seppälä, and David S. Tanenhaus for comments on an earlier draft of this chapter and Jeff Fagan for conversations about it.

1. See, e.g., H. H. Lou, *Juvenile Courts in the United States* (Chapel Hill: University of North Carolina Press, 1927). Correctional measures specifically aimed at juveniles predated the creation of juvenile courts. See, e.g., Robert M. Mennel, *Thorns and Thistles: Juvenile Delinquents in the United States, 1825–1940* (Hanover, NH: University Press of New England, 1973); Robert S. Pickett, *House of Refuge* (Syracuse, NY: Syracuse University Press, 1967); David J. Rothman and Sheila M. Rothman, *Documents Relative to the House of Refuge Instituted by the Society for the Reformation of Juvenile Delinquents in the City of New York in 1824* (New York: Garland, 1987).

2. See, e.g., S. D. Krasner, *Sovereignty: Organized Hypocrisy* (Princeton: Princeton University Press, 1999).

3. See, in this volume, Kumari, chap. 4; and Salaymeh, chap. 6.

4. See Chung, chap. 9 in this volume.

5. See, in this volume, Beloff and Langer, chap. 5; Lappi-Seppälä, chap. 2; Stańdo-Kawecka, chap. 7.

6. Máximo Langer, "Revolution in Latin American Criminal Procedure: Diffusion of Legal Ideas from the Periphery," *American Journal of Comparative Law* 55 (2007): 622–623.

7. See, in this volume, Chung, chap. 9 (explaining that South Korea adopted its own "homegrown" regulations of juvenile justice in 1958); Kumari, chap. 4 (describing the adoption of the Children Act of 1960 and its spread to Indian states); Salaymeh, chap. 6 (describing the spread and extension of the jurisdiction of juvenile courts in Muslim-majority countries in the past few decades); Skelton, chap. 8 (describing the adoption of the Child Justice Act of 2008 in South Africa).

8. See, e.g., Salaymeh, chap. 6 (appendix on Turkey).

9. See, e.g., W. Richard Scott, John W. Meyer, and Associates, *Institutional Environments and Organizations: Structural Complexity and Individualism* (Thousand Oaks, CA: Sage, 1994); Martha Finnemore, "Norms, Culture, and World Politics: Insights from Sociology's Institutionalism," *International Organization* 50 (1996): 325–347.

10. On the influence of the U.S. juvenile court model in the first half of the 20th century, see, e.g., Beloff and Langer, chap. 5 (explaining that the U.S. juvenile court was the model followed by Argentina); Kumari, chap. 4 (explaining that even though India was a British colony, it followed the U.S. model when it adopted its first juvenile act in 1920); Stańdo-Kawecka, chap. 7 (explaining how the youth court movement in Europe relied on the U.S. model of juvenile courts).

11. Joseph S. Nye, Jr., *Soft Power: The Means to Success in World Politics* (New York: Public Affairs, 2004).

12. See Gao, chap. 3 in this volume.

13. One example of undoing comes from the province of Chubut, in Argentina, where there used to be separate juvenile courts that have been recently eliminated.

14. See, e.g., Gao, chap. 3. On the relationship between urbanization and industrialization and the spreading of the concept of juvenile delinquency and the adoption of juvenile courts, see, e.g., Victor Bailey, *Delinquency and Citizenship: Reclaiming the Young Offender, 1914–1948* (New York: Oxford University Press, 1987); Anthony Platt, *The Child Savers: The Invention of Delinquency*, 2nd ed. (Chicago: University of Chicago Press, 1977); Anthony Platt, "The Child-Saving Movements and the Origins of the Juvenile Justice System," in *The Sociology of Juvenile Delinquency*, ed. Ronald J. Berger (Chicago: Nelson-Hall, 1991) 5; David J. Rothman, *The Discovery of the Asylum* (Boston: Little, Brown, 1971).

15. Among the chapters in this volume, see, e.g., Skelton, chap. 8 (describing the role of the juvenile system in the reproduction of racial oppression in South Africa). See also Geoff K. Ward, *The Black Child-Savers: Racial Democracy and Juvenile Justice* (Chicago: University of Chicago Press, 2012).

16. See, e.g., Beloff and Langer, chap. 5 (on Latin America during colonial times); Kumari, chap. 4 (on Hindu and Islamic law); Salaymeh, chap. 6 (on Islamic law). See also William Blackstone, *Commentaries on the Laws of England*, vol. 4 (1765–1769; repr., Chicago: University of Chicago Press, 1979), 22–24 (analyzing diminished responsibility regulations in civil and common law).

17. Julian Mack, "The Juvenile Court," *Harvard Law Review* 23 (1909): 107.

18. See, e.g., Beloff and Langer, chap. 5 (describing rehabilitation as one of the central goals that the introduction of juvenile courts in Latin America was supposed to advance); Stańdo-Kawecka, chap. 7 (explaining that the youth court movement in Europe coincided with the modern school of criminal law that had rehabilitation as one of its goals).

19. Francis A. Allen, "Legal Values and the Rehabilitative Ideal," in *The Borderland of Criminal Law: Essays in Law and Criminology* (Chicago: University of Chicago Press, 1964).

20. See Franklin E. Zimring, "The Common Thread: Diversion in the Jurisprudence of Juvenile Courts," in *A Century of Juvenile Justice*, ed. Margaret K. Rosenheim, Franklin E. Zimring, David S. Tanenhaus, and Bernardine Dohrn (Chicago: University of Chicago Press, 2002), 197.

21. See, e.g., in this volume, Beloff and Langer, chap. 5; Dünkel, chap. 1; Kumari, chap. 4; Stańdo-Kawecka, chap. 7 (mentioning rehabilitation as one of the goals of the 1982 Polish Juvenile Act).

22. See P. S. Cabot, "A Long-Term Study of Children: The Cambridge-Somerville Youth Study," *Child Development* 11, no. 2 (1940): 143–151; Joan McCord, "A Thirty-Year Follow-Up of Treatment Effects," in *Crime and Family: Selected Essays of Joan McCord*, 13–21 (Philadelphia: Temple University Press, 2007).

23. 397 U.S. 358 (1970). See also *In Re Gault*, 387 U.S. 1 (1967).

24. See, e.g., Beloff and Langer, chap. 5; Dünkel, chap. 1; Skelton, chap. 8; Stańdo-Kawecka, chap. 7.

25. See Lappi-Seppälä, chap. 2.

26. See, e.g., in this volume, Beloff and Langer, chap. 5 (describing the introduction of restorative justice mechanisms by the laws adopted in the past twenty-five years in Latin America); Dünkel, chap. 1 (arguing that restorative justice has been one of the main goals of juvenile justice in recent years in Europe); Skelton, chap. 8 (describing restorative justice as one of the main forces behind the South African Child Justice Bill).

27. See, e.g., Dünkel, chap. 1.

28. See, e.g., ibid.

29. On the metaphor of legal translation, see Máximo Langer, "From Legal Transplants to Legal Translations: The Globalization of Plea Bargaining and the Americanization Thesis in Criminal Procedure," *Harvard International Law Journal* 45 (2004): 1–64.

30. On the gap between due process protections on the books and the actual practice of magistrates, see, e.g., Kumari, chap. 4 (describing such a gap in India).

31. See Salaymeh, chap. 6.

32. Franklin E. Zimring, "Juvenile or Criminal Court? A Punitive Theory of Waiver," in *American Juvenile Justice* (New York: Oxford University Press, 2005), 155.

33. See, e.g., Lappi-Seppälä, chap. 2.

34. See, e.g., Kumari, chap. 4 (describing implementation problems of the Juvenile Justice Act of 2000 in India); Salaymeh, chap. 6; Skelton, chap. 8 (mentioning lack of training of police officials in the Child Justice Act as a reason for the reduction in the number of children who get into the child justice system after the passing of the act).

35. See, e.g., the contrast between the lack of meaningful programs in most of Latin America, referred to by Beloff and Langer in chapter 5, and the situation in Scandinavia, described by Lappi-Seppälä in chapter 2.

36. See Salaymeh, chap. 6.

37. Socioeconomic factors (see, e.g., Dünkel, chap. 1) and crime rates (see, e.g., Skelton, chap. 8) are other possible relevant variables.

38. See Beloff and Langer, chap. 5; Chung, chap. 9; Dünkel, chap. 1; Skelton, chap. 8; and Stańdo-Kawecka, chap. 7.

39. See Chung, chap. 9.

40. See, e.g., Dünkel, chap. 1 (describing demands for a more punitive approach to juvenile justice in many European countries, as well as the moderate impact that such demands have in fact had on European juvenile justice systems); Gao, chap. 3 (indicating that the higher rate of juvenile confinement in China than in other nations may be the result of more substantial punishment policies in Chinese juvenile courts); Kumari, chap. 4 (describing the retributivist attitudes by many Indian judges as a cause for the circumvention of the regulations of the Juvenile Justice Act of 2000); Skelton, chap. 8 (describing the introduction of new minimum-sentences legislation as a populist move to woo voters who were angry about high crime rates, as well as mentioning popular demands as a possible explanation for the increase in the number of children serving sentences between 1995 and 2004).

41. See, e.g., Beloff and Langer's chapter 5 on the case study of Chile, where they conclude that juvenile justice reform has likely increased confinement levels of juveniles.

42. See Chung, chap. 9. See also Stańdo-Kawecka, chap. 7 (arguing that the skepticism by Polish family courts about rehabilitation was one of the possible factors that explain the low use of correctional measures in that juvenile system).

43. Chung, chap. 9.

44. On the dominance of prosecutors over the juvenile justice system in the United States, see, e.g., David S. Tanenhaus, "First Things First: Juvenile Justice Reform in Historical Context," *Texas Tech Law Review* 46 (2013): 281–290.

45. See Salaymeh, chap. 6.

46. See, e.g., ibid. (on Yemen).

47. On the influence of *In Re Gault* and due process requirements on other jurisdictions, see, e.g., Beloff and Langer, chap. 5 (describing such an influence in Latin America). On the influence around the world of these recent scientific studies on the adolescent brain, see the contrast between Kumari's chapter 4 (embracing these scientific studies as a crucial component to design and implement public policy on juvenile justice in India) and Skelton's chapter 8 (explaining the strategic decision by the Centre for Child Law in South Africa not to refer to the juvenile brain studies because it was planning to challenge a law that criminalized consensual sex between adolescents). On the limits of brain studies as firm ground for future reform efforts on juvenile justice, see Terry A. Maroney, "The Once and Future Juvenile Brain," in *Choosing the Future for American Juvenile Justice*, ed. Franklin E. Zimring and David S. Tanenhaus (New York: NYU Press, 2014), 189–215.

48. For articulation of these criticisms among the chapters in this volume, see, e.g., Dünkel, chap. 1; Kumari, chap. 4.

49. The first case in this line of cases was *Tyrer v. United Kingdom* (1978) (holding that judicial corporal punishment on a juvenile was degrading treatment in violation of article 3 of the European Convention of Human Rights).

50. See, e.g., Stańdo-Kawecka, chap. 7 (describing how the European Court of Human Rights' decision in *Ademkiewicz v. Poland* of March 2, 2010, no. 54729/00, on the right to a fair and public hearing, led to an amendment of the 1982 Juvenile Act by the Polish Parliament in August 2013).

51. Among the chapters in this volume, see, e.g., Beloff and Langer, chap. 5 (describing the impact of the UN Convention on the juvenile justice reforms in Latin America); Dünkel, chap. 1 (arguing that the UN Convention has had a role in the relative invulnerability of juvenile justice systems against punitive demands in Europe); Lappi-Seppälä, chap. 2 (describing the impact that the Convention's demand of separation of juveniles from adult prisoners had in Denmark and the Convention's impact on the adoption of closed youth care in Sweden); Salaymeh, chap. 6 (describing the different strategies that Muslim-majority countries have adopted to deal with and accommodate to the UN Convention); Skelton, chap. 8 (describing the influence of the Convention and other international developments on the Child Justice Act in South Africa).

52. The Committee on the Rights of the Child also monitors implementation of two Optional Protocols to the Convention, on involvement of children in armed conflict and on the sale of children, child prostitution, and child pornography.

53. See Kumari, chap. 4 (describing the influence of the *Concluding Observations of the Committee on the Rights of the Child on India* on the adoption of a new juvenile justice act in that country in 2000); Skelton, chap. 8 (explaining that civil society organizations urged a higher age than 10 years in light of the UN Committee on the Rights of the Child's General Comment No. 10, which urged setting a minimum age of no less than 12 years); Stańdo-Kawecka, chap. 7 (considering problematic the Polish minimum age of criminal majority set at 17 years, in view of General Comment No. 10).

54. See Committee on the Rights of the Child, home page, http://www.ohchr.org/EN/HRBodies/CRC/Pages/CRCIndex.aspx; United Nations, "Optional Protocol to the Convention on the Rights of the Child on a Communications Procedure," December 19, 2011, https://treaties.un.org/pages/viewdetails.aspx?src=treaty&mtdsg_no=iv-11-d&chapter=4&lang=en.

55. See, e.g., Argentine Constitution, sec. 75.22 (giving constitutional status to the Convention on the Rights of the Child); Skelton, chap. 8 (describing South African constitutional regulations on children's rights, the constitutional obligation that courts consider international law when interpreting the Bill of Rights, and the frequent reference by the South African Constitutional Court to international documents, including the Convention).

56. See, e.g., *Roper v. Simmons*, 543 U.S. 551 (2005); *Graham v. Florida*, 560 U.S. 48 (2010).

57. See, e.g., Kumari, chap. 4.

58. See, e.g., Beloff and Langer, chap. 5.

59. See, e.g., Kumari, chap. 4 (mentioning rehabilitation as a rationale for the introduction of the Juvenile Justice Act of 2000 in India).

ABOUT THE CONTRIBUTORS

MARY BELOFF is Professor of Law at the University of Buenos Aires School of Law. She has published books and articles about children's rights in the inter-American system and was an adviser on legislative reforms concerning childhood in El Salvador, Guatemala, Honduras, Mexico, Paraguay, and the Dominican Republic. She has served as a consultant to the United Nations Fund for Children.

JAE-JOON CHUNG is Professor of Law at Shandong University law school in China. He finished his Ph.D. course at Korea University law school and received both his LL.M. and J.S.D. degrees at the University of California at Berkeley in 2010. His dissertation is about the comparative study of juvenile justice between Korea and Japan. He specializes in the comparative study of juvenile justice, and his translation into Korean of *American Juvenile Justice* was published in 2010.

FRIEDER DÜNKEL is Professor of Criminology at the Ernst Moritz Arndt University in Greifswald. He has advised both the German government and the Council of Europe on juvenile justice policy and the development of laws and guidelines in this field. Among his many publications is the four-volume *Juvenile Justice Systems in Europe: Current Situation and Reform Developments* (2010; 2nd ed., 2011).

WEIJIAN GAO is Professor of Law at Southwest University of Political Science and Law. He has written about juvenile and criminal justice in China and has translated the leading works on American juvenile justice into Chinese. Professor Gao can be reached at 54577367@qq.com or wjgao2001@sohu.com.

VED KUMARI is Professor of Law in the Faculty of Law, University of Delhi, India, and has published widely in the fields of juvenile justice,

gender justice, criminal law, and clinical legal education. She is a Ful-
bright Scholar and Commonwealth Fellow. She was also Chairperson
of the Delhi Judicial Academy. She was given the Best Social Scientist
Award in 2011 by the Indian Society of Criminology. She is the author of
Treatise on the Juvenile Justice Act 1986 (1993) and *Juvenile Justice System
in India: From Welfare to Rights* (2nd ed., 2010) and has coedited, with
Susan Brooks, *Creative Child Advocacy Global Perspectives* (2004).

MÁXIMO LANGER is Professor of Law at UCLA and a leading authority on domestic, comparative, and international criminal law and procedure. He regularly lectures in Asia, Europe, Latin America, and the
United States on criminal law and procedure issues. His work has been
translated into Chinese, German, and Spanish and has received awards
from different professional associations, including the 2007 Hessel
Yntema Prize by the American Society of Comparative Law, the 2007
Margaret Popkin Award by the Latin American Studies Association,
and the 2012 Deák Prize by the American Society of International Law.
He also serves on several editorial boards, including the executive editorial board of the *American Journal of Comparative Law*.

TAPIO LAPPI-SEPPÄLÄ is Director of the National Research Institute
of Legal Policy. Alongside his current position, he has been acting as a
part-time professor in criminology and sociology of law at the University of Helsinki. His long career as a senior legislative adviser in criminal law in the Ministry of Justice includes membership on the Board
of the Task Force for the Penal Law Reform in Finland (1989–1999),
chairmanship of the working group preparing the general part of the
criminal code (1993–1999), membership on the committee preparing
new prison law (1999–2001), and vice chairmanship for the committee
reforming the juvenile sanction system (2001–2003). He has published
several books, research reports, and articles in the fields of criminal law,
criminology, and penal policy.

LENA SALAYMEH is Assistant Professor of Law at Tel Aviv University.
She researches and teaches Islamic and Jewish jurisprudence and legal
history, as well as law in contemporary Southwest Asia (i.e., the "Middle

East") and North Africa. She currently serves as Associate Research Fellow for the Robbins Mediterranean Law Project at UC Berkeley School of Law. Her past publications have appeared in *Law and History Review*, the *Journal of Legal Education* and the *UC Irvine Law Review*.

ANN SKELTON is Professor of Law and Director of the Centre for Child Law at the University of Pretoria. Previously she served as Public Prosecutor with the Department of Justice; worked for Lawyers for Human Rights holding different positions, namely, Regional Director for the Pietermaritzburg Region, Director of the Applied Criminal Justice Project, and National Coordinator in the Child Rights Project; and served as National Project Coordinator of the UN Child Justice Project in 1999. Her contributions to children's rights, which included developing the South African juvenile justice system after apartheid, earned her the World's Children's Honorary Prize (2012).

BARBARA STAŃDO-KAWECKA is Professor of Law in the Department of Criminology at Jagiellonian University. Her research activities focus on juvenile crime and juvenile justice systems, criminal policy, penitentiary law, and penitentiary policy. She has taken part in several international research projects concerning the protection of rights of persons deprived of liberty and the execution of prison sentences as well as juvenile justice systems. She has also worked with the Helsinki Foundation of Human Rights in Poland and written reports for the Ministry of Justice.

DAVID S. TANENHAUS is Professor of History and James E. Rogers Professor of History and Law at the William S. Boyd School of Law, University of Nevada, Las Vegas. He studies one of the fundamental and recurring problems in the history of law and society—how to treat the young. His books include *Juvenile Justice in the Making* (2004) and *The Constitutional Rights of Children: In re Gault and Juvenile Justice* (2011). He coedited, with Margaret K. Rosenheim, Franklin E. Zimring, and Bernardine Dohrn, *A Century of Juvenile Justice* (2002). He also served as Editor in Chief of *The Encyclopedia of the Supreme Court of the United States* (2008).

FRANKLIN E. ZIMRING is William G. Simon Professor of Law at the University of California, Berkeley, School of Law. He has served on the National Academy of Science Panels on Violence, Deterrence, and Juvenile Justice and as director of research of the Task Force on Violence of the National Commission on the Causes and Prevention of Violence. He has written on issues of youth crime and sentencing policy, penal confinement and the restraint of crime, and gun- and drug-control policy. Recent books include *An American Travesty: Legal Responses to Adolescent Sex Offending* (2004), *American Juvenile Justice* (2005), *The Great American Crime Decline* (2006), and *The City That Became Safe: New York's Lessons for Urban Crime and Its Control* (2012).

INDEX

Page numbers in italics refer to tables and figures.

CPSIA information can be obtained
at www.ICGtesting.com
Printed in the USA
LVOW03s2052280318
571484LV00003B/294/P